Bloom's Shakespeare Through the Ages

OTHELLO

Edited and with an introduction by
Harold Bloom
Sterling Professor of the Humanities
Yale University

Volume Editor
Neil Heims

BLOOM'S
LITERARY CRITICISM
An imprint of Infobase Publishing

Bloom's Shakespeare Through the Ages: Othello

Copyright © 2008 by Infobase Publishing

Introduction © 2008 by Harold Bloom

Bloom's Literary Criticism
An imprint of Infobase Publishing
132 West 31st Street
New York NY 10001

Library of Congress Cataloging-in-Publication Data
Othello / edited and with an introduction by Harold Bloom ; volume editor, Neil Heims.
    p. cm. — (Bloom's Shakespeare through the ages)
  Includes bibliographical references and index.
  ISBN 978-0-7910-9575-1 (acid-free paper) 1. Shakespeare, William, 1564-1616. Othello. 2. Othello (Fictitious character) I. Bloom, Harold. II. Heims, Neil. III. Shakespeare, William, 1564–1616. Othello.
  PR2829.O77 2008
  822.3'3—dc22   2007026815

Bloom's Literary Criticism books are available at special discounts when purchased in bulk quantities for businesses, associations, institutions, or sales promotions. Please call our Special Sales Department in New York at (212) 967-8800 or (800) 322-8755.

You can find Bloom's Literary Criticism on the World Wide Web at
http://www.chelseahouse.com

Series design by Erika K. Arroyo
Cover design by Ben Peterson
Cover photo © The Granger Collection, New York

Printed in the United States of America

Bang EJB 10 9 8 7 6 5 4 3 2 1

This book is printed on acid-free paper.

CONTENTS

❧

SERIES INTRODUCTION

✌︎

Shakespeare Through the Ages presents not the most current of Shakespeare criticism, but the best of Shakespeare criticism, from the seventeenth century to today. In the process, each volume also charts the flow over time of critical discussion of a particular play. Other useful and fascinating collections of historical Shakespearean criticism exist, but no collection that we know of contains such a range of commentary on each of Shakespeare's greatest plays and at the same time emphasizes the greatest critics in our literary tradition: from John Dryden in the seventeenth century, to Samuel Johnson in the eighteenth century, to William Hazlitt and Samuel Coleridge in the nineteenth century, to A.C. Bradley and William Empson in the twentieth century, to the most perceptive critics of our own day. This canon of Shakespearean criticism emphasizes aesthetic rather than political or social analysis.

Some of the pieces included here are full-length essays; others are excerpts designed to present a key point. Much (but not all) of the earliest criticism consists only of brief mentions of specific plays. In addition to the classics of criticism, some pieces of mainly historical importance have been included, often to provide background for important reactions from future critics.

These volumes are intended for students, particularly those just beginning their explorations of Shakespeare. We have therefore also included basic materials designed to provide a solid grounding in each play: a biography of Shakespeare, a synopsis of the play, a list of characters, and an explication of key passages. In addition, each selection of the criticism of a particular century begins with an introductory essay discussing the general nature of that century's commentary and the particular issues and controversies addressed by critics presented in the volume.

Shakespeare was "not of an age, but for all time," but much Shakespeare criticism is decidedly for its own age, of lasting importance only to the scholar who wrote it. Students today read the criticism most readily available to them, which means essays printed in recent books and journals, especially those journals made available on the Internet. Older criticism is too often buried in out-of-print books on forgotten shelves of libraries or in defunct periodicals. Therefore, many students, particularly younger students, have no way of knowing that some of the most profound criticism of Shakespeare's plays was written decades or centuries ago. We hope this series remedies that problem, and, more importantly, we hope it infuses students with the enthusiasm of the critics in these volumes for the beauty and power of Shakespeare's plays.

INTRODUCTION BY
HAROLD BLOOM

Iago is the genius or bad angel of *Othello* and of Othello. It marks us that we know more readily how to assimilate Iago than to value Othello. Even my best students are wary of sympathizing with Othello. He baffles them: how can the great captain-general so rapidly collapse into incoherence, murderousness, and apparent self-pity?

If each of us had an Iago as personal spirit, would we do better?

The tragedy *Othello* suffers because it is preceded by *Hamlet*, and followed by *King Lear, Macbeth, Antony and Cleopatra*. Othello does not match the protagonists of those dramas, and yet Iago does. The imbalance between Othello and his devilish Ancient or ensign unsettles us these days. But that is part of Shakespeare's design in a play whose peculiar painfulness rivals *King Lear*'s.

Iago has been a fecund ancestor in high literature. His progeny include Satan in Milton's *Paradise Lost*, Claggart in Melville's *Billy Budd*, and Judge Holden in Cormac McCarthy's *Blood Meridian*. Coleridge spoke of Iago's "motiveless malignancy", but when Satan speaks of his Sense of Injured Merit we encounter Iago's fierce motive. He has been passed over for promotion and Cassio, a staff officer and not a warrior, has been given the post by Othello.

The wound to Iago, as we discern, is onto-theological. He had worshipped Othello as war-god. Betrayed, Iago activates his pyromaniac drive to carry war into the camp of peace. A true believer bereft of his fiery faith, Iago uncovers in himself a genius for destroying his captain-general.

Edmund in *King Lear* is the grand strategist of catastrophe, composing the play with the lives of the other characters. Iago, an extraordinary improviser, is rather the tactician of absolute evil. He does not set out with the object of Desdemona's murder by Othello, but embraces the horror when the Moor warns him that he must prove Desdemona a whore or else himself be slain by the overlord of mercenary soldiers.

Magnificent as his triumphalism becomes, Iago remains secondary to the tragic hero, Othello. In the twentieth century, critics like the abominable T. S. Eliot and the equally dogmatic F. R. Leavis deprecated Othello, denying him tragic stature. We can learn from them how not to go about reading so painful a drama as Shakespeare writes.

Othello, like Lear, has never known himself well. A fighter since childhood, he has fully earned his professional eminence. His gift is for commanding others, and for maintaining the separation of war from peace. Serene in his own sublimity, he believes in the honor of arms, and cannot believe that his trust is ever wrongly bestowed. Affinities abound with Antony and with Coriolanus, two other sad captains who fall apart as the contradictions in their own natures encounter overwhelming stress.

How can tragic dignity be maintained if one is reduced to incoherence by Iago's subtle art? Shakespeare is uncanny in preserving a residue of Othello's self-identity which can be reaffirmed in his suicidal final speech. Eliot and Leavis thought that Othello was only cheering himself up at the end, but that is caricature and not accurate analysis.

Hegel, who valued Shakespeare above all other writers, famously thought that tragedy came about as a conflict "between right and right". A. C. Bradley endorsed the Hegelian theory of tragedy, but I find it remote from Shakespearean actuality. There is no right on either side of the contraries that rend Othello apart. The Moor is victimized by a devil, and has no chance whatsoever.

What was Shakespeare trying to do for himself as poet-dramatist by writing *The Tragedy of Othello?* After the impasse of *Hamlet*, *Othello* clears the way for the incredible breakthrough in which *Antony and Cleopatra* followed the composition first of *King Lear* and then of *Macbeth*, thus concluding just fourteen consecutive months in which three masterworks were brought forth. I surmise that the agony of Othello was a kind of ritual sacrifice to the dark gods of creativity so as to enable Lear, Macbeth and Antony to rise up out of the maelstrom of Shakespeare's capacious spirit.

Times go by turns, and *The Tragedy of Othello* has come back from Eliotic disapproval. Since Eliot was every kind of a racist, including a virulent anti-Semitic, we can suppose that Othello's African background also provoked the poet-critic of *The Waste Land*. To this day, there is no critical agreement upon what does or does not happen in the play. I do not believe that the marriage between Desdemona and the Moor ever is consummated. Elliptical at his subtlest, Shakespeare is content to leave it uncertain. The profound sadness of *Othello* is appropriately increased by this dubiety. As readers we must construe for ourselves, and bear the play's shadows as they throng among us.

Biography of
William Shakespeare
❦

WILLIAM SHAKESPEARE was born in Stratford-on-Avon in April 1564 into a family of some prominence. His father, John Shakespeare, was a glover and merchant of leather goods who earned enough to marry Mary Arden, the daughter of his father's landlord, in 1557. John Shakespeare was a prominent citizen in Stratford, and at one point, he served as an alderman and bailiff.

Shakespeare presumably attended the Stratford grammar school, where he would have received an education in Latin, but he did not go on to either Oxford or Cambridge universities. Little is recorded about Shakespeare's early life; indeed, the first record of his life after his christening is of his marriage to Anne Hathaway in 1582 in the church at Temple Grafton, near Stratford. He would have been required to obtain a special license from the bishop as security that there was no impediment to the marriage. Peter Alexander states in his book *Shakespeare's Life and Art* that marriage at this time in England required neither a church nor a priest or, for that matter, even a document—only a declaration of the contracting parties in the presence of witnesses. Thus, it was customary, though not mandatory, to follow the marriage with a church ceremony.

Little is known about William and Anne Shakespeare's marriage. Their first child, Susanna, was born in May 1583 and twins, Hamnet and Judith, in 1585. Later on, Susanna married Dr. John Hall, but the younger daughter, Judith, remained unmarried. When Hamnet died in Stratford in 1596, the boy was only 11 years old.

We have no record of Shakespeare's activities for the seven years after the birth of his twins, but by 1592 he was in London working as an actor. He was also apparently well known as a playwright, for reference is made of him by his contemporary Robert Greene in *A Groatsworth of Wit*, as "an upstart crow."

Several companies of actors were in London at this time. Shakespeare may have had connection with one or more of them before 1592, but we have no record that tells us definitely. However, we do know of his long association with the most famous and successful troupe, the Lord Chamberlain's Men. (When James I came to the throne in 1603, after Elizabeth's death, the troupe's name

1

changed to the King's Men.) In 1599 the Lord Chamberlain's Men provided the financial backing for the construction of their own theater, the Globe.

The Globe was begun by a carpenter named James Burbage and finished by his two sons, Cuthbert and Robert. To escape the jurisdiction of the Corporation of London, which was composed of conservative Puritans who opposed the theater's "licentiousness," James Burbage built the Globe just outside London, in the Liberty of Holywell, beside Finsbury Fields. This also meant that the Globe was safer from the threats that lurked in London's crowded streets, like plague and other diseases, as well as rioting mobs. When James Burbage died in 1597, his sons completed the Globe's construction. Shakespeare played a vital role, financially and otherwise, in the construction of the theater, which was finally occupied sometime before May 16, 1599.

Shakespeare not only acted with the Globe's company of actors; he was also a shareholder and eventually became the troupe's most important playwright. The company included London's most famous actors, who inspired the creation of some of Shakespeare's best-known characters, such as Hamlet and Lear, as well as his clowns and fools.

In his early years, however, Shakespeare did not confine himself to the theater. He also composed some mythological-erotic poetry, such as *Venus and Adonis* and *The Rape of Lucrece*, both of which were dedicated to the earl of Southampton. Shakespeare was successful enough that in 1597 he was able to purchase his own home in Stratford, which he called New Place. He could even call himself a gentleman, for his father had been granted a coat of arms.

By 1598 Shakespeare had written some of his most famous works, *Romeo and Juliet, The Comedy of Errors, A Midsummer Night's Dream, The Merchant of Venice, Two Gentlemen of Verona*, and *Love's Labour's Lost*, as well as his historical plays *Richard II, Richard III, Henry IV*, and *King John*. Somewhere around the turn of the century, Shakespeare wrote his romantic comedies *As You Like It, Twelfth Night*, and *Much Ado About Nothing*, as well as *Henry V*, the last of his history plays in the Prince Hal series. During the next 10 years he wrote his great tragedies, *Hamlet, Macbeth, Othello, King Lear*, and *Antony and Cleopatra*.

At this time, the theater was burgeoning in London; the public took an avid interest in drama, the audiences were large, the plays demonstrated an enormous range of subjects, and playwrights competed for approval. By 1613, however, the rising tide of Puritanism had changed the theater. With the desertion of the theaters by the middle classes, the acting companies were compelled to depend more on the aristocracy, which also meant that they now had to cater to a more sophisticated audience.

Perhaps this change in London's artistic atmosphere contributed to Shakespeare's reasons for leaving London after 1612. His retirement from the theater is sometimes thought to be evidence that his artistic skills were waning. During this time, however, he wrote *The Tempest* and *Henry VIII*. He also wrote the "tragicomedies," *Pericles, Cymbeline,* and *The Winter's Tale.* These were thought to be inspired by Shakespeare's personal problems and have sometimes been considered proof of his greatly diminished abilities.

However, so far as biographical facts indicate, the circumstances of his life at this time do not imply any personal problems. He was in good health and financially secure, and he enjoyed an excellent reputation. Indeed, although he was settled in Stratford at this time, he made frequent visits to London, enjoying and participating in events at the royal court, directing rehearsals, and attending to other business matters.

In addition to his brilliant and enormous contributions to the theater, Shakespeare remained a poetic genius throughout the years, publishing a renowned and critically acclaimed sonnet cycle in 1609 (most of the sonnets were written many years earlier). Shakespeare's contribution to this popular poetic genre are all the more amazing in his break with contemporary notions of subject matter. Shakespeare idealized the beauty of man as an object of praise and devotion (rather than the Petrarchan tradition of the idealized, unattainable woman). In the same spirit of breaking with tradition, Shakespeare also treated themes previously considered off limits—the dark, sexual side of a woman as opposed to the Petrarchan ideal of a chaste and remote love object. He also expanded the sonnet's emotional range, including such emotions as delight, pride, shame, disgust, sadness, and fear.

When Shakespeare died in 1616, no collected edition of his works had ever been published, although some of his plays had been printed in separate unauthorized editions. (Some of these were taken from his manuscripts, some from the actors' prompt books, and others were reconstructed from memory by actors or spectators.) In 1623 two members of the King's Men, John Hemings and Henry Condell, published a collection of all the plays they considered to be authentic, the First Folio.

Included in the First Folio is a poem by Shakespeare's contemporary Ben Jonson, an outstanding playwright and critic in his own right. Jonson paid tribute to Shakespeare's genius, proclaiming his superiority to what previously had been held as the models for literary excellence—the Greek and Latin writers. "Triumph, my Britain, thou hast one to show / To whom all scenes of Europe homage owe. / He was not of an age, but for all time!"

Jonson was the first to state what has been said so many times since. Having captured what is permanent and universal to all human beings at all times, Shakespeare's genius continues to inspire us—and the critical debate about his works never ceases.

Summary of
Othello
୬୬

Act I

The action of *Othello* begins late at night, in the middle of an argument between two men as they walk through the empty streets of Venice. Roderigo has been wooing Desdemona and has trusted Iago to be his go-between. He has given him quite a bit of money, too, which was to be used to buy gifts for Desdemona. But now Roderigo has learned that Desdemona has married Othello, that very night. He suspects that Iago has known about their alliance all along and has been using him. Iago protests his ignorance and, to further his credibility as well as to deflect Roderigo's wrath, tells him how much he hates Othello. He complains that he was passed over for the position of Othello's lieutenant and made his ensign, or standard bearer, and the position was given to Cassio, whom Iago describes as an inferior man and a sort of dandy. Not quite placated, Roderigo challenges Iago to explain why he remains in the service of a general, Othello, whom he loathes. Iago explains to Roderigo that he is only biding his time, that he is not serving Othello, but himself, and that he has a scheme. He does not say what particular end he is pursuing. But he does identify his principal way of proceeding, by deceit and dissimulation:

> [W]hen my outward action doth demonstrate
> The native act and figure of my heart
> In compliment extern, 'tis not long after
> But I will wear my heart upon my sleeve
> For daws to peck at: I am not what I am.

Roderigo's only response to Iago's very revealing speech is to wonder about how rich Othello must be if he could get Desdemona. He refers to Othello not by name, but by using a racial slur, "the thick-lips."

As they speak, Iago and Roderigo are walking toward the house of Brabantio, Desdemona's father. Under his windows, Iago prompts Roderigo to wake Brabantio, and they both begin loudly calling his name. When Brabantio comes onto his balcony, Iago addresses him, under cover, using Roderigo as a front, asking if his house is safe and all his family inside. He cries out,

5

using the image of sheep mating, that Desdemona and Othello are married, characterizing Othello as an old black ram and Desdemona as a white ewe who are together "making the beast with two backs." When Brabantio demands to know who is there, Roderigo identifies himself and Iago remains in the shadows. Convinced that his daughter is not at home, Brabantio calls for the arrest of Othello, which, as a member of the Venetian senate, he has the power to do.

As Brabantio is dressing to join Roderigo in the street, Iago slips away to join Othello at the inn where he and Desdemona plan to spend their wedding night. Brabantio goes to round up his relatives and police officers in order to follow Roderigo to where Othello is and arrest him.

The scene shifts to the inn. Outside, Iago is telling Othello how he restrained himself from killing a man who had been speaking maliciously of Othello. The audience has just seen that he himself was the man. (But Othello has not.) He then turns to the topic of Othello's marriage and asks if it has been performed, warning him of the power Desdemona's father wields. Othello responds with confidence and dignity that he is not afraid of what Brabantio can do, that he has faith that the senate of Venice will recognize the considerable service he has done as its general, and that he is proud of his own lineage. Moreover, he points out, his motive in the marriage is love—otherwise he would not have forfeited the freedom of bachelorhood.

A troop of men approaches the inn. Iago warns it must come from Brabantio to take Othello and advises Othello to go inside. Othello rebuffs him, stating, "Not I. I must be found. / My parts, my title, and my perfect soul / Shall manifest me rightly." It is not a troop sent out by Brabantio, however, but an escort, headed by Cassio, sent by the Venetian senate. The senate is in emergency session because news has arrived that the Turkish fleet is headed to Cyprus, a Venetian stronghold. Othello is being summoned to the senate, in his capacity as general, to lead a Venetian force to Cyprus and repel the Turks. Othello goes inside for a moment, and Cassio asks Iago what Othello is doing at the inn. When Iago tells him Othello has been married, Cassio asks, "To who?" Before Iago can answer, Othello returns. As they are about to proceed to the senate house, Brabantio's band enters, and Brabantio commands his men to seize Othello. Iago, with drawn sword, challenges Roderigo (who had not long before been his companion and whom he had set on to do what he is now challenging him for doing, leading Brabantio to the inn in order to apprehend Othello), and a general melee threatens. Iago is trying to make chaos. Appearing to be protecting Othello, he is, in fact, endangering him. But Othello calms everything. "Keep up your bright swords," he says, and adds, showing his ability to speak with a courtier's wit, "for the dew will rust them." He adds, respectfully, addressing Desdemona's father, "Good signior, you shall more command with years / Than with your weapons."

Brabantio is not pacified by this deference, which, after all, comes after the deed. He calls Othello a thief and accuses him of being an enchanter who used magic and drugs to bind Desdemona to him. Brabantio makes the case against Othello that Iago will later hypothesize and Othello will finally internalize. How could Desdemona go against her nature and marry a black man whom she would be more inclined to fear than to love? At this point, however, Othello stands his ground calmly and once again halts an outbreak of violence. He asks Brabantio where he would like him to go to answer his charges. "To prison," he retorts. Othello is almost teasing in his response, so full of confidence is he. If I go with you to prison, he replies, how can I appear before the Duke, who has summoned me on important state business? Brabantio does not relent but orders that they proceed to the senate, where he may present his case.

At the senate the Duke is analyzing the information he is receiving regarding the strength of the Turkish fleet headed for Cyprus when a messenger arrives to announce that the Turkish fleet has veered and is heading for Rhodes. The senators determine this must be a trick, "a pageant / To keep us in false gaze." It turns out to be just that, and the senators learn that the first fleet was merely joining a larger fleet near Rhodes and returning with it to Venice. Here is a mirroring of Iago's deceptions, which make Othello's gaze false and thus make him see things falsely.

Brabantio and Othello arrive at the senate, and the Duke greets each man, telling Othello that he is dispatching him to fight against the Turks. Brabantio informs the senate he has come on private, not state, business. When he cries out in grief, "My daughter," the senators think she is dead, but he says it is worse: She has been enchanted and stolen from him by Othello. The Duke remains calm and asks Othello what he can say in his defense. Othello delivers a short oration, admitting that he has married Desdemona and minimizing his skill as a speaker because of his life as a soldier; he says he will try to show how he won Desdemona. Despite Brabantio's interruption and repeated accusations that he used witchcraft, Othello is allowed to continue. He tells the senate to call for Desdemona at the inn and let her speak to them herself. While messengers are sent to bring Desdemona to the senate, Othello tells his story of their wooing. The significant aspects are: 1) that he had originally been Brabantio's friend, and 2) that it was Desdemona who made her love known to him and solicited his in return. His summation, "She loved me for the dangers I had passed, / And I loved her that she did pity them," must give the audience or readers pause. The eloquence of his formulation belies its fatality. He did not love her for herself alone but for the way he found himself nobly and heroically reflected in her. When he will not find the image of himself there that he seeks, that exists only because it is reflected in her, "chaos is come again."

The Duke's response is that he thinks Othello's tale would win his daughter, too. That remark highlights the power of language, and Iago's corruption of language, upon which the plot of *Othello* is so dependent. Before Desdemona speaks, Brabantio concedes that if her marriage to Othello is not the result of some magical practice, he will yield, especially since he no longer has any choice in the matter.

Brabantio asks Desdemona "Where most you owe obedience," and she responds that she "perceive[s] . . . a divided duty," that the duty her mother owed to Brabantio she now owes to Othello, her husband. Brabantio, withdrawing in defeat, nevertheless delivers a fatal warning: "Look to her Moor, if thou hast eyes to see. / She has deceived her father, and may thee." It is fatal not because it is true but precisely because it is not. Brabantio's ill-meant and angry warning is harmful because it supports Othello's chaotic mistake later.

The domestic issue apparently resolved, the senate returns to the matter of Cyprus and the Turks. Desdemona entreats the senate to allow her to live with her husband in Cyprus and not be left behind in Venice. In her petition, she begins by acknowledging what marrying Othello involved. She calls it "My downright violence." She says she "saw Othello's visage in his mind" (significantly for the arguments Iago will later use to undermine Othello, she does not say she found what to like about him in his actual face but rather in his mind) and wants to share his adventures, for which she loved him, so that they can be hers, too. The senate adjourns after deciding the fleet's departure should be that night and that Desdemona should be entrusted to Iago's care on the voyage while Othello travels on another ship.

As they were the first to appear in the only act of *Othello* that takes place in Venice, so Roderigo and Iago are the last. Remaining after the senators have filed out, Roderigo laments that he will kill himself now that he has definitively lost Desdemona. Iago convinces him not to despair but rather to turn his property into money and follow the fleet to Cyprus, continuing his quest for Desdemona. She will not, Iago assures him, stay faithful to someone as distasteful as the Moor must become to her, considering her youth and her Venetian tastes. During the formation of this intrigue, Shakespeare also continues to develop Iago's religion, as it were, the things he holds as fundamental to his self-definition—primarily that he is the creator of himself and of the way others perceive reality. The scene ends with a soliloquy in which Iago promises to use his power in order to create complete chaos.

Act II

Act II begins on the seashore of Cyprus as several Venetians from the fortress look to the sea, which is tempestuous, and speculate about the fate of the Turkish fleet. A messenger enters, bearing the news that the storm confounded the Turkish fleet and, consequently, their design on Cyprus has been frustrated.

One after another, then, ships arrive from Venice. The first brings Cassio and his party. Cassio reports that the Turkish fleet has indeed been destroyed, but his happy news is tempered by his anxiety for the safety of Othello's ship, which was separated from the rest of the fleet during the storm. Next to arrive is the vessel carrying Desdemona, who is accompanied by Iago and his wife, Emilia, who also acts as Desdemona's maid and companion.

All the chief actors, except for Othello himself, are now collected onstage, awaiting the arrival of Othello's ship. During this interval of apparent comic relief, they pass the time, as Desdemona says of herself in an aside, "not merry" but to "beguile" their anxiety about Othello by seeming so. In this context they reveal their essential characteristics outside the context of the plot. Cassio shows himself to be a refined gentleman, a courtier in the tradition prescribed by Baldassare Castiglione in his handbook *The Courtier*. A soldier, he is also accomplished in the use of fine, decorated, and refined language and in gallant behavior—especially behavior that shows his devotion to women. On Desdemona's arrival, he greets her after asking the "men of Cypress, let her have your knees" as "the grace of heaven." When Emilia, Iago's wife, emerges, he kisses her, explaining to Iago that it ought not "gall your patience . . . That I extend my manners. 'Tis my breeding."

Iago then begins an interlude of comic ribaldry. He tells Cassio that he would have enough of Emilia if he got as much of her lip as Iago gets of her tongue. But all the while Emilia is silent, while Desdemona quietly supports her. "Alas, she has no speech," Desdemona says, countering Iago's portrayal of her as outspoken or a scold. This unspeaking Emilia, who can go through the play hardly noticed, as a sort of machinery of the plot, will burst forth with a torrent of searing and honest language in the last act of *Othello*.

Desdemona reveals herself, too, in her aside. She tells the audience that she is not actually merry but seems the thing she is not in order to "beguile," to trick, the oppressive feeling away. Desdemona is not a one-dimensional or passive character. She is a complex figure whom Shakespeare draws much more by innuendo, from her responses in particular situations, than by probing her the way he does Othello. The ways of her personality—not her virtue or her love—are what lend fuel to Iago's later assault upon her husband. There hangs over any reading of Desdemona the sense that she did dissemble, even if innocently, as her father claims. And later (III, iii, 20–26), when she promises aid to Cassio, she exclaims,

> assure thee,
> If I do vow a friendship, I'll perform it
> To the last article: my lord shall never rest;
> I'll watch him tame and talk him out of patience;
> His bed shall seem a school, his board a shrift;

I'll intermingle every thing he does
With Cassio's suit.

When she goes about her task, it is with an ardor that might irritate the fondest husband—even one who has not already been subverted, like Othello, in his ability to see straight. She persists in her demand to know when Othello will see Cassio: "tomorrow night, or Tuesday morn, / On Tuesday noon, or night, or Tuesday morn. / I prithee, name the time, but let it not / extend three days." She begs and bargains and stipulates. And then she begins the middle section of what is becoming a short oration, lecturing Othello on the insignificance of Cassio's fault, even recognizing that the conditions of war can change the way things are done. When Othello does not respond, she reminds him, "I wonder in my soul / What you should ask me, that I should deny you." When he finally yields and says, "Let him come when he will; / I will deny thee nothing," and she has won her suit, she is yet not content. "Why, this is not a boon; / 'Tis I should entreat you wear your gloves / Or feed on nourishing dishes or keep you warm / . . . Nay, when I have a suit / Wherein I mean to touch your love indeed, / It shall be full of poise and weight, / And fearful to be granted." Othello reassures her that he will grant her suit regarding Cassio and asks her to leave him for a while. She obeys, but not without a sharp riposte: "Shall I deny you? No. Farewell, my lord." It is this side of Desdemona that is foreshadowed in the character in Act II, scene 1, who banters with Iago.

As the interlude of waiting ends, Iago observes Cassio speaking to Desdemona and notices his gestures, how he takes her by the hand or kisses his three fingers as he speaks, and formulates his plot, incorporating the material he has just seen. When Othello arrives, there is more for him to observe. Othello takes Desdemona in his arms and renews his vow of love to her. They are both roused to such an ecstatic passion of joy that they nearly totter in their happiness. Iago notices that, too. "I cannot speak enough of this content," Othello exclaims after describing the ecstasy of his soul, "It stops me here [*touching his heart*]; it is too much of joy." In an aside, blending his voice with their experience, Iago says, "O, you are well-tuned now! / But I'll set down the pegs that make this music."

Before Iago does, however, Shakespeare devotes 10 lines to a picture of peace. Othello declares, "Our wars are done," greets old friends, speaks sweetly to Desdemona, and orders Iago to supervise the unloading of his ship. Before Iago obeys, when all the other actors have left the stage, again there appear on it only the stage manager and his principal prop, Roderigo, and Iago begins to set his plot and the rest of *Othello* itself in motion.

Honing the arguments he will later employ directly to Othello—particularly that for a young woman of Desdemona's complexion and class, marriage with Othello is against nature—Iago convinces Roderigo that Desdemona is in love with Cassio. He explains that Cassio is to command the guard that keeps order in Cyprus that night and instructs Roderigo to provoke him into a fight. By this strategy, Iago says, Roderigo will advance his cause with Desdemona. He agrees and Iago continues to develop the script of his plot, working himself up to carry it out in a soliloquy that ends the scene.

A herald appears and reads Othello's proclamation, which announces a triumphant celebration of the defeat of the Turkish fleet and of his marriage, with dances, bonfires, feasting, and reveling that night in Cyprus between five o'clock and eleven.

As Othello parts from Cassio that evening, leaving him responsibility for the watch, he confirms that "Iago is most honest" when Cassio mentions that he has already given instructions about the watch to Iago. Othello leaves and Iago enters. Rather than setting down to business, as Cassio orders, Iago counters merrily, "Not this hour, lieutenant; 'tis not yet ten o' the clock. Our general cast us thus early for the love of his Desdemona; who let us not therefore blame: he hath not yet made wanton the night with her; and she is sport for Jove." Cassio politely corrects him when he counters Iago's lascivious description of Desdemona, saying, "She's a most exquisite lady." But Iago transforms his effort with another debasing comment: "And I'll warrant her full of game." Once again Cassio goes on the defensive, saying, "Indeed, she's a most fresh and delicate nature." Their contest in verbal representation continues for a few more rounds, finally ending in Iago's triumphant, "well, happiness to their sheets!" He then invites Cassio to take a stoup of wine with him. When Cassio declines, citing his inability to hold his liquor, Iago persists and prevails, especially after Montano has given Cassio a little to drink. Once Cassio is inebriated, the plot unfolds as Iago had planned it earlier with Roderigo. Casio is seen drunk on duty. Roderigo gets Cassio into a skirmish. Drunken, brawling, and derelict in his duty, Cassio is disgraced. Iago, in testifying about him to Othello, twists rhetoric to make himself sound as if he were advocating for him when he is, in actuality, testifying against him. It is Othello, with his authority, who quells the riot instigated by Cassio's brawling, who questions his ensign, who rebukes his lieutenant, who sees to the care of the wounded, who deputizes Iago with authority while Cassio is in disgrace, and who comforts Desdemona, who had been awakened by the hubbub.

After everyone has departed, once again Iago remains, but rather than have Roderigo as his dupe/marionette, now he has Cassio. Like Roderigo bewailing his failure to win Desdemona, Cassio now bewails his drunken behavior and its consequences. As he used Roderigo's desires to further his own ends, so Iago uses Cassio's and advises him to sue to Desdemona to intervene with Othello for him. Iago knows the materials he is working with and which he must transform to seem other than they are in Othello's mind, for his description of Desdemona is remarkably true. That he knows what she is really like and how good she is—yet is unaffected by it except in as much as he wishes to crush her—is what gives fearsomeness to his strength. He says of her, as he explains to Cassio why it would be a good idea to petition Desdemona's intervention, that "[s]he is of so free, so kind, so apt, so blessed a disposition, she holds it a vice in her goodness not to do more than she is requested." He will use this goodness in her and make it look like evil, defining "debased ardor" rather than "blessed disposition" as the reason for her advocacy for Cassio.

Cassio leaves, grateful to Iago for his ear and his advice (unable to see him for what he is, the man who maneuvered him into his troubles). In a devilishly charming soliloquy, Iago then tries his art directly on the audience, acting delightful as he delights in the subversiveness of his evil. He makes the audience, by enjoying or fearing him, aware of his power; the viewers are complicit with him, nearly co-conspirators. Roderigo enters and interrupts his soliloquy, once again complaining: He is accomplishing nothing in Cyprus, he is spending his money, and tonight he was beaten up in a brawl. No longer needing him to move his plot forward, Iago puts Roderigo off by telling him to be patient. Once alone, Iago schemes. Now he needs his wife, Emilia, not Roderigo, to go to Desdemona with entreaties from Cassio. He also needs to guide Othello to the spot where Cassio will solicit Desdemona's aid. In other words, he has just outlined Act III, scene 3, of *Othello*.

Act III

The third act begins the next morning, when Cassio, following Iago's advice with Venetian excess, plants a band of musicians under their window to serenade Othello and Desdemona when they rise. A clown, also present, makes ribald jokes as he mocks the musicians and drives them out. He then teases Cassio, first changing the meaning of his words, giving an innocuous comic foreshadowing of Iago's sinister device. "Do you hear me, mine honest friend," Cassio says to the clown. The clown twists his words to be able to respond, "I hear not your honest friend. I hear you." As the clown parts with Cassio, further mocking his florid eloquence, Iago enters, making sure the stage is set. He is assured Cassio is ready to play his part, and he says he'll send Desdemona to him immediately; he will also take Othello aside so that "your converse and business / May be more free." It is just this tactic of his that Othello's character has made him shun every time Iago has advised him to be secretive. But Cassio accepts Iago's assurance of privacy with humble thanks, even after Emilia assures him that in the conversation she has just overheard between Desdemona and Othello, Othello was favorably inclined toward him.

Scene 2 is but six lines long. It shows the public Othello guiding a delegation inspecting the fortress and handing letters addressed to the Venetian senate to Iago. Othello instructs Iago to give these letters to the pilot of the ship leaving for Venice. It shows Othello in control and Iago subordinate.

As is his way, Iago is playing a double game and does not, in fact, provide Cassio with privacy when he speaks with Desdemona. As he has planned it, Iago steers Othello to their interview. As the interview ends and Desdemona has promised to use her full art and influence with Othello to help Cassio, Emilia announces that she sees Othello approaching. Cassio does not choose to stay. By this action he becomes the image of suspicion when Iago mutters, as if to himself, but loud enough for Othello to hear, "Ha! I like not that." When Othello asks what he said, Iago, rather than answering, responds with the vaguely unsettling, "Nothing my lord; or if," but breaks off with a dismissive, "I know not what." He has framed the situation so that when Othello says, "Was not that Cassio parted from my wife?" there is something ominous surrounding his words. Iago's response is a deft "Cassio, my lord? No, sure, I cannot think it / That he would steal away so guilty-like, / Seeing you coming." In the rhetorical act of seeming to exculpate Cassio, he actually incriminates him.

The strength of Desdemona's solicitation, to an unjaundiced eye, would only give it greater credibility. But because Othello's perspective is being shaped by Iago, Desdemona's ardor only suggests the wrong kind of attachment to Cassio. While Othello is apparently not alarmed by the ardor and insistence with which Desdemona argues in Cassio's favor in the first part of Act III, scene 3, its after-impression helps Iago when he later shapes Othello's thoughts to doubt her honesty and faithfulness. In Act III, scene 3, Othello assures Desdemona that he will grant her suit and asks her to leave him for a while. Alone with Othello now, Iago asks insinuatingly if Cassio knew about Othello's love for Desdemona before their marriage, while Othello was wooing her. Othello answers he did, "from first to last." When he then asks, "Why dost thou ask?" Iago's apparently innocuous answer, "but for a satisfaction of my thought, / No further harm," rings with the sound of something sinister. When Othello adds, defensively, that Cassio had been their go-between, Iago only says the puzzling, "Indeed?," which rattles Othello. "Indeed?" Othello repeats and then asserts, "Ay, indeed!" Othello asks, "Discern'st thou aught in that? / Is he not honest?" But Iago replies only by repeating his word, "Honest, my lord?" "Honest? Ay, honest," Othello states again. When Iago equivocates in his answer, Othello demands of him what he thinks, but Iago only repeats Othello's word as he had before: "Think, my lord?" At the end of his rope, Othello pushes his words back at him, crying out, "Think, my lord! By heaven, thou echoest me." Othello is nearly hooked now. "What are you hiding from me?" is the gist of his tirade, and he is ready to hear and accept anything Iago might reveal. Iago keeps taking him in circles, seeming to speak as his friend and protector, until he infects him with the idea that Desdemona has been unfaithful to him with Cassio and that she could *not possibly not have been*, given the disparity between her and Othello, given Othello's inferiority, given his race and age. Othello's very struggle not to believe what Iago insinuates brings him nearer belief. In order to reject Iago's estimate of him, he must entertain it. In order to struggle against the idea of Desdemona's infidelity, he must imagine it. Once imagined, it looms over him and finally consumes him.

Iago leaves Othello to a tormented reflection on his own inadequacies. Then Desdemona enters, seeing him in his debilitated state, and asks if he is not well. When he says with bitter self-mockery that he has "a pain upon my forehead," which she understands as a headache, he means to suggest that he feels the horns of a cuckolded husband growing upon his forehead. She attempts to tie her handkerchief around his head in order to soothe the ache, but her gesture only annoys him. As he pushes her away, she drops the handkerchief and follows him out, confused by his ill-tempered response. Emilia, who has been with her, sees the handkerchief and picks it up. She mentions she is glad to find it because Iago has repeatedly asked her to steal it, although she says she has no idea why. She resolves to have the handkerchief copied, give her husband the copy, and return the original to Desdemona, thus betraying neither her duty to her husband nor to her mistress.

When Iago reenters and finds Emilia alone, he begins to scold her, but she says she has "a thing for you," and he teases her, saying it's "a common thing to have a foolish wife." Goaded, she shows him the handkerchief to tease him but not yet to give it. He snatches it from her, however, and bids her to think no more about it and to leave him. She obeys, and Iago begins to weave the next strands of his plot, which involve dropping the handkerchief in Cassio's room and cementing Othello's jealousy with "trifles light as air." When Othello returns, Iago sees that his subversion is nearly accomplished. In the remainder of the scene, he wins Othello's trust entirely through innuendo, feigned reluctance to say what he knows, and outright lies. He succeeds in bringing Othello to the full rage of tormenting jealousy and simultaneously forges a bond of enduring service to him.

The fourth scene of Act III shifts locations to a street in Cyprus. Desdemona and Emilia are looking for Cassio's house so Desdemona can tell him that she has won his suit for him. In the context of Iago's lies about her and Cassio, it is telling that Shakespeare immediately makes it clear that Desdemona does not even know where Cassio lives. The clown, of whom she asks directions, plays with her words rather than answering her questions. She asks him where Cassio "lies," using the word in the sense of where he lodges. But the clown takes it in the sense of "where does he tell a falsehood" and refuses to answer for fear of calling a soldier a liar. When Desdemona changes her language, the clown says that he would lie if he answered because he does not know. This interlude offers comic relief in the midst of the painful unfolding of a man's destruction and the murder of a youthful spirit. But it also reflects the problem of the malleability of language, which is a theme at the heart of the play, since Iago fashions reality in Othello's mind with words falsely used.

The clown is dispatched to see if he can find where Cassio resides. Alone with Emilia, Desdemona is upset that she cannot find her handkerchief. She tells what great value it is to Othello and how such a lost handkerchief could make a husband jealous—therefore, she is grateful that Othello is not a jealous man. She defends him against Emilia's challenge, but the scene that follows—in which Othello demands the handkerchief from Desdemona with increasing jealous fury—allows Emilia to say of him, "Is not this man jealous?" Desdemona herself is confused, saying, "I never saw this before." As Emilia retorts how women are in general ill-used by their husbands, Iago enters, directing Cassio to speak with Desdemona. She tells him that she cannot do anything right now, but she will help when she can, and he must be patient, because Othello is displeased with her. Hearing this, Iago intervenes, "Is my lord angry?" and says he will go to attend to him.

Speaking by themselves, Desdemona and Emilia wonder what is troubling Othello, praying that it is not that "monster," jealousy. As they leave, Cassio remains onstage, and Bianca, a prostitute in love with Cassio, enters. She chides him for avoiding her, and he tells her that he has "with leaden thoughts been pressed" but will make up for it in the future. He gives her the handkerchief to take out and copy, since he likes the work. She protests that it was given him by a beloved, but he tells her not to be "vile," that he found it in his room and does not know how it got there. When he asks her then to leave him, she protests, but he says he does not want Othello to see him with a woman. He says he will walk a little way with her and then leave her. With the acceptance of circumstances women are expected to grant, she says, "'Tis very good. I must be circumstanced" [accept circumstances].

Act IV

Like the first act of the play, Act IV of *Othello* begins in the middle of a conversation. Now, however, it is not between Iago and Roderigo but rather Iago and Othello. Othello has taken Roderigo's place as Iago's gull, or dupe. Iago has so deeply penetrated Othello's consciousness that he can fabricate reality in his mind simply by stringing words together and making up painful erotic scenarios that trumpet Othello's betrayal:

Iago: Will you think so?
Othello: Think so, Iago!

Iago: What,
To kiss in private?

Othello: An unauthorized kiss.

Iago: Or to be naked with her friend in bed
An hour or more, not meaning any harm?

Othello: Naked in bed, Iago, and not mean harm!
It is hypocrisy against the devil:
They that mean virtuously, and yet do so,
The devil their virtue tempts, and they tempt heaven.

Iago: So they do nothing, 'tis a venial slip:
But if I give my wife a handkerchief, —

Brilliant psychologist that he is, Iago segues from these imaginings to the concrete matter of the missing handkerchief, yoking the truthfulness of those images to that apparent fact. The success of his assault is obvious when Othello, raving, "falls in a trance." While he is in a fit, Cassio enters. Iago explains that Othello is subject to such fit but tells Cassio he wants to speak with him once Othello has recovered.

Iago leaves and sets up the next scene. Othello, hidden and unobserved, will eavesdrop on a scene of Iago and Cassio talking lasciviously, he thinks, about Desdemona. It is actually Bianca, however, who is the butt of their ribaldry. Othello then watches as Bianca angrily returns Desdemona's handkerchief, insulted that she is being used to copy "some minx's token."

Alone with Iago, Othello cries of Cassio, "How shall I murder him, Iago?" Regarding Desdemona, he orders, "Get me some poison, Iago, this night." He is delighted to be overruled by Iago's injunction: "Do it not with poison. Strangle her in her bed, even the bed she has contaminated." Othello repeats, "Good, good! . . . Very good." Into the midst of this conversation, Desdemona and a deputation from Venice on state business, led by Lodovico, enter. As Othello reads letters from the senate ordering him to leave Cyprus for Mauritania, he overhears the polite conversation between Desdemona and Lodovico, in which she tells him regretfully of the falling out between her husband and Cassio. It angers him. When Lodovico tells her that he thinks the letters order Othello away, making Cassio governor of Cyprus, she responds, "Trust me. I am glad on't." Othello explodes, yells, and strikes her, shocking all who behold the blow. Lodovico intervenes and asks Othello to "make her amends." But Othello only continues to rage, claiming she weeps "crocodile" tears and ordering her "out of my sight," blind to the terrible irony that she already is: He can no longer see her. He only sees Iago's phantom, with which Iago has replaced her in Othello's mind. Iago, thereby, has subverted Desdemona as well as Othello, for each word or action of hers will be interpreted not in the context of herself but in the context of Iago's version of her, which has replaced her in Othello's mind.

Desdemona starts to leave, saying to Othello, "I will not stay to offend you." Lodovico implores Othello to call her back, and Othello does, using the opportunity to further humiliate Desdemona and himself. "What would you with her, sir?" he asks Lodovico once Desdemona has returned. Lodovico is surprised, as he did not desire anything with her but only that she should be called back and be asked forgiveness. Othello speaks of her as disobedient and a "whore" and leaves, cursing to himself. When Lodovico is alone with Iago, he voices his astonishment and questions him about Othello. Iago begins to attempt to ensnare him with innuendo against Othello, assurances of his own reluctance to speak, and suggestions that Lodovico look for himself.

The scene shifts. Othello is questioning Emilia about Desdemona. Emilia assures him with all her eloquence that Desdemona is pure and faithful. But when Othello bids her go fetch Desdemona, he thinks to himself that Emilia is nothing but a brothel mistress who will speak well of any of her girls. Of Desdemona he is convinced,

> This is a subtle whore,
> A closet lock and key of villanous secrets
> And yet she'll kneel and pray; I have seen her do't.

In this way Desdemona is negated, and her good actions are transformed, in his mind, into indications of her falseness. She pleads with him on her knees, but he merely sees her further damning herself with denials. He brands her a whore and, when she pleads she is none, he apologizes by saying he made a mistake when he took her for his wife. When he leaves, he summons Emilia and treats her as a brothel keeper, throwing her some coins. He is in a rage of perverse pleasure, enjoying the wit with which he accompanies his and his wife's degradation.

Alone with her mistress, Emilia begins to show concern for Desdemona. The quiet presence she had exhibited up to this point changes under the weight of circumstances. Emilia now becomes a strong, sure, and comic voice in the play. Even in front of Iago she curses the man who might infect another man's mind to jealousy and drive him to the madness that now torments Othello and his wife. Foreshadowing their interplay in Act V, scene 2, Iago tells his wife to be quiet. Now she is. Then she will not be.

When Desdemona and Emilia leave, Roderigo steps forward. Now he is at his wit's end, he tells Iago. He fears Iago is cheating him, his money is gone, and he will not put up with it any longer. He wants restitution of the monies he has given Iago in the attempt to corrupt Desdemona. Iago disarms him by congratulating him for his pluck in asserting himself. Iago tells Roderigo after one such act of real assertion, killing Cassio, Desdemona will be his. Roderigo leaves, mulling over Iago's plot.

Scene 3 begins at the Citadel, where Othello and Desdemona live. Othello is leaving with Lodovico and ordering Desdemona to get ready for bed. Alone and preparing for bed, Desdemona feels herself haunted by a song of unfaithfulness that she remembers her mother's maid, Barbary, singing after her own lover "proved mad / And did forsake her." Reflective after her song, Desdemona asks Emilia if there really are women who are unfaithful to their husbands and if she would do so "for all the world." Emilia responds, taking the words "for all the world" literally, and says she would "for the whole world." But Desdemona says she would not be unfaithful for anything. Starting by speaking of women's faults, Emilia quickly turns to their husbands and shows that they are the real cause of their wives' faults. She offers a category of similarities women share with men and concludes by reiterating that the ills women commit are in response to ill-treatment by men. But Desdemona says she prays for the strength and the ability not to do "bad" because bad was done to her "but by bad mend"—somehow to bring good from evil.

Act V

Out in the street, Iago readies Roderigo for the part he will play in what must be a climax in the drama Iago has directed: Cassio's murder in a street brawl. Iago plans Roderigo's, too, out of fear that Roderigo might try to regain the sums he gave Iago and tell what he knows of Iago's machinations. Cassio passes by. Roderigo lunges out at him, sword drawn. Cassio responds with his sword. They fight. Roderigo is injured; Cassio, cut in the leg and maimed. Othello enters to survey the results of the fight and is pleased to hear "The voice of Cassio" crying out, "I am maimed forever. Help, ho! Murder! Murder!" Othello blesses Iago's "noble sense of thy friend's wrong" and leaves for Desdemona's bedchamber, where he vows, "Thy bed, lust stained, shall with lust's blood be spotted."

After Othello withdraws, Lodovico and Gratiano pass by and hear Cassio's and Roderigo's cries for help. Iago then enters, carrying a light and a weapon, an irreproachable representative of authority. He is the first to put forth a question. "Who's there?" he demands. "What noise is this that cries on murder?" Hearing Cassio's voice, he asks him who has done this. Cassio does not know but says he thinks that one of them is nearby. Iago asks Lodovico and Gratiano for help. Seeing the wounded Roderigo, Iago falls upon him, crying, "That's one of them," and, stabbing Roderigo, calls "O murd'rous slave! O villain!" Roderigo, only upon being fatally wounded, fully realizes how he has been abused. "O Damned Iago! O inhuman dog!" he curses. After he dies, attention is then paid to Cassio, whose wound is bound. When Bianca passes by and hears Cassio's cries, she approaches him with comfort, but Iago apprehends her, saying she is a strumpet, a prostitute who may somehow be involved in the crime. Cassio is removed in a chair, and Iago follows to see him cared for. He orders Emilia to hasten to the Citadel to tell Othello and Desdemona of the night's events.

Scene 2, the final scene of *Othello*, is breathtaking for its dramatic and verbal poetry. Othello enters to find Desdemona asleep beside a still-burning candle and, with great delicacy, grieves over what he is about to do. He is convinced he is impelled by honor, not by a base impulse. He realizes the weight of a human life: He can relight a candle he snuffs out, but he cannot make breath he has stopped breathe again. He kisses Desdemona in her sleep, torn between his love for her and his diseased sense of love and justice, which demands her death. She wakes. With a sense that he is performing a holy action, he asks Desdemona if she has prayed. She says she has, and he asks her to remember "any crime / Unreconciled as yet to heaven and grace," so that she may add it to her prayers because he "would not kill thy unprepared spirit . . . / I would not kill thy soul." Alarmed, Desdemona says, "Talk you of killing?" His acknowledgement triggers her cry of "heaven / have mercy on me!" He replies, "Amen, with all my heart." She then begs him not to kill her. He tells her to remember her sins. She protests, "They are loves I bear to you." "For that thou diest," he answers. Desdemona pleads with him, but he tells her to "be still." Saying she will, nevertheless, she asks him, "What's the matter?" He tells her: "The handkerchief which I so loved and gave thee, / Thou gav'st to Cassio." He responds to her denial by warning her that she is on her deathbed and, therefore, must not perjure herself. Her protestations have no effect. He is beyond believing anything she says. He saw the handkerchief in Cassio's hands, he says. "He found it then," she counters. She swears she never gave it to him and implores Othello: "Send for him hither. / Let him confess the truth." Othello responds that Cassio has confessed "[t]hat he has used thee," and Iago has killed him. When Desdemona groans, "Alas, he is betrayed, and I undone," Othello storms, "Out strumpet! Weep'st thou for him to my face?" Enraged, he then strangles her as she struggles. As Desdemona's resistance melts and she lies dying, Emilia calls from outside the bedroom door. Othello hears her and guesses she has come "to speak of Cassio's death." He hesitates to admit her to the bedchamber, for "If she come in, she'll sure speak to my wife." And then the enormity, finality, and horror of what he has done hit him:

> My wife! my wife! what wife? I have no wife.
> O insupportable! O heavy hour!
> Methinks it should be now a huge eclipse
> Of sun and moon, and that the affrighted globe
> Should yawn at alteration.

When Emilia enters, she does not, at first, see Desdemona murdered on her bed but instead tells Othello that Cassio has killed Roderigo. Othello, not hearing what she actually said, responds, "Roderigo killed? And Cassio killed?" When she responds, "No, Cassio is not killed," Othello cries out, "Not Cassio killed? Then murder's out of tune, / And sweet revenge grows harsh." Significantly, almost as if it were a slip of the tongue, Othello, in his fury that Cassio has not been killed, reveals that revenge, not justice or sacrifice, was the motive for his murdering Desdemona. As he speaks, Emilia hears a dying cry from Desdemona, "falsely, falsely murdered." Emilia cries for help, and when she demands to know "who hath done this deed," Desdemona responds in her last breaths, "Nobody—I myself. Farewell. / Commend me to my kind lord," and dies, even in death maintaining her absolute loyalty to her husband. It is the only falsehood that she utters in the course of the play. Othello, at first, tries to deny his responsibility: "Why, how should she be murdered?" he asks; "You heard her say herself, it was not I." But then he confronts himself and groans, "She's like a liar gone to burning hell! / 'Twas I that killed her." His confession is not yet acknowledgment of a wrong, however, for he justifies himself by saying that Desdemona was false, "a whore." Emilia calls him a devil and says he lies. Othello insists that "Cassio did top her" and, in corroboration, she ought to "[a]sk thy husband." The exchange between them mirrors and reverses the exchange between Iago and Othello in Act III, scene 3, beginning at line 99, in which Iago echoes Othello's words to make him doubtful of what he thinks. In Act V, scene 2, when Emilia hears Othello implicate Iago in the murder of Desdemona and the attack on Cassio, she replies, dumbfounded, "My husband?" Othello repeats, "Thy husband." With each further revelation that Othello makes against Iago, Emilia repeats with greater alarm, "My husband," until Othello says to her—as he had once said to Iago, "By heaven, thou echoest me"—"What needs this iterance? Woman, I say thy husband."

"If he say so," Emilia retorts, "may his pernicious soul / Rot half a grain a day. He lies to the heart. / She was too fond of her most filthy bargain." Provoked by her words, Othello draws his sword against her to quiet her, but she is fearless with outrage and cries out for "Help! / The Moor hath killed my mistress! Murder! murder!" Her cry brings Montano and Gratiano, two Venetian nobles deployed in the administration of Cyprus, as well as Iago. Immediately upon seeing her husband, she scolds him, "You have done well, / That men must lay their murders on your neck." She orders him to "[d]isprove this villain" [Othello] and deny that he told him Desdemona was false. Equivocation being useless under her grilling, Iago admits, "I did." Emilia cries out, "You told a lie, an odious damned lie! / Upon my soul, a lie! A wicked lie!" Her honest and open denunciation of Iago breaks the hold he has had on language throughout the play. Despite the actual horror of the events upon the stage, the audience and readers can now experience the opposite of the dread that Iago's speech invites, the relief of hearing truth proclaimed and crooked things made straight. Strengthened by the very act of speaking, Emilia asks Iago, "She false with Cassio? Did you say with Cassio?" He confesses he did but attempts to use his husband's prerogative and instructs her, "Go to, charm your tongue." She defies him: "I will not charm my tongue; I am bound to speak: / My mistress lies murdered in her bed." While the attendants in the chamber respond in amazement and Othello says, "It is true, indeed," Emilia continues to pour forth her anger and defiance, calling out "villany" and refusing to obey Iago's command to go home.

In his grief, Othello attempts to explain his act and justify it, thus assuring himself, if his explanation is credited, that he has not fallen from his position of honor. He tells how a handkerchief he gave Desdemona was then given by Desdemona to Cassio. Emilia continues her magnificent aria, beginning, "O God! O heavenly God!" Iago interrupts, telling her to be quiet. She refuses, and he draws his sword. But she continues,

> O thou dull Moor! that handkerchief thou speak'st of
> I found by fortune and did give my husband;
> For often, with a solemn earnestness,
> More than indeed belong'd to such a trifle,
> He begg'd of me to steal it.

Iago calls her a "villainous whore," ironically the same slander he sought to attach to Desdemona. But Emilia continues to defy him and explains that Desdemona did not give the handkerchief to Cassio; that she, Emilia, found it "And I did give't my husband." Now enlightened, complete darkness overcomes Othello. He runs, sword drawn, at Iago but is prevented from stabbing him; however, during this business, Iago stabs Emilia, joining Othello in wife murder. Emilia is laid beside Desdemona in death. Iago flees. As Emilia lies dying, singing the willow song Desdemona had sung when preparing for bed, Othello decides to kill himself, for his "honor" ought not to outlive the "honesty" of Desdemona's chastity and the faithfulness and "honesty" of Emilia's revelation.

At this point, nearly everything that is going to happen in *Othello* has happened. Iago will be captured, refuse to speak further, and be removed to be tortured and made to confess. Cassio will be deputed in Othello's place, and Lodovico will return to Venice to make a report to the senate. The only thing remaining is Othello himself. He kills himself. But as he suffers his pre-death agony, in the most exquisite and powerful verse, Othello bares himself and finds himself unbearable. He tears himself apart, convinced that the last service he can do for the Venetian state is to kill himself as one who has offended, in his fall, the city-state of Venice itself.

KEY PASSAGES IN
OTHELLO

☙

Act I, i, 58–66

Were I the Moor, I would not be Iago:
In following him, I follow but myself;
Heaven is my judge, not I for love and duty,
But seeming so, for my peculiar end:
For when my outward action doth demonstrate
The native act and figure of my heart
In compliment extern, 'tis not long after
But I will wear my heart upon my sleeve
For daws to peck at: I am not what I am.

Shakespeare begins *Othello* in the middle of a conversation between Iago and Roderigo. As they speak, the spectator or reader becomes aware of the issues that drive each. For Roderigo, it is love for Desdemona. For Iago, it is hatred of Othello. Iago has just told Roderigo that Othello has that very night married Desdemona. Roderigo is incensed that Iago has not let him know of the impending marriage sooner, especially because Iago has represented himself to Roderigo as a go-between for him and has taken money from him, presumably to buy gifts for Desdemona in support of Roderigo's courtship.

This passage occurs just after Iago tells Roderigo that he hates Othello for having promoted Michael Cassio, instead of himself, to be his lieutenant. Roderigo challenges him, saying that he would not serve Othello under such circumstances. After Iago explains, "I follow him to serve my turn upon him," he talks about himself, giving this sharply defined and accurate description of himself.

The great western Socratic belief encapsulated in the phrase "Know thyself" is usually thought of as a key to virtue. Given this speech of his, it is clear that Iago does know himself. In his case, however, the Socratic maxim is subverted by a Machiavellian duplicity. Iago knows himself because, he believes, he constructs himself through the power of his own will. Iago's knowledge of himself is not a mark of virtue but rather a technique of evil. Yet in his ambiguous formula,

23

"Were I the Moor, I would not be Iago," he reveals something about himself that he may not know. If he were Othello, he seems to be saying, he would not want to have a person like Iago around him, because of the illwill Iago bears him and the evil he will commit. But there is the sense of another meaning in his words, too. If he were Othello, whom he would prefer to be and regrets not being, he would not have to be Iago.

What he does say clearly, and what will inform the ways in which the audience or reader perceives his every word and deed—and which the characters in the play, to their great disadvantage, do not know—is that he is not what he seems to be and that everything he says and does is calculated to deceive.

Act I, i, 68–74

Call up her father,
Rouse him: make after him, poison his delight,
Proclaim him in the streets; incense her kinsmen,
And, though he in a fertile climate dwell,
Plague him with flies: though that his joy be joy,
Yet throw such changes of vexation on't,
As it may lose some colour.

With these words directing Roderigo to arouse Brabantio, Iago begins the action of the play and reveals the depths of his delight in causing and observing painful suffering.

Act I, i, 83–89

'Zounds, sir, you're robb'd; for shame, put on your gown;
Your heart is burst, you have lost half your soul;
Even now, now, very now, an old black ram
Is tupping your white ewe. Arise, arise;
Awake the snorting citizens with the bell,
Or else the devil will make a grandsire of you:
Arise, I say.

Here is Iago, in his role as author/director of the action of the play, telling Brabantio what to feel, what to do, what his motivation is, and what action he must take. To start off his campaign against Othello, Iago rouses Desdemona's father to let him know his daughter has eloped with Othello. He speaks in graphically obscene language. Nevertheless, in its raw eloquence it is a linguistic delight and presents an indelibly defining image of the marriage of Othello and Desdemona.

Despite what the audience or readers know about Iago, he insinuates himself into an intimate relationship with them. He charms them as he will Othello and the other characters in the play. He is full of brio and vitality. When he refers to the act of sexual intercourse between Othello and Desdemona as "an old black ram / . . . tupping your white ewe," he is, despite his maliciousness, nearly irresistible, just as he is when he describes them, at line 112, as "making the beast with two backs."

In addition to telling Brabantio what has happened, Iago also instructs him in how to react and rouses him to heightened feeling, not only with his graphic obscenity but also by his narration of those feelings, as if he were a director motivating an actor: "Your heart has burst, you have lost your soul. / Even now, now, very now . . ."

―――――――――――

Act I, ii, 29–30

Iago: You were best go in.
Othello: Not I; I must be found.

Iago's first attempt to practice upon Othello fails. Despite the approach of a troop of men possibly sent by Brabantio, Othello stands firm, exhibiting no sense of guilt. He faces situations; he does not run from them. And that is true of him even to the manner of his death. In contrast, Cassio, in Act III, scene 3, line 30, at the end of his interview with Desdemona, does the opposite. He leaves when Othello approaches, consequently making himself look guilty. Had he stayed, as Desdemona suggested, things would have gone better all around, and Iago would have been robbed of material to further his deception.

―――――――――――

Act I, ii, 59–86

Othello: Keep up your bright swords, for the dew will rust them.
Good signior, you shall more command with years
Than with your weapons.
Brabantio: O thou foul thief, where hast thou stow'd my daughter?
Damn'd as thou art, thou hast enchanted her;
For I'll refer me to all things of sense,
If she in chains of magic were not bound,
Whether a maid so tender, fair and happy,
So opposite to marriage that she shunned

The wealthy curled darlings of our nation,
Would ever have, to incur a general mock,
Run from her guardage to the sooty bosom
Of such a thing as thou, to fear, not to delight.
Judge me the world, if 'tis not gross in sense
That thou hast practised on her with foul charms,
Abused her delicate youth with drugs or minerals
That weaken motion: I'll have't disputed on;
'Tis probable and palpable to thinking.
I therefore apprehend and do attach thee
For an abuser of the world, a practiser
Of arts inhibited and out of warrant.
Lay hold upon him: if he do resist,
Subdue him at his peril.
Othello: Hold your hands,
Both you of my inclining, and the rest:
Were it my cue to fight, I should have known it
Without a prompter. Where will you that I go
To answer this your charge?

This early depiction of Othello in the midst of confusion shows not only the strength of his character, the clarity of his mind, his confidence in himself, and the firmness of his authority but also the commanding eloquence and authentic grandeur of his speech.

Act I, iii, 76–109

Othello: Most potent, grave, and reverend signiors,
My very noble and approved good masters,
That I have ta'en away this old man's daughter,
It is most true; true, I have married her:
The very head and front of my offending
Hath this extent, no more. Rude am I in my speech,
And little bless'd with the soft phrase of peace:
For since these arms of mine had seven years' pith,
Till now some nine moons wasted, they have used
Their dearest action in the tented field,
And little of this great world can I speak,
More than pertains to feats of broil and battle,
And therefore little shall I grace my cause
In speaking for myself. Yet, by your gracious patience,

I will a round unvarnish'd tale deliver
Of my whole course of love; what drugs, what charms,
What conjuration and what mighty magic,
For such proceeding I am charged withal,
I won his daughter.
Brabantio: A maiden never bold;
Of spirit so still and quiet, that her motion
Blush'd at herself; and she, in spite of nature,
Of years, of country, credit, every thing,
To fall in love with what she fear'd to look on!
It is a judgment maim'd and most imperfect
That will confess perfection so could err
Against all rules of nature, and must be driven
To find out practises of cunning hell,
Why this should be. I therefore vouch again
That with some mixtures powerful o'er the blood,
Or with some dram conjured to this effect,
He wrought upon her.
Duke of Venice: To vouch this, is no proof,
Without more wider and more overt test
Than these thin habits and poor likelihoods
Of modern seeming do prefer against him.

These 33 lines, in which Othello, Brabantio, and the Duke speak, not only set forward the present business and project the characteristics of each of the speakers. They also serve as an overture to the play itself, introducing the themes that will provide the matter for the action of the play.

Othello, in his address to the senators, shows the probity of his character, his faith in himself, and his ability to deny Brabantio's accusations that he subverted Desdemona's will with drugs and magic. But what Othello does not say shows there is something about himself that gives him pause and, if it were to be excavated, could undermine his self-confidence. The issue of Brabantio's objection to his color and culture, although akin to it, displaces it. But Othello, after all, did *elope* with Desdemona rather than openly marry her after properly requesting her hand of her father, whom, he says at line 128, "loved me." Why he chose not to get married openly he does not address, and he is not asked to.

The troubling undercurrent that will eventually drown Othello and Desdemona in its upsurge is referred to by Brabantio as he interrupts Othello in the above passage. Desdemona, Brabantio says, could not "fall in love with what she fear'd to look on!" The marriage goes "[a]gainst all rules of nature." He is, of course, referring to their racial disparity. While it is true that Desdemona's response was not as her father describes it, the elopement suggests that Othello sensed that asking her father for her hand would have brought forth resistance to his blackness, which, so far in Venice, he had managed to avoid and which his pride required him not to confront.

Brabantio's indictment, moreover, unintended though it is, is also an indictment of Desdemona—one that will prove ominous later on. She may have appeared to her father, at least, as a "maiden never bold, / Of spirit so still and quiet that her motion / Blushed at herself." Such seeming, however, is contradicted by her own bold and freely chosen behavior. While she appeared one way to her father, she was, in fact, not at all that way. She had a will of her own. It is that aspect of her that Brabantio will hurl at Othello at line 289 when he surrenders his opposition to her marriage but warns, "Look to her, Moor, if thou hast eyes to see: / She has deceived her father, and may thee." All the ingredients necessary for Iago's plot are here presented.

When the Duke intervenes, his admonition to Brabantio, that "To vouch this, is no proof," is not only wise and temperate but also foreshadows Othello's own unwise temperance when he demands of Iago "ocular proof" of Desdemona's infidelity.

—◦◦◦— —◦◦◦— —◦◦◦—

Act I, iii, 316–329

'Tis in ourselves that we are thus or thus. Our bodies are our gardens,
to the which our wills are gardeners: so that if we will plant nettles, or
sow lettuce, set hyssop and weed up thyme, supply it with one gender of
herbs, or distract it with many, either to have it sterile with idleness, or
manured with industry, why, the power and corrigible authority of this
lies in our wills. If the balance of our lives had not one scale of reason to
poise another of sensuality, the blood and baseness of our natures would
conduct us to most preposterous conclusions: but we have reason to cool
our raging motions, our carnal stings, our unbitted lusts, whereof I take
this that you call love to be a sect or scion.

In this passage, using the image of a gardener tending a garden, Iago sets forth his credo of human freedom. He imagines each person divided into a garden and a gardener who tends him or her. He suggests that it is up to each person to create his or her own identity. He asserts the atheistic notion that individuals are not bound or defined by the will and shaping of a higher creator. Not bound by or to anything, people are, Iago determines, free creatures who, by intellect, create themselves as they choose to, self-advantage being their truest guide.

—◦◦◦— —◦◦◦— —◦◦◦—

Act II, i, 177–195

Othello: It gives me wonder great as my content
To see you here before me. O my soul's joy!
If after every tempest come such calms,
May the winds blow till they have waken'd death!
And let the labouring bark climb hills of seas
Olympus-high and duck again as low
As hell's from heaven! If it were now to die,
'Twere now to be most happy; for, I fear,
My soul hath her content so absolute
That not another comfort like to this
Succeeds in unknown fate.
Desdemona: The heavens forbid
But that our loves and comforts should increase,
Even as our days do grow!
Othello: Amen to that, sweet powers!
I cannot speak enough of this content;
It stops me here; it is too much of joy:
    They kiss
And this, and this, the greatest discords be
That e'er our hearts shall make!
Iago: [aside]   O, you are well tuned now!
But I'll set down the pegs that make this music,
As honest as I am.

Othello's meeting with Desdemona when he arrives safely in Cyprus is scored like a trio. Othello and Desdemona embrace as he pours forth his delight in "see[ing] you here before me. O my soul's joy!" In his exaltation there is, however buried, the slightest measure of anxiety: "My soul hath her content so absolute / That not another comfort like to this/ Succeeds in unknown fate." Desdemona answers him, "The heavens forbid / But that our loves and comforts should increase / Even as our days do grow." Othello says "Amen," and speaking of his overwhelming happiness, he kisses her, praying that these kisses "the greatest discords be."

Iago, the third voice of the trio, then enters, conjoining himself with the lovers by usurping the musical metaphor in Othello's word "discord," saying, "O, you are well tuned now! / But I'll set down the pegs that make this music." This cluster shows how the very height of Othello's emotion is just what is necessary for the vertigo Iago will induce. The trio ends with Iago's charming, disarming joke at his own expense. He makes the audience complicit in his plot by the wicked self-mockery of his words: "As honest as I am."

Act II, i, 276–303

That Cassio loves her, I do well believe it;
That she loves him, 'tis apt and of great credit:
The Moor, howbeit that I endure him not,
Is of a constant, loving, noble nature,
And I dare think he'll prove to Desdemona
A most dear husband. Now, I do love her too;
Not out of absolute lust, though peradventure
I stand accountant for as great a sin,
But partly led to diet my revenge,
For that I do suspect the lusty Moor
Hath leap'd into my seat; the thought whereof
Doth, like a poisonous mineral, gnaw my inwards;
And nothing can or shall content my soul
Till I am even'd with him, wife for wife,
Or failing so, yet that I put the Moor
At least into a jealousy so strong
That judgment cannot cure. Which thing to do,
If this poor trash of Venice, whom I trash
For his quick hunting, stand the putting on,
I'll have our Michael Cassio on the hip,
Abuse him to the Moor in the rank garb—
For I fear Cassio with my night-cap too—
Make the Moor thank me, love me, and reward me.
For making him egregiously an ass
And practising upon his peace and quiet
Even to madness. 'Tis here, but yet confused:
Knavery's plain face is never seen tin used.

Iago's soliloquy here is not an honest *expression* of his inner mind, nor is it meant to be. It is an *exposition of the workings* of his inner mind. It shows him brainstorming, spinning a plot, making an outline. It shows how he "psychs himself up" for the project at hand by imagining Othello and Cassio sleeping with his wife, Emilia, and by imagining himself desiring Desdemona. He is setting forth a series of suppositions and testing their reasonableness. He is putting together a story. Whether the story is true or not is irrelevant as long as it is believable and as long as he can get himself into the state of believing it himself. Why should Cassio not love Desdemona? Why should she not love him? Why should he not believe his own wife has been unfaithful? All these things are possible. What makes them impossible is only the nature of the two people, Desdemona and Cassio, but his scheme must override their natures, which it does by focusing on Othello's insecurity and by subverting their speech via Othello's prejudiced judgment. He must "put the Moor / . . . into a jealousy so strong / That judgment cannot cure."

Act II, iii, 106

The lieutenant is to be saved before the ancient.

This is Cassio speaking, drunk on the wine with which Iago has plied him. He is shown to be argumentative, and in the argument his own sense of pride and position asserts itself. It makes the motive for his fight with Roderigo credible when, in angry confusion, he cries at line 144, "A knave teach me my duty?"

Act II, iii, 343–350

For whiles this honest fool
Plies Desdemona to repair his fortunes
And she for him pleads strongly to the Moor,
I'll pour this pestilence into his ear,
That she repeals him for her body's lust;
And by how much she strives to do him good,
She shall undo her credit with the Moor.
So will I turn her virtue into pitch . . .

In a nutshell, Iago presents his plot and the plot of the play. It is his genius to make things seem like what they are not and to subvert meaning, making good appear to be evil. Iago will frame Desdemona in order to control Othello's mind by influencing how Othello understands the meaning of her words and actions.

Act III, iii

This scene, in its entirety, is pivotal in *Othello*. In 475 lines Shakespeare transforms the self-possessed, confident, and disciplined Othello into a distraught prisoner, bound to Iago and tormented by a jealous rage. The scene is constructed as a smooth and seamless progression of several encounters flowing one into the other. In it Shakespeare not only deepens the portrayal of each of the major characters, but he also makes their characters the driving force of the plot. Cassio's mixture of pride and shame, Desdemona's innocent

boldness, Othello's fear that his social standing and self-regard are funda-
mentally inauthentic, Iago's skill as a rhetorician who can insinuate himself
into his auditor's consciousness through verbal manipulation, Emilia's acceptance of her subjugation to her husband: All are depicted and employed as
the elements that move the action of the play forward.

At line 30, Cassio has just finished asking Desdemona if she will intercede
with Othello for him. Desdemona has assured him, with a determined spirit,
that she will. Emilia announces Othello's entrance. Guilty about his misconduct
and ashamed of himself, Cassio says he will not stay. It is precisely the wrong
move. It is not what Othello did earlier in the play when Iago advised him, "You
were best go in," as Brabantio and his men came in search of him (I, ii, 29).
There Othello responded, "Not I. I must be found," and by that stand he asserted
his assurance of his virtue and pride. Unlike Cassio, Othello was sure of his
worth and aware of the service he had performed for the state.

Iago uses Cassio's departure to begin his work of infecting Othello with
jealousy. Seeing him leave, Iago mutters, half inaudibly, "I like not that." When
Othello asks him what he just said, Iago acts confused: "Nothing, my lord; or
if—I know not what," which arouses Othello's curiosity and suspicion. Thus,
when Othello asks, "Was not that Cassio parted from my wife?" his question
has an uneasiness it would not have had without Iago's previous observation.
Iago's response deepens Othello's uneasiness. He repeats Othello's question with
a question, "Cassio, my lord?" It's a technique he continues to use throughout the
scene, as if he were holding something back for Othello's own good. Asserting
something by denying it, he says, "I cannot think it / That he would steal away
so guilty-like / Seeing you coming."

With these few words Iago frames the way Othello hears whatever
Desdemona says to him. She, of course, begins to plead Cassio's cause. Not yet
entirely subverted by Iago, Othello hears her but delays yielding immediately to
her request. In consequence, she presses harder.

At line 93, after Desdemona has pleaded her case for Cassio and then departed,
Iago begins his work on Othello in earnest, asking if Cassio, as Desdemona has
just said, had acted as a go-between for the couple. He insinuates that there
is something disturbing in this, that there was a troubling intimacy, perhaps,
between them. Throughout, he uses the same technique of interrupting himself
and of repeating Othello's words, as if preventing himself from saying things
that might hurt Othello and yet he seems duty-bound to reveal. His aim is to
make Othello unsure of himself.

Implicitly contrasting Cassio and Othello and speculating about Desdemona's
character, Iago uses the same arguments against the possibility of Desdemona's
loving Othello (i.e., for Desdemona to marry him, it would go against nature,
for she must find his blackness appalling and his age unsatisfying) that her
father had previously used and Othello had so well withstood. Iago's genius is

to undermine Othello's self-regard so subtly that these arguments now trouble him. Iago insinuates rather than declares things; he does not tell Othello to be jealous but rather to beware of being jealous. By leading Othello to deny that he is jealous, Iago forces Othello to entertain the possibility that he is jealous.

Iago's coup de grace is to urge Othello to put off restoring Cassio's office. He shrewdly admits Cassio deserves reinstatement, but he suggests the delay will give Othello the opportunity to measure how ardently Desdemona intercedes for him. Once Iago leaves him alone, Othello, in a painful soliloquy, worries over the things Iago has said as if they were his own thoughts, mulling about his blackness, regretting having married, and vowing to cast Desdemona aside despite his great love for her should she prove false.

As he is plagued by these thoughts, Desdemona returns. Seeing her, he cannot believe that she is dishonest. Nevertheless, his ordeal has weakened him, and when he tells her his head aches—bitterly implying that he feels the horns of a cuckold, a betrayed husband—she offers to bind it with her handkerchief. He stops her, probably pushing her hand away from his head, and she drops the handkerchief. Focused on him, she does not even notice she has dropped it. They exit together, leaving Emilia, who had accompanied Desdemona, alone onstage. Emilia sees the handkerchief, picks it up, and notes that it is the one Iago had been asking her to steal from Desdemona. She says she will have the handkerchief copied, give the copy to Iago, and return the original to Desdemona. But when Iago teases her at line 297, she teases him back by saying she has something he wants. When she dangles the handkerchief in front of him, he grabs it from her and sends her away, ordering her to forget about the handkerchief.

When Othello reenters at line 327, tormenting himself with jealous fears, Iago notes with satisfaction how he has destroyed Othello's peace of mind. "Not poppy nor mandragora / Nor all the drowsy syrups of the world / Shall ever medicine thee to that sweet sleep / Which thou owedst yesterday," he says to himself, his words aimed at Othello. He continues to work upon Othello, telling him that he has slept beside Cassio lately and that in his sleep Cassio had called Desdemona's name. In addition, he says he has seen Cassio using Desdemona's handkerchief to wipe his beard. Othello is inflamed with jealous rage and longs to avenge himself.

The scene ends with Othello making Iago his lieutenant and Iago vowing his loyalty to Othello: "I am your own for ever."

—◊◊◊—　—◊◊◊—　—◊◊◊—

Act IV, i, 264–283

Lodovico: Is this the noble Moor whom our full senate
Call all in all sufficient? Is this the nature

Whom passion could not shake? whose solid virtue
The shot of accident, nor dart of chance,
Could neither graze nor pierce?
Iago: He is much changed.
Lodovico: Are his wits safe? Is he not light of brain?
Iago: He's that he is: I may not breathe my censure
What he might be: if what he might he is not,
I would to heaven he were!
Lodovico: What, strike his wife!
Iago: 'Faith, that was not so well; yet would I knew
That stroke would prove the worst!
Lodovico: Is it his use?
Or did the letters work upon his blood,
And new-create this fault?
Iago: Alas, alas!
It is not honesty in me to speak
What I have seen and known. You shall observe him,
And his own courses will denote him so
That I may save my speech: do but go after,
And mark how he continues.

Lodovico, the emissary sent by the Venetian senate to recall Othello, has just seen unbelievable things. Othello, in a confused passion, has struck Desdemona and spoken of her in sexually abusive language. Lodovico's astonishment reminds the audience of what Othello was, a man "whose solid virtue / The shot of accident nor dart of chance / Could neither graze nor pierce." The irony is that he is speaking of the change in Othello to Iago, the engineer of that change. When he asks if Othello's "wits" are "safe" and "Is he not light of brain?" Iago responds with the same rhetorical trick he used on Othello, presenting himself as reluctant to speak a truth that might reflect badly on the person of whom he speaks, only overcoming his reluctance for the sake of his interlocutor. Additionally, he strengthens his own position by saying to Lodovico, essentially, not to take his word for it but to see the truth for himself. Iago is masterful at manipulating appearances and making what is seen appear to corroborate his own words.

Act IV, ii, 46–63

Had it pleased heaven
To try me with affliction; had they rain'd
All kinds of sores and shames on my bare head.

Steep'd me in poverty to the very lips,
Given to captivity me and my utmost hopes,
I should have found in some place of my soul
A drop of patience: but, alas, to make me
A fixed figure for the time of scorn
To point his slow unmoving finger at!
Yet could I bear that too; well, very well:
But there, where I have garner'd up my heart,
Where either I must live, or bear no life;
The fountain from the which my current runs,
Or else dries up; to be discarded thence!
Or keep it as a cistern for foul toads
To knot and gender in! Turn thy complexion there,
Patience, thou young and rose-lipp'd cherubin,—
Ay, there, look grim as hell!

In the midst of a scene in which he discharges his rage, branding Desdemona a whore, and is unable to accept her avowal of faithfulness and obedience, Othello focuses these lines upon himself, revealing what it is about her presumed infidelity that so undermines him. He is a soldier and as such capable of confronting adversity with heroism, which can be defined by his behavior rather than by its outcome. Affliction, poverty, captivity—these he could have met with patience. What is intolerable is the shame at being recognized as a fool who has given his heart unwisely. Outside affliction would not undermine how he appeared, but his own participation in his affliction does. The irony is that Othello is just such a dupe, not of Desdemona but of Iago, surrendering his heart foolishly to him, not to Desdemona.

Act IV, iii, 103–104

Good night, good night: Heaven me such uses send,
Not to pick bad from bad, but by bad mend!

The last scene of Act IV of *Othello* offers an apparently tranquil interlude following Desdemona's public humiliation and preceding her murder. Yet it is not, actually, particularly tranquil in itself. Desdemona cannot keep her head from drooping and from remembering a servant girl from her childhood, a girl who was betrayed by her lover and died of it. She sings "Willow," the melancholy song of the girl's betrayal. When she and Emilia discuss the disparity between men and women, Emilia eloquently lists women's grievances and supports a kind of war between the sexes to assert equality for women. But Desdemona concludes from all the ills enumerated in the scene that she wishes "Heaven me such uses send, / Not to pick bad from bad, but by bad mend!" She would be something like a gardener-magician turning weeds to flowers, evil to good. She does not fail entirely in *Othello*, however, for of the two principles, evil did not ever subvert good. Despite being murdered, Desdemona remained faithful, even in death. While evil triumphed in action, good triumphed in principle, its spirit incarnated in Desdemona.

Act V, ii, 1–3

It is the cause, it is the cause, my soul,—
Let me not name it to you, you chaste stars!—
It is the cause.

Othello utters these lines upon entering the bedchamber and finding Desdemona asleep, with a burning candle by the bed. The vagueness of these three lines—in which "it" has no reference, "cause" no specificity—gives them a deep emotional resonance and makes them the likely mantra of a spinning and tormented mind. What Othello probably means is that Desdemona's infidelity (and not his jealousy) is the cause of her murder, that this death is a sacrifice and not a revenge killing.

Act V, ii, 6

Yet she must die, else she'll betray more men.

This is a strange thing for Othello to say, for it makes it seem like he is killing her in order to prevent other men ("more men") from having to suffer betrayal by her as he has. It shows how removed from rationality he has become and how lost in a tangle of words.

Act V, ii, 40–84

Othello: Think on thy sins.
Desdemona: They are loves I bear to you.
Othello: Ay, and for that thou diest.
Desdemona: That death's unnatural that kills for loving.
Alas, why gnaw you so your nether lip?

Some bloody passion shakes your very frame:
These are portents; but yet I hope, I hope,
They do not point on me.
Othello: Peace, and be still!
Desdemona: I will so. What's the matter?
Othello: That handkerchief which I so loved and gave thee
Thou gavest to Cassio.
Desdemona: No, by my life and soul!
Send for the man, and ask him.
Othello: Sweet soul, take heed,
Take heed of perjury; thou art on thy deathbed.
Desdemona: Ay, but not yet to die.
Othello: Yes, presently:
Therefore confess thee freely of thy sin;
For to deny each article with oath
Cannot remove nor choke the strong conception
That I do groan withal. Thou art to die.
Desdemona: Then Lord have mercy on me!
Othello: I say, amen.
Desdemona: And have you mercy too! I never did
Offend you in my life; never loved Cassio
But with such general warranty of heaven
As I might love: I never gave him token.
Othello: By heaven, I saw my handkerchief in's hand.
O perjured woman! thou dost stone my heart,
And makest me call what I intend to do
A murder, which I thought a sacrifice:
I saw the handkerchief.
Desdemona: He found it then;
I never gave it him: send for him hither;
Let him confess a truth.
Othello: He hath confess'd.
Desdemona: What, my lord?
Othello: That he hath used thee.
Desdemona: How? unlawfully?
Othello: Ay.
Desdemona: He will not say so.
Othello: No, his mouth is stopp'd;
Honest Iago hath ta'en order for't.
Desdemona: O! my fear interprets: what, is he dead?
Othello: Had all his hairs been lives, my great revenge
Had stomach for them all.

Desdemona: Alas! he is betray'd and I undone.
Othello: Out, strumpet! weep'st thou for him to my face?
Desdemona: O, banish me, my lord, but kill me not!
Othello: Down, strumpet!
Desdemona: Kill me to-morrow: let me live to-night!
Othello: Nay, if you strive—
Desdemona: But half an hour!
Othello: Being done, there is no pause.
Desdemona: But while I say one prayer!
Othello: It is too late.

Beginning at Othello's command to Desdemona, "Think on thy sins," is this scene of frustrated exhilaration. Finally confronted with what was bothering Othello, Desdemona openly refutes his fears, but he is incapable of hearing her clearly. The passionate exchanges in their conversation as she begs and he repulses grow shorter and ever more intense. Rage overcomes him and he ultimately suffocates her.

—⁓— —⁓— —⁓—

Act V, ii, 177–181

Emilia: But did you ever tell him she was false?
Iago: I did.
Emilia: You told a lie, an odious, damned lie;
Upon my soul, a lie, a wicked lie!
She false with Cassio!—did you say with Cassio?

Emilia brings a burst of true words to lay the false ones that have polluted the speakers of the play. Her repetition of the word "lie," repeatedly throwing it in Iago's face, is exhilarating. The once silent and obedient Emilia, who is hardly noticed earlier in the play, is replaced by this searingly honest character.

—⁓— —⁓— —⁓—

Act V, ii, 257–279

Behold, I have a weapon;
A better never did itself sustain
Upon a soldier's thigh: I have seen the day,
That, with this little arm and this good sword,
I have made my way through more impediments
Than twenty times your stop: but, O vain boast!
Who can control his fate? 'Tis not so now.

Be not afraid, though you do see me weapon'd;
Here is my journey's end, here is my butt,
And very sea-mark of my utmost sail.
Do you go back dismay'd? 'Tis a lost fear;
Man but a rush against Othello's breast,
And he retires. Where should Othello go?
Now, how dost thou look now? O ill-starr'd wench!
Pale as thy smock! When we shall meet at compt,
This look of thine will hurl my soul from heaven,
And fiends will snatch at it. Cold, cold, my girl!
Even like thy chastity. O cursed slave!
Whip me, ye devils,
From the possession of this heavenly sight!
Blow me about in winds! Roast me in sulphur!
Wash me in steep-down gulfs of liquid fire!
O Desdemona! Desdemona! Dead! Oh! Oh!

Othello's final speeches in the play reveal the depths of his torment, but they delight as much as they pain because of the overwhelming magnificence of their poetry. Lines like "I have made my way through more impediments / Than twenty times your stop" and "Be not afraid though you do see me weapon'd; / Here is my journey's end" and "Man but a rush against Othello's breast, / And he retires" and "Where should Othello go? / Now, how dost thou look now. O ill-starr'd wench! / Pale as thy smock!" are crowded closely together, each following the next in quick succession. No matter that he is mistaken in his last imaging of her: Desdemona would plead for him with a greater intensity than she did for Cassio.

Act V, ii, 334–352

Soft you; a word or two before you go.
I have done the state some service, and they know't.
No more of that. I pray you, in your letters,
When you shall these unlucky deeds relate,
Speak of me as I am; nothing extenuate,
Nor set down aught in malice: then must you speak
Of one that loved not wisely but too well;
Of one not easily jealous, but being wrought
Perplex'd in the extreme; of one whose hand,
Like the base Indian, threw a pearl away
Richer than all his tribe; of one whose subdued eyes,

Albeit unused to the melting mood,
Drop tears as fast as the Arabian trees
Their medicinal gum. Set you down this;
And say besides, that in Aleppo once,
Where a malignant and a turban'd Turk
Beat a Venetian and traduced the state,
I took by the throat the circumcised dog,
And smote him, thus.

In his last speech, his death oration, Othello starts by seeking to justify himself and save his reputation. He quickly comes to revile himself, however, for he "threw a pearl away / Richer than all his tribe." It is, then, in a combination of pride and self-loathing that Othello speaks his death lines, which conclude with him stabbing himself.

Othello's dying words, exceptional and expressive as they are as poetry, are also significant and revealing for what they do not say. Othello is concerned with his honor and with his own stupidity in allowing himself to be gulled. But he has not grasped any more fully now the independent existence of Desdemona as her own person than he did when he told the Venetian senate in Act I that "She loved me for the dangers I had passed, / And I loved her that she did pity them." In short, he loved her love of him. To him, the story of Desdemona's death is the story of his tragic beguilement rather than the story of her fatal marriage.

LIST OF CHARACTERS IN
OTHELLO

Othello is the head of the Venetian military forces. He is not a Venetian, however, but a Moor—a black man, Arab rather than Christian. He is a proud, strong, experienced, and disciplined soldier who is dispatched to Cypress, a Venetian stronghold, by the Venetian senate when the island falls under attack by a Turkish fleet.

Desdemona is a beautiful young Venetian woman who encourages Othello's love and marries him without her father's knowledge. She accompanies him to Cypress.

Brabantio is Desdemona's father. He is broken by her marriage.

Iago is Othello's ensign. Embittered when he is passed over by Othello for a promotion, he plots to gain Othello's confidence and, by causing him to become insecure about Desdemona's love, to destroy him.

Emilia is Iago's wife and a lady-in-waiting to Desdemona. She seems at first to be obedient to Iago, but upon discovering the extent of his villainy, she rebels.

Michael Cassio is the man Othello promotes, instead of Iago, to be his lieutenant. He is handsome, debonair, and courteous, but rather self-regarding, and he has trouble holding his liquor. Iago convinces Othello that Desdemona is really in love with Cassio.

Roderigo is a fop in love with Desdemona. Iago, promising to help him win Desdemona away from Othello, uses him in his plot against Othello and Cassio.

Bianca is a prostitute who is in love with Cassio.

The **Duke of Venice** takes Othello's side when Brabantio accuses him of winning Desdemona through charms and drugs. He sends him to Cypress as leader of his military forces.

Montano is the governor of Cypress.

Lodovico is a Venetian nobleman. The senate sends him to Cypress as a messenger, to recall Othello from his post.

The **clown** appears briefly at the beginning of the third act, mocking the **musicians** whom Cassio has hired to serenade Othello as he wakes. The clown then mocks Cassio himself for his gentlemanly flourishes and courtly speech.

CRITICISM
THROUGH THE AGES
❧

OTHELLO
IN THE SEVENTEENTH CENTURY
❧

The first recorded performance of *Othello* was on November 1, 1604, in the Banqueting House at Whitehall before King James I. Scholars believe that *Othello* was written no earlier than 1604, because it seems that Shakespeare took the matter of the Turkish invasion of Cypress, which is the cause of the midnight convocation of the Venetian senate in the first act of *Othello*, from Richard Knolles's *History of the Turks,* published at the end of 1603. The underlying story of *Othello* can be found in the Italian collection of tales called the *Hecatommithi,* by Giambattista Cinzio Giraldi, published in 1565. Shakespeare added the figures of Roderigo, Desdemona's hapless Venetian suitor and Iago's gull; Brabantio, Desdemona's father; and Bianca, Cassio's mistress. Richard Burbage, a partner in Shakespeare's acting company, played the role of Othello. The force of his performance, in addition to a statement of the plot, is indicated by these lines from a eulogy after Burbage's death in 1619:

> . . . But let me not forget one chiefest part
> Wherein beyond the rest, he moved the heart,
> The grieved Moor, made jealous by a slave,
> Who sent his wife to fill a timeless grave.

An extant letter of 1610, written in Latin, offers a review of a performance given by Shakespeare's company in Oxford that year. The players, it says, "drew tears not only by their speech, but also by their action. Indeed Desdemona, though always excellent, moved us especially in her death when, as she lay on her bed, her face itself implored the pity of the audience" (Marvin Rosenberg, *The Masks of Othello,* 5). The writer's tone suggests, too, that the story and characters of the play were already familiar by 1610. In fact, *Othello* has been from the first one of Shakespeare's most popular and frequently performed plays.

The play was first published in 1622 in quarto format. Another version of some 160 lines more—and with various expletives, such as "zounds" (by God's wounds) and "'sblood" (by God's blood), expurgated in accordance with a parliamentary act of 1606 forbidding the use of profane references to God—was printed in the first Folio edition of Shakespeare's plays in 1623.

On September 2, 1642, by order of the Long Parliament, all the theaters in London were shut down by the Puritan-dominated government. *Othello* was one of the first plays presented when the theaters reopened in 1660 after the restoration of the monarchy with the return of Charles II from France. Margaret Hughes, who played Desdemona, was the first woman to appear upon the English stage. Until then, boys had played women's parts. The innovation was significant enough for a prologue attached to *Othello* to proclaim:

> The Woman plays to day: mistake me not;
> No man in gown, or Page in petty-coat.
> (Rosenberg 18)

In an entry in 1666, the famous London diarist Samuel Pepys mentions reading a copy of the play, which he liked (though not as much as the now-forgotten play *The Adventures of Five Houres*).

The first significant critical attention given to *Othello* was by Thomas Rymer in his 1693 study *A Short View of Tragedy*. It is a mocking attack upon the play, calling it "a bloody farce" and asserting that it "may be a warning to all good Wives, that they look well to their Linnen." Rymer's essay has stimulated a great deal of opposition through the centuries, as it did even in his own time. Included here is the most important contemporary response to his attack on *Othello*, written by the critic Charles Gildon.

Rymer's book served to be the spur for others in turn to write about Shakespeare. It was also important in that it applied the authority of the Aristotelian principle of "the unities," of time, place, and action, which so significantly influenced the critical standards of the eighteenth century.

1666—Samuel Pepys. *The Diary of Samuel Pepys*

Samuel Pepys (1633–1703), an English naval administrator and member of Parliament, is most famous for his diary, which is considered an invaluable primary source about daily life in the Restoration period.

Up, and to Deptford by water, reading *Othello, Moore of Venice*, which I ever heretofore esteemed a mighty good play, but having so lately read

The Adventures of Five Houres (by Samuel Tuke), it seems a mean thing. (August 20, 1666)

1693—Thomas Rymer.
From *A Short View of Tragedy*

Thomas Rymer (1641–1713) was an early English critic who wrote *The Tragedies of the Last Age* (1678) and *A Short View of Tragedy* (1693). Here Rymer condemns *Othello* for many reasons, including its supposedly implausible characters.

From all the Tragedies acted on our English Stage, *Othello* is said to bear the Bell away. The *Subject* is more of a piece, and there is indeed something like, there is, as it were, some phantom of a *Fable.* The *Fable* is always accounted the *Soul* of Tragedy. And it is the *Fable* which is properly the *Poets* part. Because the other three parts of Tragedy, to wit, the *Characters* are taken from the Moral Philosopher; the *thoughts* or sence, from them that teach *Rhetorick:* And the last part, which is the *expression,* we learn from the Grammarians.

This Fable is drawn from a Novel, compos'd in Italian by *Giraldi Cinthio,* who also was a Writer of Tragedies. And to that use employ'd such of his Tales, as he judged proper for the Stage. But with this of the Moor, he meddl'd no farther.

Shakespear alters it from the Original in several particulars, but always, unfortunately, for the worse. He bestows a name on his Moor; and styles him the Moor of *Venice:* a Note of pre-eminence, which neither History nor Heraldry can allow him. *Cinthio,* who knew him best, and whose creature he was, calls him simply a *Moor.* We say the Piper of *Strasburgh;* the Jew *of Florence;* And, if you please, the Pindar *of Wakefield:* all upon Record, and memorable in their Places. But we see no such Cause for the *Moors* preferment to that dignity. And it is an affront to all Chroniclers, and Antiquaries, to top upon 'urn a Moor, with that mark of renown, who yet had never fain within the Sphere of their Cognisance.

Then is the Moors *Wife,* from a simple Citizen, in *Cinthio,* dress'd up with her Top knots, and rais'd to be *Desdemona,* a Senators Daughter. All this is very strange; And therefore pleases such as reflect not on the improbability. This match might well be without the Parents Consent. Old *Horace* long ago forbad the Banes.

Sed non ut placidis Coeant immitia, non ut Serpentes avibus geminentur, tigribus agni.

The Fable

Othello, *a Blackmoor Captain, by talking of his Prowess and Feats of War, makes* Desdemona *a Senators Daughter to be in love with him; and to be married to him, without her Parents knowledge; And having preferred* Cassio, *to be his Lieutenant, (a place which his Ensign* Jago *sued for)* Jago *in revenge, works the Moor into a jealousy that* Cassio *Cuckolds him: which he effects by stealing and conveying a certain Handkerchief, which had, at the Wedding, been by the Moor presented to his Bride. Hereupon,* Othello *and* Jago *plot the Deaths of* Desdemona *and* Cassio, Othello *Murders her, and soon after is convinced of her Innocence. And as he is about to be carried to Prison, in order to be punish'd for the Murder, He kills himself.*

What ever rubs or difficulty may stick on the Bark, the Moral, sure, of this Fable is very instructive.

1. First, This may be a caution to all Maidens of Quality how, without their Parents consent, they run away with Blackamoors.

Di non si accompagnare con huomo, cui la natura & *il cielo,* & *il modo della vita, disgiunge da noi.* Cinthio.

Secondly, This may be a warning to all good Wives, that they look well to their Linnen.

Thirdly, This may be a lesson to Husbands, that before their Jealousie be Tragical, the proofs may be Mathematical.

Cinthio affirms that *She was not overcome by a Womanish Appetite, but by the Vertue of the Moor.* It must be a good-natur'd Reader that takes *Cinthio's* word in this case, tho' in a Novel. *Shakespear,* who is accountable both to the Eyes, and to the *Ears,* And to convince the very heart of an Audience, shews that *Desdemona* was won, by hearing *Othello* talk,

> *Othello:* I spake of most disastrous chances,
> of Moving accidents, by flood and field;
> of hair-breadth scapes i' th' imminent deadly breach;
> of being taken by the insolent foe;
> and sold to slavery: of my redemption thence;
> and portents in my Travels History:
> wherein of Antars vast, and Desarts idle,
> rough Quarries, Rocks, and Hills, whose heads touch Heaven,
> It was my hint to speak, such was my process·
> and of the *Cannibals* that each others eat:
> the *Anthropophagi,* and men whose heads
> do grow beneath their shoulders—

This was the Charm, this was the philtre, the love-powder that took the Daughter of this Noble Venetian. This was sufficient to make the Black-amoor White, and reconcile all, tho' there had been a Cloven-foot into the bargain.

A meaner woman might be as soon taken by *Aqua Tetrachymagogon.*

Nodes, Cataracts, Tumours, Chilblains, Carnosity, *Shan-kers,* or any *Cant* in the Bill of an High-German Doctor is as good *fustian Circumstance,* and as likely to charm a Senators Daughter. But, it seems, the noble Venetians have an other sence of things. The *Doge* himself tells us;

Doge: I think this Tale wou'd win my Daughter too.

Horace tells us,

Intererit Multum—
Colchus an Assyrius, Thebis nutritus, an Argis.

Shakespear in this Play calls 'em the *supersubtle Venetians.* Yet examine throughout the Tragedy there is nothing in the noble *Desdemona,* that is not below any Countrey Chamber-maid with us.

And the account he gives of their Noblemen and Senate, can only be calculated for the latitude of *Gotham.*

The Character of that State is to employ strangers in their Wars; But shall a Poet thence fancy that they will set a Negro to be their General; or trust a *Moor* to defend them against the *Turk?* With us a Black-amoor might rise to be a Trumpeter; but *Shakespear* would not have him less than a Lieutenant-General. With us a *Moor* might marry some little drab, or Small-coal Wench: *Shakespear,* would provide him the Daughter and Heir of some great Lord, or Privy-Councellor: And all the Town should reckon it a very suitable match: Yet the English are not bred up with that hatred and aversion to the *Moors,* as are the Venetians, who suffer by a perpetual Hostility from them,

Littora littoribus contraria—

Nothing is more odious in Nature than an improbable lye; And, certainly, never was any Play fraught, like this of *Othello,* with improbabilities.

The *Characters* or Manners, which are the second part in a Tragedy, are not less unnatural and improper, than the Fable was improbable and absurd.

Othello is made a Venetian General. We see nothing done by him, nor related concerning him, that comports with the condition of a General, or, indeed, of a Man, unless the killing himself, to avoid a death the Law was about to inflict upon him. When his Jealousy had wrought him up to a resolution of's taking revenge for the suppos'd injury, He sets *Jago* to the fighting part, to kill *Cassio;*

And chuses himself to murder the silly Woman his Wife, that was like to make no resistance.

His Love and his Jealousie are no part of a Souldiers Character, unless for Comedy.

But what is most intolerable is *Jago*. He is no Black-amoor Souldier, so we may be sure he should be like other Souldiers of our acquaintance; yet never in Tragedy, nor in Comedy, nor in Nature was a Souldier with his Character; take it in the Authors own words;

> *Emilia.*   some Eternal Villain,
> Some busie, and insinuating Rogue,
> Some cogging, couzening Slave, to get some Office.

Horace Describes a Souldier otherwise:

> Impiger, iracundus, inexorabilis, acer.

Shakespear knew his Character of *Jago* was inconsistent. In this very Play he pronounces,

> If thou dost deliver more or less than Truth,
> Thou art no Souldier.

   This he knew, but to entertain the Audience with something new and surprising, against common sense, and Nature, he would pass upon us a close, dissembling, false, insinuating rascal, instead of an open-hearted, frank, plain-dealing Souldier, a character constantly worn by them for some thousands of years in the World.

Tiberius Caesar[1] had a Poet Arraign'd for his Life: because *Agamemnon* was brought on the Stage by him, with a character unbecoming a Souldier.

Our Ensigns and Subalterns, when disgusted by the Captain, throw up their Commissions, bluster, and are bare-fac'd. *Jago*, I hope, is not brought on the Stage, in a Red Coat. I know not what Livery the Venetians wear: but am sure they hold not these conditions to be *alia soldatesca*.

> Non sia egli per fare la vendetta con insidie, ma con
> la spada in mano. (Cinthio.)

Nor is our Poet more discreet in his *Desdemona*, He had chosen a Souldier for his Knave: And a Venetian Lady is to be the Fool.

This Senators Daughter runs away to (a Carriers Inn) the *Sagittary*, with a Black-amoor: is no sooner wedded to him, but the very night she Beds him, is importuning and teizing him for a young smock-fac'd Lieutenant, *Cassio*. And tho' she perceives the Moor Jealous of *Cassio*, yet will she not forbear, but still rings *Cassio, Cassio* in both his Ears.

Roderigo is the Cully of *Jago*, brought in to be murder'd by *Jago*, that *Jago's* hands might be the more in Blood, and be yet the more abominable Villain: who without that was too wicked on all Conscience; And had more to answer for, than any Tragedy, or Furies could inflict upon him. So there can be nothing in the *characters*, either for the profit, or to delight an Audience.

The third thing to be consider'd is the *Thoughts*. But from such *Characters*, we need not expect many that are either true, or fine, or noble.

And without these, that is, without sense or meaning, the fourth part of Tragedy, which is the *expression* can hardly deserve to be treated on distinctly. The verse rumbling in our Ears are of good use to help off the action.

In the *Neighing* of an Horse, or in the *growling* of a Mastiff, there is a meaning, there is as lively expression, and, may I say, more humanity, than many times in the Tragical flights of *Shakespear*.

Step then amongst the Scenes to observe the Conduct in this Tragedy.

The first we see are *Jago* and *Roderigo*, by Night in the Streets of *Venice*. After growling a long time together, they resolve to tell *Brabantio* that his Daughter is run away with the Black-a-moor. *Jago* and *Roderigo* were not of quality to be familiar with *Brabantio*, nor had any provocation from him, to deserve a rude thing at their hands. *Brabantio* was a Noble Venetian one of the Sovereign Lords, and principal persons in the Government, Peer to the most Serene *Doge*, one attended with more state, ceremony and punctillio, than any English Duke, or Nobleman in the Government will pretend to. This misfortune in his Daughter is so prodigious, so tender a point, as might puzzle the finest Wit of the most *supersubtle* Venetian to touch upon it, or break the discovery to her Father. See then how delicately *Shakespear* minces the matter:

Rod.: What ho, Brabantio, Signior Brabantio, ho.
Jago: Awake, what ho, Brabantio,
Thieves, thieves, thieves:
Look to your House, your Daughter, and your Bags
Thieves, thieves.
(Brabantio *at a Window.*)
Bra.: What is the reason of this terrible summons?
What is the matter there?
Rod.: Signior, is all your Family within?
Jago: Are your Doors lockt?

Bra.: Why, wherefore ask you this?
Jago: Sir, you are robb'd, for shame put on your Gown,
Your Heart is burst, you have lost half your Soul,
Even now, very now, an old black Ram
Is tupping your white Ewe: arise, arise,
Awake the snorting Citizens with the Bell,
Or else the Devil will make a Grandsire of you, arise I say.
Jago: Sir, you are one of those that will not serve God, if the Devil bid
you; because we come to do you service, you think us Ruffians, you'le
have your Daughter covered with a Barbary Stallion. You'le have your
Nephews neigh to you; you'le have Coursers for Cousins, and Gennets
for Germans.
Bra.: What prophane wretch art thou?
Jago: I am one, Sir, that come to tell you, your Daughter and the Moor,
are now making the Beast with two backs.

In former days there wont to be kept at the Courts of Princes some body in
a Fools Coat, that in pure simplicity might let slip something, which made way
for the ill news, and blunted the shock, which otherwise might have come too
violent upon the party.

Aristophanes puts *Nicias* and *Demosthenes* into the disguise of Servants, that
they might, without indecency, be Drunk; And Drunk he must make them that
they might without reserve lay open the *Arcana* of State; And the Knavery of
their *Ministers.*

After King *Francis* had been taken Prisoner at *Pavia, Rabelais* tells of a
Drunken bout between *Gargantua* and Fryer *John;* where the valiant Fryer,
bragging over his Cups, amongst his other flights, says he, *Had I liv'd in the days
of Jesus Christ, I would ha guarded* Mount Olivet *that the Jews should never ha' tane
him. The Devil fetch me, if I would not have ham string'd those Mr. Apostles, that after
their good Supper, ran away so scurvily and left their Master to shift for himself. I hate
a Man should run away, when he should play at sharps. Pox on't, that I shou'd not be
King of* France *for an hundred years or two. I wou'd curtail all our French Dogs that
ran away at* Pavia.

This is address, this is truly Satyr, where the preparation is such, that the thing
principally design'd, falls in, as it only were of course.

But *Shakespear* shews us another sort of address, his manners and good
breeding must not be like the rest of the Civil World. *Brabantio* was not in
Masquerade, was not *incognito; Jago* well knew his rank and dignity.

Jago: The *Magnifico* is much beloved,
And hath in his effect, a voice potential
As double as the Duke—

But besides the Manners to a *Magnifico*, humanity cannot bear that an old Gentleman in his misfortune should be insulted over with such a rabble of Skoundrel language, when no cause or provocation. Yet thus it is on our Stage, this is our School of good manners, and the *Speculum Vitae*.

But our *Magnifico* is here in the dark, nor are yet his Robes on: attend him to the Senate house, and there see the difference, see the effects of Purple.

So, by and by, we find the Duke of *Venice* with his Senators in Councel, at Midnight, upon advice that the Turks, or Ottamites, or both together, were ready in transport Ships, put to Sea, in order to make a Descent upon *Cyprus*. This is the posture, when we see *Brabantio*, and *Othello* join them. By their Conduct and manner of talk, a body must strain hard to fancy the Scene at *Venice;* And not rather in some of our Cinq-ports, where the Baily and his Fisher-men are knocking their heads together on account of some Whale; or some terrible broil upon the Coast. But to shew them true Venetians, the Maritime affairs stick not long on their hand; the publick may sink or swim. They will sit up all night to hear a Doctors Commons, Matrimonial, Cause. And have the Merits of the Cause at large laid open to 'em, that they may decide it before they Stir. What can be pleaded to keep awake their attention so wonderfully?

Never, sure, was *form* of *pleading* so tedious and so heavy, as this whole Scene, and midnight entertainment. Take his own words: says the *Respondent.*

> *Oth.:* Most potent, grave, and reverend Signiors,
> My very noble, and approv'd good Masters:
> That I have tane away this old mans Daughter;
> It is most true: true, I have Married her,
> The very front and head of my offending,
> Hath this extent, no more: rude I am in my speech.
> And little blest with the set phrase of peace,
> For since these Arms of mine had seven years pith,
> Till now some nine Moons wasted, they have us'd
> Their dearest action in the Tented Field:
> And little of this great World can I speak,
> More than pertains to Broils and Battail,
> And therefore little shall I grace my Cause,
> In speaking of my self; yet by your gracious patience
> I would a round unravish'd Tale deliver,
> Of my whole course of love, what drugs, what charms
> What Conjuration, and what mighty Magick,
> (for such proceedings am I charg'd withal)
> I won his Daughter.

All this is but *Preamble,* to tell the Court that He wants words. This was the Eloquence which kept them up all Night, and drew their attention, in the midst of their alarms.

One might rather think the novelty, and strangeness of the case prevail'd upon them: no, the Senators do not reckon it strange at all. Instead of starting at the Prodigy, every one is familiar with *Desdemona,* as he were her own natural Father, rejoice in her good fortune, and wish their own several Daughters as hopefully married. Should the Poet have provided such a Husband for an only Daughter of any noble Peer in *England,* the Black-amoor must have chang'd his Skin, to look our House of Lords in the Face.

Aeschylus is noted in *Aristophanes* for letting *Niobe* be two or three Acts on the Stage, before she speaks. Our Noble Venetian, sure, is in the other more unnatural extreme. His words flow in abundance; no Butter-Quean can be more lavish. Nay: he is for talking of State-Affairs too, above any body:

Bra.: Please it your Grace, on to the State Affairs—

Yet is this *Brabantio* sensible of his affliction; before the end of the Play his Heart breaks, he dies.

Gra.: Poor *Desdemona,* I am glad thy Father's dead,
Thy match was mortal to him, and pure grief
Shore his old thread in twain—

A third part in a Tragedy is the *Thoughts:* from Venetians, Noblemen, and Senators, we may expect fine *Thoughts.* Here is a tryal of skill: for a parting blow, the *Duke,* and *Brabantio* Cap *sentences.* Where then shall we seek for the *thoughts,* if we let slip this occasion? says the Duke:

Duke: Let me speak like your self and lay a *Sentence,*
Which like a greese or step, may help these lovers
Into your favour.
When remedies are past the grief is ended,
By seeing the worst which late on hopes depended,
To mourn a mischief that is past and gone,
Is the next way to draw more mischief on;
What cannot be preserv'd when Fortune takes,
Patience her injury a Mocker makes.
The rob'd that smiles, steals something from a Thief,
He robs himself, that spends an hopeless grief.
Bra.: So let the Turk of *Cyprus* us beguile
We lose it not so long as we can smile;

He bears the sentence well, that nothing bears
But the free comfort which from thence he hears,
But he bears both the sentence and the sorrow,
That to pay grief must of poor patience borrow:
These *Sentences* to Sugar, or to Gall,
Being strong on both sides are equivocal.
But words are words, I never yet did hear,
That the bruis'd Heart was pierced through the Ear.
Beseech you now to the affairs of State.

How far wou'd the Queen of *Sheba* have travell'd to hear the Wisdom of our Noble Venetians? or is not our *Brentford* a *Venetian* Colony, for methinks their talk is the very same?
What says Prince *Volscius?*

Volscius: What shall I do, what conduct shall I find
To lead me through this twy light of my mind?

What says *Amaryllis?*

Ama.: I hope its slow beginning will portend
A forward *exit* to all future end.

What says Prince *Pretty-man?*

Pre.: Was ever Son yet brought to this distress,
To be, for being a Son, made Fatherless?
Ah, you just gods, rob me not of a Father,
The being of a Son take from me rather.

Panurge, sadly perplexed, and trying all the means in the World, to be well advised, in that knotty point *whether he should Marry, or no;* Amongst the rest, consults *Raminigrobis,* an old Poet; as one belonging to *Apollo;* And from whom he might expect something like an Oracle. And he was not disappointed. From *Raminigrobis* he had this Answer:

Prenez la, ne la prenez pas.
Si vous la prenez, c'est bien fait.
Si ne la prenez, en effet
Ce sera ouvre par compas.
Gallopez, mais allez le pas.
Recullez, entrés y de fait.

Prenez la, ne.
Take, or not take her, off or on:
Handy dandy is your Lot.
When her name you write, you blot.
'Tis undone, when all is done,
Ended, ere it is begun.
Never Gallop whilst you Trot.
Set not forward, when you run,
Nor be single, tho' alone,
Take, or not take her, off, or on.

What provocation, or cause of malice our Poet might have to Libel the most *Serene Republick,* I cannot tell: but certainly, there can be no wit in this representation.

For the *Second Act,* our Poet having dispatcht his affairs at *Venice,* shews the Action next (I know not how many leagues off) in the Island of *Cyprus.* The Audience must be there too: And yet our *Bays* had it never in his head, to make any provision of Transport Ships for them.

In the days that the *Old Testament* was Acted in *Clerkenwell,* by the *Parish Clerks* of *London,* the Israelites might pass through the Red *sea:* but alass, at this time, we have no Moses to bid the Waters *make way,* and to Usher us along. Well, the absurdities of this kind break no Bones. They may make Fools of us; but do not hurt our Morals.

Come a-shoar then, and observe the Countenance of the People, after the dreadful Storm, and their apprehensions from an Invasion by the Ottomites, their succour and friends scatter'd and tost, no body knew whither. The first that came to Land was Cassio, his first Salutation to the Governour, *Montanio,* is:

Cas.: Thanks to the valiant of this Isle:
That so approve the Moor, and let the Heavens
Give him defence against their Elements,
For I have lost him on the dangerous Sea.

To him the Governour speaks, indeed, like a Man in his wits.

Mont.: Is he well Shipt?

The Lieutenant answers thus.

Cas.: His Bark is stoutly Tymber'd, and his Pilot
Of very expert, and approv'd allowance,

Therefore my hopes (not surfeited to death)
Stand in bold care.

The Governours first question was very proper; his next question, in this posture of affairs, is:

Mont.: But, good Lieutenant, is our general Wiv'd?

A question so remote, so impertinent and absurd, so odd and surprising never entered *Bayes's Pericranium*. Only the answer may Tally with it.

Cas.: Most fortunately, he hath atcheiv'd a Maid,
That Parragons description, and wild fame:
One that excels the quirks of blasoning Pens:
And in the essential vesture of Creation,
Does bear an excellency—

They who like this Authors writing will not be offended to find so much repeated from him. I pretend not here to tax either the Sense, or the *Language;* those *Circumstances* had their proper place in the Venetian Senate. What I now cite is to shew how probable, how natural, how reasonable the Conduct is, all along.

I thought it enough that Cassio should be acquainted with a Virgin of that rank and consideration in *Venice,* as *Desdemona.* I wondred that in the Senate-house every one should know her so familiarly: yet, here also at *Cyprus,* every body is in a rapture at the name of *Desdemona:* except only *Montanio* who must be ignorant; that Cassio, who has an excellent cut in shaping an Answer, may give him the satisfaction:

Mont.: What is she?
Cas.: She that I spoke of: our Captains Captain,
Left in the Conduct of the bold *Jago,*
Whose footing here anticipates our thoughts
A Sennets speed: great *Jove Othello* guard,
And swell his Sail with thine own powerful breath,
That he may bless this Bay with his Tall Ship,
And swiftly come to *Desdemona's* Arms,
Give renewed fire to our extincted Spirits,
And bring all *Cyprus* comfort:
(Enter *Desdemona,* &c.)
O behold,
The riches of the Ship is come on shoar.

Ye men of *Cyprus,* let her have your Knees:
Hail to the Lady: and the Grace of Heaven
Before, behind thee, and on every hand.
Enwheel the round—

In the name of phrenzy, what means this Souldier? or would he talk thus, if
he meant any thing at all? Who can say *Shakespear* is to blame in his *Character* of
a Souldier? Has he not here done him reason? When cou'd our *Tramontains* talk
at this rate? but our *Jarsey* and *Garnsey* Captains must not speak so fine things,
nor compare with the Mediterranean, or Garrisons in *Rhodes* and *Cyprus.*

The next thing our Officer does, is to salute *Jago's* Wife, with this *Conge* to
the Husband,

> *Cas.:* Good Ancient, you are welcome, welcome Mistriss,
> Let it not Gall your Patience, good *Jago,*
> That I extend my Manners, 'tis my Breeding,
> That gives me this bold shew of Curtesy.
> *Jago:* Sir, would she give you so much of her lips,
> As of her tongue she has bestow'd on me,
> You'd have enough.
> *Desd.* Alass! she has no speech.

Now follows a long rabble of Jack-pudden farce betwixt *Jago* and *Desdemona,*
that runs on with all the little plays, jingle, and trash below the patience of any
Countrey Kitchin-maid with her Sweet-heart. The Venetian *Donna* is hard put
to't for pastime! And this is all, when they are newly got on shoar, from a dismal
Tempest, and when every moment she might expect to hear her Lord (as she
calls him) that she runs so mad after, is arriv'd or lost. And moreover.

> In a Town of War,
> the peoples Hearts brimful of fear.

Never in the World had any Pagan Poet his Brains turn'd at this Monstrous
rate. But the ground of all this Bedlam-Buffoonry we saw, in the case of the
French *Strolers,* the Company for Acting *Christs Passion,* or the *Old Testament,*
were Carpenters, Coblers, and illiterate fellows; who found that the Drolls, and
Fooleries interlarded by them, brought in the rabble, and lengthened their time,
so they got Money by the bargain.

Our *Shakespear,* doubtless, was a great Master in this craft. These Carpenters
and Coblers were the guides he followed. And it is then no wonder that we find
so much farce and *Apochryphal Matter* in his Tragedies. Thereby un-hallowing
the Theatre, profaning the name of Tragedy; And instead of representing Men

and Manners, turning all Morality, good sence, and humanity into mockery and derision.

But pass we to something of a more serious air and Complexion. *Othello* and his Bride are the first Night, no sooner warm in Bed together, but a Drunken Quarrel happening in the Garison, two Souldiers Fight; And the General rises to part the Fray: He swears.

> *Oth.:*   Now by Heaven,
> My blood begins my safer guides to rule,
> And passion, having my best judgment cool'd,
> Assays to lead the way: if once I stir,
> Or do but lift this arm, the best of you
> Shall sink in my rebuke: give me to know
> How this foul rout began; who set it on,
> And he that is approv'd in this offence,
> Tho' he had rwin'd with me both at a birth,
> Should lose me: what, *in a Town of War,*
> *Yet wild, the peoples Hearts brimful of fear,*
> To manage private, and domestick quarrels,
> In Night, and on the Court, and guard of safety,
> Tis Monstrous, *Jago,* who began?

In the days of yore, Souldiers did not swear in this fashion. What should a Souldier say farther, when he swears, unless he blaspheme? action shou'd speak the rest. What follows must be *ex oregladii;* He is to rap out an Oath, not Withdraw and Spin it out: by the style one might judge that *Shakespears* Souldiers were never bred in a Camp, but rather had belong'd to some Affidavit-Office. Consider also throughout this whole Scene, how the Moorish General proceeds in examining into this *Rout;* No Justice *Clod-pate* could go on with more Phlegm and deliberation. The very first night that he lyes with the Divine *Desdemona* to be thus interrupted, might provoke a Mans Christian Patience to swear in another style. But a Negro General is a Man of strange Mettle. Only his Venetian Bride is a match for him. She understands that the Souldiers in the Garison are by th' ears together: And presently she at midnight, is in amongst them.

> *Desd.:* What's the matter there?
> *Othel.:* All's well now Sweeting—
> Come away to Bed—

In the beginning of this *second Act,* before they had lain together, *Desdemona* was said to be, *our Captains Captain;* Now they are no sooner in Bed together, but *Jago* is advising *Cassio* in these words.

Jago: Our Generals Wife is now the General, I may say so in this respect, for that he hath devoted, and given up himself to the contemplation, mark, and devotement of her parts and graces. Confess your self freely to her, importune her; she'll help to put you in your place again: she is so free, so kind, so apt, so blessed a disposition, that she holds it a vice in her goodness, not to do more than she is requested. This broken joint between you and her Husband, intreat her to splinter—

And he says afterwards.

Jago: Tis most easie
The inclining *Desdemona* to subdue,
In any honest suit. She's fram'd as fruitful,
As the free Elements: And then for her
To win the Moor, were't to renounce his Baptism,
All seals and symbols of redeemed sin,
His soul is so enfetter'd to her love,
That she may make, unmake, do what she list:
Even as her appetite shall play the God
With his weak function—

This kind of discourse implies an experience and long conversation, the Honey-Moon over, and a Marriage of some standing. Would any man, in his wits, talk thus of a Bridegroom and Bride the first night of their coming together?

Yet this is necessary for our Poet; it would not otherwise serve his turn. This is the source, the foundation of his Plot; hence is the spring and occasion for all the Jealousie and bluster that ensues.

Nor are we in better circumstances for *Roderigo.* The last thing said by him in the former *Act* was,

Rod.: I'll go sell all my Land.

A fair Estate is sold to *put money in his Purse,* for this adventure. And lo here, the next day.

Rod.: I do follow here in the Chace, not like a Hound that hunts, but one that fills up the cry: My Money is almost spent. I have been tonight exceedingly well cudgell'd, I think the issue will be, I shall have so much experience for my pains, and so no Money at all, and with a little more wit return to *Venice.*

The Venetian squire had a good riddance for his Acres. The Poet allows him just time to be once drunk, a very conscionable reckoning!

In this *Second Act*, the face of affairs could in truth be no other, than

> in a Town of War,
> Yet wild, the peoples Hearts brim-ful of fear.

But nothing either in this *Act*, or in the rest that follow, shew any colour or complexion, any resemblance or proportion to that face and posture it ought to bear. Should a Painter draw any one *Scene* of this Play, and write over it, *This is a Town of War*; would any body believe that the Man were in his senses? would not a *Goose*, or *Dromedary* for it, be a name as just and suitable? And what in Painting would be absurd, can never pass upon the World of Poetry.

Cassio having escaped the Storm comes on shoar at *Cyprus*, that night gets Drunk, Fights, is turn'd out from his Command, grows sober again, takes advice how to be restor'd, is all Repentance and Mortification: yet before he sleeps, is in the Morning at his Generals door with a noise of Fiddles, and a Droll to introduce him to a little Mouth-speech with the Bride.

> *Cassio:* Give me advantage of some brief discourse
> With *Desdemona* alone.
> *Em.:* Pray you come in,
> I will bestow you, where you shall have time
> To speak your bosom freely.

So, they are put together: And when he had gone on a good while *speaking his bosom, Desdemona* answers him.

> *Desd.:* Do not doubt that, before *Emilia* here,
> I give thee warrant of thy place; assure thee,
> If I do vow a friendship, I'll perform it,
> To the last article—

Then after a ribble rabble of fulsome impertinence, She is at her Husband slap dash:

> *Desd.:* Good love, call him back.
> *Othel.:* Not now, sweet *Desdemona*, some other time.
> *Desd.:* But shall't shortly?
> *Othel:* The sooner, sweet, for you.
> *Desd.:* Shall't be to-night at Supper?
> *Othel:* No, not tonight.

Desd.: To-morrow Dinner then?
Othel. I shall not dine at home,
I meet the Captains at the Citadel.
Desd.: Why then to morrow night, or Tuesday morn,
Or night, or Wednesday morn?

After forty lines more, at this rate, they part, and then comes the wonderful Scene, where *Jago* by shrugs, half words, and ambiguous reflections, works *Othello* up to be Jealous. One might think, after what we have seen, that there needs no great cunning, no great poetry and address to make the *Moor* Jealous. Such impatience, such a rout for a handsome young fellow, the very morning after her Marriage must make him either to be jealous, or to take her for a *Changeling*, below his Jealousie. After this *Scene*, it might strain the Poets skill to reconcile the couple, and allay the Jealousie. *Jago* now can only *actum agere,* and vex the audience with a nauseous repetition.

Whence comes it then, that this is the top scene, the Scene that raises *Othello* above all other Tragedies on our Theatres? It is purely from the Action; from the Mops and the Mows, the Grimace, the Grins and Gesticulation. Such scenes as this have made all the World run after *Harlequin* and *Scaramuccio*.

The several degrees of *Action* were amongst the Ancients distinguish'd by the *Cothurnus,* the *Soccus,* and by the *Planipes.*

Had this scene been represented at old *Rome, Othello* and *Jago* must have quitted their Buskins; They must have played *bare-foot:* the spectators would not have been content without seeing their Podometry; And the Jealousie work at the very Toes of 'em. Words, be they Spanish, or Polish, or any inarticulate sound, have the same effect, they can only serve to distinguish, and, as it were, beat time to the *Action.* But here we see a known Language does wofully encumber, and clog the operation: as either forc'd, or heavy, or trifling, or incoherent, or improper, or most what improbable. When no words interpose to spoil the conceipt, every one interprets as he likes best. So in that memorable dispute betwixt *Panurge* and our English Philosopher in *Rabelais,* perform'd without a word speaking; The Theologians, Physicians, and Surgeons, made one inference; the Lawyers, Civilians, and Canonists, drew another conclusion more to their mind.

Othello the night of his arrival at *Cyprus,* is to consummate with *Desdemona,* they go to Bed. Both are rais'd and run into the Town amidst the Souldiers that were a fighting: then go to Bed again, that morning he sees *Cassio* with her; She importunes him to restore *Cassio. Othello* shews nothing of the Souldiers Mettle: but like a tedious, drawling, tame Goose, is gaping after any paultrey insinuation, labouring to be jealous; And catching at every blown surmize.

Jago: My Lord, I see you are moved.
Oth.: No, not much moved.

Do not think but *Desdemona* is honest.
Jago: Long live she so, and long live you to think so.
Oth.: And yet how Nature erring from it self,
Jago: I, There's the point: as to be bold with you,
Not to affect many proposed Matches
Of her own clime, complexion, and degree,
Wherein we see, in all things. Nature tends,
Fye, we may smell in such a will most rank,
Foul disproportion, thoughts unnatural—

The Poet here is certainly in the right, and by consequence the foundation of the Play must be concluded to be Monstrous; And the constitution, all over, to be

> *most rank,*
> Foul disproportion, thoughts unnatural.

Which instead of moving pity, or any passion Tragical and Reasonable, can produce nothing but horror and aversion, and what is odious and grievous to an Audience. After this fair Mornings work, the Bride enters, drops a Cursey.

Desd.: How now, my dear *Othello,*
Your Dinner, and the generous Islanders
By you invited, do attend your presence.
Oth.: I am to blame.
Desd.: Why is your speech so faint? Are you not well.
Oth.: I have a pain upon my Fore-head, dear.

Michael Cassio came not from *Venice* in the Ship with *Desdemona,* nor till this Morning could be suspected of an opportunity with her. And 'tis now but Dinner time; yet the *Moor* complains of his Fore-head. He might have set a Guard on *Cassio,* or have lockt up *Desdemona,* or have observ'd their carriage a day or two longer. He is on other occasions phlegmatick enough: this is very hasty. But after Dinner we have a wonderful flight:

Othel.: What sense had I of her stoln hours of lust?
I saw't not, thought it not, it harm'd not me:
I slept the next night well, was free and merry,
I found not *Cassio's* kisses on her lips—

A little after this, says he,

Oth.: Give me a living reason that she's disloyal.
Jago: I lay with *Cassio* lately,
And being troubled with a raging Tooth, I could not sleep;
There are a kind of men so loose of Soul,
That in their sleeps will mutter their affairs,
One of this kind is *Cassio:*
In sleep I heard him say: sweet *Desdemona,*
Let us be wary, let us hide our loves:
And then, Sir, wou'd he gripe, and wring my hand,
Cry out, sweet Creature; and then kiss me hard,
As if he pluckt up kisses by the roots,
That grew upon my Lips, then laid his Leg
Over my Thigh, and sigh'd, and kiss'd, and then
Cry'd, cursed fate, that gave thee to the Moor.

By the Rapture of *Othello,* one might think that he raves, is not of sound Memory, forgets that he has not yet been two nights in the Matrimonial Bed with his *Desdemona.* But we find *Jago,* who should have a better memory, forging his lies after the very same Model. The very night of their Marriage at *Venice,* the Moor, and also Cassio, were sent away to *Cyprus.* In the *Second Act, Othello* and his Bride go the first time to Bed; The *Third Act* opens the next morning. The parties have been in view to this moment. We saw the opportunity which was given for *Cassio* to *speak his bosom* to her; *once,* indeed, might go a great way with a Venetian. But *once,* will not do the Poets business; The *Audience* must suppose a great many bouts, to make the plot operate. They must deny their senses, to reconcile it to common sense: or make it any way consistent, and hang together.

Nor, for the most part, are the single thoughts more consistent, than is the economy: The Indians do as they ought in painting the Devil White: but says *Othello:*

Oth.:   Her name that was as fresh
As *Dion's* Visage, is now begrim'd and black,
As mine own face—

There is not a Monky but understands Nature better; not a Pug in *Barbury* that has not a truer taste of things.

Othel.:   O now for ever
Farewel the tranquil mind, farewel content;
Farewel the plumed troop, and the big Wars,
That make Ambition Vertue: O farewel,
Farewel the neighing Steed, and the shrill Trump,

The spirit stirring Drum, th' ear-piercing Fief,
The royal Banner, and all quality,
Pride, Pomp, and Circumstance of glorious War,
And O ye Mortal Engines, whose wide throats
Th' immortal Joves great clamours counterfeit,
Farewel, *Othello's* occupation's gone.

These lines are recited here, not for any thing Poetical in them, besides the sound, that pleases. Yet this sort of imagery and amplification is extreamly taking, where it is just and natural. As in *Gorboduck,* when a young Princess on whose fancy the personal gallantry of the Kings Son then slain, had made a strong impression, thus, out of the abundance of her imagination, pours forth her grief:

Marcella: Ah noble Prince! how oft have I beheld
Thee mounted on thy fierce, and trampling Steed,
Shining in Armour bright before the Tilt,
Wearing thy Mistress sleeve ty'd on thy helm.
Then charge thy staff, to please thy Ladies Eye,
That bow'd the head piece of thy friendly Foe?
How oft in arms, on Horse to bend the Mace,
How oft in arms, on foot, to break the Spear;
Which never now these Eyes may see agen?

Notwithstanding that this Scene had proceeded with fury and bluster sufficient to make the whole Isle ring of his Jealousy, yet is *Desdemona* diverting her self with a paultry buffoon and only solicitous in quest of *Cassio.*

Desd.: Seek him, bid him come hither, tell him—
Where shou'd I lose that Handkerchief, *Emilia?*
Believe me I had rather lose my Purse,
Full of Crusado's: And but my noble Moor
Is true of mind, and made of no such baseness,
As Jealous Creatures are; it were enough
To put him to ill thinking.
Em.: Is he not Jealous?
Desd.: Who he? I think the Sun, where he was born,
Drew all such humours from him.

By this manner of speech one wou'd gather the couple had been yoak'd together a competent while, what might she say more, had they cohabited, and had been Man and Wife seven years?
    She spies the Moor.

Desd.: I will not leave him now,
Till *Cassio* is recall'd.
I have sent to bid *Cassio* come speak with you.
Othel: Lend me thy Handkerchief.
Desd.:   This is a trick to put me from my suit.
I pray let *Cassio* be receiv'd agen.
Em.: Is not this man Jealous?
    'tis not a year or two shews us a man—

As if for the first year or two, *Othello* had not been jealous? The *third Act* begins in the morning, at noon she drops the Handkerchief, after dinner she misses it, and then follows all this outrage and horrible clutter about it. If we believe a small Damosel in the last *Scene* of this *Act*, this day is effectually seven days.

Bianca: What keep a week away! seven days,
seven nights,
Eightscore eight hours, and lovers absent hours,
More tedious than the Dial eightscore times.
O weary reckoning!

Our Poet is at this plunge, that whether this *Act* contains the compass of one day, of seven days, or of seven years, or of all together, the repugnance and absurdity would be the same. For *Othello*, all the while, has nothing to say or to do, but what loudly proclaim him jealous: her friend and confident *Emilia* again and again rounds her in the Ear that *the Man* is Jealous: yet this Venetian dame is neither to see, nor to hear; nor to have any sense or understanding, nor to strike any other note but *Cassio, Cassio.*

The Scotchman hearing *trut Scot, trut Scot,* when he saw it came from a Bird, checkt his Choler, and put up his *Swerd* again, with a *Braad O God, G. Ifthaa'dst ben a Maan, as th' art ane Green Geuse, I sud ha stuck tha' to thin heart.* Desdemona and that Parrot might pass for Birds of a Feather; and if *Sauney* had not been more generous than *Othello,* but continued to insult the poor Creature after this beastly example, he would have given our Poet as good stuff to work upon: And his *Tragedy of the Green Geuse,* might have deserv'd a better audience, than this of *Desdemona,* or *The* Moor *of Venice.*

Act IV

Enter *Jago* and *Othello*

Jago: Will you think so?
Othel: Think so, *Jago.*

Jago: What, to kiss in private?
Othel: An unauthorised kiss.
Jago: Or to be naked with her friend a-bed,
An hour or more, not meaning any harm?
Othel.: Naked a-bed, *Jago,* and not mean harm?—

At this gross rate of trifling, our General and his Auncient March on most heroically; till the Jealous Booby has his Brains turn'd; and falls in a Trance. Would any imagine this to be the Language of Venetians, of Souldiers, and mighty Captains? no *Bartholomew* Droll cou'd subsist upon such trash. But lo, a Stratagem never presented in Tragedy.

Jago: Stand you a while a part—
Incave your self;
And mark the Jeers, the Gibes, and notable scorns,
That dwell in every region of his face,
For I will make him tell the tale a new,
Where, how, how oft, how long ago, and when
He has, and is again to Cope your Wife:
I say, but mark his gesture—

With this device *Othello* withdraws. Says *Jago* aside.

Jago: Now will I question *Cassio* of *Bianca,*
A Huswife—
That doats on *Cassio*—
He when he hears of her cannot refrain
From the excess of Laughter—
As he shall smile, *Othello* shall go mad,
And his unbookish jealousy must conster
Poor *Cassio's* smiles, gesture, and light behaviour
Quite in the wrong—

So to work they go: And *Othello* is as wise a commentator, and makes his applications pat, as heart cou'd wish—but I wou'd not expect to find this Scene acted nearer than in *Southwark* Fair. But the *Hankerchief* is brought in at last, to stop all holes, and close the evidence. So now being satisfied with the proof, they come to a resolution, that the offenders shall be murdered.

Othel: But yet the pity of it, *Jago,* ah the pity.
Jago: If you be so fond over her iniquity give her

Patent to offend. For if it touches not you, it comes near no Body.
Do it not with poison, strangle her in her Bed; Even the Bed she has
contaminated.
Oth.: Good, good, the Justice of it pleases, very good.
Jago: And for *Cassio*, let me be his undertaker—

Jago had some pretence to be discontent with *Othello* and *Cassio:* And what
passed hitherto, was the operation of revenge. *Desdemona* had never done him
harm, always kind to him, and to his Wife; was his Country-woman, a Dame
of quality: for him to abet her Murder, shews nothing of a Souldier, nothing
of a Man, nothing of Nature in it. The *Ordinary* of *Newgate* never had the
like Monster to pass under his examination. Can it be any diversion to see a
Rogue beyond what the Devil ever finish'd? Or wou'd it be any instruction to
an Audience? *Jago* cou'd desire no better than to set *Cassio* and *Othello*, his two
Enemies, by the Ears together; so he might have been reveng'd on them both
at once: And chusing for his own share, the Murder of *Desdemona*, he had the
opportunity to play booty, and save the poor harmless wretch. But the Poet
must do every thing by contraries: to surprize the Audience still with something
horrible and prodigious, beyond any human imagination. At this rate he must
out-do the Devil, to be a Poet in the rank with *Shakespear.*

Soon after this, arrives from *Venice, Ludovico,* a noble Cousin of *Desdemona,*
presently she is at him also, on the behalf of *Cassio.*

Desd.: Cousin there's fallen between him and my
Lord An unkind breach, but you shall make all well.
Lud.: Is there division 'twixt my Lord and *Cassio.*
Desd.: A most unhappy one, I wou'd do much
To attone them, for the love I bear to *Cassio.*

By this time, we are to believe the couple have been a week or two Married:
And *Othello's* Jealousie that had rag'd so loudly, and had been so uneasie to
himself, must have reach'd her knowledge. The *Audience* have all heard him more
plain with her, than was needful to a Venetian capacity: And yet she must still be
impertinent in her suit for *Cassio*, well, this *Magnifico* comes from the *Doge,* and
Senators, to displace *Othello.*

Lud.: Deputing *Cassio* in his Government.
Desd.: Trust me, I am glad on't.
Oth.: Indeed.
Desd.: My Lord.
Oth.: I am glad to see you mad.
Desd.: How, sweet *Othello.*

Oth.: Devil.

Desd.: I have not deserved this.

Oth.. O Devil, Devil—

Out of my sight.

Desd.: I will not stay to offend you.

Lud.: Truly, an obedient Lady.

I do beseech your Lordship call her back.

Oth.: Mistress.

Desd.: My Lord.

Oth.: What would you with her sir?

Lud.: Who, I, my Lord?

Oth.: I, you did wish that I wou'd make her turn.

Sir, she can turn, and turn, and yet go on,

And turn agen, and she can weep, Sir, weep.

And she is obedient, as you say, obedient:

Very obedient—

Lud.: What strike your Wife?

Of what flesh and blood does our Poet make these noble Venetians? the men without Gall; the Women without either Brains or Sense? A Senators Daughter runs away with this Black-amoor; the Government employs this Moor to defend them against the Turks, so resent not the Moors Marriage at present, but the danger over, her Father gets the Moor Cashier'd, sends his Kinsman, Seignior *Ludovico*, to *Cyprus* with the Commission for a new General; who, at his arrival, finds the Moor calling the Lady his Kinswoman, Whore and Strumpet, and kicking her: what says the *Magnifico*?

Lud.: My Lord this would not be believ'd in *Venice*,

Tho' I shou'd swear I saw't, 'tis very much;

Make her amends: she weeps.

The Moor has no body to take his part, no body of his Colour: *Ludovico* has the new Governour Cassio, and all his Countrymen Venetians about him. What Poet wou'd give a villanous Black-amoor this Ascendant? What Tramontain could fancy the Venetians so low, so despicable, or so patient? this outrage to an injur'd Lady, the Divine *Desdemona*, might in a colder Climate have provoked some body to be her Champion: but the Italians may well conclude we have a strange Genius for Poetry. In the next Scene *Othello* is examining the supposed Bawd; then follows another storm of horrour and outrage against the poor Chicken, his Wife. Some Drayman or drunken Tinker might possibly treat his drab at this sort of rate, and mean no harm by it: but for his excellency, a My lord General, to Serenade a Senator's Daughter with such a volly of scoundrel filthy Language, is sure the most absurd Maggot that ever bred from any Poets addle Brain.

And she is in the right, who tells us,

Emil.: A Begger in his Drink,
Cou'd not have laid such terms upon his Callet.

This is not to describe passion. *Seneca* had another notion in the Case:

Parvae loquuntur curae, ingentes stupent.

And so had the Painter, who drew *Agamemnon* with his Face covered. Yet to make all worse, her Murder, and the manner of it, had before been resolv'd upon and concerted. But nothing is to provoke a Venetian; she takes all in good part; had the Scene lain in *Russia,* what cou'd we have expected more? With us a Tinkers Trull wou'd be Nettled, wou'd repartee with more spirit, and not appear so void of spleen.

Desd.: O good *Jago,*
What shall I do to win my Lord agen?

No Woman bred out of a Pig-stye, cou'd talk so meanly. After this, she is call'd to Supper with *Othello, Ludovico,* &c. after that comes a filthy sort of Pastoral Scene, where the *Wedding Sheets,* and Song of *Willow,* and her Mothers Maid, poor *Barbara,* are not the least moving things in this entertainment. But that we may not be kept too long in the dumps, nor the melancholy Scenes lye too heavy, undigested on our Stomach, this *Act* gives us for a farewell, the *salsa, O picante,* some quibbles, and smart touches, as Ovid had Prophecied:

Est & in obscenos deflexa Tragoedia risus.

The last *Act* begins with *Jago* and *Roderigo;* Who a little before had been upon the huff:

Rod.: I say it is not very well: I will make my self known to *Desdemona;*
if she will return me my Jewels, I will give over my suit, and repent my
unlawful sollicitation, if not, assure your self, I'll seek satisfaction of you.

Roderigo, a Noble Venetian had sought *Desdemona* in Marriage, is troubled to find the Moor had got her from him, advises with *Jago,* who wheadles him to sell his Estate, and go over the Sea to *Cyprus,* in expectation to Cuckold *Othello,* there having cheated *Roderigo* of all his Money and Jewels, on pretence of presenting them to *Desdemona*, our Gallant grows angry, and would have satisfaction from *Jago;* who sets all right, by telling him *Cassio* is to be Governour, *Othello* is going with *Desdemona* into *Mauritania:* to prevent this, you are to murder *Cassio*, and then all may be well.

> *Jago:* He goes into *Mauritania*, and takes with him the fair *Desdemona*, unless his abode be lingred here by some accident, wherein none can be so determinate, as the removing of Cassio.

Had *Roderigo* been one of the *Banditi*, he might not much stick at the Murder. But why *Roderigo* should take this for payment, and risque his person where the prospect of advantage is so very uncertain and remote, no body can imagine. It had need be a *super-subtle* Venetian that this Plot will pass upon. Then after a little spurt of villany and Murder, we are brought to the most lamentable, that ever appear'd on any Stage. A noble Venetian Lady is to be murdered by our Poet; in sober sadness, purely for being a Fool. No Pagan Poet but wou'd have found some *Machine* for her deliverance. *Pegasus* wou'd have strain'd hard to have brought old *Perseus* on his back, time enough, to rescue this *Andromeda* from so foul a Monster. Has our Christian Poetry no generosity, nor bowels? Ha, Sir *Lancelot!* ha St. *George!* will no Ghost leave the shades for us in extremity, to save a distressed Damosel?

But for our comfort, however felonious is the Heart, hear with what soft language, he does approach her, with a Candle in his Hand:

> *Oth.:* Put out the light and then put out the light;
> If I quench thee, thou flaming Minister,
> I can again thy former light restore—

Who would call him a Barbarian, Monster, Savage? Is this a Black-amoor?

> Soles occidere & redire possunt—

The very Soul and Quintessence of Sir *George Etheridge.*

One might think the General should not glory much in this action, but make an hasty work on't, and have turn'd his Eyes away from so unsouldierly an Execution: yet is he all pause and deliberation; handles her as calmly: and is as careful of her Souls health, as it had been her *Father Confessor. Have you prayed to Night,* Desdemona? But the suspence is necessary, that he might have a convenient while so to *roul his Eyes,* and so to *gnaw* his *nether lip* to the spectators. Besides the greater cruelty—*sub tarn lentis maxillis.*

But hark, a most tragical thing laid to her charge.

Oth.: That Handkerchief, that I so lov'd, and gave thee,
Thou gav'st to *Cassio.*
Desd.: No by my Life and Soul;
Send for the man and ask him.
Oth.: By Heaven, I saw my Handkerchief in his hand—
—I saw the Handkerchief.

So much ado, so much stress, so much passion and repetition about an Handkerchief! Why was not this call'd the *Tragedy of the Handkerchief?* What can be more absurd than (as *Quintilian* expresses it) *in parvis litibus has Tragoedias movere?* We have heard of *Fortunatus his Purse,* and of the *Invisible Cloak,* long ago worn thread bare, and stow'd up in the Wardrobe of obsolete Romances: one might think, that were a fitter place for this Handkerchief, than that it, at this time of day, be worn on the Stage, to raise every where all this clutter and turmoil. Had it been *Desdemona's* Garter, the Sagacious Moor might have smelt a Rat: but the Handkerchief is so remote a trifle, no Booby, on this side *Mauritania,* cou'd make any consequence from it.

We may learn here, that a Woman never loses her Tongue, even tho' after she is stifl'd.

Desd.: O falsly, falsly murder'd.
Em.: Sweet *Desdemona,* O sweet Mistress, speak.
Desd.: A guiltless death I dye.
Em.: O who has done the deed?
Desd.: No body, I my self, farewel.
Commend me to my kind Lord, O farewel.

This *Desdemona* is a black swan; or an old Black-amoor is a bewitching Bed-fellow. If this be Nature, it is a *laschete* below what the English Language can express.

For *Lardella,* to *make love, like an Humble Bee,* was, in the Rehearsal, thought a fancy odd enough.

But hark what follows:

Oth.: O heavy hour!
Methinks it shou'd be now a huge Eclipse
Of Sun and Moon, and that the affrighted globe
Shou'd yawn at Alteration.

This is wonderful. Here is Poetry to *elevate* and *amuse.* Here is sound All-sufficient. It wou'd be uncivil to ask *Flamstead,* if the Sun and Moon can both together be so hugely eclipsed, in any *heavy hour* whatsoever. Nor must the Spectators consult *Gresham* Colledge, whether a body is naturally *frighted* till he *Yawn* agen. The Fortune of Greece is not concern'd with these Matters. These are Physical circumstances a Poet may be ignorant in, with out any harm to the publick. These slips have no influence on our Manners and good Life; which are the Poets Province.

Rather may we ask here what unnatural crime *Desdemona*, or her Parents had committed, to bring this Judgment down upon her; to Wed a Black-amoor, and innocent to be thus cruelly murder'd by him. What instruction can we make out of this Catastrophe? Or whither must our reflection lead us? Is not this to envenome and sour our spirits, to make us repine and grumble at Providence; and the government of the World? If this be our end, what boots it to be Vertuous?

Desdemona dropt the Handkerchief, and missed it that very day after her Marriage; it might have been rumpl'd up with her Wedding sheets: And this Night that she lay in her wedding sheets, the *Fairey* Napkin (whilst *Othello* was stifling her) might have started up to disarm his fury, and stop his ungracious mouth. Then might she (in a Traunce for fear) have lain as dead. Then might he, believing her dead, touch'd with remorse, have honestly cut his own Throat, by the good leave, and with the applause of all the Spectators. Who might thereupon have gone home with a quiet mind, admiring the beauty of Providence; fairly and truly represented on the Theatre.

Oth.: Why, how shou'd she be murdered?
Em.: Alas, who knows?
Oth.: You heard her say her self it was not I.
Em.. She did so, I must needs report a truth.
Oth.: She's like a liar gone to burn in Hell.
Twas I that did it.
Em.: O, the more Angel she!
And you the blacker Devil.
Oth.: She turn'd to folly, and she was an Whore.
Em.: Thou dost belye her, and thou art a Devil.
Oth.: She was false as Water.
Em.: Thou art rash as Fire,
To say that she was false: O she was heavenly true.

In this kind of Dialogue they continue for forty lines farther, before she bethinks her self, to cry Murder.

Em.: Help, help, O help,
The Moor has kill'd my Mistress, murder, Murder.

But from this Scene to the end of the Play we meet with nothing but blood and butchery, described much-what to the style of *the last Speeches and Confessions of the persons executed at Tyburn:* with this difference, that there we have the *fact,* and the due course of Justice, whereas our Poet against all Justice and Reason, against all Law, Humanity and Nature, in a barbarous arbitrary way, executes and makes havock of his subjects, *Hab-nab,* as they come to hand. *Desdemona* dropt her Handkerchief; therefore she must be stifl'd. *Othello,* by law to be broken on the Wheel, by the Poets cunning escapes with cutting his own Throat. *Cassio,* for I know not what, comes off with a broken shin. *Jago* murders his Benefactor *Roderigo,* as this were poetical gratitude. *Jago* is not yet kill'd, because there never yet was such a villain alive. The Devil, if once he brings a man to be dipt in a deadly sin, lets him alone, to take his course: and now when the *Foul Fiend* has done with him, our wise Authors take the sinner into their poetical service; there to accomplish him, and do the Devils drudgery.

Philosophy tells us it is a principle in the Nature of Man *to be grateful.*

History may tell us that *John an Oaks, John a Stiles,* or *Jago* were ungrateful; *Poetry* is to follow Nature; Philosophy must be his guide: history and *fact* in particular cases *of John an Oaks,* or *John of Styles,* are no warrant or direction for a Poet. Therefore *Aristotle* is always telling us Poetry is *spoudaioteron kai philosophoteron,* is more general and abstracted, is led more by the Philosophy, the reason and nature of things, than History: which only records things higlety, piglety, right or wrong as they happen. History might without any preamble or difficulty, say that *Jago* was ungrateful. Philosophy then calls him unnatural; But the Poet is not, without huge labour and preparation to expose the Monster; and after shew the Divine Vengeance executed upon him. The Poet is not to add willful Murder to his ingratitude: he has not antidote enough for the Poison: his Hell and Furies are not punishment sufficient for one single crime, of that bulk and aggravation.

> *Em.:* O   thou dull Moor, that Handkerchief thou speakest on,
> I found by Fortune, and did give my Husband:
> For often with a solemn earnestness,
> (More than indeed belong'd to such a trifle)
> He beg'd of me to steal it.

Here we see the meanest woman in the Play takes this *Handkerchief* for a *trifle* below her Husband to trouble his head about it. Yet we find, it entered into our Poets head, to make a Tragedy of this *Trifle.*

Then for the *unraveling of the Plot,* as they call it, never was old deputy Recorder in a Country Town, with his spectacles in summoning up the evidence, at such a puzzle: so blunder'd, and bedoultefied: as is our Poet, to have a good riddance: And get the *Catastrophe* off his hands.

What can remain with the Audience to carry home with them from this sort of Poetry, for their use and edification? how can it work, unless (instead of settling the mind, and purging our passions) to delude our senses, disorder our thoughts, addle our brain, pervert our affections, hair our imaginations, corrupt our appetite, and fill our head with vanity, confusion, *Tintamarre*, and Jingle-jangle, beyond what all the Parish Clarks of *London*, with their *old Testament* farces, and interludes, in *Richard* the seconds time cou'd ever pretend to? Our only hopes, for the good of their Souls, can be, that these people go to the Playhouse, as they do to Church, to sit still, look on one another, make no reflection, nor mind the Play, more than they would a Sermon.

There is in this Play, some burlesk, some humour, and ramble of Comical Wit, some shew, and some *Mimickry* to divert the spectators: but the tragical part is, plainly none other, than a Bloody Farce, without salt or savour.

NOTES

1. Sueton. *in Tib.*
2. *Rehearsal..*

—⟨∿∿⟩— —⟨∿∿⟩— —⟨∿∿⟩—

1694—Charles Gildon. "Some Reflections on Mr. Rymer's *Short View of Tragedy* and an Attempt at a Vindication of *Shakespeare*," from "Remarks on the Plays of Shakespear"

Charles Gildon (1665–1724)—translator, biographer, essayist, playwright, and poet—wrote a series of notes and essays to accompany Rowe's edition of Shakespeare, providing the first extensive commentaries of the plays. He counted among his literary enemies Alexander Pope and Jonathan Swift.

To begin with the *Fable* (as our Critic has done) I must tell him he has as falsly as ridiculously represented it, which I shall endeavour to put in a Juster light.

Othello a Noble *Moor*, or *Negro*, that had by long Services and brave Acts establish'd himself in the Opinion of the *Senate* of VENICE, wins the Affections of *Desdemona*, Daughter to *Brabantio* (one of the *Senators*), by the moving account he gives of the imminent Dangers he had passed and hazards he had ventured through, a belief of which his known Virtue confirmed; and unknown to her Father Marries her, and carries her (with the leave of the Senate) with him to *Cyprus*, his Province. He makes *Cassio* his Lieutenant, tho' *Iago* had sollicited it by his Friends for himself; which Refusal, joyn'd with a jealousie that *Othello* had had to do with his Wife, makes him contrive the destruction of *Cassio* and the *Moor*, to gratifie his Revenge and Ambition. But having no way to revenge himself sufficiently on the *Moor* (from whom he suppos'd he had receiv'd a double *Wrong*) proportionable to the injury but this, he draws him with a great deal of Cunning into a Jealousie of his Wife, and that by a chain of Circumstances contriv'd to that purpose, and urg'd with all the taking insinuations imaginable; particularly by a Handkerchief he had convey'd to *Cassio* (which *Iago's* Wife stole from *Desdemona*) to convince the *Moor* his Wife was too familiar with him, having parted with such a favour to him (which she had on her Marriage receiv'd from *Othello* with the strictest charge of preserving, it being a Gift of his Mother, of Curious Work and secret Virtue). *Othello*, by these means won to a belief of his own Infamy, resolves the Murder of those he concluded guilty, *viz. Cassio* and his Wife. *Iago* officiously undertakes the dispatching of *Cassio*, having got his Commission already, but is disappointed of his design, employing one *Roderigo* to that purpose, who had follow'd him from *Venice* in hopes by his means to enjoy *Desdemona*, as *Iago* had promis'd him. But the *Moor* effectually puts his Revenge in Execution on his Wife, which is no sooner done but he's convinc'd of his Error, and in remorse kills himself, whilst *Iago*, the Cause of all this Villany, having slain his Wife for discovering it, is borne away to a more ignominious Punishment, as more proportion'd to his *Villanies*.

The *Fable* to be perfect must be *Admirable* and *Probable*, and as it approaches those two 'tis more or less perfect in its kind. *Admirable* is what is *uncommon* and *extraordinary*. *Probable* is what is agreeable to common Opinion. This must be the Test of this *Fable* of *Othello*; but then we must not take it as given us by our Drolling Critic (who very truely confesseth in his former Book—and in that he is no Changeling—he must be merry out of Season, as he always is) but as I have laid it down, else we shou'd do *Shakespeare* a great deal of Injustice.

I suppose none will deny that it is *Admirable*: that is, compos'd of Incidents that happen not e'ery day. His Antagonist confesses as much; there is therefore nothing but the *Probability* of it attaqu'd by him, which I question not either wholly to prove, or at least to set it on the same bottom with the best of *Sophocles*, that of his *Oedipus*.

First, to see whether he have sinn'd against Probability, let us consider what our Caviller objects, all which may be reduced to two Points. First, that 'tis not probable that the Senate of *Venice* (tho' it usually employ Strangers) should employ a *Moor* against the *Turk*, neither is it in the next place *probable* that *Desdemona* shou'd be in Love with him. On this turns all the Accusation, this is the very Head of his offending.

All the Reason he gives, or rather implies, for the first Improbability is that 'tis not likely the State of *Venice* wou'd employ a *Moor* (taking him for a *Mahometan*) against the *Turk*, because of the mutual Bond of Religion. He indeed says not so, but takes it for granted that *Othello* must be rather for the *Turkish* interest than the *Venetian*, because a *Moor*. But, I think (nor does he oppose it with any reason), the Character of the *Venetian State* being to employ Strangers in their Wars, it gives sufficient ground to our Poet to suppose a *Moor* employ'd by 'em as well as a *German*; that is, a *Christian Moor*, as *Othello* is represented by our Poet, for from such a *Moor* there cou'd be no just fear of treachery in favour of the *Mahometans*. He tells us—

I fetch my Life and Being from Men of Royal Siege.

Supposing him therefore the Son or Nephew of the Emperor of *Monomotopa*, *Aethiopia* or *Congo*, forc'd to leave his Country for Religion (or any other occasion), coming to *Europe* by the convenience of the *Portugueze* Ships, might after several Fortunes serve first as a Voluntier till he had signaliz'd himself and prov'd himself worthy of Command; part of this may very reasonably be drawn from what the Poet makes him say. Now upon this Supposition it appears more rational and probable the *Venetians* shou'd employ a Stranger who wholly depended on themselves, and whose Country was too remote to influence him to their prejudice, than other Strangers whose Princes may in some measure direct their Actions for their own Advantage. But that *Othello* is suppos'd to be a Christian is evident from the Second Act, and from these words of *Iago*:

—And then for her
To Win the Moor, *were't to renounce his* Baptism, &c.

Why therefore an *African* Christian may not by the *Venetians* be suppos'd to be as zealous against the *Turks* as an *European* Christian, I cannot imagine. So that this Bustle of *Littora littoribus Contraria*, &c. is only an inconsiderate Amusement to shew how little the Gentleman was troubled with thought when he wrote it.

No more to the purpose is that Heat he expresses against *Shakespeare's* giving a Name to his *Moor*, though *Cinthio* did not, though History did not warrant it. For this can be no more objected to our Poet, than the perverting the Character of *Dido*, and confounding the Chronology to bring her to the time of *Aeneas*, is to *Virgil*; the first as 'tis not mention'd in History, so it does not contradict it; but the last is a plain opposition to express History and Chronology. If *Virgil* be allow'd his Reason for doing that, *Shakespeare* is not to seek for one for what he has done. 'Twas necessary to give his *Moor* a place of some Figure in the World to give him the greater Authority and to make his Actions the more Considerable, and what place more likely to fix on than *Venice*, where Strangers are admitted to the highest Commands in Military Affairs?

'Tis granted, a *Negro* here does seldom rise above a Trumpeter, nor often perhaps higher at *Venice*. But then that proceeds from the Vice of Mankind, which is the Poet's Duty, as he informs us, to correct, and to represent things as they should be, not as they are. Now 'tis certain, there is no reason in the nature of things why a *Negro* of equal Birth and Merit should not be on an equal bottom with a *German, Hollander, French-man,* &c. The Poet, therefore, ought to show justice to Nations as well as Persons, and set them to rights, which the common course of things confounds. The same reason stands in force for this as for punishing the Wicked and making the Virtuous fortunate, which as *Rapin* and all the Critics agree, the Poet ought to do though it generally happens otherways. The Poet has therefore well chosen a polite People to cast off this customary Barbarity of confining Nations, without regard to their Virtue and Merits, to slavery and contempt for the meer Accident of their Complexion.

I hope I have brought by this time as convincing proofs for the probability in this particular as Mr. *Rymer* has against it, if I have not wholly gain'd my Point. Now therefore I shall proceed to the probability of *Desdemona*'s Love for the *Moor*, which I think is something more evident against him.

Whatever he aims at in his inconsistent Ramble against this may be reduc'd to the *Person* and the *Manner*. Against the *Person* he quotes you two Verses out of *Horace* that have no more reference to this than—*in the Beginning God made the Heaven and the Earth* has to the proof of the *Jus Divinum* of lay Bishops. The Verses are these:

> Sed non ut placidis coeant immitia, non ut
> Serpentes avibus geminentur, tigribus agni.

Unless he can prove that the Colour of a Man alters his Species and turns him into a *Beast* or *Devil* 'tis such a vulgar Error, so criminal a fondness of our Selves, to allow nothing of Humanity to any but our own Acquaintance of the fairer hew that I wonder a Man that pretends to be at all remov'd from the very Dreggs of the thoughtless Mob should espouse it in so public a manner! A Critic, too, who puts the Poet in mind of correcting the common corruptions of Custom. Any Man that has convers'd with the best Travels, or read any thing of the History of those parts on the continent of *Africa* discover'd by the *Portugueze*, must be so far from robbing the *Negroes* of some Countrys there of *Humanity* that they must grant them not only greater Heroes, nicer observers of Honour and all the Moral Virtues that distinguish'd the old *Romans*, but also much better Christians (where Christianity is profess'd) than we of *Europe* generally are. They move by a nobler Principle, more open, free and generous, and not such slaves to sordid Interest.

After all this, *Othello* being of *Royal Blood*, and a Christian, where is the disparity of the Match? If either side is advanc'd, 'tis *Desdemona*. And why must this Prince, though a Christian and of known and experienc'd *Virtue, Courage*, and *Conduct*, be made such a Monster that the *Venetian* Lady can't love him without perverting Nature? Experience tells us that there's nothing more common than Matches of this kind where the Whites and Blacks cohabit, as in both the *Indies*.

And Even here at home Ladys that have not wanted white Adorers have indulg'd their Amorous Dalliances with their Sable Lovers, without any of *Othello's* Qualifications, which is proof enough that Nature and Custom have not put any such unpassable bar betwixt Creatures of the same kind because of different colors; which I hope will remove the improbability of the Person, especially when the powerful Auxilarys of extraordinary Merit and Vertues come to plead with a generous Mind.

The probability of the *Person* being thus confirmed, I shall now consider that of the *Manner* of his obtaining her *Love*. To this end we must still keep in mind the known and experienc'd Virtue of the *Moor*, which gave Credit and Authority to what he said; and then we may easily suppose the story of his Fortunes and Dangers would make an impression of Pity and admiration, at least on the bosom of a Woman of a noble and generous Nature. No *Man* of any generous Principle but must be touch'd at suff'ring Virtue, and value the noble sufferer whose Courage and Bravery bears him through uncommon Trials and extraordinary Dangers. Nor would it have less force on a Woman of any principle of Honour and tenderness. She must be mov'd and pleas'd with the Narration, she must admire his constant Virtue; and Admiration is the first step to Love, which will easily gain upon those who have once entertain'd it.

Dido in *Virgil* was won by the *Trojan* stranger she never saw before by the relation of his fortunes and Escapes; and some particulars of the Narration of *Aeneas* carry full as ridiculous and absurd a Face as any thing *Othello* says; the most trifling of which is,

And of the Cannibals that each other eat,
The *Anthropophagi*, and Men whose Heads
Do grow beneath their Shoulders.

for all the rest is admirably fine, though our wonderful Critic can't relish it. There is a moving Beauty in each Line, the words are well chosen, and the Image they give great and Poetical; what an Image does *Desarts* IDLE give? That very Epithet is a perfect *Hypotyposis*, and seems to place me in the midst of one where all the active hurry of the World is lost; but all that I can say will not reach the excellence of that Epithet, so many properties of such a place meet in it. But as for the *Cannibals*, &c. *and the Men whose Heads grow beneath their Shoulders*, I have heard it condemn'd by Men whose tast I generally approve; yet must they give me leave to dissent from them here and permit me either wholly to justifie *Shakespeare*, even here, or at least to put him on an equal bottom with *Virgil* in his most beautiful part. For the fault lyes either in the *Improbability* of those things, or their *Impertinence* to the business in Hand. First, Probability we know is built on common Opinion; but 'tis certain the *Cannibals* have been generally believed, and that with very good grounds of Truth; so that there can be no doubt of the probability of that. Next for the *Men whose Heads grow beneath their Shoulders*: though that is not establish'd on so good a Foundation as Truth yet the general Traditionary belief of it in those days is sufficient to give it a poetical probability. As this was not *Improbable*, so neither was it *Impertinent*, for 'tis certain that whatever contributed to the raising her Idea of his Dangers and Escapes must conduce to his aim. But to fall into the Hands of those whom not only the fury of War but that of Custom makes Cruel, heightens the danger and by consequence the Concern, especially in a young Lady possess'd with the legend of the Nursery, whence she must have amazing Ideas of the Danger of the brave *Moor* from them.

But at worst, *Shakespeare* is on as good a bottom as *Virgil* in this particular. The Narrative of *Aeneas* that won the Heart of *Dido* has many things full as trifling and absurd as this, if not far more! . . .

. . . The Absurdities in *Homer* are much more numerous than those in *Virgil* (I mean those that must pass for such if this in *Shakespeare* is so), but because they relate not to this particular I shall say nothing of them here. All these I have remark'd in the Narration of *Aeneas* hinder'd not but that it won the Heart of *Dido*, though firmly bent against a second Amour (. . .) especially one that was not like to be so very Honorable. *Desdemona* had no such tye to steel her Heart against *Othello*'s Tongue, no reason to curb that Passion she ne'er felt before when the prevailing Virtue of the *Moor* attaqu'd her Heart; well may we therefore believe *Desdemona* shou'd yield to the same force that conquer'd *Dido*, with all her Resolutions and Engagements to the memory of *Sychaeus* [Dido's deceased husband] . . . . Cou'd *Aeneas's* Story, not one jot more moving or probable, make a meer stranger pass for a God with the Carthaginian Queen at first hearing; and must it be incredible that the same shall not make *Othello* pass for so much as a Man? The Parallel is so exact that I am apt to think *Shakespeare* took the Copy from *Virgil*. Nor can it justly be urg'd that these things were believ'd by the *Romans*, since they were so far from believing these trifles that *Seneca* in his Epistles laughs at those Fables that constituted their Hell, which was of much greater consequence. But supposing they were believ'd, the same will hold good for *Shakespeare* in this particular I vindicate him in: for 'tis built on as vulgar and general a tradition as these Fables of old were, so that the advantage is equal betwixt these two great Poets in this particular.

By this time, I hope, our *Drolling Caviller* will grant It no such monstrous absurdity for the *Doge* to say:

I think this Tale wou'd win my Daughter too.

since without doubt that short summing-up of what was only the subject of his tale to *Desdemona*, with only the supposition of the particulars, must move any generous Brest.

But should all I have said fail of clearing the *Probability* of the *Fable* from Mr. *Rymer's* Objections, yet ought not that to rob *Shakespeare* of his due Character of being a *Poet*, and a great *Genius*: unless he will for the same reason deny those prerogatives to *Homer* and *Sophocles* . . . .

. . . The whole *Fable* of *Oedipus*, tho' so much admir'd, is so very *singular* and *improbable* that 'tis scarce possible it ever cou'd have happen'd. On the other hand, the fatal Jealousie of *Othello* and the Revenge of *Iago* are the natural Consequences of our ungovern'd Passions, which by a prospect of such Tragical effects of their being indulg'd may be the better regulated and govern'd by us. So that tho' *Othello* ends not so formally with a moral Sentence as *Oedipus* does yet it sets out one of much greater Value. If it be a fault in *Shakespeare* that it end not with such a sentence, *Sophocles* is guilty of no less in his *Philoctetes*, which not only concludes without any Moral but is also incapable of being reduc'd to any, at least of any moment. Whereas the Morals of *Hamlet, Macbeth*, and most of *Shakespeare's* Plays prove a lesson of mightier consequence than any in *Sophocles* except the *Electra, viz.* that Usurpation, tho' it thrive a while, will at last be punish'd, *&c*. . . .

. . . What I have said in the beginning of my Vindication of *Shakespeare* must here be recollected on *Iago's* behalf; besides which I have some other considerations to offer, which I hope will lighten the insupportable load of Contempt and Ridicule cast on him by our Caviller . . . .

. . . We are not only to respect the profession of the Man in our Judgment of the Character but we must also have an Eye to his Nation, the Country he was born in, and the prevailing temper of the People, with their National Vices. By this Rule we shall find *Iago* an *Italian*, by Nature *Selfish, Jealous, Reserved, Revengeful* and *Proud*, nor can I see any reason to suppose his Military Profession shou'd too powerfully influence him to purge away all these Qualities and establish contrary in their room. . . .

OTHELLO
IN THE EIGHTEENTH CENTURY

"Restore the lock!" she cries; and all around
"Restore the lock!" the vaulted roofs rebound.
Not fierce Othello in so loud a strain
Roared for the handkerchief that caused his pain.

From *The Rape of the Lock* (1714)

That Alexander Pope could include such a broad and comical allusion to *Othello* in his famous satirical epic testifies not only to the widespread familiarity of the play among his readers but also to the bombastic manner in which the role of Othello was played in Pope's time. Contemporary readers can get a sense of what a performance of *Othello* was like from Richard Steele's description of the way the noted actor Thomas Betterton played the part in this comment, written at the time of the actor's death in 1770:

> The wonderful agony which he appeared in when he examined the Circumstance of the Handkerchief of *Othello*, the Mixture of Love that intruded upon his Mind upon the innocent answers *Desdemona* makes, betrayed in his Gesture such a Variety and Vicissitude of Passions as would admonish a Man to be afraid of his own Heart, and perfectly convince him that it is to stab it to admit that worst of Daggers, Jealousy. Whoever reads in his Closet this admirable Scene will find that he cannot, except he has as warm an Imagination as *Shakespeare* himself, find any but dry, incoherent, and broken Sentences. But a Reader that has seen Betterton act it . . . .

For many eighteenth-century devotees, Shakespeare was better as theater than on the page; by contrast, many nineteenth-century commentators, such as Samuel Taylor Coleridge and Charles Lamb, preferred Shakespeare on the page, unsullied by dramatic interpretation.

Nonetheless, some of the most important Shakespearean commentary in the eighteenth century came from the editors who collected and published new editions of Shakespeare's texts. These editors appended notes and commentary, discussing not only textual matters but also the shape and circumstances of the plot, the nature of the characters, and the moral wisdom to be found in the plays. Samuel Johnson, the most important of these editor-critics and one of the greatest critics ever, supplied some general comments on *Othello*, giving it high praise—particularly for its magnificent characters. Later in the century, Elizabeth Griffith, in a book on the "morality" of Shakespeare's plays, would praise *Othello* as the author's masterpiece.

Other critics, however, expressed reservations. Many believed that great drama should follow the classical "unities," rules set forth in Aristotle's *Poetics* and derived from the tragedies of his time. For example, plays should feature a single setting and not roam widely. *Othello* was thus considered to be flawed, in part because its first act takes place in Venice, while the rest of the play is set in Cyprus. Even Samuel Johnson remarked that *Othello* could be improved if the first act were simply lopped off and its matter presented in expository narration later on. (In the nineteenth century, this is exactly what Arrigo Boito did when he turned *Othello* into a libretto for Giuseppe Verdi's opera *Otello*.) Some critics, such as John Hughes, also had reservations about the probability of the action. These "failings" were balanced, however, by a sense that despite his lack of adherence to the "Rules," as Hughes felt, Shakespeare "penetrated deeply into the Nature of the Passions" in *Othello*. Similarly, Lewis Theobald called the play "most faulty and regular" but still praised it as "excellent" in its depiction of Othello's "agonies."

To many critics, Shakespeare was cavalier, even savage, in his disregard for convention but also deeply perceptive and beautifully expressive. In France, Voltaire, the great voice of reason and liberty, also found Shakespeare guilty of barbarity. In one of his "Letters on the English" (1733), he sarcastically called *Othello* "a most tender piece," in which a "Man strangles his Wife on the Stage"—a violation of the classical practice of keeping actual violence out of the audience's view. Voltaire also found it ridiculous that Desdemona, "that poor Woman, whilst she is strangling [i.e., being strangled] cries aloud, that she dies very unjustly."

Voltaire was not alone in his distress. Some producers of the play in Europe, such as Jean-François Ducis in France and Friedrich Ludwig Schröder in Germany, altered the painful ending, permitting Desdemona to live. In England, the original stood, but the play was consistently cut for purposes of "refinement." Bawdy, vulgar, graphic, and overly passionate language was excised. The great editions of Shakespeare by Alexander Pope, Samuel Johnson, and Edmund Malone sold less well than the edition of Francis Gentleman, expurgated for propriety's sake. Cutting possibly "offensive" matter was a practice continued and expanded in the following century, but it had begun in the previous one. Extant prompt books of *Othello*, used at the Smock Alley Theater in Dublin during the last decades of the seventeenth century, show a number of such excisions.

1710—Sir Richard Steele.
"On the Funeral of Betterton," from *The Tatler*

Richard Steele (1672–1729), an essayist, playwright, and politician, is best known for founding two magazines: *The Tatler*, in 1709, and, with Joseph Addison, *The Spectator*, in 1711.

Having received Notice that the famous Actor Mr. *Betterton* was to be interred this Evening in the Cloysters near *Westminster Abbey*, I was resolved to walk thither and see the last Office done to a Man whom I had always very much admired, and from whose Action I had received more strong Impressions of what is great and noble in Human Nature than from the Arguments of the most solid Philosophers or the Descriptions of the most charming Poets I have ever read. As the rude and untaught Multitude are no Way wrought upon more effectually than by seeing publick Punishments and Executions, so Men of Letters and Education feel their Humanity most forcibly exercised when they attend the Obsequies of Men who had arrived at any Perfection in Liberal Accomplishments. Theatrical Action is to be esteemed as such, except it be objected that we cannot call that an Art which cannot be attained by Art. Voice, Stature, Motion, and other Gifts must be very bountifully bestowed by Nature, or Labour and Industry will but push the unhappy Endeavourer in that Way the further off his Wishes . . . .

I have hardly a Notion that any Performer of Antiquity could surpass the Action of Mr. *Betterton* in any of the Occasions in which he has appeared on our Stage. The wonderful Agony which he appeared in when he examined the Circumstance of the Handkerchief of *Othello*, the Mixture of Love that intruded upon his Mind upon the innocent Answers *Desdemona* makes, betrayed in his Gesture such a Variety and Vicissitude of Passions as would admonish a Man to be afraid of his own Heart, and perfectly convince him that it is to stab it to admit that worst of Daggers, Jealousy. Whoever reads in his Closet this admirable Scene will find that he cannot, except he has as warm an Imagination as *Shakespeare* himself, find any but dry, incoherent, and broken Sentences. But a Reader that has seen *Betterton* act it observes there could not be a Word added, that longer Speech had been unnatural, nay impossible to be uttered in *Othello's* Circumstances. The charming Passage in the same Tragedy where he tells the Manner of winning the Affection of his Mistress was urged with so moving and graceful an Energy that, while I walked in the Cloysters, I thought of him with the same Concern as if I waited for the Remains of a Person who had in real Life done all that I had seen him represent . . . .

1713—John Hughes.
"On the Tragedy of Othello," from *The Guardian*

John Hughes (1677-1720) was a poet, translator, editor, playwright, and essayist. In his *Lives of the Poets*, Samuel Johnson (quoting Jonathan Swift) describes him as "among the mediocrists, in prose as well as verse."

Me duce damnosas, homines, conpescite curas. (Ovid, *Rem. Amor.* v. 69.)
Learn, mortals, from my precepts to control
The furious passions that disturb the soul.

It is natural for an old man to be fond of such entertainments as revive in his imagination the agreeable impressions made upon it in his youth: the set of wits and beauties he was first acquainted with, the balls and drawing-rooms in which he made an agreeable figure, the music and actors he heard and saw, when his life was fresh, and his spirits vigorous and quick, have usually the preference in his esteem to any succeeding pleasures that present themselves when his taste is grown more languid. It is for this reason I never see a picture of Sir Peter Lely's, who drew so many of my first friends and acquaintance, without a sensible delight; and I am in raptures when I reflect on the compositions of the famous Mr. Henry Lawes, long before Italian music was introduced into our nation. Above all, I am pleased in observing that the tragedies of Shakspeare, which in my youthful days have so frequently filled my eyes with tears, hold their rank still, and are the great support of our theatre.

It was with this agreeable prepossession of mind, I went, some time ago, to see the old tragedy of *Othello,* and took my female wards with me, having promised them a little before to carry them to the first play of Shakspeare's which should be acted. Mrs. Cornelia, who is a great reader, and never fails to peruse the play-bills, which are brought to her every day, gave me notice of it early in the morning. When I came to my Lady Lizard's at dinner, I found the young folks all dressed, and expecting the performance of my promise. I went with them at the proper time, placed them together in the boxes, and myself by them in a corner seat. As I have the chief scenes of the play by heart, I did not look much on the stage, but formed to myself a new satisfaction in keeping an eye on the faces of my little audience, and observing, as it were by reflection, the different passions of the play represented in their countenances. Mrs. Betty told us the names of several persons of distinction, as they took their places in their boxes, and entertained us with the history of a new marriage or two, till the curtain drew up. I soon perceived that Mrs. Jane was touched with the love of Desdemona, and in a concern to see how she would come off with her parents. Annabella had a rambling eye, and for some time was more taken up with observing what gentlemen looked at her, and with criticising the dress of the ladies, than with any thing that passed on the stage. Mrs. Cornelia, who I have often said is addicted to the study of romances, commended that speech in the play in which Othello mentions his "hair-breadth scapes in th' imminent deadly breach," and recites his travels and adventures with which he had captivated the heart of Desdemona. The Sparkler looked several times frighted: and as the distress of the play was heightened, their different attention was collected, and fixed wholly on the stage, till I saw them all, with a secret satisfaction, betrayed into tears.

I have often considered this play as a noble, but irregular, production of a genius, who had the power of animating the theatre beyond any writer we have ever known. The touches of nature in it are strong and masterly; but the economy of the fable, and in some particulars the probability, are too much neglected. If I would speak of it in the most severe terms, I should say as Waller does of the Maid's *Tragedy,*

Great are its faults, but glorious is its flame.

But it would be poor employment in a critic to observe upon the faults, and shew no taste for the beauties, in a work that has always struck the most sensible part of our audiences in a very forcible manner.

The chief subject of this piece is the passion of jealousy, which the poet hath represented at large, in its birth, its various workings and agonies, and its horrid consequences. From this passion, and the innocence and simplicity of the person suspected, arises a very moving distress.

It is a remark, as I remember, of a modern writer, who is thought to have penetrated deeply into the nature of the passions, "that the most extravagant love is nearest to the strongest hatred." The Moor is furious in both these extremes. His love is tempestuous, and mingled with a wildness peculiar to his character, which seems very artfully to prepare for the change which is to follow.

How savage, yet how ardent, is that expression of the raptures of his heart, when, looking after Desdemona as she withdraws, he breaks out,

Excellent wench! Perdition catch my soul,
But I do love thee; and when I love thee not,
Chaos is come again.

The deep and subtle villany of Iago, in working this change from love to jealousy, in so tumultuous a mind as that of Othello, prepossessed with a confidence in the disinterested affection of the man who is leading him on insensibly to his ruin, is likewise drawn with a masterly hand. Iago's broken hints, questions, and seeming care to hide the reason of them; his obscure suggestions to raise the curiosity of the Moor: his personated confusion, and refusing to explain himself while Othello is drawn on, and held in suspense till he grows impatient and angry; then his throwing in the poison, and naming to him in a caution, the passion he would raise,

—O beware of jealousy!—

are inimitable strokes of art, in that scene which has always been justly esteemed one of the best which was ever represented on the theatre.

To return to the character of Othello; his strife of passions, his starts, his returns of love, and threatenings to Iago, who had put his mind on the rack, his relapses afterward to jealousy, his rage against his wife, and his asking pardon of Iago, whom he thinks he had abused for his fidelity to him, are touches which no one can overlook that has the sentiments of human nature, or has considered the heart of man in its frailties, its penances, and all the variety of its agitations. The torments which the Moor suffers are so exquisitely drawn, as to render him as much an object of compassion, even in the barbarous action of murdering Desdemona, as the innocent person herself who falls under his hand.

But there is nothing in which the poet has more shewn his judgment in this play, than in the circumstance of the handkerchief, which is employed as a confirmation to the jealousy of Othello already raised. What I would here observe is, that the very slightness of this circumstance is the beauty of it. How finely has Shakspeare expressed the nature of jealousy in those lines, which, on this occasion, he puts into the mouth of Iago,

Trifles light as air
Are to the jealous, confirmation strong
As proofs of holy writ.

It would be easy for a tasteless critic to turn any of the beauties I have here mentioned into ridicule; but such a one would only betray a mechanical judgment, formed out of borrowed rules and common-place reading, and not arising from any true discernment in human nature, and its passions.

As the moral of this tragedy is an admirable caution against hasty suspicions, and the giving way to the first transports of rage and jealousy, which may plunge a man in a few minutes into all the horrors of guilt, distraction, and ruin, I shall farther enforce it, by relating a scene of misfortunes of the like kind, which really happened some years ago in Spain; and is an instance of the most tragical hurricane of passion I have ever met with in history. It may be easily conceived, that a heart ever big with resentments of its own dignity, and never allayed by reflections which make us honour ourselves for acting with reason and equality, will take fire precipitantly. It will, on a sudden, flame too high to be extinguished. The short story I am going to tell is a lively instance of the truth of this observation, and a just warning to those of jealous honour, to look about them, and begin to possess their souls as they ought, for no man of spirit knows how terrible a creature he is, till he comes to be provoked.

Don Alonzo, a Spanish nobleman, had a beautiful and virtuous wife, with whom he had lived for some years in great tranquillity. The gentleman, however, was not free from the faults usually imputed to his nation; he was proud, suspicious, and impetuous. He kept a Moor in his house, whom, on a complaint from his lady, he had punished for a small offence with the utmost severity. The slave vowed revenge, and communicated his resolution to one of the lady's women with whom he lived in a criminal way. This creature also hated her mistress, for she feared she was observed by her; she therefore undertook to make Don Alonzo jealous, by insinuating that the gardener was often admitted to his lady in private, and promising to make him an eye-witness of it. At a proper time agreed on between her and the Morisco, she sent a message to the gardener, that his lady, having some hasty orders to give him, would have him come that moment to her in her chamber. In the mean time she had placed Alonzo privately in an outer room, that he might observe who passed that way. It was not long before he saw the gardener appear. Alonzo had not patience, but, following him into the apartment, struck him at one blow with a dagger to the heart; then dragging his lady by the hair, without inquiring farther, he instantly killed her.

Here he paused, looked on the dead bodies with all the agitations of a demon of revenge; when the wench who had occasioned these terrors, distracted with remorse, threw herself at his feet, and in a voice of lamentation, without sense of the consequence, repeated all her guilt. Alonzo was overwhelmed with all the violent passions at one instant, and uttered the broken voices and emotions of each of them for a moment, till at last he recollected himself enough to end his agony of love, anger, disdain, revenge, and remorse, by murdering the maid, the Moor, and himself.

—◦◦◦— —◦◦◦— —◦◦◦—

1717—Lewis Theobald. From *The Censor*

Lewis Theobald (1688–1744), editor and author of essays and poetry, produced an edition of Shakespeare in 1734. He also attacked Alexander Pope's earlier edition. Pope got his revenge by depicting Theobald as the epitome of dullness in *The Dunciad*.

I have frequently perus'd with Satisfaction the *Othello* of *Shakespeare*, a Play most faulty and irregular in many Points but Excellent in one Particular. For the Crimes and Misfortunes of the *Moor* are owing to an impetuous Desire of having his Doubts clear'd, and a Jealousie and Rage, native to him, which he cannot controul and which push him on to Revenge. He is otherwise in his Character brave and open, generous and full of Love for *Desdemona,* but stung with the subtle Suggestions of *Iago* and impatient of a Wrong done to his Love and Honour. Passion at once o'erbears his Reason and gives him up to Thoughts of bloody Reparation. Yet after he has determin'd to murther his Wife his Sentiments of her suppos'd Injury and his Misfortune are so pathetick that we cannot but forget his barbarous Resolution, and pity the Agonies which he so strongly seems to feel.

> *Oth.:* Had it pleas'd Heav'n
> To try me with Affliction, had it rain'd
> All kind of Sores and Shames on my bare Head . . . .
> But there, where I have treasur'd up my Heart,
> Where either I must live or bear no Life,
> The Fountain from the which my Current runs,
> Or else dries up—to be discarded thence!

1733—Voltaire. "The Orphan," from *Philosophical Letters*

Voltaire (1694-1778), author of *Candide,* was one of the towering figures of the European Enlightenment and one of the greatest thinkers in French history. He wrote poetry, history, philosophy, drama, and fiction. The passage below is taken from a different source from the brief remarks cited in the introduction to this section, but it is similar to them in nature; here, Voltaire sarcastically describes several of the play's most indecorous scenes.

. . . We cannot sufficiently lament that the translator has, with the same cruelty, deprived us of the finest scenes of Shakespeare's "Othello." With what pleasure should we have seen the first scene at Venice, and the last at Cyprus! First of all, a Moor runs away with the daughter of a senator: Iago, the Moor's officer, runs to the window of the father's house; the father appears in his shirt at the window. "Zounds," says he, "put on your clothes; a black ram has got upon your white ewe; come, come, rise and come down, or the devil will make you a grandsire."

SENATOR.—"What's the matter, what would you be at? Are you a mad man?"
IAGO—"Zounds, sir, are you one of those who would not serve God if the devil forbade them? We are come to do you a service, and you take us for ruffians; I tell you your daughter will be covered by a Barbary horse; your grandchildren will neigh after you, and African nags will be your cousins-german."
SENATOR—"What profane rogue talks to me at this rate?"
IAGO—"Know that your daughter Desdemona and the Moor Othello now make the beast with two backs."

This same Iago accompanies to Cyprus the Moor Othello and the lady Desdemona, whom the senate of Venice kindly grants, in spite of the father, for a wife to the Moor, whom they appoint governor of Cyprus.

Scarcely have they arrived in that island, when Iago undertakes to make the Moor jealous of his wife, and to inspire him with a suspicion of her fidelity. The Moor begins to feel some inquietude, he makes the following reflections. "After all," says he, "what sense had I of the pleasure that others had given her, and of her debauchery? I did not see it, it did not hurt me; I slept as well as usual. When a thing has been stolen from us of which we had no occasion, if we are ignorant of the theft, we have lost nothing. I had been happy if the whole army, and even the pioneers, had enjoyed her, so as I had known nothing of the matter. Oh no—farewell all content—farewell the plumed troops, farewell the proud war that makes a virtue of ambition; farewell the neighing steeds and the shrill trumpets; the fife that pierces the ear, and the drum that excites the courage, the royal banner; and all the rank, pride, pomp, and various circumstances of glorious war; and you, you mortal engines, whose rude throats imitate those of the immortal Jupiter; farewell, Othello has now no occupation."

This is another of the admirable passages distinguished by [Alexander] Pope's commas.

IAGO—"Is it possible, my lord?"
OTHELLO *(taking him by the throat)*—"Villain, prove that my wife's a whore, give me an ocular proof of it; or by the worth of the eternal soul of man, it would have been better for you, you had been born a dog."
IAGO—"This office by no means pleases me; but since I have gone so far through pure honesty and friendship for you, I will proceed. I lay the other night with your lieutenant Cassio; and could not sleep for the toothache. You cannot but know that there are people so loose of soul, that in their sleep they talk of their affairs; Cassio is one of

these: he said in his sleep, 'Dear Desdemona, let us be careful, let us hide our loves.' In speaking, he took me by the hand, he patted me, he cried, 'Oh, charming creature!' he kissed me with transport, as if he had by the roots torn up kisses planted upon my lips, he put his thighs upon my legs, he sighed, he breathed short, he kissed me, he cried out, 'Cursed fate which has given you to the Moor!'"

Upon these proofs, so very decently related, and the handkerchief of Othello, which Cassio had found by accident, the Moorish general strangles his wife in her bed; but he kisses her before he puts her to death. "Come," says he, "die, thou whore." "Ah, kill me to-morrow, let me live to-night," says she. "Wretch, if you stir," cries he. "Give me but one half hour," says she. "No," answers he. "After that I will delay you no longer; let me at least say my prayers," says she. "No, it is too late," answers Othello. He strangles her; and Desdemona, after she is strangled, cries out that she is innocent.

When Desdemona is dead, the senate recalls Othello: he is seized in order to be carried to Venice to take his trial. "Hold," says he, "a word or two. Tell the senate, that one day at Aleppo I found a turbaned Turk, who beat a Venetian, and made a jest of the republic; I took by the beard, the circumcised dog, and smote him thus." At these words he stabs himself.

A French translator, who has given us sketches of several English pieces, and among others, of the "Moor of Venice," partly in verse, partly in prose, has not translated any of these important passages which we have laid before our readers; he makes Othello express himself thus:

> *L'art n'est pas fait pour moi; c'est un fard que je hais,*
> *Dites leur qu'Othello plus amoureux que sage,*
> *Quoique époux adoré, jaloux jusques à la rage,*
> *Trompé par un esclave, aveuglé par l'erreur*
> *Immola son épouse, & se perça le cœur.*
> Art I detest, I all disguise abhor.
> Say that Othello, more in love than wise,
> Imposed on by a slave, with error blind,
> Murdered his wife, then pierced his guilty breast.

There is not a word of this in the original; "*l'art n'est pas fait pour moi,*" is taken from the tragedy of "*Zaïre,*" but the rest is not.

The reader now has it in his power to decide the dispute for pre-eminence between the tragedies of London and Paris.

1765—Samuel Johnson. *Othello* (notes), from *The Plays of William Shakespear*

Samuel Johnson (1709-1784) is thought by many to be the greatest critic in the English language. He was a poet, critic, prose writer, lexicographer, editor, and celebrated raconteur. His edition of the works of Shakespeare contained some of his famous thoughts on the plays. The following comments are taken from annotations he supplied to his text of *Othello*.

...Act V. Scene vi. (v. ii. 63–5.)

Oh perjur'd woman! Thou dost stone my heart,
And mak'st me call, what I intent to do,
A murder, which I thought a sacrifice.

This line is difficult. *Thou hast hardened my heart, and makest me* kill thee with the rage of a *murderer*, when *I thought to have sacrificed* thee to justice with the calmness of a priest striking a victim.

It must not be omitted, that one of the elder quartos reads, *thou dost stone* thy *heart*; which I suspect to be genuine. The meaning then will be, *thou forcest me* to dismiss thee from the world in the state of the *murdered* without preparation for death, *when I intended* that thy punishment should have been a *sacrifice* atoning for thy crime.

I am glad that I have ended my revisal of this dreadful scene. It is not to be endured . . .

General Observation

The beauties of this play impress themselves so strongly upon the attention of the reader, that they can draw no aid from critical illustration. The fiery openness of Othello, magnanimous, artless, and credulous, boundless in his confidence, ardent in his affection, inflexible in his resolution, and obdurate in his revenge; the cool malignity of Iago, silent in his resentment, subtle in his designs, and studious at once of his interest and his vengeance; the soft simplicity of Desdemona, confident of merit, and conscious of innocence, her artless perseverance in her suit, and her slowness to suspect that she can be suspected, are such proofs of Shakespeare's skill in human nature, as, I suppose, it is vain to seek in any modern writer. The gradual progress which Iago makes in the Moor's conviction, and the circumstances which he employs to inflame him, are so artfully natural, that, though it will perhaps not be said of him as he says of himself, that he is "a man not easily jealous," yet we cannot but pity him when at last we find him "perplexed in the extreme."

There is always danger lest wickedness conjoined with abilities should steal upon esteem, though it misses of approbation but the character if Iago is so conducted, that he is from the first scene to the last hated and despised.

Even the inferiour characters of this play would be very conspicuous in any other piece, not only for their justness but their strength. Cassio is brave, benevolent, and honest, ruined only by his want of stubbornness to resist an insidious invitation of Roderigo's suspicious credulity, and impatient submission of the cheats which he sees practised upon him, and which by persuasion he suffers to be repeated, exhibit a strong picture of a weak mind betrayed by unlawful desires, to a false friend and the virtue of Aemilia is such as we often find, worn loosely but not cast off, easy to commit small crimes, but quickened and alarmed at atrocious villanies.

The Scenes from the beginning to the end are busy, varied but happy interchanges, and regularly promoting the progression of the story; and the narrative in the end, though it tells but what is known already, yet is necessary to produce the death of Othello.

Had the scene opened in Cyprus, and the preceding incidents been occasionally related, there had been little wanting of a drama of the most exact and scrupulous regularity.

1775—Elizabeth Griffith.
From *The Morality of Shakespeare's Drama Illustrated*

Elizabeth Griffith was an actress, dramatist, fiction writer, essayist, and translator. She is best known for *A Series of Genuine Letters between Henry and Frances*, a collection of letters published with her husband. She also wrote a critical study of the morality of Shakespeare's plays.

. . . Shakespeare has written three pieces on the subject of jealousy; the *Winter's Tale, Cymbeline,* and this one, besides the character of Ford, in the *Merry Wives*. But such was the richness of his genius that he has not borrowed a single thought, image, or expression, from any one of them to assist him in any of the others. The subject seems rather to have grown progressively out of itself, to have inspired its own sentiments and have dictated its own language. This Play, in my opinion, is very justly considered as the last and greatest effort of our Author's genius, and may therefore be looked upon as the *chef d'œuvre* of dramatic composition.

. . . It has often surprized me to find the character of Desdemona so much mistaken and slighted as it too generally is. It is simple, indeed, but that is one of its merits: for the simplicity of it is that of *innocence* not of *folly*. In my opinion, she seems to be as perfect a model of a wife as either this author, or any other writer, could possibly have framed. She speaks little; but whatever she says is sensible, pure, and chaste . . . .

OTHELLO
IN THE NINETEENTH CENTURY

📚

In 1826, in London, Ira Aldridge became the first black man to play the role of Othello. Until then, Othello had been performed by white actors, usually in blackface. In 1814, Edmund Kean established the tradition of playing Othello as olive-skinned. So firmly was this a precedent for white actors playing the Moor that Laurence Olivier's *Othello* at the National Theater in London in the late 1960s was noted for Olivier's full-body black makeup as well as for the intensity of his acting.

For nineteenth-century critics, Othello's skin color continued to be an issue of aesthetic and dramatic significance. The German critic August Wilhelm Schlegel insisted that Othello was a "negro," with a "wild nature," moved by a poison in his blood rather than by a passion of his heart. He described Othello's "blackness" as a surface characteristic, in contrast to Iago, who was "black," meaning "evil," to his depth. Other critics also employed a type of racial analysis that we might find disturbing today. Samuel Taylor Coleridge stated that Shakespeare could not have drawn Othello as a "negro," or sub-Saharan African, as opposed to a lighter-skinned North African. "Can we imagine him [Shakespeare] so utterly ignorant as to make a barbarous negro plead royal birth—at a time, too, when negros were not known except as slaves?"

To his credit, Coleridge, whose mind usually showed a greater generosity of thought than his racial observations suggest, also provided a number of striking insights regarding the play. For example, he challenged Samuel Johnson's assertion that if the first act of *Othello* were cut, the play would be a "regular tragedy," following the traditional "unities," and therefore superior. "In all acts of judgment," Coleridge wrote, "it can never be too often recollected, and scarcely too often repeated, that rules are means to ends, and, consequently, that the end must be determined and understood before it can be known what the rules are or ought to be." Throughout his "lecture" on Othello, Coleridge explores the text as a moral psychologist, with such lucid comments as this, derived from his observation of Iago: "a wicked man will employ real feelings, as well as assume those most alien from his own, as instruments of his purposes." Regarding Iago's statement, "'Tis in ourselves that we are thus, or thus," Coleridge observes that such "speech comprises the passionless character of Iago. It is all will in intellect; and therefore he is here a bold partizan of a truth, but yet of a truth converted into a falsehood by the absence of all the necessary modifications caused by the frail nature of man."

Charles Lamb, also entangled in the prejudice of his age, argued that the offensiveness of seeing a black man as the object of a white woman's love made *Othello* more suitable for reading than for viewing.

> Nothing can be more soothing, more flattering to the nobler parts of our natures, than to read of a young Venetian lady of highest extraction, through the force of love and from a sense of merit in him whom she loved, laying aside every consideration of kindred, and country, and colour, and wedding with a coal-black Moor . . . it is the perfect triumph of virtue over accidents, of the imagination over the senses . . . But upon the stage, when the imagination is no longer the ruling faculty, but we are left to our poor unassisted senses, I appeal to every one that has seen Othello played, whether he did not . . . find something extremely revolting in the courtship and wedded caresses of Othello and Desdemona.

Few today would admit to sharing Lamb's reaction to the union of Othello and Desdemona. His response, nevertheless, can remind readers of the powerful psychic tensions Shakespeare confronted in *Othello*.

The perceptive essayist William Hazlitt was less concerned with color than with the play's brilliant depiction of contrasting characters. He also saw the play as closer to the concerns of everyday life than any of Shakespeare's other tragedies.

Other critics were similarly admiring. Toward the century's end, Algernon Charles Swinburne wrote that "in Othello we get the pure poetry of natural and personal emotion . . . . [A]s a creator, a revealer, and an interpreter, infinite in his insight and his truthfulness, his tenderness and his wisdom, his justice and his mercy, no man who ever lived can stand beside the author of *Othello*."

As is often the case regarding Shakespeare, the famous playwright George Bernard Shaw provided a dissenting view. He called the play "pure melodrama," adding, "there is not a touch of character in it that goes below the skin." However, he also wrote: "But when the worst has been said of *Othello* that can be provoked by its superficiality and staginess, it remains magnificent by the volume of its passion and the splendor of its word-music."

Othello was also popular outside of Britain. In France, Alfred de Vigny made a French translation of *Othello* in 1829. Later, Victor Hugo famously compared Othello to night and Iago to "evil, the other form of darkness." In fact, the play had permeated French cultural imagination so effectively that it also became subject matter for other types of artists, who in effect provided their commentary via a different medium. In 1825, the great French painter Delacroix saw Edmund Kean perform *Othello* in London. "No words are strong enough to express one's admiration for the genius of Shakespeare, who created Othello and Iago," he wrote. In 1827, an English acting company headed by Charles Kimble performed *Othello* at the Odéon in Paris. Delacroix was among those in the audience, and he later wrote: "The English have opened their theatre. They have worked miracles, for they draw such crowds to the Odéon that all the paving-stones in the neighborhood rattle under the carriage wheels. In a word, they are all the rage. The most stubborn classicists have had to strike their flag. Our actors go to school to the English, and stare in astonishment." Delacroix painted *Othello and Desdemona* in 1849 and *The Death of Desdemona* in 1858. An equally sumptuous painting showing the death of Desdemona was painted by Alexandre-Marie Colin in 1829. All three are canvases swollen with texture, rich in claret, turquoise, and sky-blue tints, the paint vaporously and moodily applied. The drama of the pictures relies on the familiarity of the spectators with the story the scene depicts. The paintings not only present but also dramatize the play, offering, in romantic fashion, a voluptuousness of pain.

The greatest translation of *Othello* from one medium to another, however, was not in painting but in music. In February 1887, Giuseppe Verdi's opera *Otello*, using an Italian-language adaptation of *Othello* by Arrigo Boito, was first produced at La Scala in Milan.

In the United States, *Othello* drew the attention of former president John Quincy Adams. Even this consistently anti-slavery politician couldn't help but express his revulsion at the idea of Desdemona's attraction to Othello. He declared that Desdemona was actually an unsympathetic character because of it: "I must believe that, in exhibiting a daughter of a Venitian nobleman of the highest rank eloping in the dead of the night to marry a thick-lipped wool-headed Moor, opening a train of consequences which lead to her own destruction by her husband's hands, and to that of her father by a broken heart, he did not intend to present her as an example of the perfection of female virtue." Such attitudes were sadly persistent at the time.

1809—August Wilhelm Schlegel.
"Criticisms on Shakspeare's Tragedies," from
Lectures on Dramatic Art and Literature

August Wilhelm Schlegel (1767–1845) was a scholar, critic, poet, and professor. He translated a number of Shakespeare's plays into the German language and was one of the most influential disseminators of the ideas of the German Romantic movement.

If *Romeo and Juliet* shines with the colours of the dawn of morning, but a dawn whose purple clouds already announce the thunder of a sultry day, *Othello* is, on the other hand, a strongly shaded picture: we might call it a tragical Rembrandt. What a fortunate mistake that the Moor (under which name in the original novel, a baptized Saracen of the Northern coast of Africa was unquestionably meant), has been made by Shakespeare in every respect a negro! We recognize in Othello the wild nature of that glowing zone which generates the most ravenous beasts of prey and the most deadly poisons, tamed only in appearance by the desire of fame, by foreign laws of honour, and by nobler and milder manners. His jealousy is not the jealousy of the heart, which is compatible with the tenderest feeling and adoration of the beloved object; it is of that sensual kind which, in burning climes, has given birth to the disgraceful confinement of women and many other unnatural usages. A drop of this poison flows in his veins, and sets his whole blood in the wildest ferment. The Moor "seems" noble, frank, confiding, grateful for the love shown him; and he is all this, and, moreover, a hero who spurns at danger, a worthy leader of an army, a faithful servant of the state; but the mere physical force of passion puts to flight in one moment all his acquired and mere habitual virtues, and gives the upper hand to the savage over the moral man. This tyranny of the blood over the will betrays itself even in the expression of his desire of revenge upon Cassio. In his repentance, a genuine tenderness for his murdered wife, and in the presence of the damning evidence of his deed, the painful feeling of annihilated honour at last bursts forth; and in the midst of these painful emotions he assails himself with the rage wherewith a despot punishes a runaway slave. He suffers as a double man; at once in the higher and the lower sphere into which his being was divided.—While the Moor bears the nightly colour of suspicion and deceit only on his visage, Iago is black within. He haunts Othello like his evil genius, and with his light (and therefore the more dangerous,) insinuations, he leaves him no rest; it is as if by means of an unfortunate affinity, founded however in nature, this influence was by necessity more powerful over him than the voice of his good angel Desdemona. A more artful villain than this Iago was never portrayed; he spreads his nets with a skill which nothing can escape. The repugnance inspired by his aims becomes tolerable from the attention of the spectators being directed to his means: these furnish endless employment to the understanding. Cool, discontented, and morose, arrogant where he dare be so, but humble and insinuating when it suits his purposes, he is a complete master in the art of dissimulation; accessible only to selfish emotions, he is thoroughly skilled in rousing the passions of others, and of availing himself of every opening which they give him: he is as excellent an observer of men as any one can be who is unacquainted with higher motives of action from his own experience; there is always some truth in his malicious observations on them. He does not merely pretend an obdurate incredulity as to the virtue of women, he actually entertains it; and this, too, falls in with his whole way of thinking, and makes him the more fit for the execution of his purpose.

As in every thing he sees merely the hateful side, he dissolves in the rudest manner the charm which the imagination casts over the relation between the two sexes: he does so for the purpose of revolting Othello's senses, whose heart otherwise might easily have convinced him of Desdemona's innocence. This must serve as an excuse for the numerous expressions in the speeches of Iago from which modesty shrinks. If Shakespeare had written in our days he would not perhaps have dared to hazard them; and yet this must certainly have greatly injured the truth of his picture. Desdemona is a sacrifice without blemish. She is not, it is true, a high ideal representation of sweetness and enthusiastic passion like Juliet; full of simplicity, softness, and humility, and so innocent, that she can hardly form to herself an idea of the possibility of infidelity, she seems calculated to make the most yielding and tenderest of wives. The female propensity wholly to resign itself to a foreign destiny has led her into the only fault of her life, that of marrying without her father's consent. Her choice seems wrong; and yet she has been gained over to Othello by that which induces the female to honour in man her protector and guide,— admiration of his determined heroism, and compassion for the sufferings which he had undergone. With great art it is so contrived, that from the very circumstance that the possibility of a suspicion of her own purity of motive never once enters her mind, she is the less reserved in her solicitations for Cassio, and thereby does but heighten more and more the jealousy of Othello. To throw out still more clearly the angelic purity of Desdemona, Shakspeare has in Emilia associated with her a companion of doubtful virtue. From the sinful levity of this woman it is also conceivable that she should not confess the abstraction of the handkerchief when Othello violently demands it back: this would otherwise be the circumstance in the whole piece the most difficult to justify.

Cassio is portrayed exactly as he ought to be to excite suspicion without actual guilt—amiable and nobly disposed, but easily seduced. The public events of the first two acts show us Othello in his most glorious aspect, as the support of Venice and the terror of the Turks: they serve to withdraw the story from the mere domestic circle, just as this is done in *Romeo and Juliet* by the dissensions between the Montagues and the Capulets. No eloquence is capable of painting the overwhelming force of the catastrophe in *Othello*,—the pressure of feelings which measure out in a moment the abysses of eternity.

1811—Charles Lamb.
"On the Tragedies of Shakespeare," from *The Reflector*

Charles Lamb (1775–1834), poet and essayist, is most famous for his "Elia" essays and his children's book *Tales from Shakespear*, which he wrote with his sister, Mary Lamb.

. . . Lear is essentially impossible to be represented on a stage. But how many dramatic personages are there in Shakspeare, which though more tractable and feasible (if I may so speak) than Lear, yet from some circumstance, some adjunct to their character, are improper to be shewn to our bodily eye. Othello for instance. Nothing can be more soothing, more flattering to the nobler parts of our natures, than to read of a young Venetian lady of highest extraction, through the force of love and from a sense of merit in him whom she loved, laying aside every consideration of kindred, and country, and colour, and wedding with a coal-black Moor—(for such he is represented, in the imperfect state of knowledge respecting foreign countries in those days, compared with our own, or in compliance with popular notions, though the Moors are now well enough known to be by many shades less unworthy of a white woman's fancy)—it is the perfect triumph of virtue over accidents, of the imagination over the senses. She sees Othello's colour in his mind. But upon the stage, when the imagination is no longer the ruling faculty, but we are left to our poor unassisted senses, I appeal to every one that has seen Othello played, whether he did not, on the contrary, sink Othello's mind in his colour; whether he did not find something extremely revolting in the courtship and wedded caresses of Othello and Desdemona; and whether the actual sight of the thing did not over-weigh all that beautiful compromise which we make in reading;—and the reason it should do so is obvious, because there is just so much reality presented to our senses as to give a perception of disagreement, with not enough of belief in the internal motives,—all that which is unseen,—to overpower and reconcile the first and obvious prejudices. What we see upon a stage is body and bodily action; what we are conscious of in reading is almost exclusively the mind, and its movements . . . .

1817—William Hazlitt. "Othello,"
from *Characters of Shakespear's Plays*

William Hazlitt (1778–1830) was an English essayist and one of the finest Shakespeare critics of the nineteenth century. He also examined the work of poets, dramatists, essayists, and novelists of his own and earlier times. His essays appeared in such volumes as *English Poets*, *English Comic Writers*, and *A View of the English Stage*.

It has been said that tragedy purifies the affections by terror and pity. That is, it substitutes imaginary sympathy for mere selfishness. It gives us a high and permanent interest, beyond ourselves, in humanity as such. It raises the great, the remote, and the possible to an equality with the real, the little and the near. It makes man a partaker with his kind. It subdues and softens the stubbornness of his will. It teaches him that there are and have been others like himself, by showing him as in a glass what they have felt, thought, and done. It opens the chambers of the human heart. It leaves nothing indifferent to us that can affect our common nature. It excites our sensibility by exhibiting the passions wound up to the utmost pitch by the power of imagination or the temptation of circumstances; and corrects their fatal excesses in ourselves by pointing to the greater extent of sufferings and of crimes to which they have led others. Tragedy creates a balance of the affections. It makes us thoughtful spectators in the lists of life. It is the refiner of the species; a discipline of humanity. The habitual study of poetry and works of imagination is one chief part of a well-grounded education. A taste for liberal art is necessary to complete the character of a gentleman, Science alone is hard and mechanical. It exercises the understanding upon things out of ourselves, while it leaves the affections unemployed, or engrossed with our own immediate, narrow interests.—*Othello* furnishes an illustration of these remarks. It excites our sympathy in an extraordinary degree. The moral it conveys has a closer application to the concerns of human life than that of any other of Shakespeare's plays. 'It comes directly home to the bosoms and business of men.' The pathos in *Lear* is indeed more dreadful and overpowering: but it is less natural, and less of every day's occurrence. We have not the same degree of sympathy with the passions described in *Macbeth*. The interest in *Hamlet* is more remote and reflex. That of *Othello* is at once equally profound and affecting.

The picturesque contrasts of character in this play are almost as remarkable as the depth of the passion. The Moor Othello, the gentle Desdemona, the villain Iago, the good-natured Cassio, the fool Roderigo, present a range and variety of character as striking and palpable as that produced by the opposition of costume in a picture. Their distinguishing qualities stand out to the mind's eye, so that even when we are not thinking of their actions or sentiments, the idea of their persons is still as present to us as ever. These characters and the images they stamp upon the mind are the farthest asunder possible, the distance between them is immense: yet the compass of knowledge and invention which the poet has shown in embodying these extreme creations of his genius is only greater than the truth and felicity with which he has identified each character with itself, or blended their different qualities together in the same story. What a contrast the character of Othello forms to that of Iago: at the same time, the force of conception with which these two figures are opposed to each other is rendered still more intense by the complete consistency with which the traits of each character are brought out in a state of the highest finishing. The making one black and the other white, the one unprincipled, the other unfortunate in the extreme, would have answered the common purposes of effect, and satisfied the ambition of an ordinary painter of character. Shakespeare has laboured the finer shades of difference in both with as much care and skill as if he had had to depend on the execution alone for the success of his design. On the other hand, Desdemona and Aemilia are not meant to be opposed with anything like strong contrast to each other. Both are, to outward appearance, characters of common life, not more distinguished than women usually are, by difference of rank and situation. The difference of their thoughts and sentiments is, however, laid as open, their minds are separated from each other by signs as plain and as little to be mistaken as the complexions of their husbands.

The movement of the passion in *Othello* is exceedingly different from that of *Macbeth*. In *Macbeth* there is a violent struggle between opposite feelings, between ambition and the stings of conscience, almost from first to last: in *Othello*, the doubtful conflict between contrary passions, though dreadful, continues only for a short time, and the chief interest is excited by the alternate ascendancy of different passions, the entire and unforeseen change from the fondest love and most unbounded confidence to the tortures of jealousy and the madness of hatred. The revenge of Othello, after it has once taken thorough possession of his mind, never quits it, but grows stronger and stronger at every moment of its delay. The nature of the Moor is noble, confiding, tender, and generous; but his blood is of the most inflammable kind; and being once roused by a sense of his wrongs, he is stopped by no considerations of remorse or pity till he has given a loose to all the dictates of his rage and his despair. It is in working his noble nature up to this extremity through rapid but gradual transitions, in raising passion to its height from the smallest beginnings and in spite of all obstacles, in painting the expiring conflict between love and hatred, tenderness and resentment, jealousy and remorse, in unfolding the strength and the weaknesses of our nature, in uniting sublimity of thought with the anguish of the keenest woe, in putting in motion the various impulses that agitate this our mortal being, and at last blending them in that noble tide of deep and sustained passion, impetuous but majestic, that 'flows on to the Propontic, and knows no ebb', that Shakespeare has shown the mastery of his genius and of his power over the human heart. The third act of *Othello* is his masterpiece, not of knowledge or passion separately, but of the two combined, of the knowledge of character with the expression of passion, of consummate art in the keeping up of appearances with the profound workings of nature, and the convulsive movements of uncontrollable agony, of the power of inflicting torture and of suffering it. Not only is the tumult of passion heaved up from the very bottom of the soul, but even the slightest undulation of feeling is seen on the surface, as it arises from the impulses of imagination or the different probabilities maliciously suggested by Iago. The progressive preparation for the catastrophe is wonderfully managed from the Moor's first gallant recital of the story of his love, of 'the spells and witchcraft he had used', from his unlooked-for and romantic success, the fond satisfaction with which he dotes on his own happiness, the unreserved tenderness of Desdemona and her innocent importunities in favour of Cassio, irritating the suspicions instilled into her husband's mind by the perfidy of Iago, and rankling there to poison, till he loses all command of himself, and his rage can only be appeased by blood. She is introduced, just before Iago begins to put his scheme in practice, pleading for Cassio with all the thoughtless gaiety of friendship and winning confidence in the love of Othello.

> What! Michael Cassio?
> That came a wooing with you, and so many a time,
> When I have spoke of you dispraisingly,
> Hath ta'en your part, to have so much to do
> To bring him in?—Why this is not a boon:
> 'Tis as I should entreat you wear your gloves,
> Or feed on nourishing meats, or keep you warm;
> Or sue to you to do a peculiar profit
> To your person. Nay, when I have a suit,
> Wherein I mean to touch your love indeed,
> It shall be full of poise, and fearful to be granted.

Othello's confidence, at first only staggered by broken hints and insinuations, recovers itself at sight of Desdemona; and he exclaims

> If she be false, O then Heav'n mocks itself:
> I'll not believe it.

But presently after, on brooding over his suspicions by himself, and yielding to his apprehensions of the worst, his smothered jealousy breaks out into open fury, and he returns to demand satisfaction of Iago like a wild beast stung with the envenomed shaft of the hunters. 'Look where he comes', &c. In this state of exasperation and violence, after the first paroxysms of his grief and tenderness have had their vent in that passionate apostrophe, 'I felt not Cassio's kisses on her lips,' Iago by false aspersions, and by presenting the most revolting images to his mind, [See the passage beginning, 'It is impossible you should see this, Were they as prime as goats,' .] easily turns the storm of Passion from himself against

Desdemona, and works him up into a trembling agony of doubt and fear, in which he abandons all his love and hopes in a breath.

> Now do I see'tis true. Look here, Iago,
> All my fond love thus do I blow to Heav'n. Tis gone.
> Arise, black vengeance, from the hollow hell;
> Yield up, O love, thy crown and hearted throne
> To tyrannous hate! Swell, bosom, with thy fraught;
> For'tis of aspicks' tongues.

From this time, his raging thoughts 'never look back, ne'er ebb to humble love' till his revenge is sure of its object, the painful regrets and involuntary recollections of past circumstances which cross his mind amidst the dim trances of passion, aggravating the sense of his wrongs, but not shaking his purpose. Once indeed, where Iago shows him Cassio with the handkerchief in his hand, and making sport (as he thinks) of his misfortunes, the intolerable bitterness of his feelings, the extreme sense of shame, makes him fall to praising her accomplishments and relapse into a momentary fit of weakness, 'Yet, oh, the pity of it, Iago, the pity of it!' This returning fondness, however, only serves, as it is managed by Iago, to whet his revenge, and set his heart more against her. In his conversations with Desdemona, the persuasion of her guilt and the immediate proofs of her duplicity seem to irritate his resentment and aversion to her; but in the scene immediately preceding her death, the recollection of his love returns upon him in all its tenderness and force; and after her death, he all at once forgets his wrongs in the sudden and irreparable sense of his loss:

> My wife! My wife! What wife? I have no wife.
> Oh insupportable! Oh heavy hour!

This happens before he is assured of her innocence; but afterwards his remorse is as dreadful as his revenge has been, and yields only to fixed and death like despair. His farewell speech, before he kills himself, in which he conveys his reasons to the senate for the murder of his wife, is equal to the first speech in which he gave them an account of his courtship of her, and 'his whole course of love'. Such an ending was alone worthy of such a commencement.

If anything could add to the force of our sympathy with Othello, or compassion for his fate, it would be the frankness and generosity of his nature, which so little deserve it. When Iago first begins to practise upon his unsuspecting friendship, he answers:

> —Tis not to make me jealous,
> To say my wife is fair, feeds well, loves company,

Is free of speech, sings, plays, and dances well;
Where virtue is, these are most virtuous.
Nor from my own weak merits will I draw
The smallest fear or doubt of her revolt,
For she had eyes and chose me.

This character is beautifully (and with affecting simplicity) confirmed by what Desdemona herself says of him to Aemilia after she has lost the handkerchief, the first pledge of his love to her:

Believe me, I had rather have lost my purse
Full of cruzadoes. And but my noble Moor
Is true of mind, and made of no such baseness,
As jealous creatures are, it were enough
To put him to ill thinking.
Aemilia. Is he not jealous?
Desdemona. Who he? I think the sun where he was
born drew all such humours from him.

In a short speech of Aemilia's there occurs one of those side-intimations of the fluctuations of passion which we seldom meet with but in Shakespeare. After Othello has resolved upon the death of his wife, and bids her dismiss her attendant for the night, she answers:

I will, my Lord.
Aemilia. How goes it now? HE LOOKS GENTLER THAN HE
DID.

Shakespeare has here put into half a line what some authors would have spun out into ten set speeches.

The character of Desdemona herself is inimitable both in itself, and as it contrasts with Othello's groundless jealousy, and with the foul conspiracy of which she is the innocent victim. Her beauty and external graces are only indirectly glanced at; we see 'her visage in her mind'; her character everywhere predominates over her person:

A maiden never bold:
Of spirit so still and quiet, that her motion
Blushed at itself.

There is one fine compliment paid to her by Cassio, who exclaims triumphantly when she comes ashore at Cyprus after the storm:

Tempests themselves, high seas, and howling winds,
As having sense of beauty, do omit
Their mortal natures, letting safe go by
The divine Desdemona.

In general, as is the case with most of Shakespeare's females, we lose sight of
her personal charms in her attachment and devotedness to her husband. 'She is
subdued even to the very quality of her lord'; and to Othello's 'honours and his
valiant parts her soul and fortunes consecrates'. The lady protests so much herself,
and she is as good as her word. The truth of conception, with which timidity
and boldness are united in the same character, is marvellous. The extravagance of
her resolutions, the pertinacity of her affections, may be said to arise out of the
gentleness of her nature. They imply an unreserved reliance on the purity of her
own intentions, an entire surrender of her fears to her love, a knitting of herself
(heart and soul) to the fate of another. Bating the commencement of her passion,
which is a little fantastical and headstrong (though even that may perhaps
be consistently accounted for from her inability to resist a rising inclination
[Footnote: Iago. Ay, too gentle. Othello. Nay, that's certain.]) her whole character
consists in having no will of her own, no prompter but her obedience. Her
romantic turn is only a consequence of the domestic and practical part of her
disposition; and instead of following Othello to the wars, she would gladly have
'remained at home a moth of peace', if her husband could have stayed with her.
Her resignation and angelic sweetness of temper do not desert her at the last.
The scenes in which she laments and tries to account for Othello's estrangement
from her are exquisitely beautiful. After he has struck her, and called her names,
she says:

—Alas, Iago,
What shall I do to win my lord again?
Good friend, go to him; for by this light of heaven,
I know not how I lost him. Here I kneel;
If e'er my will did trespass 'gainst his love,
Either in discourse, or thought, or actual deed,
Or that mine eyes, mine ears, or any sense
Delighted them on any other form
Or that I do not, and ever did
And ever will, though he do shake me off
To beggarly divorcement, love him dearly,
Comfort forswear me. Unkindness may do much,
And his unkindness may defeat my life,
But never taint my love.
Iago. I pray you be content: 'tis but his humour.

The business of the state does him offence.
Desdemona. If 'twere no other!—

The scene which follows with Aemilia and the song of the Willow are equally beautiful, and show the author's extreme power of varying the expression of passion, in all its moods and in all circumstances;

Aemilia. Would you had never seen him.
Desdemona. So would not I: my love doth so approve him,
That even his stubbornness, his checks, his frowns,
Have grace and favour in them.

Not the unjust suspicions of Othello, not Iago's treachery, place Desdemona in a more amiable or interesting light than the casual conversation (half earnest, half jest) between her and Aemilia on the common behaviour of women to their husbands. This dialogue takes place just before the last fatal scene. If Othello had overheard it, it would have prevented the whole catastrophe; but then it would have spoiled the play.

The character of Iago is one of the supererogations of Shakespeare's genius. Some persons, more nice than wise, have thought this whole character unnatural, because his villainy is WITHOUT A SUFFICIENT MOTIVE. Shakespeare, who was as good a philosopher as he was a poet, thought otherwise. He knew that the love of power, which is another name for the love of mischief, is natural to man. He would know this as well or better than if it had been demonstrated to him by a logical diagram, merely from seeing children paddle in the dirt or kill flies for sport. Iago in fact belongs to a class of characters common to Shakespeare and at the same time peculiar to him; whose heads are as acute and active as their hearts are hard and callous. Iago is, to be sure, an extreme instance of the kind; that is to say, of diseased intellectual activity, with an almost perfect indifference to moral good or evil, or rather with a decided preference of the latter, because it falls more readily in with his favourite propensity, gives greater zest to his thoughts and scope to his actions. He is quite or nearly as indifferent to his own fate as to that of others; he runs all risks for a trifling and doubtful advantage; and is himself the dupe and victim of his ruling passion—an insatiable craving after action of the most difficult and dangerous kind. 'Our ancient' is a philosopher, who fancies that a lie that kills has more point in it than an alliteration or an antithesis; who thinks a fatal experiment on the peace of a family a better thing than watching the palpitations in the heart of a flea in a microscope; who plots the ruin of his friends as an exercise for his ingenuity, and stabs men in the dark to prevent ennui. His gaiety, such as it is, arises from the success of his treachery; his ease from the torture he has inflicted on others. He is an amateur of tragedy in real life; and instead of employing his invention on imaginary characters, or long-forgotten incidents, he takes the bolder and more desperate course of getting up his plot at home, casts the principal parts among his nearest friends and connexions, and rehearses it in downright earnest, with steady nerves and unabated resolution. We will just give an illustration or two.

One of his most characteristic speeches is that immediately after the marriage of Othello.

> *Roderigo.* What a full fortune does the thick lips owe,
> If he can carry her thus!
> *Iago.* Call up her father:
> Rouse him [Othello], make after him, poison his delight,
> Proclaim him in the streets, incense her kinsmen,
> And tho' he in a fertile climate dwell,
> Plague him with flies: Tho' that his joy be joy,
> Yet throw such changes of vexation on it,
> As it may lose some colour.

In the next passage, his imagination runs riot in the mischief he is plotting, and breaks out into the wildness and impetuosity of real enthusiasm.

> *Roderigo.* Here is her father's house: I'll call aloud.
> *Iago.* Do, with like timorous accent and dire yell,
> As when, by night and negligence, the fire
> Is spied in populous cities.

One of his most favourite topics, on which he is rich indeed, and in descanting on which his spleen serves him for a Muse, is the disproportionate match between Desdemona and the Moor. This is a clue to the character of the lady which he is by no means ready to part with. It is brought forward in the first scene, and he recurs to it, when in answer to his insinuations against Desdemona, Roderigo says:

> I cannot believe that in her—she's full of most blest conditions.
> *Iago.* Bless'd fig's end. The wine she drinks is made of grapes. If she had
> been blest, she would never have married the Moor.

And again with still more spirit and fatal effect afterwards, when he turns this very suggestion arising in Othello's own breast to her prejudice.

> *Othello.* And yet how nature erring from itself—
> *Iago.* Aye, there's the point;—as to be bold with you,

Not to affect many proposed matches
Of her own clime, complexion, and degree.

This is probing to the quick. Iago here turns the character of poor Desdemona, as it were, inside out. It is certain that nothing but the genius of Shakespeare could have preserved the entire interest and delicacy of the part, and have even drawn an additional elegance and dignity from the peculiar circumstances in which she is placed. The habitual licentiousness of Iago's conversation is not to be traced to the pleasure he takes in gross or lascivious images, but to his desire of finding out the worst side of everything, and of proving himself an over-match for appearances. He has none of 'the milk of human kindness' in his composition. His imagination rejects everything that has not a strong infusion of the most unpalatable ingredients; his mind digests only poisons. Virtue or goodness or whatever has the least 'relish of salvation in it' is, to his depraved appetite, sickly and insipid: and he even resents the good opinion entertained of his own integrity, as if it were an affront cast on the masculine sense and spirit of his character. Thus at the meeting between Othello and Desdemona, he exclaims, 'Oh, you are well tuned now: but I'll set down the pegs that make this music, AS HONEST AS I AM'—his character of bonhommie not sitting at all easily upon him. In the scenes where he tries to work Othello to his purpose, he is proportionably guarded, insidious, dark, and deliberate. We believe nothing ever came up to the profound dissimulation and dexterous artifice of the well-known dialogue in the third act, where he first enters upon the execution of his design.

Iago. My noble lord.
Othello. What dost thou say, Iago?
Iago. Did Michael Cassio,
When you woo'd my lady, know of your love?
Othello. He did from first to last.
Why dost thou ask?
Iago. But for a satisfaction of my thought,
No further harm.
Othello. Why of thy thought, Iago?
Iago. I did not think he had been acquainted with it.
Othello. O yes, and went between us very oft--
Iago. Indeed!
Othello. Indeed? Ay, indeed. Discern'st thou aught of that?
Is he not honest?
Iago. Honest, my lord?
Othello. Honest? Ay, honest.

> *Iago.* My lord, for aught I know.
> *Othello.* What do'st thou think?
> *Iago.* Think, my lord!
> *Othello.* Think, my lord! Alas, thou echo'st me,
> As if there was some monster in thy thought
> Too hideous to be shown.

The stops and breaks, the deep workings of treachery under the mask of love and honesty, the anxious watchfulness, the cool earnestness, and if we may so say, the PASSION of hypocrisy marked in every line, receive their last finishing in that inconceivable burst of pretended indignation at Othello's doubts of his sincerity.

> O grace! O Heaven forgive me!
> Are you a man? Have you a soul or sense?
> God be wi' you; take mine office. O wretched fool,
> That lov'st to make thine honesty a vice!
> Oh monstrous world! take note, take note, O world!
> To be direct and honest, is not safe.
> I thank you for this profit, and from hence
> I'll love no friend, since love breeds such offence.

If Iago is detestable enough when he has business on his hands and all his engines at work, he is still worse when he has nothing to do, and we only see into the hollowness of his heart. His indifference when Othello falls into a swoon, is perfectly diabolical.

> *Iago.* How is it. General? Have you not hurt your head?
> *Othello.* Dost thou mock me?
> *Iago.* I mock you not, by Heaven.

The part indeed would hardly be tolerated, even as a foil to the virtue and generosity of the other characters in the play, But for its indefatigable industry and inexhaustible resources, Which divert the attention of the spectator (as well as his own) from the end he has in view to the means by which it must be accomplished.—Edmund the Bastard in *Lear* is something of the same character, placed in less prominent circumstances. Zanga is a vulgar caricature of it.

—~~~— —~~~— —~~~—

1818—Samuel Taylor Coleridge. "Notes on *Othello*," from *Lectures and Notes on Shakspere and Other English Poets*

Samuel Taylor Coleridge (1772–1834) was an English poet, philosopher, and critic. In collaboration with his good friend William Wordsworth, he published *Lyrical Ballads*, which included his enduring poem "The Rime of the Ancient Mariner." His best-known critical work is *Biographia Literaria*.

Act I. sc. 1. Admirable is the preparation, so truly and peculiarly Shakspearian, in the introduction of Roderigo, as the dupe on whom Iago shall first exercise his art, and in so doing display his own character. Roderigo, without any fixed principle, but not without the moral notions and sympathies with honor, which his rank and connections had hung upon him, is already well fitted and predisposed for the purpose; for very want of character and strength of passion, like wind loudest in an empty house, constitute his character. The first three lines happily state the nature and foundation of the friendship between him and Iago,—the purse,—as also the contrast of Roderigo's intemperance of mind with Iago's coolness,—the coolness of a preconceiving experimenter. The mere language of protestation—

> If ever I did dream of such a matter, abhor me,—

which falling in with the associative link, determines Roderigo's continuation of complaint—

> Thou told'st me, thou didst hold him in thy hate—

elicits at length a true feeling of Iago's mind, the dread of contempt habitual to those, who encourage in themselves, and have their keenest pleasure in, the expression of contempt for others. Observe Iago's high self-opinion, and the moral, that a wicked man will employ real feelings, as well as assume those most alien from his own, as instruments of his purposes:—

> —And, by the faith of man, I know my place,
> I am worth no worse a place.

I think [scholar Thomas] Tyrwhitt's reading of 'life' for 'wife'—

> A fellow almost damn'd in a fair *wife*—

the true one, as fitting to Iago's contempt for whatever did not display power, and that intellectual power. In what follows, let the reader feel how by and through the glass of two passions, disappointed vanity and envy, the very vices of which he is complaining, are made to act upon him as if they were so many excellences, and the more appropriately, because cunning is always admired and wished for by minds conscious of inward weakness;—but they act only by half, like music on an inattentive auditor, swelling the thoughts which prevent him from listening to it.

> *Roderigo:* What a full fortune does the 'thick-lips' owe,
> If he can carry't thus.

Roderigo turns off to Othello; and here comes one, if not the only, seeming justification of our blackamoor or negro Othello. Even if we supposed this an uninterrupted tradition of the theatre, and that Shakspeare himself, from want of scenes, and the experience that nothing could be made too marked for the senses of his audience, had practically sanctioned it,—would this prove aught concerning his own intention as a poet for all ages? Can we imagine him so utterly ignorant as to make a barbarous negro plead royal birth,—at a time, too, when negros were not known except as slaves?

—As for Iago's language to Brabantio, it implies merely that Othello was a Moor, that is, black. Though I think the rivalry of Roderigo sufficient to account for his wilful confusion of Moor and Negro,—yet, even if compelled to give this up, I should think it only adapted for the acting of the day, and should complain of an enormity built on a single word, in direct contradiction to Iago's 'Barbary horse.' Besides, if we could in good earnest believe Shakspeare ignorant of the distinction, still why should we adopt one disagreeable possibility instead of a ten times greater and more pleasing probability? It is a common error to mistake the epithets applied by the 'dramatis personae' to each other, as truly descriptive of what the audience ought to see or know. No doubt Desdemona saw Othello's visage in his mind; yet, as we are constituted, and most surely as an English audience was disposed in the beginning of the seventeenth century, it would be something monstrous to conceive this beautiful Venetian girl falling in love with a veritable negro. It would argue a disproportionateness, a want of balance, in Desdemona, which Shakspeare does not appear to have in the least contemplated.

> *Brabantio's speech:*—This accident is not unlike my dream:—
> The old careful senator, being caught careless, transfers his caution to his dreaming power at least.

Iago's speech:—
    —For their souls,
Another of his fathom they have not,
To lead their business:—

The forced praise of Othello followed by the bitter hatred of him in this speech! And observe how Brabantio's dream prepares for his recurrence to the notion of philtres, and how both prepare for carrying on the plot of the arraignment of Othello on this ground.

[In act 1, scene 2]
Othello: 'Tis better as it is.

How well these few words impress at the outset the truth of Othello's own character of himself at the end—'that he was not easily wrought!' . . .

   . . .

[In act 1, scene 3]
Brabantio: Look to her, Moor; have a quick eye to see;
She has deceiv'd her father, and may thee.
Othello: My life upon her faith.

In real life, how do we look back to little speeches as presentimental of, or contrasted with, an affecting event! Even so, Shakspeare, as secure of being read over and over, of becoming a family friend, provides this passage for his readers, and leaves it to them.

Iago's speech:—
Virtue? a fig! 'tis in ourselves, that we are thus, or thus, &c.

This speech comprises the passionless character of Iago. It is all will in intellect; and therefore he is here a bold partizan of a truth, but yet of a truth converted into a falsehood by the absence of all the necessary modifications caused by the frail nature of man.

   . . .

Note Iago's pride of mastery in the repetition of 'Go, make money!' to his anticipated dupe, even stronger than his love of lucre: and when Roderigo is completely won—

I am chang'd. I'll go sell all my land—

when the effect has been fully produced, the repetition of triumph—

Go to; farewell; put money enough in your purse!

The remainder—Iago's soliloquy—the motive-hunting of a motiveless malignity —how awful it is! Yea, whilst he is still allowed to bear the divine image, it is too fiendish for his own steady view,—for the lonely gaze of a being next to devil, and only not quite devil,—and yet a character which Shakspeare has attempted and executed, without disgust and without scandal!

Dr. Johnson has remarked that little or nothing is wanting to render the *Othello* a regular tragedy, but to have opened the play with the arrival of Othello in Cyprus, and to have thrown the preceding act into the form of narration. Here then is the place to determine, whether such a change would or would not be an improvement;—nay, (to throw down the glove with a full challenge) whether the tragedy would or not by such an arrangement become more regular,—that is, more consonant with the rules dictated by universal reason, on the true common-sense of mankind, in its application to the particular case. For in all acts of judgment, it can never be too often recollected, and scarcely too often repeated, that rules are means to ends, and, consequently, that the end must be determined and understood before it can be known what the rules are or ought to be.

... Observe in how many ways Othello is made, first, our acquaintance, then our friend, then the object of our anxiety, before the deeper interest is to be approached!

...

> *Montano:* But, good lieutenant, is your general wiv'd?
> *Cassio:* Most fortunately: he hath achiev'd a maid
> That paragons description, and wild fame;
> One that excels the quirks of blazoning pens,
> And, in the essential vesture of creation,
> Does bear all excellency.

Here is Cassio's warm-hearted, yet perfectly disengaged, praise of Desdemona, and sympathy with the 'most fortunately' wived Othello;—and yet Cassio is an enthusiastic admirer, almost a worshipper, of Desdemona. O, that detestable code that excellence cannot be loved in any form that is female, but it must needs be selfish! Observe Othello's "honest," and Cassio's "bold" Iago, and Cassio's full guileless-hearted wishes for the safety and love-raptures of Othello and "the divine Desdemona." And also note the exquisite circumstance of Cassio's kissing Iago's wife, as if it ought to be impossible that the dullest auditor should not feel Cassio's religious love of Desdemona's purity. Iago's answers are the sneers which a proud bad intellect feels towards woman, and expresses to a wife. Surely it ought to be considered a very exalted compliment to women, that all the sarcasms on them in Shakspeare are put in the mouths of villains.

. . .

Iago, aside: He takes her by the palm: Ay, well said, whisper; with as little a web as this, will I ensnare as great a fly as Cassio. Ay, smile upon her, do, &c.

The importance given to trifles, and made fertile by the villainy of the observer.

. . .

Act v. last scene. *Othello's speech:*—
—Of one, whose hand,
Like the base Indian, threw a pearl away
Richer than all his tribe, &c.

. . .

Othello wishes to excuse himself on the score of ignorance, and yet not to excuse himself,—to excuse himself by accusing. This struggle of feeling is finely conveyed in the word "base," which is applied to the rude Indian, not in his own character, but as the momentary representative of Othello's . . . .

Finally, let me repeat that Othello does not kill Desdemona in jealousy, but in a conviction forced upon him by the almost superhuman art of Iago, such a conviction as any man would and must have entertained who had believed Iago's honesty as Othello did. We, the audience, know that Iago is a villain from the beginning; but in considering the essence of the Shakspearian Othello, we must perseveringly place ourselves in his situation, and under his circumstances . . . .

Othello had no life but in Desdemona:—the belief that she, his angel, had fallen from the heaven of her native innocence, wrought a civil war in his heart. She is his counterpart; and, like him, is almost sanctified in our eyes by her absolute unsuspiciousness, and holy entireness of love. As the curtain drops, which do we pity the most?

———————

1836—John Quincy Adams. "The Character of Desdemona," from *The American Monthly Magazine*

John Quincy Adams was elected president of the United States in 1824. After his defeat in the 1828 election, he served eight consecutive terms as a member of Congress, during which time he became a staunch opponent of the expansion of slavery. He also wrote his memoirs, poetry, and a number of essays.

There are critics who cannot bear to see the virtue and delicacy of Shakspeare's Desdemona called in question; who defend her on the ground that Othello is not an Ethiopian, but a Moor; that he is not black, but only tawny; and they protest against the sable mask of Othello upon the stage, and against the pictures of him in which he is always painted black. They say that prejudices have been taken against Desdemona from the slanders of Iago, from the railings of Roderigo, from the disappointed paternal rancour of Brabantio, and from the desponding concessions of Othello himself.

I have said, that since I entered upon the third of Shakspeare's seven ages, the first and chief capacity in which I have read and studied him is as a *teacher of morals;* and that I had scarcely ever seen a player of his parts who regarded him as a *moralist* at all. I further said, that in my judgment no man could understand him who did not study him preeminently as a teacher of morals. These critics say they do not incline to put Shakspeare on a level with Aesop! Sure enough *they* do not study Shakspeare as a teacher of morals. To *them*, therefore, Desdemona is a perfect character; and her love for Othello is not unnatural, because he is not a Congo negro but only a sooty Moor, and has royal blood in his veins.

My objections to the character of Desdemona arise not from what Iago, or Roderigo, or Brabantio, or Othello says of her; but from what she herself *does*. She absconds from her father's house, in the dead of night, to marry a blackamoor. She breaks a father's heart, and covers his noble house with shame, to gratify—what? Pure love, like that of Juliet or Miranda? No! unnatural passion; it cannot be named with delicacy. Her admirers now say this is criticism of 1835; that the color of Othello has nothing to do with the passion of Desdemona. No? Why, if Othello had been white, what need would there have been for her running away with him? She could have made no better match. Her father could have made no reasonable objection to it; and there could have been no tragedy. If the color of Othello is not as vital to the whole tragedy as the age of Juliet is to her character and destiny, then have I read Shakspeare in vain. The father of Desdemona charges Othello with magic arts in obtaining the affections of his daughter. Why, but because her passion for him is *unnatural*, and why is it unnatural, but because of his color? In the very first scene, in the dialogue between Roderigo and Iago, before they rouse Brabantio to inform him of his daughter's elopement, Roderigo contemptuously calls Othello "the thick lips." I cannot in decency quote here—but turn to the book, and see in what language Iago announces to her father his daughter's shameful misconduct. The language of Roderigo is more supportable. *He* is a Venitian gentleman, himself a rejected suitor of Desdemona; and who has been forbidden by her father access to his house. Roused from his repose at the dead of night by the loud cries of these two men, Brabantio spurns, with indignation and scorn, the insulting and beastly language of Iago; and sharply chides Roderigo, whom he supposes to be hovering about his house in defiance of his prohibitions and in a state of intoxication. He threatens him with punishment. Roderigo replies—

> Sir, I will answer any thing. But I beseech you,
> If't be your pleasure, and most wise consent,
> (As partly, I find, it is,) that your fair daughter
> At this odd-even and dull watch o' the night, Transported—with no worse nor better guard,
> But with a knave of common hire, a gondolier,—
> To the gross clasps to a lascivious Moor,—
> If this be known of you, and your allowance,
> We then have done you bold and saucy wrongs;
> But if you know not this, my manners tell me,
> We have your wrong rebuke. Do not believe,
> That, from the sense of all civility,
> I thus would play and trifle with your reverence:
> Your daughter—if you have not given her leave,—
> I say again, hath made a gross revolt;
> Tying her duty, beauty, wit, and fortunes,
> In an extravagant and wheeling stranger,
> Of here and every where: Straight satisfy yourself:
> If she be in her chamber, or your house,
> Let loose on me the justice of the state
> For thus deluding you.

Struck by this speech as by a clap of thunder, Brabantio calls up his people, remembers a portentous dream, calls for light, goes and searches with his servants, and comes back saying—

> It is too true an evil: gone she is:
> And what's to come of my despised time,
> Is nought but bitterness.

The father's heart is broken; life is no longer of any value to him; he repeats this sentiment time after time whenever he appears in the scene; and in the last scene of the play, where Desdemona lies dead, her uncle Gratiano says—

> Poor Desdemona! I am glad thy father's dead,
> Thy match was mortal to him, and pure grief
> Shore his old thread in twain.

Indeed! indeed! I must look at Shakspeare in this as in all his pictures of human life, in the capacity of a teacher of morals. I must believe that, in exhibiting a daughter of a Venitian nobleman of the highest rank eloping in the dead of the night to marry a thick-lipped wool-headed Moor, opening a train of consequences which lead to her own destruction by her husband's hands, and to that of her father by a broken heart, he did not intend to present her as an example of the perfection of female virtue. I must look first at the action, then at the motive, then at the consequences, before I inquire in what light it is received and represented by the other persons of the drama. The first action of Desdemona discards all female delicacy, all filial duty, all sense of ingenuous shame. So I consider it—and so, it is considered, by her own father. Her offence is not a mere elopement from her father's house for a clandestine marriage. I hope it requires no unreasonable rigour of morality to consider even *that* as suited to raise a prepossession rather unfavorable to the character of a young woman of refined sensibility and elevated education. But an elopement for a clandestine marriage with a blackamoor!—That is the measure of my estimation of the character of Desdemona from the beginning; and when I have passed my judgment upon it, and find in the play that from the first moment of her father's knowledge of the act it made him loathe his life, and that it finally broke his heart, I am then in time to inquire, what was the deadly venom which inflicted the immedicable wound:—and what is it, but the color of Othello?

> Now, Roderigo,
> Where did'st thou see her?—Oh, unhappy girl!—
> *With the Moor, say'st thou?*—Who would be a father?

These are the disjointed lamentations of the wretched parent when the first disclosure of his daughter's shame is made known to him. This scene is one of the inimitable pictures of human passion in the hands of Shakspeare, and that half line,

> With the MOOR say'st thou?

comes from the deepest recesses of the soul.

Again, when Brabantio first meets Othello, he breaks out:

> O, thou foul thief, where hast thou stow'd my daughter?
> Damn'd as thou art, thou hast enchanted her:
> For I'll refer me to all things of sense,
> If she, in chains of magic were not bound,
> Whether a maid so tender, fair, and happy,
> So opposite to marriage that she shunn'd

> The wealthly *curled* darlings of our nation,
> Would ever have to incur our general mock,
> Run from her guardage *to the sooty bosom*
> Of such a thing as thou; to fear, not to delight.

Several of the English commentators have puzzled themselves with the inquiry why the epithet "curled" is here applied to the wealthy darlings of the nation; and Dr. Johnson thinks it has no reference to the hair; but it evidently has. The *curled* hair is in antithetic contrast to the sooty bosom, the thick lips, and the woolly head. The contrast of color is the very hinge upon which Brabantio founds his charge of magic, counteracting the impulse of nature.

At the close of the same scene (the second of the first act) Brabantio, hearing that the duke is in council upon public business of the State, determines to carry Othello before him for trial upon the charge of magic. "Mine," says he,

> Mine's not a middle course; the duke himself
> Or any of my brothers of the state
> Cannot but feel the wrong, as 'twere their own:
> For if such actions may have passage free,
> Bond slaves and Pagans shall our statesmen be.

And Steevens, in his note on this passage, says, "He alludes to the common condition of all blacks who come from their own country, both *slaves* and *pagans;* and uses the word in contempt of Othello and his complexion. If this Moor is now suffered to escape with impunity, it will be such an encouragement to his black countrymen, that we may expect to see all the first offices of our state filled up by the Pagans and bond-slaves of Africa." Othello himself in his narrative says that he had been taken by the insolent foe and sold to slavery. He *had been* a slave.

Once more—When Desdemona pleads to the Duke and the council for permission to go with Othello to Cyprus, she says,

> That I did love the Moor, to live with him,
> My downright violence and storm of fortune
> May trumpet to the world; *my heart's subdued,*
> *Even to the very quality of my lord;*
> I saw Othello's visage in his mind;
> And to his honours and his valiant parts
> Did I my soul and fortunes consecrate.

In commenting upon this passage, Wm. Henley says, "That *quality* here signifies the Moorish *complexion* of Othello, and not his military profession (as Malone had supposed), is obvious from what immediately follows: 'I saw Othello's visage in his mind;' and also from what the Duke says to Brabantio—

> If virtue no delighted beauty lack
> Your son-in-law is far more fair than black.

The characters of Othello and Iago in this play are evidently intended as contrasted pictures of human nature, each setting off the other. They are national portraits of man—the ITALIAN and the MOOR. The Italian is *white, crafty,* and *cruel;* a consummate villain; yet, as often happens in the realities of that description whom we occasionally meet in the intercourse of life, so vain of his own artifices that he betrays himself by boasting of them and their success. Accordingly, in the very first scene he reveals to Roderigo the treachery of his own character:—

> For when my outward action doth demonstrate
> The native act and figure of my heart
> In compliment extern, 'tis not long after
> But I will wear my heart upon my sleeve
> For daws to peck at: I am not what I am.

There is a seeming inconsistency in the fact that a double dealer should disclose his own secret, which must necessarily put others upon their guard against him; but the inconsistency is in human nature, and not in the poet.

The double dealing Italian is a very intelligent man, a keen and penetrating observer, and full of ingenuity to devise and contrive base expedients. His language is coarse, rude, and obscene: his humor is caustic and bitter. Conscious of no honest principle in himself, he believes not in the existence of honesty in others. He is jealous and suspicious; quick to note every trifle light as air, and to draw from it inferences of evil as confirmed circumstances. In his dealings with the Moor, while he is even harping upon his honesty, he offers to commit any murder from extreme attachment to his person and interests. In all that Iago says of others, and especially of Desdemona, there is a mixture of truth and falsehood, blended together, in which the truth itself serves to accredit the lie; and such is the ordinary character of malicious slanders. Doctor Johnson speaks of "the soft simplicity," the "innocence," the "artlessness" of Desdemona. Iago speaks of her as a *supersubtle* Venitian; and, when kindling the sparks of jealousy in the soul of Othello, he says,

> She did deceive her father, marrying you:
> And when she seemed to shake and fear your looks,
> She loved them most.

"And so she did," answers Othello. This charge, then, was true; and Iago replies:

> Why, go to, then;
> She that so young could give out such a seeming
> To seal her father's eyes up, close as oak.—
> He thought 'twas witchcraft.

It was not witchcraft; but surely as little was it simplicity, innocence, artlessness. The effect of this suggestion upon Othello is terrible only because he knows it is true. Brabantio, on parting from him, had just given him the same warning, to which he had not then paid the slightest heed. But soon his suspicions are roused—he tries to repel them; they are fermenting in his brain: he appears vehemently moved and yet unwilling to acknowledge it. Iago, with fiend-like sagacity, seizes upon the paroxysm of emotion, and then comes the following dialogue:—

> *Iago:* My lord, I see you are mov'd.
> *Othello:* No, not much mov'd:—
> I do not think but Desdemona's honest.
> *Iago:* Long live she so! and long live you to think so!
> *Oth.:* And yet, how nature erring from itself,—
> *Iago:* Ay, there's the point:—As,—to be bold with you,—
> Not to affect many proposed matches,
> Of her own clime, complexion, and degree;
> Whereto, we see, in all things nature tends:
> Foh! one may smell, in such, a will most rank,
> Foul disproportion, thoughts unnatural.

The deadly venom of these imputations, working up to frenzy the suspicions of the Moor, consist not in their falsehood but in their truth.

I have said the character of Desdemona was deficient in delicacy. Besides the instances to which I referred in proof of this charge, observe what she says in pleading for the restoration of Cassio to his office, from which he had been cashiered by Othello for beastly drunkenness and a consequent night-brawl, in which he had stabbed Montano—the predecessor of Othello as Governor of Cypress—and nearly killed him; yet in urging Othello to restore Cassio to his office and to favor, Desdemona says—

> in faith, he's penitent;
> And yet his trespass, in our common reason,
> (Save that, they say, the wars must make examples

Out of their best,) *is not almost a fault*
To incur a private check.

Now, to palliate the two crimes of Cassio—his drunken fit and his stabbing
of Montano—the reader knows that he has been inveigled to the commission
of them by the accursed artifices of Iago; but Desdemona knows nothing of
this; she has no excuse for Cassio—nothing to plead for him but his penitence.
And is this the character for a woman of delicate sentiment to give of such a
complicated and heinous offence as that of which Cassio has been guilty, even
when pleading for his pardon? No! it is not for female delicacy to extenuate the
crimes of drunkenness and bloodshed, even when performing the appropriate
office of raising the soul-subduing voice for mercy.

Afterwards, in the same speech, she says—

What! Michael Cassio,
That came a-wooing with you; and many a time,
When I have spoke of you dispraisingly,
Hath ta'en your part; to have so much to do
To bring *him* in!

I will not inquire how far this avowal that she had been in the frequent habit
of speaking dispraisingly of Othello at the very time when she was so deeply
enamoured with his honors and his valiant parts, was consistent with sincerity.
Young ladies must be allowed a little concealment and a little disguise, even for
passions of which they have no need to be ashamed. It is the rosy pudency—the
irresistible charm of the sex; but the exercise of it in satirical censure upon the
very object of their most ardent affections is certainly no indication of innocence,
simplicity, or artlessness.

I still retain, then, the opinion—

First. That the passion of Desdemona for Othello is *unnatural,* solely and
exclusively because of his color.

Second. That her elopement *to* him, and secret marriage *with* him, indicate
a personal character not only very deficient in delicacy, but totally regardless of
filial duty, of female modesty, and of ingenuous shame.

Third. That her deficiency in delicacy is discernible in her conduct and
discourse throughout the play.

I perceive and acknowledge, indeed, the admirable address with which the
part has been contrived to inspire and to warm the breast of the spectator
with a deep interest in her fate; and I am well aware that my own comparative
insensibility to it is not in unison with the general impression which it produces
upon the stage. I shrink from the thought of slandering even a creature of
the imagination. When the spectator or reader follows, on the stage or in the

closet, the infernal thread of duplicity and of execrable devices with which Iago entangles his victims, it is the purpose of the dramatist to merge all the faults and vices of the sufferers in the overwhelming flood of their calamities, and in the unmingled detestation of the inhuman devil, their betrayer and destroyer. And in all this, I see not only the skill of the artist, but the power of the moral operator, the purifier of the spectator's heart by the agency of *terror* and *pity*.

The characters of Othello and Desdemona, like all the characters of men and women in real life, are of "mingled yarn," with qualities of good and bad—of virtues and vices in proportion differently composed. Iago, with a high order of intellect, is, in moral principle, the very spirit of evil. I have said the moral of the tragedy is, that the intermarriage of black and white blood is a violation of the law of nature. *That* is the lesson to be learned from the play. To exhibit all the natural consequences of their act, the poet is compelled to make the marriage secret. It must commence by an elopement, and by an outrage upon the decorum of social intercourse. He must therefore assume, for the performance of this act, persons of moral character sufficiently frail and imperfect to be capable of performing it, but in other respects endowed with pleasing and estimable qualities. Thus, the Moor is represented as of a free, and open, and generous nature; as a Christian; as a distinguished military commander in the service of the Republic of Venice; as having rendered important service to the State, and as being in the enjoyment of a splendid reputation as a warrior. The other party to the marriage is a maiden, fair, gentle, and accomplished; born and educated in the proudest rank of Venitian nobility.

Othello, setting aside his color, has every quality to fascinate and charm the female heart. Desdemona, apart from the grossness of her fault in being accessible to such a passion for such an object, is amiable and lovely; among the most attractive of her sex and condition. The faults of their characters are never brought into action excepting as they illustrate the moral principle of the whole story. Othello is not jealous by nature. On the contrary, with a strong natural understanding, and all the vigilance essential to an experienced commander, he is of a disposition so unsuspicious and confiding, that he believes in the *exceeding honesty* of Iago long after he has ample cause to suspect and distrust him. Desdemona, *supersubtle* as she is in the management of her amour with Othello; deeply as she dissembles to deceive her father; and, forward as she is in inviting the courtship of the Moor; discovers neither artifice nor duplicity from the moment that she is Othello's wife. Her innocence, in all her relations with him, is pure and spotless; her kindness for Cassio is mere untainted benevolence; and, though unguarded in her personal deportment towards him, it is far from the slightest soil of culpable impropriety. Guiltless of all conscious reproach in this part of her conduct, she never uses any of the artifices to which she had resorted to accomplish her marriage with Othello. Always feeling that she has given him no cause of suspicion, her endurance of his cruel treatment and brutal abuse of her through all its stages of violence, till he murders her in bed, is always marked with the most affecting sweetness of temper, the most perfect artlessness, and the most endearing resignation. The defects of her character have here no room for developement, and the poet carefully keeps them out of sight. Hence it is that the general reader and spectator, with Dr. Johnson, give her unqualified credit for soft simplicity, artless-ness, and innocence—forgetful of the qualities of a different and opposite character, stamped upon the transactions by which she effected her marriage with the Moor. The marriage, however, is the source of all her calamities; it is the primitive cause of all the tragic incidents of the play, and of its terrible catastrophe. That the moral lesson to be learned from it is of no practical utility in England, where there are no valiant Moors to steal the affections of fair and high-born dames, may be true; the lesson, however, is not the less, couched under the form of an admirable drama; nor needs it any laborious effort of the imagination to extend the moral precept resulting from the story to a salutary admonition against all ill-assorted, clandestine, and unnatural marriages.

1864—Victor Hugo. From *William Shakespeare*

Victor Hugo (1802–1885), the great French author of *Les Misérables* and *The Hunchback of Notre Dame,* also wrote a study of Shakespeare.

Now what is Othello? He is the night, An immense fatal figure. Night is amorous of day. Darkness loves the dawn. The African adores the white woman. Othello has for his light and for his frenzy, Desdemona. And then, how easy to him is jealousy! He is great, he is dignified, he is majestic, he soars above all heads; he has as an escort bravery, battle, the braying of trumpets, the banners of war, renown, glory; he is radiant with twenty victories, he is studded with stars, this Othello: but he is black. And thus how soon, when jealous, the hero becomes the monster, the black becomes the negro! How speedily has night beckoned to death!

By the side of Othello, who is night, there is Iago, who is evil—evil, the other form of darkness. Night is but the night of the world; evil is the night of the soul. How deeply black are perfidy and falsehood! It is all one whether what courses through the veins be ink or treason. Whoever has jostled against imposture and perjury, knows it: one must blindly grope one's way with knavery. Pour hypocrisy upon the break of day, and you put out the sun; and this, thanks to false religions, is what happens to God.

Iago near Othello is the precipice near the landslip. "This way!" he says in a low voice. The snare advises blindness. The lover of darkness guides the black.

Deceit takes upon itself to give what light may be required by night. Falsehood serves as a blind man's dog to jealousy. Othello the negro and Iago the traitor pitted against whiteness and candor: what more formidable? These ferocities of darkness act in unison. These two incarnations of the eclipse conspire, the one roaring, the other sneering, for the tragic suffocation of light.

Sound this profound thing. Othello is the night, and being night, and wishing to kill, what does he take to slay with? Poison? the club? the axe? the knife? No; the pillow. To kill is to lull to sleep. Shakespeare himself perhaps did not take this into account. The creator sometimes, almost unknown to himself, yields to his type, so truly is that type a power. And it is thus that Desdemona, spouse of the man Night, dies, stifled by the pillow upon which the first kiss was given, and which receives the last sigh.

⸎⸎⸎ ⸎⸎⸎ ⸎⸎⸎

1880—Algernon Charles Swinburne. From *A Study of Shakespeare*

A. C. Swinburne (1837–1909), most famous for his ornate poetry, was also an astute critic.

In the seventh story of the third decade of the Hecatommithi of M. Giovanbattista Giraldi Cinthio, "nobile Ferrarese," first published in 1565, there is an incident so beautifully imagined and so beautifully related that it seems at first inexplicable how Shakespeare, when engaged in transfiguring this story into the tragedy of Othello, can have struck it out of his version. The loss of the magic handkerchief which seals the doom of the hero and his fellow-victim is far less plausibly and far less beautifully explained by a mere accident, and a most unlikely accident, than by a device which heightens at once the charm of Desdemona and the atrocity of Iago. It is through her tenderness for his little child that he takes occasion to destroy her.

The ancient or ensign, who is nameless as every other actor in the story except the Moor's wife, is of course, if compared with Iago, a mere shadow cast before it by the advent of that awful figure. But none the less is he the remarkably powerful and original creature of a true and tragic genius. Every man may make for himself, and must allow that he cannot pretend to impose upon any other, his own image of the most wicked man ever created by the will of man or God. But Cinthio's villain is distinctly and vividly set before us: a man "of most beautiful presence, but of the wickedest nature that ever was man in the world." Less abnormal and less inhumanly intellectual than Iago, who loved Desdemona "not out of absolute lust" (perhaps the strangest and subtlest point of all that go to make up his all but inscrutable character), this simpler villain, "no whit heeding the faith given to his wife, nor friendship, nor faith, nor obligation, that he might have to the Moor, fell most ardently in love with Desdemona. And he set all his thought to see if it might become possible for him to enjoy her."

This plain and natural motive would probably have sufficed for any of those great contemporaries who found it easier to excel all other tragic or comic poets since the passing of Sophocles and Aristophanes than to equal or draw near to Shakespeare. For him it was insufficient. Neither envy nor hatred nor jealousy nor resentment, all at work together in festering fusion of conscious and contemplative evil, can quite explain Iago even to himself: yet neither Macbeth nor even Hamlet is by nature more inevitably introspective. But the secret of the abyss of this man's nature lies deeper than did ever plummet sound save Shakespeare's. The bright and restless devil of Goethe's invention, the mournfuller and more majestic devil created by Marlowe, are spirits of less deep damnation than that incarnate in the bluff plain-spoken soldier whose honesty is the one obvious thing about him, the one unmistakable quality which neither man nor woman ever fails to recognise and to trust.

And what is even the loftier Faust, whose one fitting mate was Helen, if compared with the subjects of Iago's fathomless and bottomless malice? This quarry cries on havoc louder than when Hamlet fell. Shakespeare alone could have afforded to cancel the most graceful touch, to efface the loveliest feature, in the sketch of Cinthio's heroine. But Desdemona can dispense with even this.

> The Moor's wife went often, as I have said, to the ancient's wife's house, and abode with her a good part of the day. Whence this man seeing that she sometimes bore about her a handkerchief which he knew that the Moor had given her, the which handkerchief was wrought in Moorish wise most subtly, and was most dear to the lady, and in like wise to the Moor, he bethought him to take it from her secretly, and thence to prepare against her her final ruin. And he having a girl of three years old, which child was much beloved of Disdemona, one day that the hapless lady had gone to stay at the house of this villain, he took the little girl in his arms and gave her to the lady, who took her and gathered her to her breast: this deceiver, who was excellent at sleight of hand, reft from her girdlestead the handkerchief so cunningly that she was no whit aware of it, and departed from her right joyful. Disdemona, knowing not this, went home, and being busied with other thoughts took no heed of the handkerchief. But some days thence, seeking for it and not finding it, she was right fearful lest the Moor should ask it of her, as he was often wont to do.

No reader of this terribly beautiful passage can fail to ask himself why Shakespeare forbore to make use of it. The substituted incident is as much less probable as it is less tragic. The wife offers to bind the husband's aching forehead with this especially hallowed handkerchief: "he puts it from him, and it drops," unnoticed by either, for Emilia to pick up and reflect, "I am glad I have found this napkin." What can be the explanation of what a dunce who knows better than Shakespeare might call an oversight? There is but one: but it is all-sufficient. In Shakespeare's world as in nature's it is impossible that monsters should propagate: that Iago should beget, or that Goneril or Regan should bring forth. Their children are creatures unimaginable by man. The old chronicles give sons to Goneril who vanquish Cordelia in battle and drive her to suicide in prison: but Shakespeare knew that such a tradition was not less morally and physiologically incongruous than it was poetically and dramatically impossible. And Lear's daughters are not monsters in the proper sense: their unnatural nature is but the sublimation and exaggeration of common evil qualities, unalloyed, untempered, unqualified by any ordinary admixture of anything not ravenously, resolutely, mercilessly selfish. They are devils only by dint of being more utterly and exclusively animals—and animals of a lower and hatefuller type—than usual. But any one less thoroughly intoxicated with the poisonous drug of lifelong power upon all others within reach of his royal hand would have been safe from the convincing and subjugating influence of Goneril and Regan. That is plain enough: but who will be fool enough to imagine that he would have been safe against the more deadly and inevitable influence of Iago?

The most fearful evidence of his spiritual power—for it would have been easy for a more timid nature than his wife's to secure herself beforehand against his physical violence by a warning given betimes to either of his intended victims— was necessarily suppressed by Shakespeare as unfit for dramatic service. Emilia will not believe Othello's assurance of her husband's complicity in the murder of Desdemona: the ancient's wife in Cinthio's terrible story "knew all, seeing that her husband would fain have made use of her as an instrument in the lady's death, but she would never assent, and for dread of her husband durst not tell her anything." This is not more striking and satisfying in a tale than it would have been improper and ineffectual in a tragedy. So utter a prostration of spirit, so helpless an abjection of soul and abdication of conscience under the absolute pressure of sheer terror, would have been too purely dreadful and contemptible a phase of debased nature for Shakespeare to exhibit and to elaborate as he must needs have done throughout the scenes in which Iago's wife must needs have figured: even if they could have been as dramatic, as living, as convincing as those in which the light, unprincipled, untrustworthy, loving, lying, foolish, fearless and devoted woman is made actual and tangible to our imagination as none but Shakespeare could have made her: a little afraid, it may be, of her husband, when she gives him the stolen handkerchief, but utterly dauntless when his murderous hand is lifted against her to silence her witness to the truth.

The crowning mark of difference between such a nature as this and such a nature as that of the mistress for whose sake she lays down her life too late to save her is less obvious even in their last difference of opinion—as to whether there are or are not women who abuse their husbands as Othello charges his wife with abusing him—than in the previous scene when Emilia most naturally and inevitably asks her if he has not just shown himself to be jealous, and she answers:

> Who, he? I think the sun where he was born
> Drew all such humours from him.

This would be a most noble stroke of pathos if the speaker were wrong—misled by love into loving error; but the higher Shakespearean pathos, unequalled and impossible for man to conceive as ever possibly to be equalled by man, consists in the fact that she was right. And the men of Shakespeare's age could see this: they coupled together with equally assured propriety and justice of epithet "Honest Iago" and "the jealous Moor."

The jealousy of the one and the honesty of the other must stand or fall together. Othello, when overmastered by the agony of the sudden certitude that the devotion of his love has been wasted on a harlot who has laid in ashes the honour and the happiness of his life, may naturally or rather must inevitably so bear himself as to seem jealous in the eyes of all—and they are all who know him—to whom Iago seems the living type of honesty: a bluff, gallant, outspoken fellow, no conjurer and no saint, coarse of speech and cynical of humour, but true and tried as steel: a man to be trusted beyond many a far cleverer and many a more refined companion in peril or in peace. It is the supreme triumph of his superb hypocrisy so to disguise the pride of intellect which is the radical instinct of his nature and the central mainspring of his action as to pass for a man of rather inferior than superior intelligence to the less blunt and simple natures of those on whom he plays with a touch so unerring at the pleasure of his merciless will. One only thing he cannot do: he cannot make Desdemona doubt of Othello. The first terrible outbreak of his gathering passion in a triple peal of thunder fails to convince her that she has erred in believing him incapable of jealousy. She can only believe that he has vented upon her the irritation aroused by others, and repent that she should have charged him even in thought with unkindness on no more serious account than this. "Nay, we must think men are not gods": and she had been but inconsiderate and over-exacting, an "unhandsome warrior" unfit to bear the burden and the heat of the day—of a lifelong union and a fellowship in battle and struggle against the trials and the tests of chance—to repine internally for a moment on such a score as that.

Were no other proof extant and flagrant of the palpable truth that Shakespeare excelled all other men of all time on record as a poet in the most proper and literal sense—as a creator of man and woman—there would be overflowing and overwhelming proof of it in the creation and interaction of these three characters. In the more technical and lyrical sense of the word, no less than in height of prophetic power, in depth of reconciling and atoning inspiration, he is excelled by Æschylus; though surely, on the latter score, by Æschylus alone. But if the unique and marvellous power which at the close of the Oresteia leaves us impressed with a crowning and final sense of high spiritual calm and austere consolation in face of all the mystery of suffering and of sin—if this supreme gift of the imaginative reason was no more shared by Shakespeare than by any poet or prophet or teacher of Hebrew origin, it was his and his alone to set before us the tragic problem of character and event, of all action and all passion, all evil and all good, all natural joy and sorrow and chance and change, in such fullness and perfection of variety, with such harmony and supremacy of justice and of truth, that no man known to historic record ever glorified the world whom it would have been so utterly natural and so comparatively rational to fall down before and worship as a God.

For nothing human is ever for a moment above the reach or beyond the scope or beneath the notice of his all but superhuman genius. In this very play he sets before mankind for ever not only the perfect models of heroic love and honour, of womanly sweetness and courage, of intelligent activity and joyous energy in evil, but also an unsurpassable type of the tragicomic dullard. Roderigo is not only Iago's but (in Dryden's masterly phrase) "God Almighty's fool." And Shakespeare shows the poor devil no more mercy than Iago or than God. You see at once that he was born to be plundered, cudgeled, and killed—if he tries to play the villain—like a dog. No lighter comic relief than this rather grim and pitiless exhibition of the typic fool could have been acceptable or admissible on the stage of so supreme a tragedy.

Such humorous realism—and it is excellent of its kind—as half relieves and half intensifies the horror of Cinthio's tale may serve as well as any other point of difference to show with what matchless tact of transfiguration by selection and rejection the hand of Shakespeare wrought his will and set his mark on the materials left ready for it by the hand of a lesser genius. The ancient waylays and maims the lieutenant on a dark night as he comes from the house of a harlot "with whom he was wont to solace himself"; and when the news gets abroad next morning, and reaches the ears of Disdemona, "she, who was of a loving nature and thought not that evil should thence befall her, shewed that she had right great sorrow for such a mishap. Hereof the Moor took the worst opinion that might be, and went to find the ancient, and said to him, 'Thou knowest well that my ass of a wife is in so great trouble for the lieutenant's mishap that she is like to run mad.' 'And how could you,' said he, 'deem otherwise, seeing that he is her soul?' 'Her soul, eh?' replied the Moor. 'I will pluck—that will I—the soul from her body.'" Shakespeare and his one disciple Webster alone could have afforded to leave this masterly bit of dialogue unused or untranslated. For they alone would so have elevated and ennobled the figure of the protagonist as to make it unimaginable that he could have talked in this tone of his wife and her supposed paramour with the living instrument of his revenge. Could he have done so, he might have been capable of playing the part played by the merciless Moor who allows the ancient to thrash her to death with a stocking stuffed with sand. No later master of realistic fiction can presumably have surpassed the simple force of impression and effect conveyed by this direct and unlovely narrative.

And as they debated with each other whether the lady should be done to death by poison or dagger, and resolved not on either the one or the other of these, the ancient said, "A way there is come into my mind whereby you shall satisfy yourself, and there shall be no suspicion of it whatever. And it is this. The house wherein you dwell is very old, and the ceiling of your chamber has many chinks in it. I will that with a stocking full of sand we smite Disdemona so sore that she die thereof, whereby there may seem on her no sign of blows: when she shall be dead, we will make part of the ceiling fall, and will shatter the lady's head; feigning that a beam as it fell has shattered it and killed her: and in this wise there shall be no one who may conceive any suspicion of you, every man believing that her death has befallen by accident." The cruel counsel pleased the Moor, and after abiding the time that seemed convenient to him, he being one night with her abed, and having already hidden the ancient in a little chamber that opened into the bedchamber, the ancient, according to the order taken between them, made some manner of noise in the little chamber: and, hearing it, the Moor said, suddenly, to his wife, "Hast thou heard that noise?" "I have heard it," said she. "Get up," subjoined the Moor, "and see what is the matter." Up rose the hapless Disdemona, and, as soon as she came near the little chamber, forth came thereout the ancient, who, being a strong man, and of good muscle, with the stocking which he had ready gave her a cruel blow in the middle of her back, whereby the lady instantly fell, without being able wellnigh to draw breath. But with that little voice that she could get she called on the Moor to help her, and he, risen out of bed, said to her, "Most wicked lady, thou hast the wage of thine unchastity: thus fare those women, who, feigning to love their husbands, set horns on their heads." The wretched lady, hearing this, and feeling herself come to her end, inasmuch as the ancient had given her another blow, said that in witness of her faith she called upon the divine justice, seeing that the world's failed her. And as she called on God to help her, when the third blow followed, she lay slain by the villainous ancient. Then, having laid her in bed, and shattered her head, he and the Moor made the rooftree of the chamber fall, as they had devised between them, and the Moor began to call for help, for the house was falling: at whose voice the neighbours came running, and having uncovered the bed, they found the lady under the roof-beams dead.

We are a long way off Shakespeare in this powerfully dramatic and realistic scene of butchery: it is a far cry from Othello, a nature made up of love and honour, of resolute righteousness and heroic pity, to the relentless and deliberate ruffian whose justice is as brutal in its ferocity as his caution is cold-blooded in its foresight. The sacrificial murder of Desdemona is no butchery, but tragedy—terrible as ever tragedy may be, but not more terrible than beautiful; from the first kiss to the last stab, when the sacrificing priest of retribution immolates the victim whose blood he had forborne to shed for pity of her beauty till impelled to forget his first impulse and shed it for pity of her suffering. His words can bear no other meaning, can imply no other action, that would not be burlesque rather than grotesque in its horror. And the commentators or annotators who cannot understand or will not allow that a man in almost unimaginable passion of anguish may not be perfectly and sedately mindful of consistency and master of himself must explain how Desdemona manages to regain her breath so as to speak three times and utter the most heavenly falsehood that ever put truth to shame, after being stifled to death. To recover breath enough to speak, to think, and to lie in defence of her slayer, can hardly be less than to recover breath enough to revive and live, if undespatched by some sharper and more summary method of homicide. The fitful and intermittent lack of stage directions which has caused and perpetuated this somewhat short-sighted oversight is not a more obvious evidence of the fact that Shakespeare's text has lost more than any other and lesser poet's for want of the author's revision than is the misplacing of a letter which, as far as I know, has never yet been set right. When Othello hears that Iago has instigated Roderigo to assassinate Cassio, he exclaims, 'O villain!' and Cassio ejaculates, 'Most heathenish, and most gross!' The sense is improved and the metre is rectified when we perceive that the original printer mistook the word 'villanie' for the word ' villaine.' Such corrections of an unrevised text may seem slight and trivial matters to Englishmen who give thanks for the like labour when lavished on second-rate or third-rate poets of classical antiquity: the toil bestowed by a Bentley or a Porson on Euripides or Horace must naturally, in the judgment of universities, seem wasted on Shakespeare or on Shelley.

One of the very few poets to be named with these has left on everlasting record the deliberate expression of his judgment that Othello combines and unites the qualities of King Lear, "the most tremendous effort of Shakespeare as a poet" (a verdict with which I may venture to express my full and absolute agreement), and of *Hamlet*, his most tremendous effort "as a philosopher or meditator." It may be so: and Coleridge may be right in his estimate that "*Othello* is the union of the two." I should say myself, but with no thought of setting my opinion against that of the man who at his best was now and then the greatest of all poets and all critics, that the fusion of thought and passion, inspiration and meditation, was at its height in King Lear. But in Othello we get the pure poetry of natural and personal emotion, unqualified by the righteous doubt and conscientious intelligence which instigate and impede the will and the action of Hamlet. The collision and the contrast of passion and intellect, of noble passion and infernal intellect, was never before and can never be again presented and verified as in this most tragic of all tragedies that ever the supreme student of humanity bequeathed for the study of all time. As a poet and a thinker Æschylus was the equal, if not the superior, of Shakespeare; as a creator, a revealer, and an interpreter, infinite in his insight and his truthfulness, his tenderness and his wisdom, his justice and his mercy, no man who ever lived can stand beside the author of *Othello*.

⎯⎯ ⎯⎯ ⎯⎯

1897—George Bernard Shaw. "Mainly About Shakespeare," from *London Saturday Review*

George Bernard Shaw, one of the great dramatists of his time, was also known for his sometimes idiosyncratic criticism, in which he often expressed his ambivalence toward Shakespeare. Some of his most famous plays include *Saint Joan*, *Pygmalion* (later adapted into the musical and film *My Fair Lady*), *Man and Superman*, and *Caesar and Cleopatra*.

"Othello," on the other hand, is pure melodrama. There is not a touch of character in it that goes below the skin; and the fitful attempts to make Iago something better than a melodramatic villain only make a hopeless mess of him and his motives. To any one capable of reading the play with an open mind as to its merits, it is obvious that Shakespeare plunged through it so impetuously that he had it finished before he had made up his mind as to the character and motives of a single person in it. Probably it was not until he stumbled into the sentimental fit in which he introduced the willow song that he saw his way through without making Desdemona enough of the "supersubtle Venetian" of Iago's description to strengthen the case for Othello's jealousy. That jealousy, by the way, is purely melodramatic jealousy. The real article is to be found later on in "A Winter's Tale," where Leontes is an unmistakable study of a jealous man from life. But when the worst has been said of "Othello" that can be provoked by its superficiality and staginess, it remains magnificent by the volume of its passion and the splendor of its word-music, which sweep the scenes up to a plane on which sense is drowned in sound. The words do not convey ideas: they are streaming ensigns and tossing branches to make the tempest of passion visible. In this passage, for instance:

"Like to the Pontic sea,
Whose icy current and compulsive course
Ne'er feels retiring ebb, but keeps due on
To the Propontic and the Hellespont,
E'en so my bloody thoughts, with violent pace,
Shall ne'er look back, ne'er ebb to humble love
Till that a capable and wide revenge
Swallow them up,"

if Othello cannot turn his voice into a thunder and surge of passion, he will achieve nothing but a ludicrously misplaced bit of geography. If in the last scene he cannot throw the darkness of night and the shadow of death over such lines as

"I know not where is that Promethean heat
That can thy light relume,"

he at once becomes a person who, on his way to commit a pettish murder, stops to philosophize foolishly about a candle end. The actor cannot help himself by studying his part acutely; for there is nothing to study in it. Tested by the brain, it is ridiculous: tested by the ear, it is sublime. He must have the orchestral quality in him; and as that is a matter largely of physical endowment, it follows that only an actor of certain physical endowments can play Othello. Let him be as crafty as he likes without that, he can no more get the effect than he can sound the bottom C on a violoncello. The note is not there, that is all; and he had better be content to play Iago, which is within the compass of any clever actor of normal endowments.

. . .

But the character [Iago] defies all consistency. Shakespeare, as usual, starts with a rough general notion of a certain type of individual, and then throws it over at the first temptation. Iago begins as a coarse blackguard, whose jovial bluntness passes as "honesty," and who is professionally a routine subaltern incapable of understanding why a mathematician gets promoted over his head. But the moment a stage effect can be made, or a fine speech brought off by making him refined, subtle and dignified, he is set talking like Hamlet, and becomes a godsend to students of the "problems" presented by our divine William's sham characters. Mr. [Franklin] McLeay does all that an actor can do with him. He follows Shakespeare faithfully on the rails and off them. He plays the jovial blackguard to Cassio and Roderigo and the philosopher and mentor to Othello just as the lines lead him, with perfect intelligibility and with so much point, distinction and fascination that the audience loads him with compliments, and the critics all make up their minds to declare that he shows the finest insight into the many-sided and complex character of the prince of villains . . . .

OTHELLO IN THE TWENTIETH CENTURY

In the twentieth century, commentary on *Othello* continued to build on the work of critics past. A. C. Bradley's enduring *Shakespearean Tragedy*, published in 1904, follows in the tradition of Schlegel and Coleridge, at the start of the nineteenth century, and of Swinburne, near the century's end. Bradley's work is concerned with the formal structure of Shakespeare's plays and the analysis of characters—their psychology, their motives, and their place on the moral spectrum. Bradley claimed that Iago was one of Shakespeare's four "most wonderful" characters, along with Falstaff, Hamlet, and Cleopatra.

Other critics followed Bradley in admiring Iago's diabolic brilliance. Harold C. Goddard, writing in 1951, called Iago "a moral pyromaniac." The poet W. H. Auden, however, argued that Iago is essentially a practical joker, with no identity of his own, someone who, out of envy, thrives on subverting the identity of others. In 1956, Robert B. Heilman said of Iago, "As the spiritual have-not, Iago is universal, that is, many things at once, and of many times at once." In 1992, Harold Bloom, in an introduction to a collection of criticism specifically on the character of Iago, compared him to Hamlet: "Hamlet and Iago alike are theatrical geniuses, though the Prince of Denmark's genius is universal, whereas Iago, who prides himself upon his military talents, displays throughout a dramatic grasp of the power of fantasy that rivals Shakespeare's own."

In 1927, another great poet, T. S. Eliot, spoke out against the character of Othello. He argued that Othello's last speech is simply an instance of Othello "cheering himself up," having been unable to understand and take responsibility for his terrible delusion. This line of thought, followed by other critics, such as F. R. Leavis, has not proved as persuasive as commentaries that more fully acknowledge Othello's nobility.

In 1930, G. Wilson Knight analyzed the language of *Othello*. He termed the poetic language of the main character "the Othello music." Knight, unlike Eliot, believed that "during the last scene, Othello is a nobly tragic figure." Later in the century, the poet Anthony Hecht would agree, writing, in his interesting overview of the play, of the "painful but undoubted nobility" of Othello's suicide.

In his 1983 book *The New Mimesis*, the critic A. D. Nuttall took Eliot's statement as a starting point for his own examination of the play.

In 1936, William Empson, writing about *Othello* in the periodical *Life and Letters To-Day*, sought to reveal the force of the play and the psychology of its characters through an analysis of the multiple, ironic, and puzzling ways Shakespeare manipulates the meanings of words such as "honest." In 1951, the critic Kenneth Burke provided a symbolic analysis of Othello, in his famous essay "'Othello': An Essay to Illustrate a Method." Allowing Desdemona, Othello, and Iago their full human dimensionality as characters, Burke's essay also examines them in the relation of "possession, possessor, and estrangement."

In the 1980s, the civil rights movement in the United States, the feminist movement, and the gay liberation movement all exerted a strong influence on the academic study of literature. *Othello* was examined as a play about race relations, black masculinity, the social constraints imposed upon women, and more. Some critics even saw a subconscious homoerotic bond between Iago and Othello. In his book *Renaissance Self-Fashionings*, Stephen Greenblatt examined *Othello*, among other works, as he propounded a new critical theory that became known as New Historicism.

Othello was staged frequently during the twentieth century and provided a vehicle for some of the century's great actors, such as Paul Robeson, Laurence Olivier, James Earl Jones, and Anthony Hopkins. It was also adapted for the movies. Orson Welles played Othello in a 1952 stripped-down film version, now considered a masterpiece. Olivier's National Theater production of 1965 was also filmed. In 1995, Laurence Fishburne and Kenneth Branagh played Othello and Iago in a less successful production.

The twentieth century saw the adaptation of *Othello* as the basis for new works that both re-imagine the play and use it to comment on contemporary social and sexual currents. In 1994, Paula Vogel published *Desdemona: A Play about a Handkerchief*, an exploration of female sexuality in which Desdemona is made both as promiscuous as Othello fears her to be and yet guilty of no breach of conduct. *Good Night Desdemona (Good Morning Juliet)*, by Ann-Marie MacDonald, deconstructs *Othello* (and *Romeo and Juliet*) by placing a graduate student into each play and allowing her to manipulate its plot as she seeks to come to terms with her own life and identity.

1904—A. C. Bradley.
"Othello," from *Shakespearean Tragedy*

A. C. Bradley (1851–1935) was a professor at Oxford and other institutions. His book *Shakespearean Tragedy* was one of the most significant works of Shakespeare criticism of the twentieth century.

1

Evil has nowhere else been portrayed with such mastery as in the character of Iago. Richard III., for example, beside being less subtly conceived, is a far greater figure and a less repellent. His physical deformity, separating him from other men, seems to offer some excuse for his egoism. In spite of his egoism, too, he appears to us more than a mere individual: he is the representative of his family, the Fury of the House of York. Nor is he so negative as Iago: he has strong passions, he has admirations, and his conscience disturbs him. There is the glory of power about him. Though an excellent actor, he prefers force to fraud, and in his world there is no general illusion as to his true nature. Again, to compare Iago with the Satan of *Paradise Lost* seems almost absurd, so immensely does Shakespeare's man exceed Milton's Fiend in evil . . . . It is only in Goethe's Mephistopheles that a fit companion for Iago can be found. Here there is something of the same deadly coldness, the same gaiety in destruction. But then Mephistopheles, like so many scores of literary villains, has Iago for his father. And Mephistopheles, besides, is not, in the strict sense, a character. He is half person, half symbol. A metaphysical idea speaks through him. He is earthy, but could never live upon the earth.

. . . [I]f Iago had been a person as attractive as Hamlet, as many thousands of pages might have been written about him, containing as much criticism good and bad. As it is, the majority of interpretations of his character are inadequate not only to Shakespeare's conception, but, I believe, to the impressions of most readers of taste who are unbewildered by analysis. These false interpretations, if we set aside the usual lunacies, fall into two groups. The first contains views which reduce Shakespeare to common-place. In different ways and degrees they convert his Iago into an ordinary villain. Their Iago is simply a man who has been slighted and revenges himself; or a husband who believes he has been wronged, and will make his enemy suffer a jealousy worse than his own; or an ambitious man determined to ruin his successful rival—one of these, or a combination of these, endowed with unusual ability and cruelty. These are the more popular views. The second group of false interpretations is much smaller, but it contains much weightier matter than the first. Here Iago is a being who hates good simply because it is good, and loves evil purely for itself. His action is not prompted by any plain motive like revenge, jealousy or ambition. It springs from a 'motiveless malignity,' or a disinterested delight in the pain of others; and Othello, Cassio and Desdemona are scarcely more than the material requisite for the full attainment of this delight. This second Iago, evidently, is no conventional villain, and he is much nearer to Shakespeare's Iago than the first. Only he is, if not a psychological impossibility, at any rate not a *human* being. He might be in place, therefore, in a symbolical poem like *Faust*, but in a purely human drama like *Othello* he would be a ruinous blunder. Moreover, he is not in *Othello*: he is a product of imperfect observation and analysis.

Coleridge, the author of that misleading phrase 'motiveless malignity,' has some fine remarks on Iago; and the essence of the character has been described, first in some of the best lines Hazlitt ever wrote, and then rather more fully by Mr. Swinburne,—so admirably described that I am tempted merely to read and illustrate these two criticisms. This plan, however, would make it difficult to introduce all that I wish to say. I propose, therefore, to approach the subject directly, and, first, to consider how Iago appeared to those who knew him, and what inferences may be drawn from their illusions; and then to ask what, if we judge from the play, his character really was. And I will indicate the points where I am directly indebted to the criticisms just mentioned.

But two warnings are first required. One of these concerns Iago's nationality. It has been held that he is a study of that peculiarly Italian form of villainy which is considered both too clever and too diabolical for an Englishman. I doubt if there is much more to be said for this idea than for the notion that Othello is a study of Moorish character. No doubt the belief in that Italian villainy was prevalent in Shakespeare's time, and it may perhaps have influenced him in some slight degree both here and in drawing the character of Iachimo in *Cymbeline*. But even this slight influence seems to me doubtful. If Don John in *Much Ado* had been an Englishman, critics would have admired Shakespeare's discernment in making his English villain sulky and stupid. If Edmund's father had been Duke of Ferrara instead of Earl of Gloster, they would have said that Edmund could have been nothing but an Italian. Change the name and country of Richard III., and he would be called a typical despot of the Italian Renaissance. Change those of Juliet, and we should find her wholesome English nature contrasted with the southern dreaminess of Romeo. But this way of interpreting Shakespeare is not Shakespearean. With him the differences of period, race, nationality and locality have little bearing on the inward character, though they sometimes have a good deal on the total imaginative effect, of his figures. When he does lay stress on such differences his intention is at once obvious, as in characters like Fluellen or Sir Hugh Evans, or in the talk of the French princes before the battle of Agincourt. I may add that Iago certainly cannot be taken to exemplify the popular Elizabethan idea of a disciple of Macchiavelli. There is no sign that he is in theory an atheist or even an unbeliever in the received religion. On the contrary, he uses its language, and says nothing resembling the words of the prologue to the *Jew of Malta*:

> I count religion but a childish toy,
> And hold there is no sin but ignorance.
> . . .

I come to a second warning. One must constantly remember not to believe a syllable that Iago utters on any subject, including himself, until one has tested his statement by comparing it with known facts and with other statements of his own or of other people, and by considering whether he had in the particular circumstances any reason for telling a lie or for telling the truth. The implicit confidence which his acquaintances placed in his integrity has descended to most of his critics; and this, reinforcing the comical habit of quoting as Shakespeare's own statement everything said by his characters, has been a fruitful source of misinterpretation. I will take as an instance the very first assertions made by Iago. In the opening scene he tells his dupe Roderigo that three great men of Venice went to Othello and begged him to make Iago his lieutenant; that Othello, out of pride and obstinacy, refused; that in refusing he talked a deal of military rigmarole, and ended by declaring (falsely, we are to understand) that he had already filled up the vacancy; that Cassio, whom he chose, had absolutely no practical knowledge of war, nothing but bookish theoric, mere prattle, arithmetic, whereas Iago himself had often fought by Othello's side, and by 'old gradation' too ought to have been preferred. Most or all of this is repeated by some critics as though it were information given by Shakespeare, and the conclusion is quite naturally drawn that Iago had some reason to feel aggrieved. But if we ask ourselves how much of all this is true we shall answer, I believe, as follows. It is absolutely certain that Othello appointed Cassio his lieutenant, and *nothing* else is absolutely certain. But there is no reason to doubt the statement that Iago had seen service with him, nor is there anything inherently improbable in the statement that he was solicited by three great personages on Iago's behalf. On the other hand, the suggestions that he refused out of pride and obstinacy, and that he lied in saying he had already chosen his officer, have no verisimilitude; and if there is any fact at all (as there probably is) behind Iago's account of the conversation, it doubtless is the fact that Iago himself was ignorant of military science, while Cassio was an expert, and that Othello explained this to the great personages. That Cassio, again, was an interloper and a mere closet-student without experience of war is incredible, considering first that Othello chose him for lieutenant, and secondly that the senate appointed him to succeed Othello in command at Cyprus; and we have direct evidence that part of Iago's statement is a lie, for Desdemona happens to mention that Cassio was a man who 'all his time had founded his good fortunes' on Othello's love and had 'shared dangers' with him (iii. iv. 93). There remains only the implied assertion that, if promotion had gone by old gradation, Iago, as the senior, would have been preferred. It may be true: Othello was not the man to hesitate to promote a junior for good reasons. But it is just as likely to be a pure invention; and, though Cassio was young, there is nothing to show that he was younger, in years or in service, than Iago. Iago, for instance, never calls him 'young,' as he does Roderigo; and a mere youth would not have been made Governor of Cyprus. What is certain, finally, in the whole business is that Othello's mind was perfectly at ease about the appointment, and that he never dreamed of Iago's being discontented at it, not even when the intrigue was disclosed and he asked himself how he had offended Iago.

2

It is necessary to examine in this manner every statement made by Iago. But it is not necessary to do so in public, and I proceed to the question what impression he made on his friends and acquaintances. In the main there is here no room for doubt. Nothing could be less like Iago than the melodramatic villain so often substituted for him on the stage, a person whom everyone in the theatre knows for a scoundrel at the first glance. Iago, we gather, was a Venetian soldier, eight-and-twenty years of age, who had seen a good deal of service and had a high reputation for courage. Of his origin we are ignorant, but, unless I am mistaken, he was not of gentle birth or breeding. He does not strike one as a degraded man of culture: for all his great powers, he is vulgar, and his probable want of military science may well be significant. He was married to a wife who evidently lacked refinement, and who appears in the drama almost in the relation of a servant to Desdemona. His manner was that of a blunt, bluff soldier, who spoke his mind freely and plainly. He was often hearty, and could be thoroughly jovial; but he was not seldom rather rough and caustic of speech, and he was given to making remarks somewhat disparaging to human nature. He was aware of this trait in himself, and frankly admitted that he was nothing if not critical, and that it was his nature to spy into abuses. In these admissions he characteristically exaggerated his fault, as plain-dealers are apt to do; and he was liked none the less for it, seeing that his satire was humorous, that on serious matters he did not speak lightly (iii. iii. 119), and that the one thing perfectly obvious about him was his honesty. 'Honest' is the word that springs to the lips of everyone who speaks of him. It is applied to him some fifteen times in the play, not to mention some half-dozen where he employs it, in derision, of himself. In fact he was one of those sterling men who, in disgust at gush, say cynical things which they do not believe, and then, the moment you are in trouble, put in practice the very sentiment they had laughed at. On such occasions he showed the kindliest sympathy and the most eager desire to help. When Cassio misbehaved so dreadfully and was found fighting with Montano, did not Othello see that 'honest Iago looked dead with grieving'? With what difficulty was he induced, nay, compelled, to speak the truth against the lieutenant! Another man might have felt a touch of satisfaction at the thought that the post he had coveted was now vacant; but Iago not only comforted Cassio, talking to him cynically about reputation, just to help him over his shame, but he set his wits to work and at once perceived that the right plan for Cassio to get his post again was to ask Desdemona to intercede. So troubled was he at his friend's disgrace that his own wife was sure 'it grieved her husband as if the case was his.' What wonder that anyone in sore trouble, like Desdemona, should send at once for Iago (iv. ii. 106)? If this rough diamond had any flaw, it was that Iago's warm loyal heart incited him to too impulsive action. If he merely heard a friend like Othello calumniated, his hand flew to his sword; and though he restrained himself he almost regretted his own virtue (i. ii. 1-10).

Such seemed Iago to the people about him, even to those who, like Othello, had known him for some time. And it is a fact too little noticed but most remarkable, that he presented an appearance not very different to his wife. There is no sign either that Emilia's marriage was downright unhappy, or that she suspected the true nature of her husband. No doubt she knew rather more of him than others. Thus we gather that he was given to chiding and sometimes spoke shortly and sharply to her (iii. iii. 300 f.); and it is quite likely that she gave him a good deal of her tongue in exchange (ii. i. 101 f.). He was also unreasonably jealous; for his own statement that he was jealous of Othello is confirmed by Emilia herself, and must therefore be believed (iv. ii. 145). But it seems clear that these defects of his had not seriously impaired Emilia's confidence in her husband or her affection for him. She knew in addition that he was not quite so honest as he seemed, for he had often begged her to steal Desdemona's handkerchief. But Emilia's nature was not very delicate or scrupulous about trifles. She thought her husband odd and 'wayward,' and looked on his fancy for the handkerchief as an instance of this (iii. iii. 292); but she never dreamed he was a villain, and there is no reason to doubt the sincerity of her belief that he was heartily sorry for Cassio's disgrace. Her failure, on seeing Othello's agitation about the handkerchief, to form any suspicion of an intrigue, shows how little she doubted her husband. Even when, later, the idea strikes her that some scoundrel has poisoned Othello's mind, the tone of all her speeches, and her mention of the rogue who (she believes) had stirred up Iago's jealousy of her, prove beyond doubt that the thought of Iago's being the scoundrel has not crossed her mind (iv. ii. 115-147). And if any hesitation on the subject could remain, surely it must be dispelled by the thrice-repeated cry of astonishment and horror, 'My husband!', which follows Othello's words, 'Thy husband knew it all'; and by the choking indignation and desperate hope which we hear in her appeal when Iago comes in:

> Disprove this villain if thou be'st a man:
> He says thou told'st him that his wife was false:
> I know thou did'st not, thou'rt not such a villain:
> Speak, for my heart is full.

Even if Iago *had* betrayed much more of his true self to his wife than to others, it would make no difference to the contrast between his true self and the self he presented to the world in general. But he never did so. Only the feeble eyes of the poor gull Roderigo were allowed a glimpse into that pit.

The bearing of this contrast upon the apparently excessive credulity of Othello has been already pointed out. What further conclusions can be drawn from it? Obviously, to begin with, the inference, which is accompanied by a thrill of admiration, that Iago's powers of dissimulation and of self-control must have been prodigious: for he was not a youth, like Edmund, but had worn this mask for years, and he had apparently never enjoyed, like Richard, occasional explosions of the reality within him. In fact so prodigious does his self-control appear that a reader might be excused for feeling a doubt of its possibility. But there are certain observations and further inferences which, apart from confidence in Shakespeare, would remove this doubt. It is to be observed, first, that Iago was able to find a certain relief from the discomfort of hypocrisy in those caustic or cynical speeches which, being misinterpreted, only heightened confidence in his honesty. They acted as a safety-valve, very much as Hamlet's pretended insanity did. Next, I would infer from the entire success of his hypocrisy—what may also be inferred on other grounds, and is of great importance—that he was by no means a man of strong feelings and passions, like Richard, but decidedly cold by temperament. Even so, his self-control was wonderful, but there never was in him any violent storm to be controlled. Thirdly, I would suggest that Iago, though thoroughly selfish and unfeeling, was not by nature malignant, nor even morose, but that, on the contrary, he had a superficial good-nature, the kind of good-nature that wins popularity and is often taken as the sign, not of a good digestion, but of a good heart. And lastly, it may be inferred that, before the giant crime which we witness, Iago had never been detected in any serious offence and may even never have been guilty of one, but had pursued a selfish but outwardly decent life, enjoying the excitement of war and of casual pleasures, but never yet meeting with any sufficient temptation to risk his position and advancement by a dangerous crime. So that, in fact, the tragedy of *Othello* is in a sense his tragedy too. It shows us not a violent man, like Richard, who spends his life in murder, but a thoroughly bad, *cold* man, who is at last tempted to let loose the forces within him, and is at once destroyed.

3

In order to see how this tragedy arises let us now look more closely into Iago's inner man. We find here, in the first place, as has been implied in part, very remarkable powers both of intellect and of will. Iago's insight, within certain limits, into human nature; his ingenuity and address in working upon it; his quickness and versatility in dealing with sudden difficulties and unforeseen opportunities, have probably no parallel among dramatic characters. Equally remarkable is his strength of will. Not Socrates himself, not the ideal sage of the Stoics, was more lord of himself than Iago appears to be. It is not merely that he never betrays his true nature; he seems to be master of *all* the motions that might affect his will. In the most dangerous moments of his plot, when the least slip or accident would be fatal, he never shows a trace of nervousness. When Othello takes him by the throat he merely shifts his part with his usual instantaneous adroitness. When he is attacked and wounded at the end he is perfectly unmoved. As Mr. Swinburne says, you cannot believe for a moment that the pain of torture will ever open Iago's lips. He is equally unassailable by the temptations of indolence or of sensuality. It is difficult to imagine him inactive; and though he has an obscene mind, and doubtless took his pleasures when and how he chose, he certainly took them by choice and not from weakness, and if pleasure interfered with his purposes the holiest of ascetics would not put it more resolutely by. 'What should I do?' Roderigo whimpers to him; 'I confess it is my shame to be so fond; but it is not in my virtue to amend it.' He answers: 'Virtue! a fig! 'tis in ourselves that we are thus and thus. It all depends on our will. Love is merely a lust of the blood and a permission of the will. Come, be a man .... Ere I would say I would drown myself for the love of a guinea-hen, I would change my humanity with a baboon.' Forget for a moment that love is for Iago the appetite of a baboon; forget that he is as little assailable by pity as by fear or pleasure; and you will acknowledge that this lordship of the will, which is his practice as well as his doctrine, is great, almost sublime. Indeed, in intellect (always within certain limits) and in will (considered as a mere power, and without regard to its objects) Iago *is* great.

To what end does he use these great powers? His creed—for he is no sceptic, he has a definite creed—is that absolute egoism is the only rational and proper attitude, and that conscience or honour or any kind of regard for others is an absurdity. He does not deny that this absurdity exists. He does not suppose that most people secretly share his creed, while pretending to hold and practise another. On the contrary, he regards most people as honest fools. He declares that he has never yet met a man who knew how to love himself; and his one expression of admiration in the play is for servants

> Who, trimmed in forms and visages of duty,
> Keep yet their hearts attending on themselves.

'These fellows,' he says, 'have some soul.' He professes to stand, and he attempts to stand, wholly outside the world of morality.

The existence of Iago's creed and of his corresponding practice is evidently connected with a characteristic in which he surpasses nearly all the other inhabitants of Shakespeare's world. Whatever he may once have been, he appears, when we meet him, to be almost destitute of humanity, of sympathetic or social feeling. He shows no trace of affection, and in presence of the most terrible suffering he shows either pleasure or an indifference which, if not complete, is nearly so. Here, however, we must be careful. It is important to realise, and few readers are in danger of ignoring, this extraordinary deadness of feeling, but it is also important not to confuse it with a general positive ill-will. When Iago has no dislike or hostility to a person he does *not* show pleasure in the suffering of that person: he shows at most the absence of pain. There is, for instance, not the least sign of his enjoying the distress of Desdemona. But his sympathetic feelings are so abnormally feeble and cold that, when his dislike is roused, or when an indifferent person comes in the way of his purpose, there is scarcely anything within him to prevent his applying the torture.

What is it that provokes his dislike or hostility? Here again we must look closely. Iago has been represented as an incarnation of envy, as a man who, being determined to get on in the world, regards everyone else with enmity as his rival. But this idea, though containing truth, seems much exaggerated. Certainly he is devoted to himself; but if he were an eagerly ambitious man, surely we should see much more positive signs of this ambition; and surely too, with his great powers, he would already have risen high, instead of being a mere ensign, short of money, and playing Captain Rook to Roderigo's Mr. Pigeon. Taking all the facts, one must conclude that his desires were comparatively moderate and his ambition weak; that he probably enjoyed war keenly, but, if he had money enough, did not exert himself greatly to acquire reputation or position; and, therefore, that he was not habitually burning with envy and actively hostile to other men as possible competitors.

But what is clear is that Iago is keenly sensitive to anything that touches his pride or self-esteem. It would be most unjust to call him vain, but he has a high opinion of himself and a great contempt for others. He is quite aware of his superiority to them in certain respects; and he either disbelieves in or despises the qualities in which they are superior to him. Whatever disturbs or wounds his sense of superiority irritates him at once; and in *that* sense he is highly competitive. This is why the appointment of Cassio provokes him. This is why Cassio's scientific attainments provoke him. This is the reason of his jealousy of Emilia. He does not care for his wife; but the fear of another man's getting the better of him, and exposing him to pity or derision as an unfortunate husband, is wormwood to him; and as he is sure that no woman is virtuous at heart, this fear is ever with him. For much the same reason he has a spite against goodness in men (for it is characteristic that he is less blind to its existence in men, the stronger, than in women, the weaker). He has a spite against it, not from any love of evil for evil's sake, but partly because it annoys his intellect as a stupidity; partly (though he hardly knows this) because it weakens his satisfaction with himself, and disturbs his faith that egoism is the right and proper thing; partly because, the world being such a fool, goodness is popular and prospers. But he, a man ten times as able as Cassio or even Othello, does not greatly prosper. Somehow, for all the stupidity of these open and generous people, they get on better than the 'fellow of some soul.' And this, though he is not particularly eager to get on, wounds his pride. Goodness therefore annoys him. He is always ready to scoff at it, and would like to strike at it. In ordinary circumstances these feelings of irritation are not vivid in Iago—*no* feeling is so—but they are constantly present.

4

Our task of analysis is not finished; but we are now in a position to consider the rise of Iago's tragedy. Why did he act as we see him acting in the play? What is the answer to that appeal of Othello's:

> Will you, I pray, demand that demi-devil
> Why he hath thus ensnared my soul and body?

This question Why? is *the* question about Iago, just as the question Why did Hamlet delay? is *the* question about Hamlet. Iago refused to answer it; but I will venture to say that he *could* not have answered it, any more than Hamlet could tell why he delayed. But Shakespeare knew the answer, and if these characters are great creations and not blunders we ought to be able to find it too.

Is it possible to elicit it from Iago himself against his will? He makes various statements to Roderigo, and he has several soliloquies. From these sources, and especially from the latter, we should learn something. For with Shakespeare soliloquy generally gives information regarding the secret springs as well as the outward course of the plot; and, moreover, it is a curious point of technique with him that the soliloquies of his villains sometimes read almost like explanations offered to the audience. Now, Iago repeatedly offers explanations either to Roderigo or to himself. In the first place, he says more than once that he 'hates' Othello. He gives two reasons for his hatred. Othello has made Cassio lieutenant; and he suspects, and has heard it reported, that Othello has an intrigue with Emilia. Next there is Cassio. He never says he hates Cassio, but he finds in him three causes of offence: Cassio has been preferred to him; he suspects *him* too of an intrigue with Emilia; and, lastly, Cassio has a daily beauty in his life which makes Iago ugly. In addition to these annoyances he wants Cassio's place. As for Roderigo, he calls him a snipe, and who can hate a snipe? But Roderigo knows too much; and he is becoming a nuisance, getting angry, and asking for the gold and jewels he handed to Iago to give to Desdemona. So Iago kills Roderigo. Then for Desdemona: a fig's-end for her virtue! but he has no ill-will to her. In fact he 'loves' her, though he is good enough to explain, varying the word, that his 'lust' is mixed with a desire to pay Othello in his own coin. To be sure she must die, and so must Emilia, and so would Bianca if only the authorities saw things in their true light; but he did not set out with any hostile design against these persons.

Is the account which Iago gives of the causes of his action the true account? The answer of the most popular view will be, 'Yes. Iago was, as he says, chiefly incited by two things, the desire of advancement, and a hatred of Othello due principally to the affair of the lieutenancy. These are perfectly intelligible causes;

we have only to add to them unusual ability and cruelty, and all is explained. Why should Coleridge and Hazlitt and Swinburne go further afield?' To which last question I will at once oppose these: If your view is correct, why should Iago be considered an extraordinary creation; and is it not odd that the people who reject it are the people who elsewhere show an exceptional understanding of Shakespeare?

The difficulty about this popular view is, in the first place, that it attributes to Iago what cannot be found in the Iago of the play. Its Iago is impelled by *passions*, a passion of ambition and a passion of hatred; for no ambition or hatred short of passion could drive a man who is evidently so clear-sighted, and who must hitherto have been so prudent, into a plot so extremely hazardous. Why, then, in the Iago of the play do we find no sign of these passions or of anything approaching to them? Why, if Shakespeare meant that Iago was impelled by them, does he suppress the signs of them? Surely not from want of ability to display them. The poet who painted Macbeth and Shylock understood his business. Who ever doubted Macbeth's ambition or Shylock's hate? And what resemblance is there between these passions and any feeling that we can trace in Iago? The resemblance between a volcano in eruption and a flameless fire of coke; the resemblance between a consuming desire to hack and hew your enemy's flesh, and the resentful wish, only too familiar in common life, to inflict pain in return for a slight. Passion, in Shakespeare's plays, is perfectly easy to recognise. What vestige of it, of passion unsatisfied or of passion gratified, is visible in Iago? None: that is the very horror of him. He has *less* passion than an ordinary man, and yet he does these frightful things. The only ground for attributing to him, I do not say a passionate hatred, but anything deserving the name of hatred at all, is his own statement, 'I hate Othello'; and we know what his statements are worth.

But the popular view, beside attributing to Iago what he does not show, ignores what he does show. It selects from his own account of his motives one or two, and drops the rest; and so it makes everything natural. But it fails to perceive how unnatural, how strange and suspicious, his own account is. Certainly he assigns motives enough; the difficulty is that he assigns so many. A man moved by simple passions due to simple causes does not stand fingering his feelings, industriously enumerating their sources, and groping about for new ones. But this is what Iago does. And this is not all. These motives appear and disappear in the most extraordinary manner. Resentment at Cassio's appointment is expressed in the first conversation with Roderigo, and from that moment is never once mentioned again in the whole play. Hatred of Othello is expressed in the First Act alone. Desire to get Cassio's place scarcely appears after the first soliloquy, and when it is gratified Iago does not refer to it by a single word. The suspicion of Cassio's intrigue with Emilia emerges suddenly, as an afterthought, not in the first soliloquy but the second, and then disappears for ever. Iago's 'love' of Desdemona is alluded to in the second soliloquy; there is not the faintest trace of it in word or deed either before or after. The mention of jealousy of Othello is followed by declarations that Othello is infatuated about Desdemona and is of a constant nature, and during Othello's sufferings Iago never shows a sign of the idea that he is now paying his rival in his own coin. In the second soliloquy he declares that he quite believes Cassio to be in love with Desdemona; it is obvious that he believes no such thing, for he never alludes to the idea again, and within a few hours describes Cassio in soliloquy as an honest fool. His final reason for ill-will to Cassio never appears till the Fifth Act.

What is the meaning of all this? Unless Shakespeare was out of his mind, it must have a meaning. And certainly this meaning is not contained in any of the popular accounts of Iago.

Is it contained then in Coleridge's word 'motive-hunting'? Yes, 'motive-hunting' exactly answers to the impression that Iago's soliloquies produce. He is pondering his design, and unconsciously trying to justify it to himself. He speaks of one or two real feelings, such as resentment against Othello, and he mentions one or two real causes of these feelings. But these are not enough for him. Along with them, or alone, there come into his head, only to leave it again, ideas and suspicions, the creations of his own baseness or uneasiness, some old, some new, caressed for a moment to feed his purpose and give it a reasonable look, but never really believed in, and never the main forces which are determining his action. In fact, I would venture to describe Iago in these soliloquies as a man setting out on a project which strongly attracts his desire, but at the same time conscious of a resistance to the desire, and unconsciously trying to argue the resistance away by assigning reasons for the project. He is the counterpart of Hamlet, who tries to find reasons for his delay in pursuing a design which excites his aversion. And most of Iago's reasons for action are no more the real ones than Hamlet's reasons for delay were the real ones. Each is moved by forces which he does not understand; and it is probably no accident that these two studies of states psychologically so similar were produced at about the same period.

What then were the real moving forces of Iago's action? Are we to fall back on the idea of a 'motiveless malignity;' that is to say, a disinterested love of evil, or a delight in the pain of others as simple and direct as the delight in one's own pleasure? Surely not. I will not insist that this thing or these things are inconceivable, mere phrases, not ideas; for, even so, it would remain possible that Shakespeare had tried to represent an inconceivability. But there is not the slightest reason to suppose that he did so. Iago's action is intelligible; and indeed the popular view contains enough truth to refute this desperate theory. It greatly exaggerates his desire for advancement, and the ill-will caused by his disappointment, and it ignores other forces more important than these; but it is right in insisting on the presence of this desire and this ill-will, and their presence is enough to destroy Iago's claims to be more than a demi-devil. For love of the evil that advances my interest and hurts a person I dislike, is a very different thing from love of evil simply as evil; and pleasure in the pain of a person disliked or regarded as a competitor is quite distinct from pleasure in the pain of others simply as others. The first is intelligible, and we find it in Iago. The second, even if it were intelligible, we do not find in Iago.

Still, desire of advancement and resentment about the lieutenancy, though factors and indispensable factors in the cause of Iago's action, are neither the principal nor the most characteristic factors. To find these, let us return to our half-completed analysis of the character. Let us remember especially the keen sense of superiority, the contempt of others, the sensitiveness to everything which wounds these feelings, the spite against goodness in men as a thing not only stupid but, both in its nature and by its success, contrary to Iago's nature and irritating to his pride. Let us remember in addition the annoyance of having always to play a part, the consciousness of exceptional but unused ingenuity and address, the enjoyment of action, and the absence of fear. And let us ask what would be the greatest pleasure of such a man, and what the situation which might tempt him to abandon his habitual prudence and pursue this pleasure. Hazlitt and Mr. Swinburne do not put this question, but the answer I proceed to give to it is in principle theirs.

The most delightful thing to such a man would be something that gave an extreme satisfaction to his sense of power and superiority; and if it involved, secondly, the triumphant exertion of his abilities, and, thirdly, the excitement of danger, his delight would be consummated. And the moment most dangerous to such a man would be one when his sense of superiority had met with an affront, so that its habitual craving was reinforced by resentment, while at the same time he saw an opportunity of satisfying it by subjecting to his will the very persons who had affronted it. Now, this is the temptation that comes to Iago. Othello's eminence, Othello's goodness, and his own dependence on Othello, must have been a perpetual annoyance to him. At *any* time he would have enjoyed befooling and tormenting Othello. Under ordinary circumstances he was restrained, chiefly by self-interest, in some slight degree perhaps by the faint pulsations of conscience or humanity. But disappointment at the loss of the lieutenancy supplied the touch of lively resentment that was required to overcome these obstacles; and the prospect of satisfying the sense of power by mastering Othello through an intricate and hazardous intrigue now became irresistible. Iago did not clearly understand what was moving his desire; though he tried to give himself reasons for his action, even those that had some reality made but a small part of the motive force; one may almost say they were no more than the turning of the handle which admits the driving power into the machine. Only once does he appear to see something of the truth. It is when he uses the phrase '*to plume up my will* in double knavery.'

To 'plume up the will,' to heighten the sense of power or superiority—this seems to be the unconscious motive of many acts of cruelty which evidently do not spring chiefly from ill-will, and which therefore puzzle and sometimes horrify us most. It is often this that makes a man bully the wife or children of whom he is fond. The boy who torments another boy, as we say, 'for no reason,' or who without any hatred for frogs tortures a frog, is pleased with his victim's pain, not from any disinterested love of evil or pleasure in pain, but mainly because this pain is the unmistakable proof of his own power over his victim. So it is with Iago. His thwarted sense of superiority wants satisfaction. What fuller satisfaction could it find than the consciousness that he is the master of the General who has undervalued him and of the rival who has been preferred to him; that these worthy people, who are so successful and popular and stupid, are mere puppets in his hands, but living puppets, who at the motion of his finger must contort themselves in agony, while all the time they believe that he is their one true friend and comforter? It must have been an ecstasy of bliss to him. And this, granted a most abnormal deadness of human feeling, is, however horrible, perfectly intelligible. There is no mystery in the psychology of Iago; the mystery lies in a further question, which the drama has not to answer, the question why such a being should exist.

Iago's longing to satisfy the sense of power is, I think, the strongest of the forces that drive him on. But there are two others to be noticed. One is the pleasure in an action very difficult and perilous and, therefore, intensely exciting. This action sets all his powers on the strain. He feels the delight of one who executes successfully a feat thoroughly congenial to his special aptitude, and only just within his compass; and, as he is fearless by nature, the fact that a single slip will cost him his life only increases his pleasure. His exhilaration breaks out in the ghastly words with which he greets the sunrise after the night of the drunken tumult which has led to Cassio's disgrace: 'By the mass, 'tis morning. Pleasure and action make the hours seem short.' Here, however, the joy in exciting action is quickened by other feelings. It appears more simply elsewhere in such a way as to suggest that nothing but such actions gave him happiness, and that his happiness was greater if the action was destructive as well as exciting. We find it, for instance, in his gleeful cry to Roderigo, who proposes to shout to Brabantio in order to wake him and tell him of his daughter's flight:

> Do, with like timorous accent and dire yell
> As when, by night and negligence, the fire
> Is spied in populous cities.

All through that scene; again, in the scene where Cassio is attacked and Roderigo murdered; everywhere where Iago is in physical action, we catch this sound of almost feverish enjoyment. His blood, usually so cold and slow, is racing through his veins.

But Iago, finally, is not simply a man of action; he is an artist. His action is a plot, the intricate plot of a drama, and in the conception and execution of it he experiences the tension and the joy of artistic creation. 'He is,' says Hazlitt, 'an amateur of tragedy in real life; and, instead of employing his invention on imaginary characters or long-forgotten incidents, he takes the bolder and more dangerous course of getting up his plot at home, casts the principal parts among his newest friends and connections, and rehearses it in downright earnest, with steady nerves and unabated resolution.' Mr. Swinburne lays even greater stress on this aspect of Iago's character, and even declares that 'the very subtlest and strongest component of his complex nature' is 'the instinct of what Mr. Carlyle would call an inarticulate poet.' And those to whom this idea is unfamiliar, and who may suspect it at first sight of being fanciful, will find, if they examine the play in the light of Mr. Swinburne's exposition, that it rests on a true and deep perception, will stand scrutiny, and might easily be illustrated. They may observe, to take only one point, the curious analogy between the early stages of dramatic composition and those soliloquies in which Iago broods over his plot, drawing at first only an outline, puzzled how to fix more than the main idea, and gradually seeing it develop and clarify as he works upon it or lets it work. Here at any rate Shakespeare put a good deal of himself into Iago. But the tragedian in real life was not the equal of the tragic poet. His psychology, as we shall see, was at fault at a critical point, as Shakespeare's never was. And so his catastrophe came out wrong, and his piece was ruined.

Such, then, seem to be the chief ingredients of the force which, liberated by his resentment at Cassio's promotion, drives Iago from inactivity into action, and sustains him through it. And, to pass to a new point, this force completely possesses him; it is his fate. It is like the passion with which a tragic hero wholly identifies himself, and which bears him on to his doom. It is true that, once embarked on his course, Iago *could* not turn back, even if this passion did abate; and it is also true that he is compelled, by his success in convincing Othello, to advance to conclusions of which at the outset he did not dream. He is thus caught in his own web, and could not liberate himself if he would. But, in fact, he never shows a trace of wishing to do so, not a trace of hesitation, of looking back, or of fear, any more than of remorse; there is no ebb in the tide. As the crisis approaches there passes through his mind a fleeting doubt whether the deaths of Cassio and Roderigo are indispensable; but that uncertainty, which does not concern the main issue, is dismissed, and he goes forward with undiminished zest. Not even in his sleep—as in Richard's before his final battle—does any rebellion of outraged conscience or pity, or any foreboding of despair, force itself into clear consciousness. His fate—which is himself—has completely mastered him: so that, in the later scenes, where the improbability of the entire success of a design built on so many different falsehoods forces itself on the reader, Iago appears for moments not as a consummate schemer, but as a man absolutely infatuated and delivered over to certain destruction.

5

Iago stands supreme among Shakespeare's evil characters because the greatest intensity and subtlety of imagination have gone to his making, and because he illustrates in the most perfect combination the two facts concerning evil which seem to have impressed Shakespeare most. The first of these is the fact that perfectly sane people exist in whom fellow-feeling of any kind is so weak that an almost absolute egoism becomes possible to them, and with it those hard vices—such as ingratitude and cruelty—which to Shakespeare were far the worst. The second is that such evil is compatible, and even appears to ally itself easily, with exceptional powers of will and intellect. In the latter respect Iago is nearly or quite the equal of Richard, in egoism he is the superior, and his inferiority in passion and massive force only makes him more repulsive. How is it then that we can bear to contemplate him; nay, that, if we really imagine him, we feel admiration and some kind of sympathy? Henry the Fifth tells us:

> There is some soul of goodness in things evil,
> Would men observingly distil it out;

but here, it may be said, we are shown a thing absolutely evil, and—what is more dreadful still—this absolute evil is united with supreme intellectual power. Why is the representation tolerable, and why do we not accuse its author either of untruth or of a desperate pessimism?

To these questions it might at once be replied: Iago does not stand alone; he is a factor in a whole; and we perceive him there and not in isolation, acted upon as well as acting, destroyed as well as destroying. But, although this is true and important, I pass it by and, continuing to regard him by himself, I would make three remarks in answer to the questions.

In the first place, Iago is not merely negative or evil—far from it. Those very forces that moved him and made his fate—sense of power, delight in performing a difficult and dangerous action, delight in the exercise of artistic skill—are not at all evil things. We sympathise with one or other of them almost every day of our lives. And, accordingly, though in Iago they are combined with something detestable and so contribute to evil, our perception of them is accompanied with sympathy. In the same way, Iago's insight, dexterity, quickness, address, and the like, are in themselves admirable things; the perfect man would possess them. And certainly he would possess also Iago's courage and self-control, and, like Iago, would stand above the impulses of mere feeling, lord of his inner world. All this goes to evil ends in Iago, but in itself it has a great worth; and, although in reading, of course, we do not sift it out and regard it separately, it inevitably affects us and mingles admiration with our hatred or horror.

All this, however, might apparently co-exist with absolute egoism and total want of humanity. But, in the second place, it is not true that in Iago this egoism and this want are absolute, and that in this sense he is a thing of mere evil. They are frightful, but if they were absolute Iago would be a monster, not a man. The fact is, he *tries* to make them absolute and cannot succeed; and the traces of conscience, shame and humanity, though faint, are discernible. If his egoism were absolute he would be perfectly indifferent to the opinion of others; and he clearly is not so. His very irritation at goodness, again, is a sign that his faith in his creed is not entirely firm; and it is not entirely firm because he himself has a perception, however dim, of the goodness of goodness. What is the meaning of the last reason he gives himself for killing Cassio:

> He hath a daily beauty in his life
> That makes me ugly?

Does he mean that he is ugly to others? Then he is not an absolute egoist. Does he mean that he is ugly to himself? Then he makes an open confession of moral sense. And, once more, if he really possessed no moral sense, we should never have heard those soliloquies which so clearly betray his uneasiness and his unconscious desire to persuade himself that he has some excuse for the villainy he contemplates. These seem to be indubitable proofs that, against his will, Iago is a little better than his creed, and has failed to withdraw himself wholly from the human atmosphere about him. And to these proofs I would add, though with less confidence, two others. Iago's momentary doubt towards the end whether Roderigo and Cassio must be killed has always surprised me. As a mere matter of calculation it is perfectly obvious that they must; and I believe his hesitation is not merely intellectual, it is another symptom of the obscure working of conscience or humanity. Lastly, is it not significant that, when once his plot has begun to develop, Iago never seeks the presence of Desdemona; that he seems to leave her as quickly as he can (iii. iv. 138); and that, when he is fetched by Emilia to see her in her distress (iv. ii. 110 ff.), we fail to catch in his words any sign of the pleasure he shows in Othello's misery, and seem rather to perceive a certain discomfort, and, if one dare say it, a faint touch of shame or remorse? This interpretation of the passage, I admit, is not inevitable, but to my mind (quite apart from any theorising about Iago) it seems the natural one. And if it is right, Iago's discomfort is easily understood; for Desdemona is the one person concerned against whom it is impossible for him even to imagine a ground of resentment, and so an excuse for cruelty.

There remains, thirdly, the idea that Iago is a man of supreme intellect who is at the same time supremely wicked. That he is supremely wicked nobody will doubt; and I have claimed for him nothing that will interfere with his right to that title. But to say that his intellectual power is supreme is to make a great mistake. Within certain limits he has indeed extraordinary penetration, quickness, inventiveness, adaptiveness; but the limits are defined with the hardest of lines, and they are narrow limits. It would scarcely be unjust to call him simply astonishingly clever, or simply a consummate master of intrigue. But compare him with one who may perhaps be roughly called a bad man of supreme intellectual power, Napoleon, and you see how small and negative Iago's mind is, incapable of Napoleon's military achievements, and much more incapable of his political constructions. Or, to keep within the Shakespearean world, compare him with Hamlet, and you perceive how miserably close is his intellectual horizon; that such a thing as a thought beyond the reaches of his soul has never come near him; that he is prosaic through and through, deaf and blind to all but a tiny fragment of the meaning of things. Is it not quite absurd, then, to call him a man of supreme intellect?

And observe, lastly, that his failure in perception is closely connected with his badness. He was destroyed by the power that he attacked, the power of love; and he was destroyed by it because he could not understand it; and he could not understand it because it was not in him. Iago never meant his plot to be so dangerous to himself. He knew that jealousy is painful, but the jealousy of a love like Othello's he could not imagine, and he found himself involved in murders which were no part of his original design. That difficulty he surmounted, and his changed plot still seemed to prosper. Roderigo and Cassio and Desdemona once dead, all will be well. Nay, when he fails to kill Cassio, all may still be well. He will avow that he told Othello of the adultery, and persist that he told the truth, and Cassio will deny it in vain. And then, in a moment, his plot is shattered by a blow from a quarter where he never dreamt of danger. He knows his wife, he thinks. She is not over-scrupulous, she will do anything to please him, and she has learnt obedience. But one thing in her he does not know—that she *loves* her mistress and would face a hundred deaths sooner than see her fair fame darkened. There is genuine astonishment in his outburst 'What! Are you mad?' as it dawns upon him that she means to speak the truth about the handkerchief. But he might well have applied to himself the words she flings at Othello,

> O gull! O dolt!
> As ignorant as dirt!

The foulness of his own soul made him so ignorant that he built into the marvellous structure of his plot a piece of crass stupidity.

To the thinking mind the divorce of unusual intellect from goodness is a thing to startle; and Shakespeare clearly felt it so. The combination of unusual intellect with extreme evil is more than startling, it is frightful. It is rare, but it exists; and Shakespeare represented it in Iago. But the alliance of evil like Iago's with *supreme* intellect is an impossible fiction; and Shakespeare's fictions were truth.

———ⁿⁿ⌐ ———ⁿⁿ⌐ ———ⁿⁿ⌐

1927—T. S. Eliot. "The Hero Cheering Himself Up," from "Shakespeare and the Stoicism of Seneca"

T. S. Eliot (1888-1965) was one of the great poets of the twentieth century as well as one of the most influential literary critics.

. . . I have always felt that I have never read a more terrible exposure of human weakness—of universal human weakness—than the last great speech of Othello. I am ignorant whether any one else has ever adopted this view, and it may appear subjective and fantastic in the extreme. It is usually taken on its face value, as expressing the greatness in defeat of a noble but erring nature:

> Soft you; a word or two before you go.
> I have done the state some service, and they know't—
> No more of that. —I pray you, in your letters,
> When you shall these unlucky deeds relate,
> Speak of me as I am; nothing extenuate,
> Nor set down aught in malice: then must you speak
> Of one that loved not wisely but too well;
> Of one not easily jealous, but being wrought
> Perplex'd in the extreme; of one whose hand,
> Like the base Indian, threw a pearl away
> Richer than all his tribe; of one whose subdued eyes,
> Albeit unused to the melting mood,
> Drop tears as fast as the Arabian trees
> Their medicinal gum. Set you down this;
> And say besides, that in Aleppo once,
> Where a malignant and a turban'd Turk
> Beat a Venetian and traduced the state,
> I took by the throat the circumcised dog,
> And smote him—thus.

What Othello seems to me to be doing in making this speech is cheering himself up. He is endeavoring to escape reality, he has ceased to think about Desdemona, and is thinking about himself. Humility is the most difficult of all the virtues to achieve; nothing dies harder than the desire to think well of oneself. Othello succeeds in turning himself into a pathetic figure, by adopting an *aesthetic* rather than a moral attitude, dramatising himself against his environment. He takes in the spectator, but the human motive is primarily to take in himself. I do not believe that any writer has ever exposed this *bovarysme*, the human will to see things as they are not, more clearly than Shakespeare.

⤙⫸⫷ ⫸⫷ ⫸⤚

1930—G. Wilson Knight.
"The *Othello* Music," from *The Wheel of Fire*

G. Wilson Knight was a professor of English at Leeds University and also taught at the University of Toronto. At both universities he produced and acted in Shakespeare's plays. In addition, Knight wrote plays for the British stage and television. His books include *Shakespearean Production* and *Lord Byron: Christian Virtues*, but his most famous is *The Wheel of Fire*.

In *Othello* we are faced with the vividly particular rather than the vague and universal. The play as a whole has a distinct formal beauty: within it we are ever confronted with beautiful and solid forms. The persons tend to appear as warmly human, concrete. They are neither vaguely universalized, as in *King Lear* or *Macbeth*, nor deliberately mechanized and vitalized by the poet's philosophic plan as in *Measure for Measure* and *Timon of Athens*, wherein the significance of the dramatic person is dependent almost wholly on our understanding of the allegorical or symbolical meaning. It is true that Iago is here a mysterious, inhuman creature of unlimited cynicism: but the very presence of the concrete creations around, in differentiating him sharply from the rest, limits and defines him. *Othello* is a story of intrigue rather than a visionary statement. If, however, we tend to regard Othello, Desdemona, and Iago as suggestive symbols rather than human beings, we may, from a level view of their interaction, find a clear relation existing between *Othello* and other plays of the hate-theme. Such an analysis will be here only in part satisfactory. It exposes certain underlying ideas, abstracts them from the original: it is less able to interpret the whole positive beauty of the play. With this important reservation, I shall push the interpretative method as far as possible.

 Othello is dominated by its protagonist. Its supremely beautiful effects of style are all expressions of Othello's personal passion. Thus, in first analysing *Othello*'s poetry, we shall lay the basis for an understanding of the play's symbolism: this matter of style is, indeed, crucial, and I shall now indicate

those qualities which clearly distinguish it from other Shakespearian poetry. It
holds a rich music all its own, and possesses a unique solidity and precision of
picturesque phrase or image, a peculiar chastity and serenity of thought. It is,
as a rule, barren of direct metaphysical content. Its thought does not mesh with
the reader's: rather it is always outside us, aloof. This aloofness is the resultant
of an inward aloofness of image from image, word from word. The dominant
quality is separation, not, as is more usual in Shakespeare, cohesion. Consider
these exquisite poetic movements:

> O heavy hour!
> Methinks it should be now a huge eclipse
> Of sun and moon, and that the affrighted globe
> Should yawn at alteration.
> (V. ii. 97)

Or,

> It is the very error of the moon;
> She comes more near the earth than she was wont,
> And makes men mad.
> (V. ii. 107)

These are solid gems of poetry which lose little by divorce from their context:
wherein they differ from the finest passages of *King Lear* or *Macbeth*, which are
as wild flowers not to be uptorn from their rooted soil if they are to live. In these
two quotations we should note how the human drama is thrown into sudden
contrast and vivid, unexpected relation with the tremendous concrete machinery
of the universe, which is thought of in terms of individual heavenly bodies: 'sun'
and 'moon'. The same effect is apparent in:

> Nay, had she been true,
> If Heaven would make me such another world
> Of one entire and perfect chrysolite,
> I'd not have sold her for it.
> (V. ii. 141)

Notice the single word 'chrysolite' with its outstanding and remote beauty: this
is typical of *Othello*.

The effect in such passages is primarily one of contrast. The vastness of the
night sky, and its moving planets, or the earth itself—here conceived objectively
as a solid, round, visualized object—these things, though thrown momentarily
into sensible relation with the passions of man, yet remain vast, distant, separate,

seen but not apprehended; something against which the dramatic movement may be silhouetted, but with which it cannot be merged. This poetic use of heavenly bodies serves to elevate the theme, to raise issues infinite and unknowable. Those bodies are not, however, implicit symbols of man's spirit, as in *King Lear*: they remain distinct, isolated phenomena, sublimely decorative to the play. In *Macbeth* and *King Lear* man commands the elements and the stars: they are part of him. Compare the above quotations from *Othello* with this from *King Lear*:

> You nimble lightnings, dart your blinding flames
> Into her scornful eyes! Infect her beauty,
> You fen-suck'd fogs, drawn by the powerful sun,
> To fall and blast her pride.
>   (II. iv. 167)

This is typical: natural images are given a human value. They are insignificant, visually: their value is only that which they bring to the human passion which cries out to them. Their aesthetic grandeur, in and for themselves, is not relevant to the *King Lear* universe. So, too, Macbeth cries

>   Stars, hide your fires;
> Let not light see my black and deep desires.
>   (I. iv. 50)

And Lady Macbeth:

>   Come, thick night,
> And pall thee in the dunnest smoke of Hell,
> That my keen knife see not the wound it makes,
> Nor Heaven peep through the blanket of the dark,
> To cry 'Hold, hold!'
>   (I. v. 51)

Here, and in the *King Lear* extract, there is no clear visual effect as in *Othello*: tremendous images and suggestions are evoked only to be blurred as images by the more powerful passion which calls them into being. Images in *Macbeth* are thus continually vague, mastered by passion; apprehended, but not seen. In Othello's poetry they are concrete, detached; seen but not apprehended. We meet the same effect in:

>   Like to the Pontic sea,
> Whose icy current and compulsive course
> Ne'er feels retiring ebb, but keeps due on

> To the Propontic and the Hellespont,
> Even so my bloody thoughts, with violent pace,
> Shall ne'er look back, ne'er ebb to humble love,
> Till that a capable and wide revenge Swallow them up.
> Now, by yond marble heaven,
> In the due reverence of a sacred vow
> I here engage my words.
>
> (III. iii. 454)

This is a strongly typical speech. The long comparison, explicitly made, where in *King Lear* or *Macbeth* a series of swiftly evolving metaphors would be more characteristic, is another example of the separateness obtaining throughout *Othello*. There is no fusing of word with word, rather a careful juxtaposition of one word or image with another. And there are again the grand single words, 'Propontic', 'Hellespont', with their sharp, clear, consonant sounds, constituting defined aural solids typical of the *Othello* music: indeed, fine single words, especially proper names, are a characteristic of this play—Anthropophagi, Ottomites, Arabian trees, 'the base Indian', the Egyptian, Palestine, Mauretania, the Sagittary, Olympus, Mandragora, Othello, Desdemona. This is a rough assortment, not all used by Othello, but it points the Othello quality of rich, often expressly consonantal, outstanding words. Now Othello's prayer, with its 'marble heaven', is most typical and illustrative. One watches the figure of Othello silhouetted against a flat, solid, moveless sky: there is a plastic, static suggestion about the image. Compare it with a similar *King Lear* prayer:

> O heavens,
> If you do love old men, if your sweet sway
> Allow obedience, if yourselves are old,
> Make it your cause; send down and take my part!
>
> (II. iv. 192)

Here we do not watch Lear: 'We are Lear.' There is no visual effect, no rigid subject–object relation between Lear and the 'heavens', nor any contrast, but an absolute unspatial unity of spirit. The heavens blend with Lear's prayer, each is part of the other. There is an intimate interdependence, not a mere juxtaposition. Lear thus identifies himself in kind with the heavens to which he addresses himself directly: Othello speaks of 'yond marble heaven', in the third person, and swears by it, does not pray to it. It is conceived as outside his interests.

This detached style, most excellent in point of clarity and stateliness, tends also to lose something in respect of power. At moments of great tension, the *Othello* style fails of a supreme effect. Capable of fine things quite unmatched in their particular quality in any other play, it nevertheless sinks sometimes to a studied artificiality, nerveless and without force. For example, Othello thinks of himself as:

> . . . one whose subdued eyes,
> Albeit unused to the melting mood,
> Drop tears as fast as the Arabian trees
> Their medicinal gum.
>
> (V. ii. 347)

Beside this we might place Macduff's

> O I could play the woman with mine eyes
> And braggart with my tongue! But, gentle heavens,
> Cut short all intermission . . .
>
> (IV. iii. 229)

Othello's lines here have a certain restrained, melodic beauty, like the 'Pontic sea' passage; both speeches use the typical *Othello* picturesque image or word; both compare, by simile, the passion of man with some picture delightful in itself, which is developed for its own sake, slightly overdeveloped—so that the final result makes us forget the emotion in contemplation of the image. Beauty has been imposed on human sorrow, rather than shown to be intrinsic therein. But Macduff's passionate utterance has not time to paint word pictures of 'yond marble heaven', or to search for abstruse geographical images of the Hellespont or Arabia. There is more force in his first line than all Othello's slightly over-strained phraseology of 'subdued eyes' and 'melting mood'. Its strength derives from the compression of metaphor and the sudden heightened significance of a single, very commonplace, word ('woman'), whereas the other style deliberately refuses power in the level prolixity of simile, and searches always for the picturesque. The *Othello* style is diffuse, leisurely, like a meandering river; the *Macbeth* style compressed, concentrated, and explosive; often jerky, leaping like a mountain torrent. But metaphor is not essential to intensest Shakespearian power. Another, still finer, passage from *King Lear* on the same theme might be adduced:

> *Cordelia.* How does my royal lord? How fares your majesty?
> *Lear.* You do me wrong to take me out o' the grave:
> Thou art a soul in bliss; but I am bound
> Upon a wheel of fire, that mine own tears
> Do scald like molten lead.
>
> (IV. vii. 44)

The extraordinary force of that ending is gained by simile: but there is no diffusion of content, no accent that does not carry the maximum of emotion. It is even more powerful than Macduff's speech, since it lacks excitability: it has the control and dignity of Othello's with the compressed, explosive quality of Macduff's. The *Othello* style does not compass the overpowering effects of *Macbeth* or *King Lear*: nor does it, as a rule, aim at them. At the most agonizing moments of Othello's story, however, there is apparent weakness: we find an exaggerated, false rhetoric.

There is a speech in *Othello* that begins in the typical restrained manner, but degenerates finally to what might almost be called bombast. It starts:

> Where should Othello go?
> Now, how dost thou look now? O ill-starr'd wench!
> Pale as thy smock! When we shall meet at compt,
> This look of thine will hurl my soul from Heaven,
> And fiends will snatch at it. Cold, cold, my girl!
> Even like thy chastity.
>
> (V. ii. 270)

Here we have the perfection of the *Othello* style. Concrete, visual, detached. Compare it with Lear's, 'Thou art a soul in bliss . . . ,' where the effect, though perhaps more powerful and immediate, is yet vague, intangible, spiritualized. Now this speech, started in a style that can in its own way challenge that of *King Lear*, rapidly degenerates as Othello's mind is represented as collapsing under the extreme of anguish:

> O cursed, cursed slave! Whip me, ye devils,
> From the possession of this heavenly sight!
> Blow me about in winds! roast me in sulphur!
> Wash me in steep-down gulfs of liquid fire!
> O Desdemona! Desdemona! dead!
> Oh! Oh! Oh!
>
> (V. ii. 276)

There is a sudden reversal of poetic beauty: these lines lack cogency because they exaggerate rather than concentrate the emotion. Place beside these violent eschatological images the passage from *King Lear*:

> And my poor fool is hang'd! No, no, no life!
> Why should a dog, a horse, a rat have life,
> And thou no breath at all? Thou'lt come no more,
> Never, never, never, never, never!

Pray you, undo this button: thank you, sir.
Do you see this? Look on her, look, her lips,
Look there, look there!

(V. iii. 307)

Notice by what rough, homely images the passion is transmitted—which are as truly an integral part of the naturalism of *King Lear* as the mosaic and polished phrase and the abstruse and picturesque allusion are, in its best passages, characteristic of Othello's speech. Thus the extreme, slightly exaggerated beauty of Othello's language is not maintained. This is even more true elsewhere. Othello, who usually luxuriates in deliberate and magnificent rhetoric, raves, falls in a trance:

> Lie with her! lie on her! We say lie on her, when they belie her. Lie with her! that's fulsome. Handkerchief—confession—handkerchief! To confess, and be hanged for his labour; first, to be hanged, and then to confess—I tremble at it. Nature would not invest herself in such shadowing passion without some instruction. It is not words that shake me thus. Pish! Noses, ears, and lips.—Is't possible?— Confess—handkerchief—O devil!
>
> (IV. i. 35)

Whereas Lear's madness never lacks artistic meaning, whereas its most extravagant and grotesque effects are presented with imaginative cogency, Othello can speak words like these. This is the Iago-spirit, the Iago medicine, at work, like an acid eating into bright metal. This is the primary fact of Othello and therefore of the play: something of solid beauty is undermined, wedged open so that it exposes an extreme ugliness.

When Othello is represented as enduring loss of control he is, as Macbeth and Lear never are, ugly, idiotic; but when he has full control he attains an architectural stateliness of quarried speech, a silver rhetoric of a kind unique in Shakespeare:

> It is the cause, it is the cause, my soul—
> Let me not name it to you, you chaste stars!—
> It is the cause. Yet I'll not shed her blood;
> Nor scar that whiter skin of hers than snow,
> And smooth as monumental alabaster.
> Yet she must die, else she'll betray more men.
> Put out the light, and then put out the light.
> If I quench thee, thou flaming minister,
> I can again thy former light restore,

Should I repent me: but once put out thy light,
Thou cunning'st pattern of excelling nature,
I know not where is that Promethean heat
That can thy light relume. When I have pluck'd the rose,
I cannot give it vital growth again,
It needs must wither: I'll smell it on the tree.
                                    (V. ii. 1)

This is the noble *Othello* music: highly-coloured, rich in sound and phrase, stately. Each word solidifies as it takes its place in the pattern. This speech well illustrates the *Othello* style: the visual or tactile suggestion—'whiter skin of hers than snow', 'smooth as monumental alabaster'; the slightly over-decorative phrase, 'flaming minister'; the momentary juxtaposition of humanity and the vast spaces of the night, the 'chaste stars'; the concrete imagery of 'thou cunning'st pattern of excelling nature', and the lengthy comparison of life with light; the presence of simple forward-flowing clarity of dignified statement and of simile in place of the super-logical welding of thought with molten thought as in the more compressed, agile, and concentrated poetry of *Macbeth* and *King Lear*; and the fine outstanding single word, 'Promethean'. In these respects Othello's speech is nearer the style of the aftermath of Elizabethan literature, the settled lava of that fiery eruption, which gave us the solid image of Marvell and the 'marmoreal phrase' of Browne: it is the most Miltonic thing in Shakespeare.

This peculiarity of style directs our interpretation in two ways. First, the tremendous reversal from extreme, almost over-decorative, beauty, to extreme ugliness—both of a kind unusual in Shakespeare—will be seen to reflect a primary truth about the play. That I will demonstrate later in my essay. Second, the concreteness and separation of image, word, or phrase, contrasting with the close-knit language elsewhere, suggests a proper approach to *Othello* which is not proper to *Macbeth* or *King Lear*. Separation is the rule throughout *Othello*. Whereas in *Macbeth* and *King Lear* we have one dominant atmosphere, built of a myriad subtleties of thought and phraseology entwining throughout, subduing our minds wholly to their respective visions, whereas each has a single quality, expresses as a whole a single statement, *Othello* is built rather of outstanding differences. In *Othello* all is silhouetted, defined, concrete. Instead of reading a unique, pervading, atmospheric suggestion—generally our key to interpretation of what happens within that atmosphere—we must here read the meaning of separate persons. The persons here are truly separate. Lear, Cordelia, Edmund all grow out of the *Lear* universe, all are levelled by its characteristic atmosphere, all blend with it and with each other, so that they are less closely and vividly defined. They lack solidity. Othello, Desdemona, Iago, however, are clearly and vividly separate. All here—but Iago—are solid, concrete. Contrast is raised to its highest pitch. Othello is statuesque, Desdemona most concretely human and individual, Iago, if not human or in any usual sense 'realistic', is quite unique. Within analysis of these three persons and their interaction lies the meaning of *Othello*. In *Macbeth* or *King Lear* we interpret primarily a singleness of vision. Here, confronted with a significant diversity, we must have regard to the essential relation existing between the three main personal conceptions. Interpretation must be based not on unity but differentiation. Therefore I shall pursue an examination of this triple symbolism; which analysis will finally resolve the difficulty of Othello's speech, wavering as it does between what at first sight appear an almost artificial beauty and an equally inartistic ugliness.

Othello radiates a world of romantic, heroic, and picturesque adventure. All about him is highly coloured. He is a Moor; he is noble and generally respected; he is proud in the riches of his achievement. Now his prowess as a soldier is emphasized. His arms have spent 'their dearest action in the tented field' (I. iii. 85). Again,

> The tyrant custom, most grave Senators,
> Hath made the flinty and steel couch of war
> My thrice-driven bed of down.
> (I. iii. 230)

His iron warriorship is suggested throughout. Iago says:

> Can he be angry? I have seen the cannon,
> When it hath blown his ranks into the air,
> And, like the Devil, from his very arm
> Puff'd his own brother:—and can he be angry?
> Something of moment then: I will go meet him:
> There's matter in't indeed, if he be angry.
> (III. iv. 133)

And Lodovico:

> Is this the noble nature
> Whom passion could not shake? Whose solid virtue
> The shot of accident, nor dart of chance,
> Could neither graze nor pierce?
> (IV. i. 276)

But we also meet a curious discrepancy. Othello tells us:

> Rude am I in my speech,
> And little bless'd with the soft phrase of peace.
> (I. iii. 81)

Yet the dominant quality in this play is the exquisitely moulded language, the noble cadence and chiselled phrase, of Othello's poetry. Othello's speech, therefore, reflects not a soldier's language, but the quality of soldiership in all its glamour of romantic adventure; it holds an imaginative realism. It has a certain exotic beauty, is a storied and romantic treasure-house of rich, colourful experiences. He recounts his adventures, telling of

> antres vast and desarts idle,
> Rough quarries, rocks, and hills whose heads touch heaven,
> > (I. iii. 140)

of Cannibals, and the Anthropophagi, and 'men whose heads do grow beneath their shoulders' (I. iii. 144). He tells Desdemona of the handkerchief given by 'an Egyptian' to his mother:

> 'Tis true: there's magic in the web of it:
> A sibyl, that had number'd in the world
> The sun to course two hundred compasses,
> In her prophetic fury sew'd the work;
> The worms were hallow'd that did breed the silk,
> And it was dyed in mummy which the skilful
> Conserved of maidens' hearts.
> > (III. iv. 70)

Swords are vivid, spiritualized things to Othello. There is his famous line:

> Keep up your bright swords, for the dew will rust them.
> > (I. ii. 59)

And in the last scene, he says:

> I have another weapon in this chamber;
> It is a sword of Spain, the ice-brook's temper.
> > (V. ii. 251)

In his address at the end, he speaks of himself as

> one whose hand,
> Like the base Indian, threw a pearl away
> Richer than all his tribe.
> > (V. ii. 345)

His tears flow as the gum from 'Arabian trees' (V. ii. 349); he recounts how in Aleppo he smote 'a malignant and a turban'd Turk' (V. ii. 352) for insulting Venice. Finally there is his noble apostrophe to his lost 'occupation':

> Farewell the plumed troop and the big wars,
> That make ambition virtue! O, farewell!
> Farewell the neighing steed and the shrill trump,
> The spirit-stirring drum, the ear-piercing fife,
> The royal banner and all quality,
> Pride, pomp, and circumstance of glorious war!
> And, O you mortal engines, whose rude throats
> The immortal Jove's dread clamours counterfeit,
> Farewell! Othello's occupation's gone.
>   (III. iii. 350)

Again, we have the addition of phrase to separate phrase, rather than the interdependence, the evolution of thought from thought, the clinging mesh of close-bound suggestions of other plays. This noble eulogy of war is intrinsic to the conception. War is in Othello's blood. When Desdemona accepts him, she knows she must not be 'a moth of peace' (I. iii. 258). Othello is a compound of highly-coloured, romantic adventure—he is himself 'coloured'—and war; together with a great pride and a great faith in those realities. His very life is dependent on a fundamental belief in the validity and nobility of human action—with, perhaps, a strong tendency towards his own achievement in particular. Now war, in Shakespeare, is usually a positive spiritual value, like love. There is reference to the soldiership of the protagonist in all the plays analysed in my present treatment. Soldiership is almost the condition of nobility, and so the Shakespearian hero is usually a soldier. Therefore Othello, with reference to the Shakespearian universe, becomes automatically a symbol of faith in human values of love, of war, of romance in a wide and sweeping sense. He is, as it were, conscious of all he stands for: from the first to the last he loves his own romantic history. He is, like Troilus, dedicated to these values, has faith and pride in both. Like Troilus he is conceived as extraordinarily direct, simple, 'credulous' (IV. i. 46). Othello, as he appears in the action of the play, may be considered the high-priest of human endeavour, robed in the vestments of romance, whom we watch serving in the temple of war at the altar of love's divinity.

Desdemona is his divinity. She is, at the same time, warmly human. There is a certain domestic femininity about her. She is 'a maiden never bold' (I. iii. 94). We hear that 'the house affairs' (had Cordelia any?) drew her often from Othello's narrative (I. iii. 147). But she asks to hear the whole history:

> I did consent,
> And often did beguile her of her tears,
> When I did speak of some distressful stroke
> That my youth suffer'd. My story being done,
> She gave me for my pains a world of sighs:
> She swore, in faith, 'twas strange, 'twas passing strange,
> 'Twas pitiful, 'twas wondrous pitiful:
> She wish'd she had not heard it, yet she wish'd
> That heaven had made her such a man.
>
> (I. iii. 155)

The same domesticity and gentleness is apparent throughout. She talks of 'to-night at supper' (III. iii. 57) or 'to-morrow dinner' (III. iii. 58); she is typically feminine in her attempt to help Cassio, and her pity for him. This is how she describes her suit to Othello:

> Why, this is not a boon;
> 'Tis as I should entreat you wear your gloves,
> Or feed on nourishing dishes, or keep you warm,
> Or sue to you to do a peculiar profit
> To your own person . . .
>
> (III. iii. 76)

—a speech reflecting a world of sex-contrast. She would bind Othello's head with her handkerchief—that handkerchief which is to become a terrific symbol of Othello's jealousy. The *Othello* world is eminently domestic, and Desdemona expressly feminine. We hear of her needlework (IV. i. 197), her fan, gloves, mask (IV. ii. 8). In the exquisite willow-song scene, we see her with her maid, Emilia. Emilia gives her 'her nightly wearing' (IV. iii. 16). Emilia says she has laid on her bed the 'wedding-sheets' (IV. ii. 104) Desdemona asked for. Then there is the willow-song, brokenly sung whilst Emilia 'unpins' (IV. iii. 34) Desdemona's dress:

> My mother had a maid called Barbara:
> She was in love, and he she loved proved mad
> And did forsake her . . .
>
> (IV. iii. 26)

The extreme beauty and pathos of this scene are largely dependent on the domesticity of it. *Othello* is eminently a domestic tragedy. But this element in the play is yet to be related to another more universal element. Othello is concretely human, so is Desdemona. Othello is very much the typical middle-aged bachelor entering matrimony late in life, but he is also, to transpose a phrase of Iago's, a symbol of human—especially masculine—'purpose, courage, and valour' (IV. ii. 218), and, in a final judgement, is seen to represent the idea of human faith and value in a very wide sense. Now Desdemona, also very human, with an individual domestic feminine charm and simplicity, is yet also a symbol of woman in general daring the unknown seas of marriage with the mystery of man. Beyond this, in the far flight of a transcendental interpretation, it is clear that she becomes a symbol of man's ideal, the supreme value of love. At the limit of the series of wider and wider suggestions which appear from imaginative contemplation of a poetic symbol she is to be equated with the divine principle. In one scene of *Othello*, and one only, direct poetic symbolism breaks across the vividly human, domestic world of this play.[1] As everything in *Othello* is separated, defined, so the plot itself is in two distinct geographical divisions: Venice and Cyprus. Desdemona leaves the safety and calm of her home for the stormy voyage to Cyprus and the tempest of the following tragedy. Iago's plot begins to work in the second part. The storm scene, between the two parts, is important.

Storms are continually symbols of tragedy in Shakespeare. This scene contains some most vivid imaginative effects, among them passages of fine storm-poetry of the usual kind:

> For do but stand upon the foaming shore,
> The chidden billow seems to pelt the clouds;
> The wind-shak'd surge, with high and monstrous mane,
> Seems to cast water on the burning bear,
> And quench the guards of the ever-fixed pole:
> I never did like molestation view,
> On the enchafed flood.
>
> (II. i. 11)

This storm-poetry is here closely associated with the human element. And in this scene where direct storm-symbolism occurs it is noteworthy that the figures of Desdemona and Othello are both strongly idealized:

> *Cassio.* Tempests themselves, high seas and howling winds,
> The gutter'd rocks and congregated sands—
> Traitors ensteep'd to clog the guiltless keel—
> As having sense of beauty, do omit
> Their mortal natures, letting go safely by
> The divine Desdemona.
> *Montano.*   What is she?
> *Cassio.* She that I spake of, our great captain's captain,
> Left in the conduct of the bold Iago,

Whose footing here anticipates our thoughts
A se'nnight's speed. Great Jove, Othello guard,
And swell his sail with thine own powerful breath,
That he may bless this bay with his tall ship,
Make love's quick pants in Desdemona's arms,
Give renew'd fire to our extincted spirits,
And bring all Cyprus comfort!
    Enter Desdemona, &c.
    O, behold,
The riches of the ship is come on shore!
Ye men of Cyprus, let her have your knees.
Hail to thee, lady! and the grace of Heaven,
Before, behind thee, and on every hand,
Enwheel thee round!
                (II. i. 68)

Desdemona is thus endued with a certain transcendent quality of beauty and
grace. She 'paragons description and wild fame' says Cassio: she is

One that excels the quirks of blazoning pens,
And in the essential vesture of creation
Does tire the ingener.
                (II. i. 63)

And Othello enters the port of Cyprus as a hero coming to 'bring comfort',
to 'give renewed fire' to men. The entry of Desdemona and that of Othello
are both heralded by discharge of guns: which both merges finely with the
tempest-symbolism and the violent stress and excitement of the scene as a
whole, and heightens our sense of the warrior nobility of the protagonist and
his wife, subdued as she is 'to the very quality' of her lord (I. iii. 253). Meeting
Desdemona, he speaks:

Othello. O my fair warrior!
Desdemona.   My dear Othello!
Othello. It gives me wonder great as my content
To see you here before me. O my soul's joy!
If after every tempest come such calms,
May the winds blow till they have waken'd death!
And let the labouring bark climb hills of seas
Olympus-high and duck again as low
As Hell's from Heaven! If it were now to die,
'Twere now to be most happy; for, I fear,

My soul hath her content so absolute
That not another comfort like to this
Succeeds in unknown fate.

(II. i. 185)

This is the harmonious marriage of true and noble minds. Othello, Desdemona, and their love are here apparent, in this scene of storm and reverberating discharge of cannon, as things of noble and conquering strength: they radiate romantic valour. Othello is essential man in all his prowess and protective strength; Desdemona essential woman, gentle, loving, brave in trust of her warrior husband. The war is over. The storm of sea or bruit of cannonade are powerless to hurt them: yet there is another storm brewing in the venomed mind of Iago. Instead of merging with and accompanying tragedy the storm here is to be contrasted with the following tragic events: as usual in *Othello*, contrast and separation take the place of fusion and unity. This scene is as a microcosm of the play, reflecting its action. Colours which are elsewhere softly toned are here splashed vividly on the play's canvas. Here especially Othello appears a prince of heroes, Desdemona is lit by a divine feminine radiance: both are transfigured. They are shown as coming safe to land, by Heaven's 'grace', triumphant, braving war and tempestuous seas, guns thundering their welcome. The reference of all this, on the plane of high poetic symbolism, to the play as a whole is evident.

Against these two Iago pits his intellect. In this scene too Iago declares himself with especial clarity:

O gentle lady, do not put me to't;
For I am nothing if not critical.

(II. i. 118)

His conversation with Desdemona reveals his philosophy. Presented under the cloak of fun, it exposes nevertheless his attitude to life: that of the cynic. Roderigo is his natural companion: the fool is a convenient implement, and at the same time continual food for his philosophy. Othello and Desdemona are radiant, beautiful: Iago opposes them, critical, intellectual. Like cold steel his cynic skill will run through the warm body of their love. Asked to praise Desdemona, he draws a picture of womanly goodness in a vein of mockery; and concludes:

Iago. She was a wight if ever such wight were—
Desdemona. To do what?
Iago: To suckle fools and chronicle small beer.

(II. i. 158)

Here is his reason for hating Othello's and Desdemona's love: he hates their
beauty, to him a meaningless, stupid thing. That is Iago. Cynicism is his
philosophy, his very life, his 'motive' in working Othello's ruin. The play turns on
this theme: the cynical intellect pitted against a lovable humanity transfigured by
qualities of heroism and grace. As Desdemona and Othello embrace he says:

> O you are well tuned now!
> But I'll set down the pegs that make this music,
> As honest as I am.
> (II. i. 202)

'Music' is apt: we remember Othello's rich harmony of words. Against the *Othello*
music Iago concentrates all the forces of cynic villainy.
  Iago's cynicism is recurrent:

> Virtue! a fig! 'tis in ourselves that we are thus or thus . . .
> (I. iii. 323)

Love to him is

> . . . merely a lust of the blood and a permission of the will.
> (I. iii. 339)

He believes Othello's and Desdemona's happiness will be short-lived, since he
puts no faith in the validity of love. Early in the play he tells Roderigo:

> It cannot be that Desdemona should long continue her love to the
> Moor . . . nor he his to her . . . These Moors are changeable in their wills
> . . . the food that to him now is as luscious as locusts, shall be to him
> shortly as bitter as coloquintida. She must change for youth: when she is
> sated with his body, she will find the error of her choice: she must have
> change, she must.
> (I. iii. 347)

This is probably Iago's sincere belief, his usual attitude to love: he is not
necessarily deceiving Roderigo. After this, when he is alone, we hear that he
suspects Othello with his own wife: nor are we surprised. And, finally, his own
cynical beliefs suggest to him a way of spiting Othello. He thinks of Cassio:

> After some time, to abuse Othello's ear
> That he is too familiar with his wife.
> (I. iii. 401)

The order is important: Iago first states his disbelief in Othello's and Desdemona's continued love, and next thinks of a way of precipitating its end. That is, he puts his cynicism into action. The same rhythmic sequence occurs later. Iago witnesses Cassio's meeting with Desdemona at Cyprus, and comments as follows:

> He takes her by the palm: ay, well said, whisper: with as little a web as
> this will I ensnare as great a fly as Cassio. Ay, smile upon her, do; I will
> gyve thee in thine own courtship . . .
> (II. i. 168)

Iago believes Cassio loves Desdemona. He has another cynical conversation with Roderigo as to Desdemona's chances of finding satisfaction with Othello, and the probability of her love for Cassio (II. i. 223–79). A kiss, to Iago, cannot be 'courtesy': it is

> Lechery, by this hand; an index and obscure prologue to the history of
> lust and foul thoughts.
> (II. i. 265)

Iago is sincere enough and means what he says. Cynicism is the key to his mind and actions. After Roderigo's departure, he again refers to his suspicions of Othello—and Cassio too—with his own wife. He asserts definitely—and here there is no Roderigo to impress—his belief in Cassio's guilt:

> That Cassio loves her, I do well believe it;
> That she loves him, 'tis apt and of great credit.
> (II. i. 298)

In this soliloquy he gets his plans clearer: again, they are suggested by what he believes to be truth. I do not suggest that Iago lacks conscious villainy: far from it. Besides, in another passage he shows that he is aware of Desdemona's innocence (IV. i. 48). But it is important that we observe how his attitude to life casts the form and figure of his meditated revenge. His plan arises out of the cynical depths of his nature. When, at the end, he says, 'I told him what I thought' (V. ii. 174), he is speaking at least a half-truth. He hates the romance of Othello and the loveliness of Desdemona because he is by nature the enemy of these things. Cassio, he says,

> hath a daily beauty in his life
> That makes mine ugly.
> (V. i. 19)

This is his 'motive' throughout: other suggestions are surface deep only. He is cynicism loathing beauty, refusing to allow its existence. Hence the venom of his plot: the plot is Iago—both are ultimate, causeless, self-begotten. Iago is cynicism incarnate and projected into action.

Iago is utterly devilish: no weakness is apparent in his casing armour of unrepentant villainy. He is a kind of Mephistopheles, closely equivalent to Goethe's devil, the two possessing the same qualities of mockery and easy cynicism. He is called a 'hellish villain' by Lodovico (V. ii. 367), a 'demi-devil' by Othello (V. ii. 300). Othello says:

> I look down towards his feet; but that's a fable.
> If that thou be'est a devil, I cannot kill thee.
> (V. ii. 285)

Iago himself recognizes a kinship:

> Hell and night
> Must bring this monstrous birth to the world's sight.
> (I. iii. 409)

And,

> Divinity of Hell!
> When devils will the blackest sins put on,
> They do suggest at first with heavenly shows
> As I do now.
> (II. iii. 359)

He knows that his 'poison' (III. iii. 326) will 'burn like the mines of sulphur' (III. iii. 330) in Othello. Thus Iago is, to Othello, the antithesis of Desdemona: the relation is that of the spirit of denial to the divine principle. Desdemona 'plays the god' (II. iii. 356) with Othello: if she is false, 'Heaven mocks itself' (III. iii. 278). During the action, as Iago's plot succeeds, her essential divinity changes, for Othello, to a thing hideous and devilish— that is to its antithesis:

> Her name that was as fresh
> As Dian's visage, is now begrim'd and black
> As mine own face.
> (III. iii. 387)

She is now 'devil' (IV. i. 252, 255) or 'the fair devil' (III. iii. 479); her hand, a 'sweating devil' (III. iv. 43); the 'devils themselves' will fear to seize her for her heavenly looks (IV. ii. 35). Thus Iago, himself a kind of devil, insidiously eats his way into this world of romance, chivalry, nobility. The word 'devil' occurs frequently in the latter acts: devils are alive here, ugly little demons of black disgrace. They swarm over the mental horizon of the play, occurring frequently. Iago is directly or indirectly their author and originator. 'Devil', 'Hell', 'damnation'—these words are recurrent, and continually juxtaposed to thoughts of 'Heaven', prayer, angels. We are clearly set amid 'Heaven and men and devils' (V. ii. 219). Such terms are related here primarily to sexual impurity. In *Othello*, pure love is the supreme good; impurity damnation. This pervading religious tonal significance relating to infidelity explains lines such as:

> Turn thy complexion there,
> Patience, thou young and rose-lipp'd cherubin—
> Ay, there, look grim as Hell!
> (IV. ii. 61)

Othello addresses Emilia:

> You, mistress,
> That have the office opposite to Saint Peter,
> And keep the gate of Hell!
> (IV. ii. 89)

Here faithful love is to be identified with the divine, the 'heavenly'; unfaithful love, or the mistrust which imagines it, or the cynic that gives birth to that imagination—all these are to be identified with the devil. The hero is set between the forces of Divinity and Hell. The forces of Hell win and pure love lies slain. Therefore Othello cries to 'devils' to whip him from that 'heavenly' sight (V. ii. 276). He knows himself to have been entrapped by hell-forces. The Iago–Devil association is of importance.

It will be remembered that *Othello* is a play of concrete forms. This world is a world of visual images, colour, and romance. It will also be clear that the mesh of devil-references I have just suggested show a mental horizon black, formless, colourless. They contrast with the solid, chiselled, enamelled *Othello* style elsewhere. This devil-world is insubstantial, vague, negative. Now on the plane of personification we see that Othello and Desdemona are concrete, moulded of flesh and blood, warm. Iago contrasts with them metaphysically as well as morally: he is unlimited, formless villainy. He's the spirit of denial, wholly negative. He never has visual reality. He is further blurred by the fact of his being something quite different from what he appears to the others. Is he to look like a bluff soldier, or Mephistopheles? He is a different kind of being from Othello and Desdemona: he belongs to a different world. They, by their very existence, assert the positive beauty of created forms—hence Othello's perfected style of speech, his strong human appeal, his faith in creation's values of love and war. This world of created forms, this sculptural and yet pulsing beauty, the Iago-spirit undermines, poisons, disintegrates. Iago is a demon of cynicism, colourless, formless, in a world of colours, shapes, and poetry's music. Of all these he would create chaos. Othello's words are apt:

> Excellent wretch! Perdition catch my soul
> But I do love thee! And when I love thee not,
> Chaos is come again.
>
> (III. iii. 90)

Chaos indeed. Iago works at the foundations of human values. Cassio is a soldier: he ruins him as a soldier, makes him drunk. So he ruins both Othello's love and warrior-heart. He makes him absurd, ugly. Toward the end of the play there is hideous suggestion. We hear of 'cords, knives, poison' (III. iii. 389), of lovers 'as prime as goats, as hot as monkeys' (III. iii. 404); we meet Bianca, the whore, told by Cassio to 'throw her vile guesses in the Devil's teeth' (III. iv. 183); there are Othello's incoherent mutterings, 'Pish! Noses, ears and lips!' (IV. i. 43), he will 'chop' Desdemona 'into messes' (IV. i. 210); she reminds him of 'foul toads' (IV. ii. 60). Watching Cassio, he descends to this:

> O! I see that nose of yours, but not the dog I shall throw it to.
>
> (IV. i. 144)

Othello strikes Desdemona, behaves like a raging beast. 'Fire and brimstone!' (IV. i. 246) he cries, and again, 'Goats and monkeys!' (IV. i. 274). 'Heaven stops the nose' at Desdemona's impurity (IV. ii. 76). Othello in truth behaves like 'a beggar in his drink' (IV. ii. 120). In all these phrases I would emphasize not the sense and dramatic relevance alone, but the suggestion—the accumulative effect of ugliness, hellishness, idiocy, negation. It is a formless, colourless essence, insidiously undermining a world of concrete, visual, richly-toned forms. That is the Iago-spirit embattled against the domesticity, the romance, the idealised humanity of the *Othello* world.

Here, too, we find the reason for the extreme contrast of Othello's two styles: one exotically beautiful, the other blatantly absurd, ugly. There is often no dignity in Othello's rage. There is not meant to be. Iago would make discord of the *Othello* music. Thus at his first conquest he filches something of Othello's style and uses it himself:

> Not poppy, nor mandragora,
> Nor all the drowsy syrups of the world,

Shall ever medicine thee to that sweet sleep
Which thou owed'st yesterday.

(III. iii. 331)

To him Othello's pride in his life-story and Desdemona's admiration were ever stupid:

Mark me with what violence she first loved the Moor, but for bragging and telling her fantastical lies: and will she love him still for prating?

(II. i. 225)

Iago, 'nothing if not critical', speaks some truth of Othello's style—it is 'fantastical'. As I have shown, it is somewhat over-decorative, highly-coloured. The dramatic value of this style now appears. In fact, a proper understanding of Othello's style reveals Iago's 'motive' so often questioned. There is something sentimental in Othello's language, in Othello. Iago is pure cynicism. That Iago should scheme—in this dramatic symbolism forged in terms of interacting persons—to undermine Othello's faith in himself, his wife, and his 'occupation', is inevitable. Logically, the cynic must oppose the sentimentalist: dramatically, he works his ruin by deceit and deception. That Othello often just misses tragic dignity is the price of his slightly strained emotionalism. Othello loves emotion for its own sake, luxuriates in it, like Richard II. As ugly and idiot ravings, disjointed and with no passionate dignity even, succeed Othello's swell and flood of poetry, Iago's triumph seems complete. The honoured warrior, rich in strength and experience, noble in act and repute, lies in a trance, nerveless, paralysed by the Iago-conception:

Work on, my medicine, work.

(IV. i. 45)

But Iago's victory is not absolute. During the last scene, Othello is a nobly tragic figure. His ravings are not final: he rises beyond them. He slays Desdemona finally not so much in rage, as for 'the cause' (V. ii. 1). He slays her in love. Though Desdemona fails him, his love, homeless, 'perplexed in the extreme' (V. ii. 345), endures. He will kill her and 'love her after' (V. ii. 19). In that last scene, too, he utters the grandest of his poetry. The Iago-spirit never finally envelops him, masters him, disintegrates his soul. Those gem-like miniatures of poetic movement quoted at the start of my essay are among Othello's last words. His vast love has, it is true, failed in a domestic world. But now symbols of the wide beauty of the universe enrich his thoughts: the 'chaste stars', the 'sun and moon', the 'affrighted globe', the world 'of one entire and perfect chrysolite' that may not buy a Desdemona's love. At the end we know that Othello's fault is simplicity alone. He is, indeed, 'a gull, a dolt' (V. ii. 161); he loves 'not wisely but too well' (V. ii. 343). His simple faith in himself endures: and at the end, he takes just pride in recalling his honourable service.

In this essay I have attempted to expose the underlying thought of the play. Interpretation here is not easy, nor wholly satisfactory. As all within *Othello*—save the Iago-theme—is separated, differentiated, solidified, so the play itself seems at first to be divorced from wider issues, a lone thing of meaningless beauty in the Shakespearian universe, solitary, separate, unyielding and chaste as the moon. It is unapproachable, yields itself to no easy mating with our minds. Its thought does not readily mesh with our thought. We can visualize it, admire its concrete felicities of phrase and image, the mosaic of its language, the sculptural outline of its effects, the precision and chastity of its form. But one cannot be lost in it, subdued to it, enveloped by it, as one is drenched and refreshed by the elemental cataracts of *King Lear*; one cannot be intoxicated by it as by the rich wine of *Antony and Cleopatra*. *Othello* is essentially outside us, beautiful with a lustrous, planetary beauty. Yet the Iago-conception is of a different kind from the rest of the play. This conception alone, if no other reason existed, would point the necessity of an intellectual interpretation. So we see the Iago-spirit gnawing at the root of all the *Othello* values, the *Othello* beauties; he eats into the core and heart of this romantic world, worms his way into its solidity, rotting it, poisoning it. Once this is clear, the whole play begins to have meaning. On the plane of dramatic humanity, we see a story of the cynic intriguing to ruin the soldier and his love. On the plane of poetic conception, in matters of technique, style, personification—there we see a spirit of negation, colourless, and undefined, attempting to make chaos of a world of stately, architectural, and exquisitely coloured forms. The two styles of Othello's speech illustrate this. Thus the different technique of the Othello and Iago conceptions is intrinsic with the plot of the play: in them we have the spirit of negation set against the spirit of creation. That is why Iago is undefined, devisualized, inhuman, in a play of consummate skill in concrete imagery and vivid human delineation. He is a colourless and ugly thing in a world of colour and harmony. His failure lies in this: in the final scene, at the moment of his complete triumph, Emilia dies for her mistress to the words of Desdemona's willow-song, and the *Othello* music itself sounds with a nobler cadence, a richer flood of harmonies, a more selfless and universalized flight of the imagination than before. The beauties of the *Othello* world are not finally disintegrated: they make 'a swan-like end, fading in music'.

NOTE

1. But note too the significance of the magic handkerchief *as both a symbol of domestic sanctity and the play's one link with the supernatural* (1947).

1936—William Empson.
"The Best Policy," from *Life and Letters To-Day*

William Empson (1906–1984) was a professor at Sheffield University,
a poet, and one of the finest literary critics of his time. Two of his best-
known books are *Seven Types of Ambiguity* and *Some Versions of Pastoral.*

Most people would agree with what Bradley, for example, implied, that the way
everybody calls Iago honest amounts to a criticism of the word—Shakespeare
means "a bluff forthright manner, and amusing talk, which get a man called
honest, may go with extreme dishonesty." Or indeed that this is treated as
normal, and the satire is on our nature not on language. But they would
probably maintain that Iago is not honest and does not think himself so,
and only calls himself so as a lie or an irony. It seems to me, if you leave the
matter there, that there is much to be said for what Rymer decided, when the
implications of the hearty use had become simpler and more clear-cut—that
the play is ridiculous, because that sort of villain (silly-clever, full of secret
schemes, ignorant of people) is not mistaken for that sort of honest man. This,
if true, is of course a plain fault, whatever you think about "character-analysis."
It is no use taking short cuts in these things, and I should fancy that what
Rymer said had a large truth when he said it, and also that Iago was a plausible
enough figure in his time. The only main road into this baffling subject is to
find how the characters use the term themselves.

Both Iago and Othello oppose honesty to mere truth-telling:

Oth.: I know, Iago,
Thy honesty and love doth mince this matter,
Making it light to Cassio.
Iago: It were not for our quiet, nor your good,
Nor for my manhood, honesty, or wisdom
To let you know my thoughts.

No doubt the noun tends to be more old fashioned than the adjective, but
the old "honourable" sense is as broad and vague as the new slang one; it was
easy enough to be puzzled by the word. Iago means partly "faithful to friends,"
which would go with the Restoration use, but partly I think "chaste," the version
normally used of women; what he has to say is improper. Certainly one cannot
simply treat his version of *honest* as the Restoration one—indeed, the part of the
snarling critic involves a rather puritanical view, at any rate towards other people.
It is the two notions of being ready to blow the gaff on other people and frank
to yourself about your own desires that seem to me crucial about Iago; they grow

on their own, independently of the hearty feeling that would normally humanise them; though he can be a good companion as well.

One need not look for a clear sense when he toys with the word about Cassio; the question is how it came to be so mystifying. But I think a queer kind of honesty is maintained in Iago through all the puzzles he contrives; his emotions are always expressed directly and it is only because they are clearly genuine that he can mislead Othello as to their cause.

> *Oth.*: Is he not honest? [Faithful etc.]
> *Iago*:   Honest, my lord? [Not stealing etc. Shocked.]
> *Oth.*: Honest? Ay, honest. ["Why repeat? The word is clear enough."]
> *Iago*: My lord, for aught I know. ["In *some* sense . . . ."]
>   For Michael Cassio
> I dare be sworn I think that he is honest.
> *Oth.*: I think so too.
> *Iago*:   Men should be what they seem,
> Or those that be not, would they might seem none.
> *Oth.*: Certain, men should be what they seem.
> *Iago*: Why then, I think Cassio's an honest man.

The point of these riddles is to get "not hypocritical"—"frank about his own nature" accepted as the relevant sense; Iago will readily call him honest on that basis, and Othello cannot be reassured. "Chaste" (the sense normally used of women) Cassio is not, but he is "not a hypocrite" about Bianca. Iago indeed despises him for letting her make a fool of him in public; for that and for other reasons (Cassio is young and without experience) Iago can put a contemptuous tone into the word; the feeling is genuine but not the sense it may imply. This gives room for a hint that Cassio has been "frank" to Iago in private about more things than may honestly be told. I fancy too that the idea of "not being men" gives an extra twist. Iago does not think Cassio manly nor that it is specially manly to be chaste; this allows him to agree that Cassio may be honest in the female sense about Desdemona and still keep a tone which seems to deny it—if he is, after so much encouragement, he must be "effeminate" (there is a strong idea of "manly" in *honest* and an irony on that gives its opposite). Anyway, Iago can hide what reservations he makes but show that he makes reservations: this suggests an embarrassed defence— "Taking a broad view, with the world as it is, and Cassio my friend, I can decently call him honest." This forces home the Restoration idea—"an honest dog of a fellow, straightforward about women," and completes the suspicion. It is a bad piece of writing unless you are keyed up for the shifts of the word.

The play with the feminine version is doubtful here, but he certainly does it the other way round about Desdemona, where it had more point: in the best case it is for his own amusement when alone.

> And what's he then that says I play the villain,
> When this advice is free I give and honest,
> Probal to thinking, and indeed the course
> To win the Moor again? For 'tis most easy
> The inclining Desdemona to subdue
> In any honest suit. She framed as fruitful
> As the free elements . . .

Easy, inclining, fruitful, free all push the word the same way, from "chaste" to "flat, frank and natural"; all turn the ironical admission of her virtue into a positive insult against her. The delight in juggling with the word here is close to the Machiavellian interest in plots for their own sake, which Iago could not resist and allowed to destroy him. But a good deal of the "motive-hunting" of the soliloquies must, I think, be seen as part of Iago's "honesty"; he is quite open to his own motives or preferences and interested to find out what they are.

The clear cases where Iago thinks himself honest are at a good distance from the Restoration use, they bring him into line with the series of sharp unromantic critics like Jacques and Hamlet:

> For I am nothing if not critical

he tells Desdemona to amuse her: his faults, he tells Othello, are due to an excess of this truthful virtue—

> I confess, it is my nature's plague
> To spy into abuses, and oft my virtue
> Shapes faults that are not.

There seems no doubt that he believes this and thinks it creditable, whatever policy made him say it here; indeed we know from the soliloquies it is true. Now this kind of man is really very unlike the Restoration honest fellow, and for myself I find it hard to combine them in one feeling about the word. But in a great deal of Iago's talk to Roderigo—"drown thyself! drown cats and blind puppies . . . why, thou silly gentleman, I will never love thee after"—he is a wise uncle, obviously honest in the cheerful sense, and for some time this is our main impression of him. Perhaps the main connection between the two sorts of honest men is in not being indulgent towards romantic love:

> *Oth.*: I cannot speake enough of this content,
> It stops me heere; it is too much of joye.
> And this, and this, the greatest discords be,
> That e'er our hearts shall make. (Kissing her.)
> *Iago*:   Oh you are well tun'd now;
> But ile set down the peggs that make this Musicke,
> As honeste as I am.

The grammar may read "because I am so honest" as well as "though I am so honest" and the irony may deny any resultant sense. He is ironical about the suggestions in the patronising use, which he thinks are applied to him—"low-class, and stupid, but good-natured." But he feels himself really "honest" as the kind of man who can see through nonsense; Othello's affair is a passing lust which has become a nuisance, and Iago can get it out of the way.

The suggestion of "stupid" in a patronising version of *honest* (still clear in "honest Thompson, my gardener," a Victorian, if not a present-day, use) brings it near to *fool*; there is a chance for these two rich words to overlap. Though there is an aspect of Iago in which he is the Restoration "honest fellow," who is good company because he blows the gaff, we see Iago like this mainly when he makes sport for his betters; especially when he clowns in the second act to amuse Desdemona, and she takes his real opinion of love and woman for a piece of hearty and good-natured fun. Iago's kind of honesty, he feels, is not valued as it should be: there is much in Iago of the Clown in Revolt, and the inevitable clown is almost washed out in this play to give him a free field. It is not, I think, dangerously far-fetched to take almost all Shakespeare's uses of *fool* as metaphors from the clown, whose symbolism certainly rode his imagination and was explained to the audience in most of his early plays. Now Iago's defence when Othello at last turns on him, among the rich ironies of its claim to honesty, brings in both Fool and the Vice used in *Hamlet* as an old name for the clown.

> *Iago*:   O wretched foole,
> That lou'st to make thine Honesty, a Vice!
> Oh monstrous world! Take note, take note (O World)
> To be direct and honest, is not safe.
> I thank you for this profit, and from hence
> I'll love no Friend, sith Love breeds such offence.
> *Oth.*: Nay stay: thou should'st be honest.
> *Iago*: I should be wise; for Honestie's a Foole,
> And loses that it works for.
> *Oth.*:   By the world,
> I think my wife be honeste, and thinke she is not.

What comes out here is Iago's unwillingness to be the Fool he thinks he is taken for; but it is dramatic irony as well, and that comes back to his notion of *honest*; he is fooled by the way his plans run away with him; he fails in knowledge of others and perhaps even of his own desires.

Othello swears by the world because what Iago has said about being honest in the world, suggesting what worldly people think, is what has made him doubtful; yet the senses of *honest* are quite different—chastity and truth-telling. Desdemona is called a supersubtle Venetian, and he may suspect she would agree with what Iago treats as worldly wisdom; whereas it was her simplicity that made her helpless; though again, the fatal step was her lie about the handkerchief. *Lou'st* in the second line (Folios) seems to me better than *liu'st* (Quarto), as making the frightened Iago bring in his main claim at once; the comma after *Honesty* perhaps makes the sense "loves with the effect of making" rather than "delights in making"; in any case *loue* appears a few lines down. *Breeds* could suggest sexual love, as if Iago's contempt for that has spread to his notions of friendship; Othello's marriage is what has spoilt their relations (Cassio "came a-wooing with" Othello, as a social figure, and then got the lieutenantship). In the same way Othello's two uses of *honest* here jump from "loving towards friends, which breeds honour" to (of women) "chaste." It is important I think that the feminine sense, which a later time felt to be quite distinct, is so deeply confused here with the other ones.

It is not safe to be direct either way, to be *honest* in Othello's sense or Iago's. The sanctimonious metaphor *profit* might carry satire from Iago on Puritans or show Iago to be like them. Iago is still telling a good deal of truth; the reasons he gives have always made him despise those who are faithful to their masters, if not to their friends. It is not clear that he would think himself a bad friend to his real friends. He believes there is a gaff to blow about the ideal love affair, though his evidence has had to be forced. Of course he is using *honest* less in his own way than to impose on Othello, yet there is a real element of self-pity in his complaint. It is no whitewashing of Iago—you may hate him the more for it—but he feels he is now in danger because he has gone the "direct" way to work, exposed false pretensions, and tried to be "frank" to himself about the whole situation. I do not think this is an oversubtle treatment of his words; behind his fear he is gloating over his cleverness, and seems to delight in the audience provided by the stage.

In the nightmare scene where Othello clings to the word to justify himself he comes near accepting Iago's use of it.

Emil.: My Husband!
Oth.:   Ay, 'twas he that told me first:
An honest man he is, and hates the slime
That sticks on filthy deeds . . . .

Emil.: My husband says that she was false?
Oth.:   He, woman;
I say thy husband: dost understand the word?
My friend, thy husband, honest, honest Iago.

From the sound of the last line it seems as bitter and concentrated as the previous question; to the audience it is. Yet Othello means no irony against Iago, and it is hard to invent a reason for his repetition. He may feel it painful that the coarse Iago, not Desdemona or Cassio, should be the only honest creature, or Iago's honesty may suggest the truth he told; or indeed you may call this a trick on the audience, to wind up the irony to its highest before Iago is exposed. Yet Iago would agree that one reason he was honest was that he hated the slime. The same slime would be produced, by Desdemona as well as by Othello, one would hope, if the act of love were of the most rigidly faithful character; the disgust in the metaphor is disgust at all sexuality. Iago, playing "honest" as prude, is the rat who stands up for the ideal; once Othello agrees he is finely cheated; Iago is left with his pleasures and Othello's happiness is destroyed. Iago has always despised his pleasures, always treated sex without fuss, like the lavatory; it is by this that he manages to combine the "honest dog" tone with honesty as Puritanism. The twist of the irony here is that Othello now feels humbled before such clarity. It is a purity he has failed to attain, and he accepts it as a form of honour. The hearty use and the horror of it are united in this appalling line.

The only later use comes when Othello's sword is taken from him by the State officer; a mark of disgrace, a symbol of cuckoldry; two possible negations of honour and honesty.

Oth.:   I am not valiant neither,
For every puny whipster gets my sword.
But why should honour outlive honesty?
Let it go all.

This question so sums up the play that it involves nearly all of both words; it seems finally to shatter the concept whose connecting links the play has patiently removed. There are ten other uses of *honour*. Four by Othello about himself, three by others about Othello, one by Othello about Desdemona, echoed once ironically by Iago, one ironically from Iago about heroes in general. The play has made Othello the personification of honour; if honour does not survive some test of the idea nor could Othello. And to him *honest* is "honourable," from which it was derived; a test of one is a test of the other. Outlive Desdemona's chastity, which he now admits, outlive Desdemona herself, the personification of chastity (lying again, as he insisted, with her last breath), outlive decent behaviour in, public respect for, self-respect in, Othello—all these are honour, not honesty; there is no question whether Othello outlives them. But they are not tests of an idea; what has been tested is a special sense of *honest*. Iago has been the personification of honesty, not merely to Othello but to his world; why should honour, the father of the word, live on and talk out itself; honesty, that obscure bundle of assumptions, the play has destroyed. I can see no other way to explain the force of the question here.

There is very little for anybody to add to A. C. Bradley's magnificent analysis, but one can maintain that Shakespeare, and the audience he had, and the audience he wanted, saw the thing in rather different proportions. Many of the audience were old soldiers disbanded without pension; they would dislike Cassio as the new type of officer, the boy who can displace men of experience merely because he knows enough mathematics to work the new guns. The play plays into their hands by making Cassio a young fool who can't keep his mistress in order and can't drink. Iago gets a long start at the beginning of the play, where he is enchantingly amusing and may be in the right. I am not trying to deny that by the end of the first act he is obviously the villain, and that by the end of the play we are meant to feel the mystery of his life as Othello did—

> Will you, I pray, demand that demi-devil
> Why he hath thus ensnared my soul and body?

Shakespeare can now speak his mind about Iago through the conventional final speech by the highest in rank:

> O Spartan dog,
> More fell than anguish, hunger, or the sea.

Verbal analysis is not going to weaken the main shape of the thing. But even in this resounding condemnation the *dog* is not simple. The typical Shakespearean dogmen are Apemantus and Thersites (called "dog" by Homer), malign underdogs, snarling critics, who yet are satisfactory as clowns and carry something of the claim of the disappointed idealist; on the other hand, if there is an obscure prophecy in the treatment of *honest*, surely the "honest dog" of the Restoration may cast something of his shadow before. Wyndham Lewis' interesting treatment of Iago as "fox" leaves out both these dogs, though the dog is more relevant than the fox on his analogy of tragedy to bull-baiting; indeed the clash of the two dogs goes to the root of Iago. But the *dog* symbolism is a mere incident, like that of *fool*; the thought is carried on *honest*, and I throw in the others only not to over-simplify the thing. Nor are they used to keep Iago from being a simple villain; the point is that more force was needed to make Shakespeare's audience hate Iago than to make the obviously intolerable Macbeth into a tragic hero.

There seems a linguistic difference between what Shakespeare meant by Iago and what the nineteenth century critics saw in him. They took him as an abstract term "Evil"; he is a critique on an unconscious pun. This is seen more clearly in their own personification of their abstract word; e.g. *The Turn of The Screw* and *Dr. Jekyll and Mr. Hyde*. Henry James got a great triumph over some critics who said his villains were sexual perverts (if the story meant anything they could hardly be anything else). He said "Ah, you have been letting yourself have fancies about Evil; I kept it right out of my mind." That indeed is what the story is about. Stevenson rightly made clear that *Dr. Jekyll* is about hypocrisy. You can only consider Evil as all things that destroy the good life; this has no unity; for instance, Hyde could not be both the miser and the spendthrift and whichever he was would destroy Jekyll without further accident. Evil here is merely the daydream of a respectable man, and only left vague so that respectable readers may equate it unshocked to their own daydreams. Iago may not be a "personality," but he is better than these; he is a product of a more actual interest in a word.

1951—Harold C. Goddard.
"*Othello*," from *The Meaning of Shakespeare*

Harold C. Goddard (1878-1950) was head of the English Department at Swarthmore College. One of the most important twentieth-century books on Shakespeare is his *The Meaning of Shakespeare*, published after his death.

I

Hamlet is Shakespeare's supreme interrogation, the culmination of his capacity to ask questions of life. In *Othello* life begins to answer. Not that *Hamlet* contains no answers, but they are not so much expressed as to be inferred. *Othello* speaks more directly. In it the poet's tragic genius moves from its negative to its positive phase and tragedy recovers something of that pre-Euripidean state so eloquently characterized by Nietzsche in his *Birth of Tragedy*. *Romeo and Juliet*, it is true, is always the exception. It is like an overture to the later Tragedies and contains hints and glimpses of what was to come in practically every one of them. But if Juliet is the morning star, Desdemona is the dawn—another morn risen on the mid-noon of *Hamlet*. With her, an almost unbroken line of beings begins to enter the Shakespearean world, with power not so much to solve as to put out of existence the problems which *Hamlet* propounded but to which Hamlet himself had no answer but silence.

The psychological link between *Hamlet* and *Othello* is close. The one grows out of the other as naturally as the blossom from the bud. The obvious tie between the two is that both are plays of revenge. A far subtler and more intimate one is the fact that the motifs of eavesdropping, of pouring poison in the ear ("I'll pour this pestilence into his ear"), and of the mousetrap—the sublimation of which from the literal to the figurative had already gone far in the earlier play—are in the later one carried to the psychological limit. Iago is a sort of super-eavesdropper. His plot is the last word in traps. And the scene in the third act, where he pours his vile story in the waking Othello's ear—accounted by many the most dramatic one in Shakespeare—makes the corresponding scene where Claudius murders the sleeping King Hamlet, whether as narrated by the Ghost or re-enacted in the dumb show, primitive in comparison. However, these metaphorical similarities and echoes are merely the signs of a more deep-lying organic connection. And here, again, dreams illuminate the poetic mind.

The analogy has already been noted between the successive works of a poet and the successive dreams of a dreamer. On this principle a character with a double personality in an earlier work may appear as two characters in a later one, as the promise of both Julius Caesar and Brutus, for example, may be traced in the man who was, variously, Hal, Prince Henry, and King Henry V. The imaginative energy that created Hamlet did not cease functioning when Hamlet himself expired. There could scarcely be a better example than the Prince of Denmark of the divided, or, we might better say, the dividing man. With the deep conflict within him of masculine and feminine traits, he is, as we noted, a sort of unfulfilled promise of the Platonic man-woman. It is as if the tension between these poles of his nature sought an equilibrium too unstable to be maintained, so that, like a cell that bifurcates, Hamlet in the next world—that is, in *Othello*—divides into Desdemona and Iago.

The idea must of course not he taken too literally nor pressed too far, but, within limits, it can be highly suggestive to those interested in psychic relationships of this sort. (Those who are not, or who consider them fanciful or far-fetched, may ignore this one—the rest of the argument does not depend on it.) Hamlet, it is generally admitted, is the most paradoxical mixture of good and evil. Iago is close to pure evil; Desdemona close to pure good. Hamlet's most endearing traits—his ingenuousness, his modesty, his truthfulness, his freedom, his courage, his love, his sympathetic imagination—are all Desdemona's. His darker and more detestable ones—his suspicion, his coarseness, his sarcastic wit, his critical intellect, his callousness, his cruelty, his sensuality, his savage hatred, his bloodiness, his revenge—are all Iago's. Only in dramatic imagination is the nobler Hamlet akin to Iago. But even there his final prostitution of that gift to evil[1] ties him exactly to his counterpart who notoriously did the same. What looked like an exception clinches the analogy. And the qualities of Hamlet that neither Desdemona nor Iago inherits—his melancholy, his brooding, his hesitancy, his hysteria—instead of confuting, confirm the contention: for these are the result of the strife between his two selves, and when the two have been split apart the strife naturally ceases. The strife *within* Hamlet is replaced by the strife *between* Iago and Desdemona (for the possession of Othello), or, if one prefers, is replaced by the contrast between them, the strife in that case being between Iago and that part of Othello that loves Desdemona and has faith in her. Hamlet—not quite able to slough off his atavistic traits and step into the future—divides into his components, one part going up with Desdemona, another down with Iago. (Where still other parts go will be seen later.)

It is Othello and Cassio, standing between the extremes, who in a way inherit and continue the divided nature of Hamlet. In fineness of impulse, in tenderness, in trustfulness, in openness and freedom, both of them are much like Desdemona. Shakespeare had to endow all three with these qualities to make the machinations of Iago credible. If any one of them had been lacking in faith, his plot would have been frustrated. So, in a sense, it is the triad, Othello-Cassio-Desdemona, rather than just Desdemona, with whom Iago is thrown into contrast. But Othello compared with Desdemona is vulnerable, and Cassio compared with her is common clay. Their weaknesses are Iago's opportunity and the source of the dramatic warfare.

II

And there is another bond between *Hamlet* and *Othello*—or more specifically between the Prince of Denmark and Desdemona. Both dramas emerge from a parent–child situation. Hamlet obeys his father. Desdemona disobeys hers. And the more we figure the Father to ourselves as the symbol of Authority and Force, the deeper the significance of the contrast becomes. Romeo, Hal, Brutus, and Hamlet opposed to the Father's will an energy that, viewing them as a group, steadily mounted until in Hamlet a stage of near-equilibrium was reached. Desdemona is the next term of the progression. She successfully defies the Father. It is this seemingly trifling fact that makes *Othello* the turning point of Shakespeare.

Brabantio may seem like a very diluted counterpart of the Ghost, and he is as an emissary of revenge. But his function in the play is in a negative sense the same. Like Capulet or like Portia's father, he would impose his will on the next generation. But Desdemona, unlike Hamlet, will not sacrifice her life or happiness on the altar of Authority, however willing she is to sacrifice both on the altar of Love. She stands for freedom, and her audacity in doing what she thinks right in the face of her father's opposition is sufficient answer to those incredible readers who persist in thinking her weak. We are reminded by contrast of Ophelia, in which case Brabantio falls into Polonius' place, however unfair in other respects the comparison may be. Desdemona is Ophelia choosing the other fork of the road. She is an anti-Ophelia. All we have to ask is what would have happened in *Hamlet* if Hamlet had had her love. She never would have deserted him in his critical hour. "Frailty, thy name is woman." Desdemona is a living contradiction of that indispensable premise of Hamlet's philosophy and action. In her presence his tragedy would have melted into thin air.

The significance in the fact that it is a woman who thus refuses to ruin her life by surrender to the Force of the Past—"the tyrant custom," as Othello calls it—cannot be exaggerated, for Desdemona, heralded indeed by Juliet, is the first of a series of Shakespearean women, in tragedy at least, who defy authority in this sense. Man after man has wrestled with this problem of force in vain, for force is traditionally man's method. Now, women begin to attack it not in vain—not in vain, that is, from the tragic viewpoint. The feminine pole of Shakespeare's genius is gaining ascendancy. "Shakespeare led a life of allegory: his works are the comments on it." Desdemona helps us understand that alluring sentence.

III

The audacity of Desdemona's act is at least quadrupled by the fact that the man she marries is a Moor. Which raises the old question:

Is Othello brown or black?

The controversy over this problem has been a long and heated one. Its main result has been to prove once more that learning is the least imaginative thing in the world. The argument has been in part textual: the marshaling on both sides of every passage in the play that seems in any way pertinent to the question of Othello's color; in part historical and ethnological: an attempt to determine whether Shakespeare could himself have been aware of the distinction between Moor and Ethiopian. Two things at any rate are clear: (1) Iago's statements about Othello's appearance cannot be taken at face value; (2) the word "black" is used more than once in the play—even by Desdemona herself—as a synonym for brunette in contrast with "fair" which, when put over against it, stands for blonde. These considerations may or may not be deemed decisive. The scholar who is not convinced one way or the other can still keep his mind open. But the actor and director in the case of a particular production must decide the question once for all. On the stage Othello cannot be both brown and black at the same time, and the decision, in certain places and circumstances, may be a critical one. The reader on the other hand is relatively free. He may visualize Othello more or less to suit himself.

But turn from the world of drama to the world of poetry and we perceive that all this misses the point and begs the question.

What attracted Shakespeare in the first place to this exotic story of a Moor, this blood-and-thunder novella of Cinthio's, so inferior in many ways to anything else he ever used for tragedy? A futile question, it would seem, beyond the fact that the tale had obvious theatrical qualities. Yet perhaps not so futile after all, for in one respect we can answer it with almost as much assurance as if we actually had access to Shakespeare's mind.

The moment he saw that first line, "There was once a Moor in Venice . . . ," how could he have failed to recall *The Jew of Venice*, as the public had apparently insisted on rechristening his own play laid in the same city? The scene the same, the title almost the same, and both stories centering around one alien in the midst of many native Venetians! Nor did the analogy stop there. Everything in *The Merchant of Venice* turns on the contrast between inner and outer, depth and surface, on the gilded that is mistaken for the golden, the precious that is hidden beneath the base. But here, in Cinthio's tale, is a hero with a dark skin caught in the toils of a villain with a fair and honest exterior. The casket theme exactly! the old story over again—with its implicit tragedy now explicit—only with its material symbols transmuted into the very stuff of human life, not gold and lead, but good and evil, light and shadow, black and white. Othello and Iago must have been conceived at the moment that that analogy struck the poet, one black without and white within, the other white without and black within. And to these two a third was inevitably added, Desdemona, white both without and within. These contrasts are obviously the substance and essence of the play, penetrating far under any merely ethnological or theatrical considerations to the heart of the imagination itself[2] and making even the symbolism of *The Merchant of Venice* crude in comparison. To the imagination, black, not brown, represents the shadow, evil, death. On the level of poetry that settles it beyond appeal. Othello is black.

This contrast scheme of light and dark sets everything in perspective. In a sense it predetermines the characterization.

I saw Othello's visage in his mind,

says Desdemona, and instantly we are convinced that though the two are alien in race they are akin in spirit. Throughout, she seems unconscious of his color and under the influence of her love he too forgets it. The symbolism demands that Desdemona's own visage, both without and within, be a shining white. And, symbolism or no symbolism, that is exactly what Shakespeare makes it. Which is why her role is beyond the reach of any actress. Innocence cannot be imitated. Only some Desdemona-like woman from some region uncontaminated by anything theatrical might be Desdemona momentarily on the stage, as a child becomes what he plays.

Just the opposite is true of Iago. Only a consummate actor can render him. I wonder if anyone ever has—ever has succeeded, I mean, in making him convincingly "honest" not just to Othello, Cassio, and Desdemona, but even, in its presence, to the audience that is in the secret. That would be the test. That would make everything credible. Iago is a snake—but a snake under a flower. On the surface he must not fascinate like a snake. He must charm like a flower.

What wisdom he utters, and into what depravity it turns on his lips! Take his metaphor of the garden: "Our bodies are our gardens, to the which our wills are gardeners . . . . If the balance of our lives had not one scale of reason to poise another of sensuality, the blood and baseness of our natures would conduct us to most preposterous conclusions"—like the conclusion of this play! What is that but Hamlet's speech on blood and judgment translated, significantly, from poetry into prose? But one was spoken to Horatio, the other to Roderigo. One in profound affection, the other in murderous contempt. How diametrical ideas become that are practically identical!

Iago keeps reminding us of Othello's color just as Desdemona causes us to forget it. To him Othello is "an old black ram," or worse. He loses no opportunity to keep him conscious of his supposed inferiority and he makes the most of the unnatural character of his union with Desdemona. The degree to which the ocher characters are scandalized by the marriage is a measure of their own blindness or depravity, or both. Brabantio is scandalized by it out of family pride: he wants to marry his daughter to one of the "wealthy curled darlings of our nation." Roderigo, one of those very darlings, is scandalized by it because of envy: he wants Desdemona for himself, and to him Othello is a "thick-lips." Emilia refers to the marriage as Desdemona's "most filthy bargain." (The phrase reveals her vulgar quality, but it was uttered under a tragic misunderstanding and on the brink of incredible loyalty, so we forgive it.) The Duke of Venice, on the other hand, a man of character and insight, approves the match:

> Noble signior,
> If virtue no delighted beauty lack,
> Your son-in-law is far more fair than black.

And as for Cassio, he seems scarcely more conscious of anything alien in Othello than Desdemona herself. To the end, in spite of everything, Othello remains to him just "dear general."

These characters, it is interesting to note, all conform, if less extremely, to the pattern of light and shade of the three main figures. Like those in *The Merchant of Venice* they are all one thing without, another within. Emilia: common clay concealing a capacity for devotion almost divine. Roderigo: the fine young gentleman rotten at the core. Bianca: the courtesan who falls in love. Brabantio: the unrelenting father, who, nevertheless, dies of a broken heart. Cassio: the profligate with a pure heart, the drunkard who comes through true as steel. All this cannot be chance.

IV

Iago's jealousy of Cassio is real enough, but it is the occasion rather than the cause of his plot against Othello; and the other reasons he assigns for his hatred in the course of the play are not so much motives as symptoms of a deeply underlying condition. The psychology of Iago is that of the slave-with-brains who aspires to power yet remains at heart a slave.

> We cannot all be masters, nor all masters
> Cannot be truly follow'd.

"Some cogging cozening slave," says Emilia, describing the as yet hypothetical and unidentified villain who is actually her husband. "O cursed, cursed slave!" cries Othello, at the end, to that part of himself that Iago had corrupted. We are led to conjecture that some situation or event early in Iago's life that produced a profound sense of injustice or inferiority, and instigated a revolt against it, could alone have produced so twisted a nature, as in the case of Emily Brontë's Heathcliff or Dostoevsky's Smerdyakov, figures spiritually akin to Shakespeare's villain. It would be consumingly interesting to have a peep into Iago's childhood, as we have into theirs. It must have been full of power-fantasies like those that Dostoevsky describes in *A Raw Youth*. "The secret consciousness of power is more insupportably delightful than open domination." "I don't know," the Raw Youth declares, "whether the spider perhaps does not hate the fly he has marked and is snaring. Dear little fly! It seems to me that the victim is loved, or at least may be loved. Here I love my enemy; I am delighted, for instance, that she is so beautiful." Compare this with Iago's words on Desdemona:

> Now, I do love her too;
> Not out of absolute lust, though peradventure
> I stand accountant for as great a sin,
> But partly led to diet my revenge,

or his,

> So will I turn her virtue into pitch,
> And out of her own goodness make the net
> That shall enmesh them all.

Iago is a spider whose web is spun out of his brain. (Though that is by no means all he is.) Whatever he began by being, however human the motives that at first led him on, he ends by being an image of Death revenging itself on Life through destruction. Why does a small boy knock down, in pure wantonness, the tower of blocks his younger brother has so slowly and laboriously built up? Iago is like that:

If Cassio do remain,
He hath a daily beauty in his life
That makes me ugly.

These are the most consciously self-revealing words he speaks. Ugliness cannot tolerate beauty. Death cannot tolerate life.

That that likes not me
Pleases me best.

If you are defeated, change the rules of the game, call defeat success (as if to get the fewest runs in baseball were the object), and then you win! Drag down the good—it is so much easier than rising. Define darkness as light.

Shakespeare's archvillain had many Shakespearean forerunners: the melodramatic Richard III, the casuistical Pandulph, the sly and crafty Ulysses. But they all fade before him. He is perhaps the most terrific indictment of pure intellect in the literature of the world—"pure intellect," which, as Emerson said, "is the pure devil." "Think, and die," as Enobarbus puts it, though he may not have realized all he was packing into three words. The intellect, as all the prophets have divined, should be the servant of the soul. Performing that function it is indispensable. There can scarcely be too much of it. Indeed, the primacy in the world of art of men like Beethoven, Michelangelo, and Shakespeare himself is that their imaginations are held in check by their critical power. But the moment the intellect sets up a claim of sovereignty for itself, it is the slave in revolt, the torchbearer turned incendiary, Lucifer fallen. Iago is a moral pyromaniac.

I wonder, if he had been of more limited intelligence, whether he might not have been, literally, a pyromaniac. He exhibits a dozen traits of that type of criminal, including a secret joy in being on the scene of the conflagration he has kindled. Shakespeare himself hints as much in the speech in which, of all in the play barring the soliloquies, Iago most fully reveals himself for what he is. It is in the opening scene, while his plot, if conceived, is still unconscious. And he is boasting to his dupe, Roderigo. He is off guard. But first we must recall the conscious revelation that leads up to the unconscious one:

For when my outward action doth demonstrate
The native act and figure of my heart
In compliment extern, 'tis not long after
But I will wear my heart upon my sleeve
For daws to peck at. I am not what I am.

How characteristic of Shakespeare that in his very next speech Iago should place his heart squarely on his sleeve, and put into words, and still more into tone, precisely what he is.

> *Rod.*: What a full fortune does the thick-lips owe,
> If he can carry't thus!
> *Iago*:   Call up her father:
> Rouse him, make after him, poison his delight,
> Proclaim him in the streets, incense her kinsmen,
> And, though he in a fertile climate dwell,
> Plague him with flies; though that his joy be joy,
> Yet throw such changes of vexation on 't,
> As it may lose some colour.
> *Rod.*: Here is her father's house; I'll call aloud.
> *Iago*: Do, with like timorous accent and dire yell
> As when, by night and negligence, the fire
> Is spied in populous cities.

Poison! Plague! Fire! Never again, unless to himself, do we hear Iago speak with such gusto. The bewildering shift in antecedents of the pronouns ("Rouse him, make after him"), the first referring to Brabantio, the second to Othello, is intentional on Shakespeare's part, revealing in a flash that Iago's hatred of Othello is already an obsession. For these few seconds, before he puts on his perpetual mask and cloak, Iago stands before us naked.

But if he is a moral pyromaniac, it is only morally that he is mad, and, whatever may be said of the fires he kindles in others, the fire in his own veins is an icy fire. "Now could I drink hot blood," cried Hamlet. Iago goes fathoms lower than that. "For I am nothing if not critical," he observes calmly, as he scrutinizes Desdemona's beauty on the threshold of her destruction; and as he begins to weave the web that is to enmesh her, he cries:

> By the mass, 'tis morning;
> Pleasure and action make the hours seem short.

Hot revenge is a fearful thing. But its devastation has bounds, because its passion reveals its secret, makes it act prematurely, mars its aim, and soon burns it out. Cold revenge is incredibly more awful. For it can conceal, it can calculate, it can lie in wait; it can control itself, it can coil and strike without warning at the crucial moment. Cold revenge is the union of intellect and hate—the most annihilating of all alliances. Dante was right in making his nethermost hell of ice.

V

The deliberate placing of the highest intellectual gifts and achievements at the service of the lowest human instincts is a phenomenon with which the twentieth century is acquainted on a scale never previously attained. And whether the instinct be fear (the main defensive one) or revenge, greed, cruelty, thirst to possess more power or to assert power already possessed (the main offensive ones) makes little difference in the end, so readily do they pass into one another.

It is no recent discovery that brain as well as brawn is essential to the efficient fighter. The Trojan Horse is the perennial symbol of that truth, and it is appropriate that Shakespeare put on the lips of Ulysses an encomium on the "still and mental parts" of war. But it remained for war in our time to effect the total mobilization of those still and mental parts. The ideological warfare that precedes and precipitates the physical conflict (*cold* war as it has significantly come to be called); the propaganda that prepares and unifies public opinion; the conscription, in a dozen spheres, of the nation's brains; the organization of what is revealingly known as the *intelligence* service; but most of all the practical absorption of science into the military effort: these things, apart from the knowledge and skill required for the actual fighting, permit us to define modern war, once it is begun, as an unreserved dedication of the human intellect to death and destruction.

But that is exactly what Iago is—an unreserved dedication of intellect to death and destruction. To the extent that this is true, Iago is an incarnation of the spirit of modern war.

This does not mean that those who participate in modern war are Iagos. The scientist calmly conducting his experiment in a clean laboratory without an iota of hate in his heart bears no resemblance to Shakespeare's Italian fiend. But there may be hate, and there will almost certainly be fear, in the heart of the man who months later and thousands of miles away utilizes the results of that experiment on the fighting front (not to imply for a moment that there may not be heroism in it also). Nobody wants war. No individual does, that is, or very few. But that great Composite Personality which is the nation is driven into it nevertheless against the wishes of the thousands of individuals who make it up. It is within that Personality, not generally within the individual, that the union of intellect with animal instincts takes place, the prostitution especially of man's supreme intellectual achievement, modern science, to the most destructive of his ancestral practices. It is something within this Composite Personality that is like Iago, and, like him, it did not foresee when it set out to make war efficient that it was playing with the possibility of its own extinction. The uniqueness of Iago, like the uniqueness of modern war, does not lie in the spirit of destruction. That has always been common enough. It lies in the genius he dedicates to destructive ends. Modern war would not recognize itself in the portraits of Shakespeare's classical and feudal fighters, in Hector and Hotspur, in Faulconbridge and Coriolanus, or in Othello himself. But let it look in the glass and it will behold Iago. In him Shakespeare reveals, with the clarity of nightmare, that unrestrained intellect, instead of being the opposite of force, and an antidote for it, as much of the modern world thinks, is force functioning on another plane. It is the immoral equivalent of war, and as certain to lead to it in due season as Iago's machinations were to lead to death. "All other knowledge is hurtful," says Montaigne, "to him who has not the science of honesty and goodness."

VI

To those who forget Emerson's wise observation that "perpetual modernness is the measure of merit in any work of art" all this will be an unpardonable digression from the play. To them it will be allegorizing *Othello*, reading into it what could never have entered Shakespeare's head. On the contrary, it is in this case demonstrable from the text that Shakespeare definitely intended precisely this equation between Iago and War, though, naturally, he could not have foreseen how the changes in the conduct of war between his time and ours were to sharpen and point the analogy. It is a perfect example of the nature of poetic foresight as distinguished from the popular conception of prophecy.

The opening of every one of Shakespeare's greatest Tragedies, as certainly as a Wagnerian overture, sounds the central theme or themes of the play. *Othello*, taking its cue from *Troilus and Cressida*, begins with a contrast between the physical and the mental parts of war. Iago, who is to prove himself such a master of intrigue, is cursing Othello to Roderigo for preferring Cassio as his lieutenant, with his "bookish theoric," "mere prattle, without practice," to himself with his active service in the field. However little we may suspect his sincerity at a first reading, the subject of his introductory speech portends a play in some sense about war as infallibly as their respective openings indicate that *Hamlet* will concern itself with ghosts, *Macbeth* with the nature of evil, and *King Lear* with the relations of the generations.

I doubt whether many people think of *Othello* as a play about war. But it is, even literally. Three of its four main characters are warriors. And the fourth is a warrior's wife, herself referred to by her husband at the climax of his joy as "my fair warrior." Even Cassio, whom Iago so despised, was considered worthy by the home government of taking Othello's place in Cyprus. Furthermore, the war between the Venetians and the Turks, which is the background and occasion of the action, is as indispensable to the plot and the "moral" as the feud between the Capulets and the Montagues is to *Romeo and Juliet*. It is obvious in the earlier case that if you drop out the feud the play falls to pieces. It is not so obvious, but it is just as true, that if you drop out the war from *Othello* it falls to pieces. The more closely one examines the analogy between the two plays in this respect the more impressive it becomes.

War is the royal occupation. Othello is a follower and master of it. Yet, before the play is over, "Othello's occupation's gone." Why and how it went it is vital for us to see, for in these days war is the world's occupation.

The Turk in this play, until he disappears beneath the waves, is consistently represented as the Enemy. At the beginning, his fleet is reported as bearing down on Cyprus, then on Rhodes, then again on Cyprus. The Venetians set out to head him off—or to be on hand when he appears. A terrific storm arises. The Turks are all drowned. The Venetians arrive safe in Cyprus.

All this at first sight seems of no intrinsic interest. It is mere machinery, mere scenery against which the domestic drama is to be enacted. Unless we are on guard, we skip it mentally in the reading. But we do so at our peril, for the "scenery" in Shakespearean tragedy is part of the action, and never more so, not even in *King Lear*, than here. "Be what cannot be skipped." The war in *Othello* conforms to that Emersonian injunction.

Reread the play with sharp attention to the parts in which war figures, pondering particularly every allusion to the Turks—there are many of them— and it is inescapable that what Shakespeare is bent on is an insinuation into the underconsciousness of the reader of an analogy between Iago and the Turk. Indeed, in one passage Iago openly makes the identification himself. Desdemona has dubbed him "slanderer" for his strictures upon women. "Nay, it is true," retorts Iago, "or else I am a Turk." But it is not true. And so he is a Turk.

The end crowns the whole, and Othello confirms the capital nature of the analogy in those last words that set the seal on his lips and create the metaphor he acts out in death:

And say besides, that in Aleppo once,
Where a malignant and a turban'd Turk
Beat a Venetian and traduc'd the state,
I took by the throat the circumcised dog,
And smote him—thus.

Whereupon he stabs himself, as if he would reach down with his dagger to that Turk-Iago within himself that enabled the other Iago to beat and traduce him.

The speech in which the analogy is fast set up is one of those seemingly casual, unnecessarily digressive ones that a stage director can be counted on to abbreviate or cut out. As we have repeatedly noticed, it is into such passages, when attention is suspended, that Shakespeare loves to insert his most valuable clues. So here. A sailor enters and announces that the Turkish preparation makes for Rhodes. Incredible, says a Senator, that they should not take Cyprus first, which is both easier to capture and more useful to them. The expedition to Rhodes must be a blind.

First Sen.:   This cannot be,
By no assay of reason; 'tis a pageant,
To keep us in false gaze. When we consider
The importancy of Cyprus to the Turk,
And let ourselves again but understand
That, as it more concerns the Turk than Rhodes,
So may he with more facile question bear it,
For that it stands not in such warlike brace,
But altogether lacks the abilities
That Rhodes is dress'd in; if we make thought of this,
We must not think the Turk is so unskilful
To leave that latest which concerns him first,
Neglecting an attempt of ease and gain
To wake and wage a danger profitless.

It would be prosaic to put the analogy on all fours. But who can miss it? The Turk is apparently taking one course that under cover of it he may take an entirely different one. Iago is about to do the same. "A pageant To keep us in false gaze." What better description could we ask of his plot? And the last four lines of the passage quoted—do they not fit Iago as well as they do the Turk? Indeed we are almost tempted to go on and seek analogies for Cyprus and Rhodes in Iago's story. But that would be to force what is thrown out as a suggestion rather than intended for an exact comparison. What is beyond doubt is that the passage is prophetic of the plot against Othello, and, in the light of the doom that overcame the Turks, of its ultimate spiritual defeat and of Iago's submergence under the waves of a final silence.

With this hint, the storm scene at the beginning of Act II takes on undreamed-of meanings.

When, following the tempest that has imperiled them all and engulfed the Turks, Othello at last arrives in Cyprus, he is shaken to the depths of his nature by the experience of stepping, as it were, from the embrace of death to the embrace of Desdemona. The piercing beauty of the words he speaks to her is stamped with that individual quality which Shakespeare somehow imparts to the speech of all his lovers, revealing his belief that every true love between man and woman is unique. "O my fair warrior!"—note the word, for it is Shakespeare's as well as Othello's—the Moor exclaims, as he catches sight of his wife. "My dear Othello!" she replies. And, as he takes her in his arms, he goes on:

It gives me wonder great as my content
To see you here before me. O my soul's joy!
If after every tempest come such calms,
May the winds blow till they have waken'd death!

And let the labouring bark climb hills of seas
Olympus-high, and duck again as low
As hell's from heaven! If it were now to die,
'Twere now to be most happy; for, I fear,
My soul hath her content so absolute
That not another comfort like to this
Succeeds in unknown fate.

At a first reading we enter into Othello's wonder and joy, a content so absolute that we, like him, cannot imagine it augmented; and we feel that undertone of sadness that accompanies all supreme felicity and beauty—enhanced in this instance by our knowledge of the plot against them. When, however, having finished the play, we reread these lines, we suddenly realize that Othello has prayed in them for exactly what the future was to bring him: a storm as much more terrific than the tumult of wind and wave through which he has just passed as the ocean of human emotion is more treacherous than any Mediterranean—a storm whose crest and trough should literally touch heaven and hell.

Wash me in steep-down gulfs of liquid fire!

he was to pray later, when the full fury of that storm burst on him. But little, now, does he envisage any such tragic answer to his prayer, and, having uttered it, he kisses Desdemona and exclaims contradictorily:

And this, and this, the greatest discords be
That e'er our hearts shall make!

Whereupon Turk-Iago mutters to himself,

O, you are well tuned now!
But I'll set down the pegs that make this music,
As honest as I am.

To this unoverheard diabolic comment on the situation, Othello, utterly forgetting his prayer of the instant before for a vaster war of the elements, unwittingly replies:

Our wars are done, the Turks are drown'd.
. . . I prithee, good Iago . . . .

This, to put it mildly, is premature. There is one war that is not done, one Turk that is not drowned, though he is destined before long to go down in a tempest of his own raising. Prayers are always answered, but not always in the way or in the sense that we intend.

Thus does Shakespeare tie Iago with the Turk—and so with the Enemy, and so with War. The connection is too often reiterated to be coincidence. It is too clearly contrived to be unconscious. It is plainly intentional.

So much for the first two readings of this scene. (To something else in it to be discovered only by a third or later reading I will return before I am done.)

<h1 style="text-align:center">VII</h1>

Desdemona is one of those touchstones in which Shakespeare's plays abound. Ask a group of people whether Desdemona is a weak or a strong character, and they characterize themselves by their answers. There are those who would dilute her away into a foolish and timid girl who makes a precipitate and unfortunate misalliance with a foreigner much older than herself. That is to pay scant attention to the picture Shakespeare gives of her as she was before the shadow of tragedy touched her, the girl her father referred to as "perfection." She was nearer perfection than he suspected. He never dreamed what audacity there was under her quietness and stillness. Desdemona was not absorbed merely in household duties. She loved company, could be witty, could dance, play, and sing. But her world was not bounded by these things either, and if she could do fine needlework, be sure she could dream over it too. As her response to Othello's tales of his adventures shows, she was in love with danger. It takes your shy ones to be bold. And when she says, as he reports,

> she wish'd
> That heaven had made her such a man,

whatever she meant by it and however Othello took it, Shakespeare plainly contrived that Delphic line as a preparation for Othello's own "O my fair warrior!" There was a boy within this girl, a man's courage at the heart of this maiden whose very motion blushed at herself. Desdemona is merely an extreme example of that union of feminine and masculine qualities that Shakespeare plainly held essential for either the perfect man or the perfect woman.

It is extraordinary (and especially to be noted for future reference) that Iago gives the best full-length description of Desdemona in the play. In the interlude at Cyprus before Othello's entrance after the storm, Desdemona asks Iago how he would praise a woman so deserving that malice itself would have to admit her merit. Malice itself of course is Iago and the deserving woman Desdemona. She naturally does not recognize either of these facts; he recognizes them both. And this is his description of the ideal woman he knows her to be:

She that was ever fair and never proud,
Had tongue at will and yet was never loud,
Never lack'd gold and yet went never gay,
Fled from her wish and yet said, "Now I may,"
She that being anger'd, her revenge being nigh,
Bade her wrong stay and her displeasure fly,
She that in wisdom never was so frail
To change the cod's head for the salmon's tail,
She that could think and ne'er disclose her mind,
See suitors following and not look behind,
She was a wight, if ever such wight were,—

and as Iago pauses, Desdemona asks, as he hoped she would, "To do what?"

To suckle fools and chronicle small beer.
O most lame and impotent conclusion!

she exclaims, never guessing what Iago has been up to. His picture reveals with what completeness he can appraise both truth and beauty, and then revert—as he does the next second in an aside, "with as little a web as this will I ensnare as great a fly as Cassio"—to the spider. Desdemona may be evaluated, she will never be caught—in either sense—by the intellect.

"At some thoughts," says Dostoevsky, "one stands perplexed, especially at the sight of men's sin, and wonders whether one should use force or humble love. Always decide to use humble love. If you resolve on that once for all, you may subdue the whole world. Loving humility is marvelously strong, the strongest of all things and there is nothing else like it." It would be impertinent to say that Desdemona believed that. She was it—and it is superfluous to believe what we are. Desdemona a strong or weak character? Under her spell, one is tempted to assert that she is the strongest character in all Shakespeare. Who can contend with her for that eminence? Only the transformed Cordelia. But Desdemona did not have to be transformed. While blows, physical, mental, and spiritual, rained on her head, she held to her faith in goodness and to the end helped answer her own prayer:

Heaven me such uses send,
Not to pick bad from bad, but by bad mend.

"O my fair warrior!" Othello was right. "The divine Desdemona." Cassio did not exaggerate.

And it is precisely one of her divinest acts that, curiously, is most often set down to her discredit: the dropping of the handkerchief. "That is a fault," says Othello in the next scene, when he asks his wife to lend him the handkerchief and she cannot produce it, and many readers agree that it was a fault, not noticing that Shakespeare has been careful to show that, so far as Desdemona is concerned, the loss of the handkerchief was not only not a fault, but actually a virtue of an angelic order. Indeed, there is a sense in which Desdemona tells no lie when she denies that the handkerchief is lost. Things are lost through carelessness or genuine accident—and the dropping of the handkerchief came about through neither of these. The truth, as contrasted with the fact, of the matter is that neither Desdemona, nor accident, nor Fate, dropped the handkerchief. Othello dropped it.

> *Des.*:   How now, my dear Othello!
> Your dinner, and the generous islanders
> By you invited, do attend your presence.
> *Oth.*: I am to blame.
> *Des.*:   Why do you speak so faintly?
> Are you not well?
> *Oth.*: I have a pain upon my forehead here.
> *Des.*: Faith, that's with watching; 'twill away again:
> Let me but bind it hard, within this hour
> It will be well.
> *Oth.*:   Your napkin is too little:
> Let it alone. Come, I'll go in with you.
> *Des.*: I am very sorry that you are not well.

And Othello and Desdemona go out as Emilia picks up the handkerchief.

It is vital here to visualize what has happened. The stage business is left to the actors and director, but surely there is only one right way of arranging it. Othello, his mind full of the terrible doubts Iago has poured into it, explains his embarrassed manner and faint voice as due to headache, as, indeed, they may well be. Desdemona takes out her handkerchief and starts to bind his forehead. At the moment, he cannot bear this act of affection with its physical contact from the woman he has begun to doubt, and with a gesture of impatience—"Let it alone"—he pushes her hand away, causing the handkerchief to drop, the "it," of course, referring not to the handkerchief, as it is often taken to, but to the forehead. Now if Desdemona had loved Othello less, had been less genuinely pained by his pain, or had valued a mere token of love above love itself, she would naturally have noticed the fall of the handkerchief and would, however unconsciously, have stooped and picked it up. But every fiber of her soul and body, conscious and unconscious, is so totally devoted to Othello that the handkerchief for the moment ceases to exist. The slightest deflection of her eye in its direction as it dropped would have been a subtraction from the infinity of her love—just as the movement of Othello's hand when he pushed her hand away measured his distrust of that love, gave the villain his unique opportunity, and sealed his own doom forever. Is there anything in all the drama of the world, I wonder, to equal this in its own kind? The moment when Romeo thrust his rapier between Tybalt and Mercutio is similar. But that was a rapier, the moment was patently critical, and the act, however impulsive, was a conscious one. This, on the other hand, is only a handkerchief, the situation the most ordinary, and the act one that almost anybody might be guilty of any day in his life. "Trifles light as air." Was there ever a better demonstration that everything may depend on anything? "Who can control his fate?" asks Othello when it is too late. And there have been those who think that Shakespeare is asking the same question. But in that case he is answering: Othello for one could have controlled his—and Romeo for another—if, like Desdemona's and Juliet's, their bounty had been as boundless as the sea, their love as deep. This is not fate. This is freedom.

But if the hero foredooms himself by causing the handkerchief to drop, the villain does as much for himself just twenty-seven lines further on when he snatches the handkerchief from his wife's hand. Emilia, as the event proves, was Iago's oversight. "It is in just such stupid things," says Dostoevsky (without any allusion to *Othello* of course), "that clever people are most easily caught. The more cunning a man is the less he suspects that he will be caught in a simple thing." But long before his wife turns the handkerchief against him, Iago uses it with bloody effect on Othello. When, on top of his account of Cassio's revelation in his sleep, he tells him that that very day he saw Cassio wipe his beard with it, Othello is finally convinced:

Now do I see 'tis true. Look here, Iago;
All my fond love thus do I blow to heaven.
'Tis gone.
Arise, black vengeance, from the hollow hell!
Yield up, O love, thy crown and hearted throne
To tyrannous hate! Swell, bosom, with thy fraught,
For 'tis of aspics' tongues! . . .
O, blood, blood, blood!

In the next scene where Othello demands the handkerchief and Desdemona persists in turning the subject back to Cassio—"the handkerchief," "Cassio"; "the handkerchief," "Cassio"—she is generally blamed, first, for lying, and, second, for an utterly unforgivable lack of sense and tact. But it is Othello, not Desdemona, who really lies about the handkerchief in this scene! For the express, if not conscious, purpose of frightening his wife, he invents a fabulous story of the handkerchief's origin and magical properties, the falsity of which Shakespeare is careful to bring out by having him give a true account of it at the end of the play. Desdemona is naturally awed, and like a scared child evades her husband's questions. Her "guilt" is venial compared with his. And it is precisely her utter innocence that permits her insistence about Cassio. A guilty woman would have sensed at once that she must keep clear of so dangerous a subject. But to Desdemona a chance to help another is a command to do so instantly and utterly. Truth and compassion are rare. Tact and worldliness are common. Only those who think that the transformation of a childlike and loving woman into a discreet and worldly one is a moral ascent can wish that Desdemona had acted otherwise than she did in this distressing scene. If she exhibits a deficiency of common sense, she shows an abundance of a sense utterly uncommon. If it had been a younger daughter entreating a father to forgive an older sister who had fallen out of his favor, and not allowing herself to be put off, we would have nothing but admiration for her. We should have nothing but admiration for Desdemona's persistence in behalf of Cassio.

Desdemona's "lie" about the handkerchief is not the only one that is charged against her. There is also what is generally known as her dying lie in the last words that she speaks:

> *Emil.*: O, who hath done this deed?
> *Des.*: Nobody; I myself. Farewell!
> Commend me to my kind lord. O, farewell!

"Truth sits upon the lips of dying men." Dostoevsky thought it worth while to write a novel of a thousand pages to bring home the truth that sat upon the lips of the dying Desdemona. The central doctrine of Father Zossima in *The Brothers Karamazov* is that each is "to blame for everyone and for all things." The plot of the novel was conceived to illustrate and prove that paradox. There is hardly one of its pages that has no bearing on it. Desdemona expressed it more briefly: "I myself." Into those two words she put the whole mystery of the atonement. And this is what the world chooses to call a lie.

VIII

If, so far, we have said more about Desdemona and Iago than about the one who gives the title to the play, it is because he cannot be understood without first understanding them. They are the poles between which he moves. At the opening of the story, before Iago begins to enmesh him, he seems as simple and noble as Desdemona herself, and, however black without, is rightly described as white within, made so partly by her love. But when the poison begins to work, when that simplicity and nobility begin to be contaminated, then Othello becomes an alternation of mighty opposites, not gray, but black-and-white—the poet-barbarian, the hero-murderer, the paragon of self-control gone mad, the harmonious nature to whom chaos comes again. Taking the whole play into account, he is equally susceptible, almost, to the influence of Desdemona and to that of Iago. First Desdemona wins him; then Iago; then Desdemona, dead, wins him back. There is the plot reduced to a dozen words. Though he kills her, she saves him. Perhaps that is Shakespeare's unconscious prophecy of the destiny of a mankind that in so many ways resembles Othello.

There is no other among his supreme plays against the plot and the psychology of which so many objections have been brought as against *Othello*, and they are leveled primarily against the conduct of its hero. The improbabilities of *King Lear* are another and more venial matter because of its remote and semimythical setting and atmosphere. *Othello* is domestic, it is said, and should submit to more exacting tests. A real Othello would have gone to his wife for an explanation. (And, incidentally, a real Desdemona would have found a chance to explain.) In answer, his defenders are compelled to plead his age, his brief acquaintance with his wife, his ignorance of Venetian society and consequent self-distrust and willingness to accept Iago's account of its habits.

This much is true at any rate: Othello regarded Desdemona's love for him as a dream too beautiful to be true. Hence, when it is suggested to him that it is not true, this is in a sense nothing but what he has been ready to believe all along. What wonder that it is easy for him to dismiss his happiness as an illusion! "Desdemona love *me*! Impossible!" When we waken from a dream we do not go about searching for material evidence that it was not a dream after all. Neither does Othello. It is the best things in him, his love, his imagination, his lack of suspicion, his modesty, that give Iago his chance. But such considerations will not silence the doubters. Apparently only some parallel incident from real life would convince them that a man of Othello's temperament could act as Othello is represented as acting in this play. Such an incident, it would seem, would be rather difficult to produce. And yet, strangely, it can be produced. Under the title of *A Practical Joke*, Dostoevsky's wife relates a domestic incident which occurred in the spring of 1876. If it had been expressly written to prove, a fortiori, the truth of the psychology of *Othello*, it could scarcely have been improved, as anyone who reads it will be bound to agree. It runs as follows:

> On 18th May, 1876, an incident took place which I recall almost with terror. This is how it happened. A new novel by Mme. Sophie Smirnov entitled *The Strong Character* was running as a serial then in *The Otechestvennya Zapiski*. Fiodor was on friendly terms with Sophie Smirnov and valued her talent very highly. He was interested in her latest work, and asked me to get him the numbers of the monthly as they appeared. I chose those few days, when my husband had a rest from his work on *The Journal of an Author*, and brought him the

numbers of *The Otechestvennya Zapiski*. But as journals are lent by the libraries only for two or three days, I urged my husband to read the journal quickly so as to avoid paying a fine at the library. So it was also with the April number. Fiodor read the novel and spoke to me of how our dear Sophie (whom I, too, valued very highly) had succeeded in creating a certain male character in the novel. That evening my husband went out to some gathering, and after seeing the children to bed, I began reading the novel. In it, by the way, was published an anonymous letter, sent by the villain to the hero, which ran as follows:

"Dear Sir, Noblest Peter Ivanovich,

As I am a perfect stranger to you, but take an interest in your feelings, I venture to address these lines to you. Your nobility is sufficiently well-known to me, and my heart is pained at the idea, that despite all your nobility, a certain person, who is very close to you, is so basely deceiving you. Having gone away with your blessing to a place four hundred miles off, she, like a delighted dove spreading its wings and soaring upwards, has no mind to return to the marital home. You have let her go to your own as well as to her ruin, into the claws of a man who terrifies her, but who fascinates her by his flattering addresses. He has stolen her heart, and there are no eyes more beautiful to her than his. Even her little children are loathsome to her, if she gets no loving word from him. If you want to know who this fellow the villain is, I must not reveal his name, but look for yourself among those who frequent your house, and beware of dark men. When you see the dark man, who loves haunting your doors, have a good look at him. It is now a long time since that fellow has crossed your path, and you are the only one who does not notice it.

Nothing but your nobility compels me to reveal this secret to you. And if you don't trust me, then have a look at the locket which your wife wears round her neck, and see whose portrait she wears in that locket near her heart.

YOUR EVER UNKNOWN WELL-WISHER."

I must say here that lately I had been in the best of moods; my husband had had no epileptic fits for a long time, our children were perfectly well, our debts were gradually being paid, and the success of *The Journal of an Author* was marked. All this strengthened my characteristic cheerfulness, and under the influence of the anonymous letter, just read, a playful idea flashed across my mind—to copy that letter (changing the name and striking out certain lines) and to send it by post to

Fiodor. It seemed to me that, as he had only yesterday read that letter
in Mme. Smirnov's novel, he would guess at once that it was a joke,
and we should have some fun. There also occurred another idea to me,
that my husband might take the letter seriously. In that case I was
interested to see how he would regard it: whether he would show it to
me, or throw it away into the waste-paper basket. As usual with me, I
had no sooner thought of the idea than I put it into execution. At first
I wanted to write the letter in my own handwriting; but as I had been
copying for Fiodor every day, and my handwriting was too familiar to
him, I resolved to cover up my joke and began copying out the letter in
a rounder handwriting than mine. But it turned out to be a hard job,
and I spoilt several sheets before I managed to write the whole letter in
a uniform hand. Next morning I posted it, and in the afternoon it was
delivered to us together with other letters.

That day Fiodor was out later than usual, and returned only at five
o'clock and, not wanting to keep the children waiting for their dinner, he
just changed and came straight into the dining room, without looking
at his letters. The dinner passed off merrily and noisily. Fiodor was in
a good mood; he talked a good deal and laughed, as he answered the
children's questions. After dinner, with the usual cup of tea in his hand,
he went into his study. I went into the nursery, and in about ten minutes'
time I entered the study to see the effect which my anonymous letter
had produced.

I sat down in my usual seat by the writing table, and purposely
asked Fiodor something to which he had to give an answer. But he kept
a gloomy silence, and paced the room with heavy steps. I saw he was
upset, and instantly I felt sorry. To break the silence I asked him: "Why
are you so gloomy, Fedya?"

Fiodor gave me an angry look, walked across the room a couple of
times and came to a stop just facing me.

"You wear a locket?" he asked in a choking voice.

"I do."

"Show it to me."

"What for? You have seen it many times."

"Show—me—the locket!" Fiodor shouted at the top of his voice.
I realised that my joke had gone too far, and in order to reassure him
I began undoing the collar of my dress. But I had no time to take the
locket out. Fiodor could not restrain the anger which had seized him.
He quickly rushed to me and caught my chain with all his strength. It
was a thin chain which he himself had bought for me in Venice. It broke
instantly, and the locket remained in my husband's hand. He quickly
swept round the table and with his head bent down, he began opening

the locket. Not knowing where to press the spring, he fussed over it for a long time. I saw how his hands trembled, and the locket nearly slipped from them on to the table, I was very sorry for him and terribly angry with myself. I began to speak in a friendly tone, and proposed to open the locket for him; but Fiodor with an angry nod of his head refused my help. At last my husband opened the locket and found there—on one side the portrait of our little daughter, on the other—his own portrait. He was absolutely confused, and kept on looking at the portrait in silence.

"Well, now, have you found it?" I asked him. "Fedya, you silly, how could you believe an anonymous letter?"

Fiodor instantly turned his face to me. "How do you know of the letter?"

"How? I myself sent it you!"

"What do you mean; you sent it me? It is incredible!"

"I'll prove it to you at once."

I went to the other table on which lay the copy of *The Otechestvennya Zapiski*, and got out several sheets of paper, on which I had practised my changed handwriting.

Fiodor raised his hands in astonishment. "And did you yourself compose the letter?"

"Not at all. I simply copied it from Sophie's novel. Surely you read it yesterday? I thought you would guess at once."

"Well, how could I remember! Anonymous letters are always in that style. I simply can't understand why you sent it me?"

"I just wanted to have a lark," I explained.

"How could you play such a joke? I have been in anguish for the last half hour."

"How could I know that you would be such an Othello, and get into such a rage without giving yourself time for a moment's thought?"

"One does not think in such cases. Ah, well, it is clear that you have never experienced real love and real jealousy."

"As for real love, I experience it even now, and as for my not knowing 'real jealousy,' it is your own fault. Why aren't you unfaithful to me?" I laughed, wishing to divert his mood. "Please, be unfaithful to me. Even then I would be kinder than you are. I would not touch you, but I would scratch out her eyes, the villainess . . . ."

"Well, you are laughing, Anechka," Fiodor began apologetically. "But think what a misfortune might have happened: indeed, in my anger I could have strangled you. I may indeed say: God has taken pity on our little ones. And suppose I had not found those portraits, a grain of doubt as to your faithfulness would have remained in my mind for ever, and would have tortured me all my life. I implore you, do not play with such things: in a rage I am not responsible for my actions."

During the conversation I felt a slight awkwardness in moving my neck. I passed my handkerchief over it, and there was a line of blood on it. Evidently the chain in being wrenched off by force had scratched my skin. Seeing blood on my handkerchief, my husband was in despair.

"My God," he exclaimed, "what have I done? Anechka, my dear, forgive me. I have wounded you. Does it pain you, tell me, does it pain you very much?"

I began to reassure him that there was no "wound," but just a mere scratch which would disappear by the morning. Fiodor was seriously upset, and, above all, was ashamed of his fit of anger. The whole evening was given up to his apologies and expressions of sympathy and tenderness. And I, too, was boundlessly happy that my absurd joke had ended so happily. I sincerely repented of having made Fiodor suffer, and I promised myself never again to play such a joke, having learnt from this experience to what a furious, almost irresponsible state my dear husband was capable of being reduced in moments of jealousy.

I still preserve the locket and the anonymous letter (of 18th May, 1876).

Here, then, is another case of an older and experienced man married to a younger wife, hardly able to believe, as other documents attest,[3] that his happiness is real. This man, moreover, is by general consent one of the profoundest students of human nature that ever lived, especially of its roots in the unconscious. Yet, caught in the grip of ancestral jealousy, his wisdom vanishes as if it had never existed and he becomes as helpless as a child. It would be tedious to point out all the parallels between this narrative and *Othello* (the mention of which in the narrative is itself significant) down even to such a detail as the strangling. The same readiness of a profoundly loving nature to believe the worst, the same precipitate rage and failure to give any opportunity to explain, the same centering of everything on a token of love, with the other ending only perhaps because Anna was able to produce the locket as Desdemona was not able to produce its counterpart, the handkerchief. And the startling thing is that it all happened in this later case without an Iago—the Russian Desdemona being her own Iago. Then how much more easily with him! The fact that Dostoevsky and Othello, too, were both prone to epileptic attacks is of more than passing interest, as is the antipodal reversal of emotion in the two men when the truth appears. All in all, the irrational and inundating character of jealousy has seldom been better set forth than in this incident, not even in Leontes in *The Winter's Tale*, whom it also helps us understand. I can testify from many experiments with this anecdote that it ends for good and all the doubts of those who until they heard it thought that in *Othello* Shakespeare had for once slipped up in his knowledge of human nature or, worse, had sacrificed that knowledge to theatrical effect.

IX

Though the main stumbling block to readers of *Othello* is an incapacity to realize what jealousy can be when aroused in a nature not easily jealous, there are other sources of trouble, numerous specific moments in the play where a failure to notice some "tremendous trifle" in the text is the source of grave misunderstanding. Three of them may be mentioned.

1. In the scene, staged by Iago, where Othello oversees Cassio talking with Bianca, supposedly of Desdemona, and catches fragments of their conversation, it is frequently held that the Moor is too readily duped. This sort of thing is all right on the stage, but it couldn't happen in life. Such objectors have forgotten that Othello has but a moment before emerged from an epileptic fit and is in no condition to exercise his critical faculty.

2. When Othello, near the end, declares that Cassio has admitted his guilt, he is usually taken to be speaking in general of the circumstantial case against him and, more particularly, of Iago's loathsome account of Cassio's confession to him. But he means far more than this. In the darkness and confusion Othello mistakes the voice of the wounded Roderigo—"O, villain that I am!"—for Cassio's. He hears what he fears. He thinks he has heard Cassio with his dying words admit his guilt. "It is e'en so," Othello assents. What more convincing evidence could he ask for? Fail to take that "O, villain that I am!" into account, and the mistake based on it, and the whole character of Othello's act in killing Desdemona is altered. The point is a capital one. Many must have detected it. Yet of hundreds of readers of the play I have questioned I have yet to find the first one who noticed it for himself. Even when asked to find the passage in which Othello hears with his own ears "Cassio's" confession, few, even with the text before them, can locate it.

3. And then the classic question: How could Desdemona speak after she had been strangled? Medical authority has been marshaled on both sides of this question. But Shakespeare was seeking poetical, rather than physiological or anatomical truth (not that the former violates the latter). What happens at this point should be plain—and there is an old stage tradition, it is said, to support it. Othello has failed to stifle his wife, and, perceiving signs of life, does not again try to do what he has attempted in vain, but stabs her at the words "So, so." Not only does this make understandable her speaking again before death; the irony, the contrasts, and the symbolism agree in demanding what it is natural anyway for Othello to have done in the circumstances. His earlier,

> Yet I'll not shed her blood,
> Nor scar that whiter skin of hers than snow,

makes the inference almost irresistible that he will and does shed her blood, that he will and does scar that skin. Blood, throughout Shakespeare as throughout poetry, is the symbol of passion, of the instinctive as against the rational life. It is needed here to make visible Othello's descent from the judicial and sacrificial mood in which he enters his wife's chamber—

It is the cause, it is the cause, my soul,

—to the fury at the last when he denies his victim even a moment for one prayer. The linking of Desdemona with snow at this point is a confirmation of the symbolic color scheme of the play and effects a final fearful contrast with the red for which Othello has now come to stand. Moreover, Shakespeare seems to have specifically prepared for the moment when Othello stabs Desdemona by the moment when he strikes her. In retrospect the earlier scene seems like a rehearsal of the later. They are the two most nearly unendurable moments in the play. The sharpness of the contrast depends on Othello's finally doing with a knife what he had already done with his hand.

X

Nowhere else in a single pair of characters, nor even in *King Lear*, does Shakespeare more squarely confront the diabolic and the divine than in Iago and Desdemona.

. . . do but see his vice;
'Tis to *her* virtue a just equinox.

With a change of one word, Iago himself expresses it for us perfectly.

One might expect that in order to make the most of this contrast the two would be brought into frequent contact in the course of the play. But they are not. They are never alone together, and only twice are there what might be called dialogues between them. Near the quay at Cyprus, partly to hide her fears about Othello in the storm, Desdemona indulges in light banter with Iago and, as we saw, he draws the ideal portrait which clandestinely is a picture of herself and which he brings to a "lame and impotent conclusion." No more is needed to show his sensitiveness to moral beauty. Why did Shakespeare take the trouble to demonstrate it so convincingly? What becomes of it during the rest of the play? It is almost wholly repressed. That it is capable of rising above the surface, however, is proved by that extraordinary exclamation near the end,

If Cassio do remain,
He hath a daily beauty in his life
That makes me ugly.

But if the daily beauty in Cassio's life makes Iago ugly, how about the hourly, the momentary beauty in Desdemona's? What does that do to him? The poet, if I am not mistaken, dedicates the one highly dramatic scene in which the two talk with each other to bringing that out.

It comes just after the fearful "brothel" scene in which Othello has flung all the evil he imagines straight in his wife's face. On his exit, Desdemona, stunned, sinks into a state beyond the relief of tears. She ominously bids Emilia lay her wedding sheets on her bed and summon to comfort her in her distress—of all people on earth—the very one who has caused it! At the nadir of her despair she will consult Iago on what she can do to win her lord again. Iago comes, and we have as psychologically interesting a scene as there is in the play. Desdemona's condition of semi-somnolence, just preceding it, is the correlative and opposite of Othello's epileptic seizure. In each case a scene with Iago follows. The same thing that Iago does to Othello in the earlier one is done to him, in a reversed sense, in the later one. Here, if ever, in this interview between the villain and the heroine, we have a chance to study the effect on each other of something close to pure evil and pure good. By way of mediation, Emilia, who is a paradoxical mixture of the two, is also present.

The effect of evil on good may be dismissed in a word by saying that good here not only does not resist evil, it is unaware of its presence. It acts as if it did not exist—which is another way of saying that it treats the evil man as if he were good.

Does evil reciprocate and treat good as if it did not exist? It does not. It cannot. Evil is forever uneasy in the presence of good, and it is significant to begin with that Desdemona and Emilia in this scene each speak almost twice as many words as does the usually voluble Iago. But the quality as well as the quantity of his utterances is altered.

> Do not weep, do not weep. Alas the day!
> I pray you be content.
> Go in, and weep not; all things shall be well.

In their simplicity and sympathy the words sound utterly unlike anything else in Iago's role. "Exactly!" it will be said. "Here the man's histrionic powers are at their acme. He can feign even pity and compassion perfectly. Here he sinks to his lowest point—pretending to comfort the one he is about to destroy. These, if any were ever shed, are crocodile tears." Of course they are crocodile tears. Short of throwing up his whole plot, Iago is compelled to go on acting. But what taught this crocodile-Iago to simulate sympathy so consummately? What if not the very buried sympathy that Desdemona's presence had activated in him? The words that crocodile-Iago needs for his part are the very ones that a genuinely sympathetic Iago might have spoken. It is as if an inner prompter handed them to him at a moment when he was at a loss for the next words in his role. Who is that Inner Prompter? An unconscious as well as a conscious Iago are present in this scene exactly as there were two Shylocks to offer to Antonio in one breath, as it were, the loan without interest and the bloody bond. The parallel is startling. To feign goodness successfully it is not enough that we should have had experience with goodness in the past; we must retain potential goodness. Otherwise the counterfeit will be crude. Iago's is so true it could be passed for genuine coin. It was the unconscious Iago that made it so.

Whatever unique thing, good or bad, any individual may have made out of his inherited qualities, there underneath, however deep down, the human nature into which he was born is bound to survive in its general composite trend and upshot as incarnated in the lives of all his ancestors, a mingled web of light and dark. Only let that individual be taken off guard, suddenly confronted with some circumstance or person alien to the world to which he has conditioned himself, and that fundamental human nature will reassert itself. The situation here is precisely that. Unless Shakespeare is contravening his seemingly universal practice and is making Iago a pure abstraction, the rule is bound not to fail. It does not fail. And this scene is inserted, I believe, to show that it does not fail.

Imagine any man calloused by bitterness and cruelty. If a child, especially a beautiful child, were without warning to throw her arms about his neck, nestle up to him confidingly, and speak words of piercing loveliness, is it conceivable that he would not be moved? No matter how he might try to hide it or deny it to himself, that remnant of goodness in him that nothing can eradicate would respond. Dostoevsky chose precisely this situation for the crisis of the first of his great masterpieces, *Crime and Punishment*. It is at the moment when the little girl Polenka throws her arms about the murderer Raskolnikov and kisses him that he is reborn. He reverts a moment later, as might be expected, to his most devastating power-fantasies. But the seed has been sown. Long afterward it comes to fruit. *Mutatis mutandis*, Shakespeare, if I am not mistaken, gives us the same situation here, if with the other outcome. We never see Iago repentant as we do Raskolnikov, but the effect of his brief interview with Desdemona shakes him to the foundation.

From the moment he enters he is scarcely recognizable as the same man we have known under the name of Iago, and except for three sharp sentences he speaks to his wife which make the difference the more conspicuous, the man who addresses Desdemona remains unrecognizable throughout the scene. If anyone ignorant of the story were to read it by itself, he would be utterly bewildered. One Iago is so tender and sympathetic, the other so coarse and ill-tempered.[4] But we who have read the play, if we have been attentive, will recall certain passages from Iago's own role that throw light on this moment of it, for Shakespeare is nothing if not preparatory. First, we remember his penetrating description of the moral beauty of the woman into whose intimate presence he now comes for the first time since the occasion near the quay when he uttered it. He stressed then, particularly, her power to subdue all feeling of anger or revenge, precisely the emotions that almost any woman would have given unrestrained vent to after being struck and insulted by her husband as Desdemona had been just before this very meeting. "She is of so free, so kind, so apt, so blessed a disposition, that she holds it a vice in her goodness not to do more than she is requested." That sentence, too, might well come to mind. And those strange words in soliloquy:

> Now, I do love her too,
> Not out of absolute lust,

and, finally, the words to Roderigo, "as, they say, base men being in love have then a nobility in their natures more than is native to them," which puts in a nutshell the very truth on which we are now insisting: that no matter how wicked a man may become, the nobility that is an inevitable part of his inheritance will be there underneath ready to appear under the right conditions. Are the conditions right for the appearance of the nobility in this base man? They obviously are, whether he knows it or not.

At the end of their interview Desdemona kneels. It is left to the actress and to our imaginations to decide whether she kneels just to heaven or to Iago also, whom she is beseeching to go to her lord on her behalf. If, as I believe, it should be to Iago too, we have a counterpart of the famous scene where the sainted Father Zossima kneels to the potential parricide, Dmitri Karamazov, in Dostoevsky's novel. (And if we want to press the parallel we may even believe that something deep in Desdemona's unconscious mind saw into the future and was seeking less a reconciliation between herself and her lord than one between Iago and Othello, of any breach between whom she is of course at the moment unaware.) It is noteworthy that Desdemona's final words in this interview are practically a paraphrase of Shakespeare's own confession of faith about love in the 116th sonnet, culminating, in her case, in the lines:

> Unkindness may do much;
> And his unkindness may defeat my life,
> But never taint my love.

If anything was capable of it, this longest and in many respects loveliest speech in the role of the laconic Desdemona, from which these words come, must have moved Iago to the depths, imparting a meaning he had never dreamed of to his, "Now I do love her too." If it did shake him, it is the supreme tribute to her in the entire play: even Iago could not escape the effect of her presence. That the whole interview did move him profoundly Shakespeare all but proves, where it is his habit to prove such things, in the little scene that immediately follows—in that and in the rest of the play.

When Desdemona goes out, Roderigo enters, and in the first part of what ensues we see Iago for the first time at his wit's end, unable to devise anything by way of answer to Roderigo's importunities. In his brief and stalling replies to his dupe's reiterated complaints Shakespeare is plainly registering the profound and disturbing effect that Desdemona—and incidentally Emilia—has just had on him. She has sapped his power. In thirty-four lines of text, these are Iago's speeches—Roderigo says all the rest:

> What in the contrary?
> Will you hear me, Roderigo?
> You charge me most unjustly.
> Well; go to; very well.
> Very well.
> You have said now.

Is this Iago? To paraphrase Lodovico's words about Othello: Is this the resourceful nature that obstacles could not daunt? He resembles himself as little as Falstaff does himself at the moment of his rejection, or as Falstaff resembles that other Falstaff who creeps into the basket of foul linen in the home of Mistress Ford. It is no answer to say that Iago, before the scene is over, does partly recover his wits. How came he to lose them? And such wits as he does recover resemble those of some common ruffian rather than those of the archpsychologist that Iago was at his intellectual best. The expedient he recommends to Roderigo is the desperate one of knocking out Cassio's brains. It is not coincidence, but more nearly cause and effect, that from the presence of Desdemona he steps immediately to this fatal mistake. The man has himself received a death blow. For the first time in his life he has encountered a force more powerful than his own diabolic nature. What has happened to him he doubtless does not understand. He is intelligent, but not intelligent enough for that. Never again in the play do we find him perfectly poised and sure of himself as he had been previously. He almost hesitates about Cassio's death. The final reason he gives for it, the daily beauty of Cassio's life, shows that the beauty of Desdemona has given him a mortal (or perhaps we should say an immortal) wound. He would have been incapable of offering that highly uncharacteristic reason before he had that fatal interview. He is defeated. From his first false step he goes on to another and another until he sinks into that final terrific silence that is but a prelude to the silence of death. The Turk to whom he is compared went down under the waters of the Mediterranean. He goes down under the same element in its symbolic sense.

XI

Into what element did Desdemona pass at death?

Our imaginations cannot help asking that question, however idle it may seem. If Iago went down under water, Desdemona might well have been lifted into air. If his end was silence, hers should be harmony. If he descended to hell, she should have ascended to heaven, or, as we are more prone to say today, if he reverted to the unconscious, she must have been transformed into spirit. Water, silence, hell; air, harmony, heaven: that is what the symbols seem to call for. But this is the merest fancy unless there is warrant for it in the text. These are castles in the air unless there is a Shakespearean foundation to put under them.

We have noted over and over Shakespeare's habit of concealing, in what seem like brief digressions or superfluous scenes, clues to the over- and undermeanings of his plays—as in the garden scene in *Richard II*, the dawn passage in Julius *Caesar*, or the one in *Hamlet* where the Prince teases Polonius about the cloud.

If readers of *Othello* were asked to select the most supererogatory passage in the play, they would probably be unanimous, unless some forgot its very existence, in picking the opening of Act III where Cassio comes in with some musicians who are prepared to play but are peremptorily dismissed by the Clown (for there *is* a clown in *Othello*):

> *Clown*: Then put up your pipes in your bag, for I'll away. Go; vanish into air, away! (*Exeunt Musicians*)

This brief overture to what is admittedly one of the greatest acts Shakespeare ever wrote is a tolerably obvious allegory of that sudden interruption of the music of Othello's love which is to be the subject of the act—a fact that in itself justifies us, apart from its very inconsequentiality, in searching it for other clues.

The passage emphasizes the fact that it is upon wind instruments that the musicians are prepared to play, and the Clown himself plays on that idea when he tells them to "vanish into air." Vanish into your proper element, he might have said. The other thing stressed is the idea of inaudible music:

> *Clown*: But, masters, here's money for you: and the general so likes your music, that he desires you, for love's sake, to make no more noise with it.
> *First Mus.*: Well, sir, we will not.
> *Clown*: If you have any music that may not be heard, to't again: but, as they say, to hear music the general does not greatly care.
> *First Mus.*: We have none such, sir.

This sounds like the idlest fooling, and on the surface it is just that. But when we remember Keats's

Heard melodies are sweet, but those unheard
    Are sweeter; therefore, ye soft pipes, play on;
Not to the sensual ear, but, more endear'd,
    Pipe to the spirit ditties of no tone,

we see that, so far from mere fooling, this idea of inaudible music is the idea of poetry itself brought down by the Clown to the level of burlesque and parody. The quintessence of a poem is precisely its music that may not be heard. May not, notice, nor cannot.

Where, audible or inaudible, is there music in Othello? Where, especially, if anywhere, is there wind music?

We think immediately of the storm off Cyprus. There the gale roared until Montano cried, "The wind hath spoke aloud." There it tossed water on the very stars, bringing a chaos of the elements that forecasts the chaos that "is come again" in Othello's soul when Iago loosens the moral hurricane that parts the Moor from his wife more violently than ever the physical tempest did. The Turks go down in the first storm. Turk-Iago goes down in the second one. Othello and Desdemona were parted by the first storm, but were reunited after it. They were parted by the second one. Was there a Second Cyprus?

If Shakespeare carries his symbolism through with Iago, is it inconceivable that he may have done the same with Desdemona and Othello? Here, if anywhere, it would be natural to seek the poetry of this poem, the music in this play that may not be heard.

A scientist gets his hypothesis from he does not always know where. He subjects it to the test of facts, and accepts it or rejects it accordingly. So it should be with the interpretation of a work of literary art. Where a suggested reading comes from is not the important question. The important question is whether it can pass the test of the text. If not, however alluring, it must be dismissed.

Let us look at the storm scene for a *third* time.

A Sea-port in Cyprus. An open place near the quay. (Cyprus, remember, is an island, and we know what an island came to mean to Shakespeare near the end of his life.)

Three figures with wind-blown garments and spray-spattered hair are gazing out over mountainous waves toward a misty horizon:

What from the cape can you discern at sea?

Nothing at all: it is a high-wrought flood.
I cannot, 'twixt the heaven and the main,
Descry a sail.

Methinks the wind hath spoke aloud at land;
A fuller blast ne'er shook our battlements.
If it hath ruffian'd so upon the sea,
What ribs of oak, when mountains melt on them,
Can hold the mortise? What shall we hear of this?

A segregation of the Turkish fleet.
For do but stand upon the foaming shore,
The chidden billow seems to pelt the clouds;
The wind-shak'd surge, with high and monstrous mane,
Seems to cast water on the burning Bear
And quench the guards of the ever-fixed pole:
I never did like molestation view
On the enchafed flood.

A storm that assaults heaven itself! Which storm is this? The storm in which
the Turks went down, or the storm for which Othello prayed?—

May the winds blow till they have waken'd death!
And let the labouring bark climb hills of seas
Olympus-high, and duck again as low
As hell's from heaven!

—a storm that did indeed awaken death and duck as low as hell:

Whip me, ye devils, . . .
Blow me about in winds! roast me in sulphur!
Wash me in steep-down gulfs of liquid fire!

What place in the story have we reached? On which side of death are we?
    And now, suddenly, there is a fourth speaker on the shore. "Our wars are done."
A ship has made port, he announces, bringing one Michael Cassio. The Turks are
drowned. And while that thought, the messenger declares, comforts Cassio,

yet he looks sadly
And prays the Moor be safe, for they were parted
With foul and violent tempest.

And like an echo from some remote region of

old, unhappy, far-off things,
And battles long ago,

we hear a voice saying,

> Dear general, I never gave you cause.

But the confusion—or is it the clarity?—increases. Here is Cassio himself! And as he joins the others on the shore, he cries,

> O, let the heavens
> Give him defence against the elements,
> For I have lost him on a dangerous sea.

You have indeed, Cassio, and on a vaster sea than any Mediterranean.

> "Is he well shipp'd?" a voice inquires.

> *Cas.*: His bark is stoutly timber'd, and his pilot
> Of very expert and approv'd allowance;
> Therefore my hopes, not surfeited to death,
> Stand in bold cure.

In spite of all, Cassio has kept faith.
And now there is a sudden cry within, "A sail, a sail, a sail!"

> The town is empty; on the brow o' the sea
> Stand ranks of people, and they cry, "A sail!"

We see them gazing out with tense faces over the gray oncoming waves. But who are they? Whom are they awaiting? What town have they left empty? And for a second we remember another unidentified little town that was left similarly desolate:

> What little town by river or sea shore,
>   Or mountain-built with peaceful citadel,
>   Is emptied of this folk, this pious morn?
> And, little town, thy streets for evermore
>   Will silent be; and not a soul to tell
>   Why thou art desolate, can e'er return.

Perhaps these watchers for a sail, likewise, will never return to their homes.
But the ship is in. And whom has it brought?

> Tempests themselves, high seas, and howling winds,

The gutter'd rocks and congregated sands,
Traitors ensteep'd to clog the guiltless keel,
As having sense of beauty, do omit
Their mortal natures, letting go safely by
The divine Desdemona.

Desdemona? Then she escaped the traitors? She survived the storm? It cannot
be. But it is—for here she is herself:

O, behold,
The riches of the ship is come on shore! . . .
Hail to thee, lady! and the grace of heaven,
Before, behind thee, and on every hand,
Enwheel thee round!

Heaven again? We were told it was Cyprus. But wherever she is she acknowledges
the welcome. Her brow, however, shows she is troubled.

Des.: What tidings can you tell me of my lord?
Cas.: He is not yet arriv'd . . . .
Des.: O! but I fear—How lost you company?
Cas.: The great contention of the sea and skies
Parted our fellowship.

Will her fears, this time, be justified?
Again there is a cry: "But hark! a sail" that is echoed from within. "A sail, a
sail!"
Again it cannot be. But again it is. Othello has come to port. There is an
interlude. Then he enters and takes Desdemona in his arms:

O my fair warrior!
My dear Othello!
It gives me wonder great as my content
To see you here before me. O my soul's joy!
If after every tempest come such calms . . . .

And in a kind of divine confusion we ask:
After which storm?
This is what I have long been in the habit of calling *The Sixth Act of Othello*.
Here is music played on the wind instruments of the storm, which, like the storm
itself, reaches the stars. Here, as surely as music is harmony, is music that may not
be heard. Here is form that, like the form of Keats's urn, does

     tease us out of thought
As doth eternity.

Like a face in the embers, it is there for those who see it, not there for those who do not.

Bradley speaks of *Othello* as having less cosmic sweep than the other Tragedies. "We seem to be aware in it," he says, "of a certain limitation, a partial suppression of that element in Shakespeare's mind which unites him with the mystical poets and with the great musicians and philosophers." It is true that the atmosphere of *Othello* is more realistic and "modern" than that of the other Tragedies. But that is precisely what makes such effects as his use of the storm in this play the more miraculous. It is the virtue of Othello that—like the poetry of Emily Dickinson—it synthesizes the domestic and the cosmic.

"But you have forgotten one thing," someone can be counted on to object just here. "Iago, too, survived the storm off Cyprus. It was he, indeed, under whose conduct Desdemona came safely through!" And the tone of triumph implies, "What can you say to that?"

How fortunate that there are prose and reason in the world to keep the poetry straight! Why not go even further and point out that this whole play is obviously rubbish because all the Italians in it speak English?

But the objection about Iago is overruled even on its own premise. The Turk goes down. And if Desdemona reaches heaven after the Second Storm, it is partly because of the very tempest through which Iago led her. Here Shakespeare plumbs the very depths of evil. There were two Iagos: the one who went down, and the "good Iago" whom Desdemona trusted and who drew the picture of her on the quay.

Here, if ever, we see the difference between logic and imagination, between factual and poetical truth. To the intellect this diagram is what it is, no more, no less:

But the eye inevitably supplements it by drawing two lines parallel to the right-hand sides of the inner figure, completing the outer one. To the reason, the fact that Othello and Desdemona were parted by a physical tempest, then reunited, then parted by a moral one, sets up no presumption whatever that they will again be reunited. The opposite assumption is just as logical, and probably even more convincing to the intellect, which is skeptical by nature. But, to the imagination, what may be called the transcendental reunion of Othello and Desdemona is as irresistible as the completion of the geometrical diagram is to the eye. For, as Blake is continually reminding us, imagination is more analogous to sensation than to thought. Imagination is spiritual sensation—"That most pure spirit of sense." It is its own evidence.

Beauty itself doth of itself persuade,

says Shakespeare in *Lucrece*. As Longinus saw, long ago, it does not convince by logic, it takes captive. What happens after death is strictly an unknown quantity to reason. But as certainly as the value of x in an equation can be calculated if the other quantities are known, so certainly can the imagination "calculate" the unknown factors in life from the known ones. Poetry is the art of spiritual mensuration. Its validity or lack of validity can be referred to no standard outside itself and us. It depends solely on its impact on our imaginations. So with such creations of the Imagination as heaven and hell. Whether they are true or not is the most important thing in the world. Whether or not they exist is a senseless question. "He who has never hoped shall never receive what he has never hoped for."

XII

Whoever is content to see Iago go down under water with the Turks and does not "hope," in this high Heracleitean sense, to behold Desdemona "vanish into air" or catch a glimpse of her in heaven will be compelled to admit at any rate that she is alive after death, on earth, both within the play and without it. Cassio, near the end, tells how, in a letter found in the slain Roderigo's pocket, there is a revelation of Iago's original plan to have Roderigo brave Cassio upon the watch after Iago has made him drunk.

. . . even but now he spake,

says Cassio, wondering as if at a miracle,

After long seeming dead.

But if Roderigo spoke after death, Desdemona not only spoke but, in the words of Wordsworth's great sonnet, lived, and acted, and served the future hour. That which acts is actual, and it is Desdemona who effects the final transformation in Othello that imparts to his last words their preternatural calm. In that last speech he describes himself as one who

Like the base Judean, threw a pearl away
Richer than all his tribe.

It is strange that nearly all editors have preferred to this reading of the Folio that of the Quarto,

Like the base Indian, threw a pearl away . . .

in the face of Othello's "I kiss'd thee ere I kill'd thee" a moment later, which is as clear an identification of the murderer-Othello with Judas as could be asked. (The Othello who *now* kisses her is another man.)

Who the pearl was the base Judean threw away all the world knows, final proof, were it needed, that just as the poet ties Iago and war together in this play, so he links Desdemona with the spirit that brings war to an end. "*Solitudinem faciunt, pacem appellant*," cried Tacitus, compressing into one of the compactest sentences ever written the fatal error we make in confusing *the end of war* and *what ends war*. At the end of war, if there is not a "solitude," then there is a truce, a fresh balance of power, or an imposed reign of order ("order," the counterfeit of peace) which holds until the old conflict breaks out anew. And meanwhile men go on seeking some law, or formula, or system that will end the rule of Mars. Only the simple way, that is at once the easiest and the hardest, is not tried. "Here you are teaching all the time," says a character in Chekhov, "fathoming the depths of the ocean, dividing the weak from the strong, writing books and challenging to duels—and everything remains as it is; but, behold! some feeble old man will mutter just one word with a holy spirit, . . . and everything will be topsy-turvy, and in Europe not one stone will be left standing upon another." One word with a holy spirit. It was such a word that Desdemona spoke. She is what the greatest sages from Laotse to Tolstoy have taught. She shows that to be is better than to act, for through whoever is the gods themselves act.

The secret of social and political strife, of conflict between nations, is only that of individual and domestic strife writ large. War and peace, says *Othello*, confirming *Hamlet* and carrying the thought from its negative to its positive phase, are states of the soul. War in the military sense is the outer manifestation of war in the psychological sense preexisting in the inner worlds of its fomenters and participants. That is not saying that outer conditions have nothing to do with the production of war. But it is only as those conditions first produce a military state of the soul that they secondly produce war in its more generally accepted sense. And, no matter how adverse, they do not *necessarily* produce a military state of the soul, as Desdemona shows; on the contrary, as Iago shows, that state is a most potent producer of those very conditions. It was to demonstrate this double truth that Dostoevsky wrote *Crime and Punishment*. *Othello* demonstrates it even more compactly.

NOTES

1. See the chapter on *Hamlet*.

2. All this is remarkably confirmed by a dream of a young theological student that Jung records. The dreamer saw a magician dressed wholly in black who, he nevertheless knew, was the white magician. Presently the figure was joined by another, the black magician, dressed wholly in white. It was obviously at the moment Cinthio's tale activated, as the psychologists say, the same ancestral images in Shakespeare's mind that Othello and Iago were conceived. There could scarcely be better proof that he who takes Othello as just "cheater," just realism, or even as just drama, is missing something. Another confirmation of this imagery is to be found in Blake's "The Little Black Boy" with its line: "And I am black, but O! my soul is white."

3. It is of interest that Dostoevsky proposed to this woman through the medium of an invented story, just as Othello wooed Desdemona through stories into which a considerable element of unconscious invention undoubtedly entered.

4. When Emilia suggests that some cozening slave is the author of this slander, Iago turns it off with a "Fie, there is no such man." Whereupon Desdemona exclaims, "If any such there be, Heaven pardon him." "A halter pardon him! and hell gnaw his bones!" cries Emilia. Our emotional responses to these two lines measure the respective amounts of Desdemona and Emilia there are in our own natures. Emilia is the Gratiano—on an immensely higher plane—of this scene. She is a safety valve for the crowd's feelings.

1951—Kenneth Burke. "'Othello': An Essay to Illustrate a Method," from *The Hudson Review*

Kenneth Burke, a literary critic and theorist of rhetoric, taught at Bennington College. *Kenneth Burke on Shakespeare* is a collection of his writings on the playwright. His other books include *The Philosophy of Literary Form* and *Language as Symbolic Action*.

Othello. Will you, I pray, demand that demi-devil
Why he hath thus ensnared my soul and body?
Iago. Demand me nothing: what you know, you know:
From this time forth I never will speak word.
Lodovico. What! not to pray?
Gratiano. Torments will ope your lips.

I

Iago as Katharma

OTHELLO: ACT V, SCENE II. Desdemona, fated creature, marked for a tragic end by her very name (Desdemona: "moan-death") lies smothered. Othello, just after the words cited as our motto, has stabbed himself and fallen across her body. (Pattern of Othello's farewell speech: How he spoke of a "base Indian", and we knew by that allusion he meant Othello. When it was told that he "threw a pearl away", for "threw away" we substituted "strangled", and for the pearl, "Desdemona". Hearing one way, we interpreted another. While he was ostensibly telling of a new thing, thus roundabout he induced us to sum up the entire meaning of the story. Who then was the "turban'd Turk" that Othello seized by the throat and smote? By God, it was himself—our retrospective translation thus suddenly blazing into a new present identity, a new act here and now, right before our eyes, as he stabs himself.) Iago, "Spartan dog, / More fell than anguish, hunger, or the sea", is invited by Lodovico to "look on the tragic loading of this bed." *Exeunt omnes*, with Iago as prisoner, we being assured that they will see to "the censure of this hellish villain, / The time, the place, the torture." Thus like the tragic bed, himself bending beneath a load, he is universally hated for his ministrations. And in all fairness, as *advocatus diaboli* we would speak for him, in considering the cathartic nature of his role.

Reviewing, first, the definition of some Greek words central to the ritual of cure:

Katharma: that which is thrown away in cleansing; the off-scourings, refuse, of a sacrifice; hence, worthless fellow. "It was the custom at Athens," lexicographers inform us, "to reserve certain worthless persons, who in case of plague, famine, or other visitations from heaven, were thrown into the sea," with an appropriate formula, "in the belief that they would cleanse away or wipe off the guilt of the nation." And these were *katharmata*. Of the same root, of course, are our words *cathartic* and *catharsis*, terms originally related to both physical and ritual purgation.

A synonym for *katharma* was *pharmakos*: poisoner, sorcerer, magician; one who is sacrificed or executed as an atonement or purification for others; a scapegoat. It is related to *pharmakon*: drug, remedy, medicine, enchanted potion, philtre, charm, spell, incantation, enchantment, poison.

Hence, with these terms in mind, we note that Iago has done this play some service. Othello's suspicions, we shall aim to show, arise from within, in the sense that they are integral to the motive he stands for; but the playwright cuts through that tangle at one stroke, by making Iago a voice at Othello's ear.

What arises within, if it wells up strongly and presses for long, will seem imposed from without. One into whose mind melodies spontaneously pop, must eventually "hear voices". "Makers" become but "instruments", their acts a sufferance. Hence, "inspiration", "afflatus", "angels", and "the devil". Thus, the very extremity of inwardness in the motives of Iago can make it seem an outwardness. Hence we are readily disposed to accept the dramatist's dissociation. Yet villain and hero here are but essentially inseparable parts of the one fascination.

Add Desdemona to the inseparable integer. That is: add the privacy of Desdemona's treasure, as vicariously owned by Othello in manly miserliness (Iago represents the threat implicit in such cherishing), and you have a tragic trinity of ownership in the profoundest sense of ownership, the property in human affections, as fetishistically localized in the object of possession, while the possessor is himself possessed by his very engrossment (Iago being the result, the apprehension that attains its dramatic culmination in the thought of an agent acting to provoke the apprehension). The single mine-own-ness is thus dramatically split into the three principles of possession, possessor, and estrangement (threat of loss). Hence, trust and distrust, though *living in* each other, can be shown *wrestling with* each other. *La propriété, c'est le vol.* Property fears theft because it is theft.

Sweet thievery, but thievery nonetheless. Appropriately, the first outcry in this play was of "Thieves, thieves, thieves!" when Iago stirred up Desdemona's father by shouting: "Look to your house, your daughter, and your bags! / Thieves! thieves!"—first things in a play being as telltale as last things. Next the robbery was spiritualized: "You have lost your soul." And finally it was reduced to imagery both lewd and invidious: "An old black ram is tupping your white ewe," invidious because of the social discrimination involved in the Moor's blackness. So we have the necessary ingredients, beginning from what Desdemona's father, Brabantio, called "the property of youth and maidenhood." (Nor are the connotations of *pharmakon*, as evil-working drug, absent from the total recipe, since Brabantio keeps circling about this theme, to explain how the lover robbed the father of his property in the daughter. So it is there, in the offing, as imagery, even though rationalistically disclaimed; and at one point, Othello does think of poisoning Desdemona.)

Desdemona's role, as one of the persons in this triune tension (or "psychosis"), might also be illuminated by antithesis. In the article on the Fine Arts (in the eleventh edition of the *Encyclopaedia Britannica*), the elements of pleasure "which are not disinterested" are said to be:

> the elements of personal exultation and self-congratulation, the pride of
> exclusive possession or acceptance, all these emotions, in short, which
> are summed up in the lover's triumphant monosyllable, "Mine."

Hence it follows that, for Othello, the beautiful Desdemona was not an aesthetic object. The thought gives us a radical glimpse into the complexity of her relation to the audience (her nature as a rhetorical "topic"). First, we note how, with the increased cultural and economic importance of private property, an aesthetic might arise antithetically to such norms, exemplifying them in reverse, by an idea of artistic enjoyment that would wholly transcend "mine-own-ness". The sharper the stress upon the *meum* in the practical realm, the greater the invitation to its denial in an aesthetic *nostrum*.

We are here considering the primary paradox of dialectic, stated as a maxim in the formula beloved by dialectician Coleridge: "Extremes meet." Note how, in this instance, such meeting of the extremes adds to our engrossment in the drama. For us, Desdemona is an aesthetic object: we never forget that we have no legal rights in her, and we never forget that she is but an "imitation". But *what* is she imitating? She is "imitating" her third of the total tension (the disequilibrium of monogamistic love, considered as a topic). She is imitating a major perturbation of property, as so conceived. In this sense, however aloof from her the audience may be in discounting her nature as a mere playwright's invention, her role can have a full effect upon them only insofar as it draws upon firm beliefs and dark apprehensions that not only move the audience *within* the conditions of the play, but prevail as an unstable and disturbing cluster of motives *outside* the play, or "prior to" it. Here the "aesthetic," even in negating or transcending "mine-own-ness," would draw upon it for purposes of poetic persuasion. We have such appeal in mind when speaking of the "topical" element. You can get the point by asking yourself: "So far as catharsis and wonder are concerned, what is gained by the fact that the play imitates *this particular tension* rather than some other?"[1]

In sum, Desdemona, Othello, and Iago are all partners of a single conspiracy. There were the enclosure acts, whereby the common lands were made private; here is the analogue, in the realm of human affinity, an act of spiritual enclosure. And might the final choking be also the ritually displaced effort to close a thoroughfare, as our hero fears lest this virgin soil that he had opened up become a settlement? Love, universal love, having been made private, must henceforth be shared vicariously, as all weep for Othello's loss, which is, roundabout, their own. And Iago is a function of the following embarrassment: Once such privacy has been made the norm, its denial can be but promiscuity. Hence his ruttish imagery, in which he signalizes one aspect of a total fascination.

So there is a whispering. There is something vaguely feared and hated. In itself it is hard to locate, being woven into the very nature of "consciousness"; but by the artifice of Iago it is made local. The tinge of malice vaguely diffused through the texture of events and relationships can here be condensed into a single principle, a devil, giving the audience as it were flesh to sink their claw-thoughts in. Where there is a gloom hanging over, a destiny, each man would conceive of the obstacle in terms of the instruments he already has for removing obstacles, so that a soldier would shoot the danger, a butcher thinks it could be chopped, and a merchant hopes to get rid of it by trading. But in Iago the menace is generalized. (As were you to see man-made law as destiny, and see destiny as a hag, cackling over a brew, causing you by a spell to wither.)

In sum, we have noted two major cathartic functions in Iago: (1) as regards the tension centering particularly in sexual love as property and ennoblement (monogamistic love), since in reviling Iago the audience can forget that his transgressions are theirs; (2) as regards the need of finding a viable localization for uneasiness (*Angst*) in general, whether shaped by superhuman forces or by human forces interpreted as super-human (the scapegoat here being but a highly generalized form of the over-investment that men may make in specialization). Ideally, in childhood, hating and tearing-at are one; in a directness and simplicity of hatred there may be a ritual cure for the bewilderments of complexity; and Iago may thus serve to give a feeling of integrity.

These functions merge into another, purely technical. For had Iago been one bit less rotten and unsleeping in his proddings, how could this play have been kept going, and at such a pitch? Until very near the end, when things can seem to move "of themselves" as the author need but actualize the potentialities already passed, Iago has goaded (tortured) the plot forward step by step, for the audience's villainous entertainment and filthy purgation. But his function as impresario takes us into matters that must be considered rather in terms of internal development.

II

Ideal Paradigm

As regards internal relations, let us propose the following ideal paradigm for a Shakespearean tragedy:

Act I: Setting the situation, pointing the arrows, with first unmistakable guidance of the audience's attitude towards the *dramatis personae*, and with similar setting of expectations as regards plot. Thus we learn of Cassio's preferment over Iago, of Iago's vengeful plan to trick Othello ("I follow him to serve my turn upon him . . . . But I will wear my heart upon my sleeve / for daws to peck at: I am not what I am.") Also we learn of Desdemona as the likely instrument or object of the deception. Usually, in this act, various strands that are later to be interwoven are introduced in succession, with minimum relation to one another, though an essential connection is felt: for instance, the incidents in the Council Chamber of Scene III will set up, in Othello's departure for battle, such conditions as, the audience already realizes, are suited to Iago's purposes (the situation thus implicitly containing his act).

Act II: Perhaps the most nearly "novelistic" act of a Shakespearean play? While events are developing towards the peripety, the audience is also allowed to become better acquainted with a secondary character much needed for the action. "Humanization", even possibly character-drawing for its own sake, as the second act of *Hamlet* might be entitled "Polonius" (the five being: "The Ghost", "Polonius", "The Play-within-a-Play", "Ophelia Pitiful", and "The Duel"). If Act I of Othello could be called "Iago Plans Vengeance", Act II would be "Cassio", or better, "Cassio Drunk", since his use in sharpening our understanding of all the relationships must also be eventful in itself, as well as performing some function that will serve as a potential, leading into the third act.

Or might the best way to approach the second act be to treat it as analogous to the introduction of the second theme in the classical sonata-form? Perhaps the most revealing example of the second act, thus considered, is in Corneille's *Cinna*. In the first act we have seen Cinna plotting against the life of the Emperor (Auguste). The woman whom he loves has demanded that he lead this conspiracy. The Emperor had mistreated her father, and she would have vengeance, though the Emperor has sought to make amends by being kind and generous to her personally. Hence, her lover, to prove himself "worthy" of her (what could a Cornelian tragedy do without that word, *digne!*) must conspire against the Emperor, with whom he stands in good favor. He plans the assassination for love. When officiating at a public sacrifice, he will make the Emperor the victim instead. Just before the first act ends, one of the conspirators enters with the news that Cinna and the other main conspirator, Maxime, have been summoned by the Emperor. The act ends on general consternation among the conspirators. They fear that their plot has been discovered.

In Act II, however, the plot is moved forward by a startling development. Auguste, who has not appeared in the first act at all, now confides to Cinna and Maxime that he is weary of rule. He would lay down his office, turning it over to Cinna and Maxime. (And to complete the irony of the situation, he also talks of plans for having Cinna marry Emilie, the very woman for whose love Cinna has vowed to slay him.) He "aspires to descend" (*aspire a descendre*), a good variant of the "mounting" theme which we always watch incidentally in our search for motives. Thus, one editor quotes Louis Racine, in his *Mémoires*: "'Note well that expression,' my father said with enthusiasm to my brother. 'One says *aspire to rise* (*aspirer à monter*); but you must know the human heart as well as Corneille did, to be able to say of an ambitious man that he aspires to descend.'"

The Emperor's unexpected decision, in all simplicity and affection, to make the conspirators rulers in his stead, is a *second theme* of the most startling sort. As contrasted with the expectations established at the end of Act I (the conspirators' fears that their conspiracy had been discovered), this development is so abrupt as almost to be a peripety. And the situation is so set up that, whereas Cinna and Maxime had, heretofore, been united despite a divergency of motives, they are now put at odds. Maxime would now abandon the conspiracy; but Cinna would carry it through regardless, since it is the price of his marriage to vengeance-minded Emilie.

In this kind of drama, almost each scene discloses something that jerks the characters into a new relationship (somewhat as, with the slow turning of a kaleidoscope, there is a succession of abrupt changes, each time the particles fall suddenly into a new design). But the change from the conspiracy theme of the first act to the abdication theme of the second is so exceptionally marked that it illustrates our point about the second theme even to excess.

Incidentally, as regards Shakespearean forms generally, we suppose that the relation between "second theme" and "double plot" should best be studied along the lines of Mr. Francis Fergusson's speculations about "analogy" in drama, in his recently published *Idea of a Theater*.

Act III: The peripety. In Act II, after Cassio had been established unmistakably as chivalrous in the extreme towards Desdemona, Iago had promised us in an aside: "He takes her by the palm; ay, well said, whisper; with as little a web as this I will ensnare as great a fly as Cassio. Ay, smile upon her, do; I will gyve thee in thine own courtship." Accordingly, we might call Act III "The Trap Is Laid." Or perhaps, "The Mock Disclosure", since here Iago causes Othello to see with his own eyes things that are not—and with this diabolic epiphany the play rises to a new level of engrossment.

Iago's manipulations of Othello's mind are like the catechizing of him in a black mass, as the pace of the play increases through their raging stichomythia; and in the handkerchief the solemn enunciation of the false doctrine has its corresponding revelation of the "sacred object."

Note, incidentally, how cautiously the dramatist has released the incidents of his story. Before Iago works on Othello as regards Desdemona, we have seen him duping Cassio, then Montano, and even to some extent his confederate Roderigo; also we have seen him moulding Othello's misjudgment of Cassio; and only then do the direct attacks upon Othello's confidence in Desdemona begin. Thus, through seeing Iago at work, the audience has been led carefully, step by step, to believe in the extent of his sinister resources, before the fullest dramaturgic risks (with correspondingly rich rewards) are undertaken. Only now, presumably, the dramatist feels that he has prepared the audience to accept the possibility of Othello's ensnarement.

References to the Cornelian structure might also assist us here. One Corneille editor who sums up the structure of the five acts could be translated freely thus:

> The first act makes clear the location of the action, the relations among the heroic figures (their situation), their interests, their characteristic ways, their intentions.
> The second gets the plot under way (*commence l'intrigue*).
> In the third, it reaches its full complication (literally, "it ties itself").
> The fourth prepares the untying (*dénouement*).
> And in the fifth act this resolution is completed.

The formula does not quite fit the particulars of *Cinna*. We do not know of Auguste's intentions until the second act; and we do not know until the third that Maxime is secretly in love with Emilie. So some of the development is got by *gradual revelation* of the character's designs.

However, the paradigm can help us glimpse a difference, in the third act, between a Cornelian "tying" and a Shakespearean "peripety". After all the workings at cross-purposes, the discovery that Maxime is in love with Emilie does serve to add the final complication. But this is hardly a reversal, such as we underwent at the beginning of Act II. Rather it is more like putting on "the last straw", by taking the final step in the directions already indicated. In contrast, recall the great peripety scene in *Julius Caesar*, Antony's speech to the mob. Here no such timely releasing of information is involved: as against the Cornelian transformation-by-information, we watch the transformations taking place before our eyes while we follow the effects of Antony's ingenious oratory. Similarly in *Othello*, the great scene in the third act where Iago finally springs the trap, involves no new disclosures, so far as the audience is concerned. We simply witness (with a pleasurable mixture of fear and admiration) a mounting series of upheavals, as Iago works his magic on the Moor.

Act IV: "The Pity of It." Indeed, might we not, even as a rule, call this station of a Shakespearean tragedy the "pity" act? There can be flashes of pity wherever opportunity offers, but might the fourth act be the one that seeks to say pity-pity-pity repeatedly? Thus, after the terror of Gloucester's eyes being torn out in Act III of *King Lear*, there is the pity of his blindness in Act IV, while the audience is likewise softened by the sweet tearfulness of Lear's reunion with Cordelia (father and daughter meeting like child and mother). In the same act of *Measure for Measure*, Mariana is pensively silent while the boy sings "Take, O take those lips away." In Hamlet, the corresponding stage is Ophelia's fatal bewilderment. In Macbeth, it is the killing of Macduff's son. And so on. Here, when Desdemona says to Othello, who has just struck her, "I have not deserved this," she almost literally repeats the Aristotelian formula for pity (that we pity those who suffer unjustly). And, after the slight flurry of hope when Othello, talking with Emilia, gets a report of Desdemona not at all like the one Iago had led him to expect, Desdemona's "willow" song is particularly sad because, in her preparations for Othello's return ("He says he will return incontinent") there are strong forebodings (making her rather like a victim going willingly towards sacrifice). She seems doubly frail, in both her body and her perfect forgiveness— an impression that the audience will retain to the end, so that the drama attains maximum poignancy when Othello, hugely, throttles her.

In *Cinna*, it is in the fourth act that Auguste learns of the treachery. Pity here takes the modified form of manly grief, as he in a great soliloquy first accuses himself, then gradually moves towards a monarchic resolution ("*O Romains, ô vengeance, ô pouvoir absolu . . .*"). Then it undergoes another modification, as the Empress begs Auguste to treat the conspirators with mercy. And in this tragedy, too, I believe, we might select the fourth as the "pity act."

The reference to modifications in *Cinna* also reminds us that sometimes the pity can be used purely as a device to "soften up" the audience. The pity we feel for Desdemona singing the willow song is of this sort. At other times it can be used to motivate some act of vengeance on the part of some character in the play, as with Macduff on hearing of his son's death.

Act V is, of course, the bringing of all surviving characters to a final relationship, the resolution, in accordance with the original pointing of the arrows, arrows pointed both rationalistically, by intrigue, and through a succession of ideas and images (topics) that direct the play into one channel of associations rather than another, thereby "setting the tone", and getting new implications from the sum of the many passing explicit references. When Othello says, "Put out the light, and then put out the light," is he but making the scene for the act, hence finding a device for killing her three times (for even without this, she dies twice, as were the second time a weak nervous twitch following a previous strong expulsion)? Or is this, ritually, a double darkness, imaginally saying that his enclosed mind is now engrossed with still narrower enclosure?

This analysis of the form does not cover all the important fields of investigation, even as regards the succession of acts (or succession of stages, insofar as the present explicit division into five acts may have been the work of editors, rather than of the playwright). There is a kind of ritualistic form lurking behind a drama, perhaps not wholly analyzable in terms of the intrigue. That is, the drama (like such a Platonic dialogue as the *Phaedrus*) may be treated formally as a kind of "initiation into a mystery"—and when approached exclusively in such terms, the analysis of the intrigue alone is not adequate. The mythic or ritual pattern (with the work as a viaticum for guiding us through a dark and dangerous passage) lurks behind the "rational" intrigue; and to some degree it requires a different kind of analysis, though ideally the course of the rational intrigue coincides with the course of the work, considered as viaticum.

Viewed in these terms, the first act would be "the way in". It states the primary conditions in terms of which the journey is to be localized or specified this time. The same essential journey could be taken in other terms; hence, there must be a point at which we glimpse the essence of the mystery as it lies beyond all terms; but this point can be reached only by going thoroughly into some one structure of terms. For though the ritual must always follow the same general succession of stages regardless of the intrigue, this course is repeated each time in the details proper to a particular intrigue. There is perhaps nothing essentially "irrational" about the stages of initiation; however, they may seem so, as contrasted with the rationality of the intrigue (with its need to present the natural development in terms of probability and necessity).

The second act (the introduction of the "second theme") would seem analogous to the definite pushing-off from shore. Of course, the very opening of the play was, in one sense, a pushing-off from shore, the abandoning of one realm for another. But once this decision has been taken, within its own internality there is another kind of departure when the second theme has entered, and we now do indeed feel ourselves under way (as though the bark had suddenly increased its speed, or suggested a further certainty in its movements).

In the peripety of the third act, the principle of internality confronts its very essence. Here is the withinness-of-withinness. It corresponds to the moment in the *Phaedrus* where Socrates has talked ecstatically of the soul as *self*-moving, as the "fountain and beginning of motion," and of a wing (a most unwinglike wing, by the way, with capacities that would also lend themselves well to psychoanalytic interpretation); and precisely following these topics, he arrives at "the heaven above the heavens" (the *hyperouranion*, which, by our notion, would figure the withinness-of-withinness); and he now comes forward with the enunciation of the principle that has been secretly directing our voyage: "There abides the very being with which true knowledge is concerned; the colourless, formless, intangible essence, visible only to mind, the pilot of the soul." (Before moving on from his principle of oneness to his doctrine of the hierarchic order which he would deduce from this principle, he further drives it home imaginally by talk of an ultimate feasting "in the interior of the heavens." He has thus brought together, and fused with his rational principle of oneness: flight in the sense of betterment; flight in the sense of sexual exaltation; and the notions of substantial contact that draw upon suggestions of feasting for many reasons both normal and perverse, the basic normal reason doubtless being the latent memory of the infant's sense of wholly joyous contact while feeding at the breast.)

Reverting now to the drama: In the third act, containing the peripety in a five-part form, we should arrive at some similar principle of internality. The principle is revealed at its best, perhaps, in *Hamlet*, since the play-within-a-play of the third act so clearly figures the withinness-of-withinness that we have in mind. The design is almost as clearly revealed in *Julius Caesar*, for Antony's speech before the Roman populace is similarly a kind of play-within-a-play. And to say as much is to see how the same principle informs the third act of *Othello*, with Iago here taking the role of Antony and Othello the role of the mob moved by his eloquence. However, as contrasted with the ecstatic moment of internality in the *Phaedrus*, here we confront a monstrous mock-revelation, in accordance with Iago's promise, at the end of Act I: "Hell and night / Must bring this monstrous birth to the world's light." ("O it is monstrous! monstrous!" exclaims Alonso a few lines before the end of the third act in *The Tempest*, a play so greatly unlike *Othello* in attitude, since the destinies there are all in the direction of easement, but so greatly like it in one notable dramaturgic respect, since Prospero is even more influential than Iago in overseeing the development of the plot.)

What of the rite from here out? I take it that, from this point on, we are returning. We shall get back to the starting point, though with a difference, somewhat as with a child who, having gone the magic circle in the Old Mill at the amusement park, steps from the boat, walks past the same ticket booth that he had passed before entering: everything is literally the same as it was before, yet somehow everything is, in essence, altered.

There is presumably to be some kind of splitting, a "separating out." Something is to be dropped away, something retained, the whole history thereby becoming a purification of a sort. Seen from this point of view, the "pity act" reveals further possibilities. From the standpoint of intrigue, we noted how it might serve to motivate vengeance in one of the *dramatis personae*, or how it might serve to "soften up" the audience so that they would be more thoroughly affected by the butchery still to come. But from the standpoint of the "initiation," the pity may be viewed as one aspect of the "separating out," preparing us, in one way or another, to relinquish those figures who are to die for our edification.

The last act would complete this process. And it would "release" us in the sense that it would transform the passion into an assertion. For in a tragedy of sacrifice, the assertion need not be got through the *rescuing* of a character; more often it comes through the playwright's felicity in making sure that the character "dies well" (within the conditions of the fiction)—or, as regards the "separating out," the character whom we would disclaim must in some ultimate sense be destroyed, threatened, or branded. But, all told, the rite is complete when one has become willing to abandon the figures who vicariously represent his own tension. The work thus parallels what we have elsewhere cited a sociologist as terming a "ritual of riddance." It is a requiem in which we participate at the ceremonious death of a portion of ourselves. And whatever discomforts we may have experienced under the sway of this tension in life itself, as thus "imitated" in art it permits us the great privilege of being present at our own funeral. For though we be lowly and humiliated, we can tell ourselves at least that, as a corpse, if the usual rituals are abided by, we are assured of an ultimate dignity, that all men must pay us tribute insofar as they act properly, and that a sermon doing the best possible by us is in order.

III

Dramatis Personae

First, as regards the rationality of the intrigue, the *dramatis personae* should be analyzed with reference to what we have elsewhere called the agent-act ratio. That is, the over-all action requires contributions by the characters whose various individual acts (and their corresponding passions) must suit their particular natures. And these acts must mesh with one another, in a dialectic of cooperative competition. So, in filling out the analysis of the *dramatis personae*, we should look for the acts, attitudes, ideas, and images that typify each of the characters (citing from the text, and discounting with regard to the role of the person that makes the statement). By the principle of the agent-act ratio, the dramatist prepares for an agent's act by building up the corresponding properties in that agent, properties that fit him for the act. Often, Shakespeare's great economy in attributing to a character only the traits needed for his action has led to misunderstanding about his methods: he is praised as though he aimed at "character-drawing" in the more novelistic sense. His characters' "life-like" quality, the illusion of their being fully rounded out as people, really derives from his dramaturgic skill in finding traits that act well, and in giving his characters only traits that suit them for the action needed of them. Often, purely situational aids are exploited here. Thus, much of Lucio's saliency in *Measure for Measure* derives from his ironic situation in forever slandering the Duke, or telling the Duke lies about his relations to the Duke, not knowing (as the audience does know) that he is talking to the Duke.

If the drama is imitating some tension that has its counterpart in conditions outside the drama, we must inquire into the dramatic analysis of this tension, asking ourselves what it might be, and how the dramatist proceeds to break down the psychosis into a usable spectrum of differentiated roles. That is, we must ask how many voices are needed to provide a sufficient range of "analogies" (with the overall tension being variously represented in each of them). Though Iago-Othello-Desdemona are obviously the major trio here, a complete analysis would require us also to ask how each of the minor characters reflects some fragment of the tension (while serving, from the standpoint of the intrigue, to help the three major persons dramatically communicate with one another).

Thus, briefly, Brabantio is handy in relating the tension to an earlier stage, when Desdemona was her father's property. We follow a change from father-daughter to husband-wife—and this history also supplies a kind of tragic flaw for Desdemona, a magic mark against her, and one that Iago will use likewise, to further the intrigue. For the first suspicion of Desdemona had been uttered by none other than her own father:

Look to her, Moor, if thou hast eyes to see:
She has deceiv'd her father, and may thee.

Dramaturgically speaking, there had been this one false note, as regards Desdemona. Even if it had escaped the notice of the audience, the dramatist reconstructs it when Iago says to Othello: "She did deceive her father, marrying you ..." etc.

The Duke, besides his convenience for details of the plot, provides ways for better identifying the psychosis, or tension, with matters of State (a dignification that, as we shall show later, is particularly important in this play).

Roderigo (marked by Iago's line, "put money in thy purse"), helps build up by contrast Desdemona's *spirituality* of property. (Emilia's coarseness similarly contributes, as does Bianca's disreputableness.) Roderigo is also handy in providing Iago with a confidant (and thereby allowing for a further mark against Iago, who is seen to be deceiving even him).

Cassio's role as "second theme" is obvious. We should also note how he bridges the high motives and the low, as his reverence for Desdemona is matched by his cynical attitude towards Bianca. Though we shall not here study the relations and functions of the minor characters in detail, perhaps we could most quickly indicate what we are here aiming at, if we noted two possible directly contrasting ways of dealing with Cassio.

In accordance with what we might call the "novelistic" approach to the *dramatis personae* (as a set of character-portraits), one might remark that, although Cassio was in many ways an admirable man, unfortunately he could not hold his liquor. Then one might remark that Iago, who happened to be a scheming wretch, took advantage of Cassio's weakness, to set him at odds with Othello.

But for our purposes the observations should be reversed thus: If Iago is to set Cassio at odds with Othello, the playwright must provide for Iago some plausible way of getting a hold on Cassio. And he can provide such a hold by endowing Cassio with this weakness (whereby Cassio's necessary befuddlement will be "characteristic" of him, while the playwright can further motivate the development situationally by staging the scene at a time of general revelry, when Cassio might be most likely, in the audience's opinion, to take a drink against his better judgment, at Iago's prodding).

It has been suggested that Othello's motives might have been explained on the basis of his status as a parvenu. By antithesis, this notion serves excellently to indicate the sort of approach we think should be employed in this section of the dramatis personae. The notion gains further credence from the fact that Iago himself discusses such a condition with relation to his disgruntlement with Cassio: "Preferment goes by letter and affection, / And not by the old gradation, where each second / Stood heir to the first." (I, i, 36). And though such unsettlement is certainly to be considered always, as a possible motive complicating the magic of class relationships in Elizabethan times, for our purposes we should turn the matter around, putting it thus:

One notable aspect of the tension Shakespeare is exploiting is the lover's sense of himself as a parvenu. For ennoblement through love is a new richness (a notable improving of one's status, a destiny that made love a good symbol for secretly containing the political aspirations of the bourgeois as *novus homo*). Hence, in breaking the proprieties of love into their components, in dramatically carving this idea at the joints, we should encounter also in Othello as lover the theme of the newly rich, the marriage above one's station. And misgivings (which could be dramatized as murderous suspicions) would be proper to this state, insofar as the treasured object stands for many things that no human being could literally be. So, in contrast with the notion of the play as the story of a black (low-born) man cohabiting with (identified with) the high-born (white) Desdemona, we should say rather that the role of Othello as "Moor" draws for its effects upon the sense of the "black man" in every lover. There is a converse ennoblement from Desdemona's point of view, in that Othello is her unquestioned "lord". And could we not further say that such categorical attributing of reverence to the male (in a social context of double sexual standards) necessarily implies again some suspicions of inadequacy. The very sovereignty that the male absolutely arrogates to himself, as an essential aspect of private property in human affection, introduces a secret principle of self-doubt—which would be properly "imitated" in the ascribing of "inferior" origins to Othello, even in the midst of his nobility. And though the reader might not agree with this explanation in detail, it can serve in principle to indicate the *kind* of observation we think the analysis of the dramatis personae requires. For, in contrast with the novelistic "portrait gallery" approach to Shakespeare's characters, so prevalent in the nineteenth century, one should here proceed not from character-analysis to the view of the character in action, but from the logic of the *action as a whole*, to the analysis of the character as a recipe fitting him for his proper place in the action (as regards both the details of the intrigue and the imitating of the tension by dramatic dissociation into interrelated roles).

Since A. C. Bradley was one of the best critics who tended to approach Shakespeare "novelistically", we might develop our position best by commenting on some of his comments. Thus, when Bradley writes, "Desdemona's sweetness and forgiveness are not based on religion," I can think of no remark better fitted to deflect attention from the sort of approach I have in mind. To arouse our pity here, Shakespeare places Desdemona in a sacrificial situation wherein she gives herself up as a gentle victim, with malice towards none. We have mentioned Aristotle's formula, that men pity those who suffer unjustly. But Shakespeare's usage involves a further motive. For pity is extracted most effectively from the spectacle of suffering if the tormented, at the very height of the torment, forgives the tormentor. The scene in which she sings the willow song casts her perfectly in the role of one preparing meekly for sacrifice. And her sorrow is in the same mode when, having been fatally attacked by her husband, she speaks as her parting words: "Commend me to my kind lord. O! farewell!" Here Shakespeare goes as far as he can towards making her conduct Christlike. And this *exploiting* of a religious pattern as a part of the playwright's design upon the audience's sympathies is a much more important detail about Desdemona as a character-recipe than the fact that, literally, she is not strong on theological references.

On the other hand, the playwright is always careful to see that, however austere the perfectly piteous offering may be, the audience is not confined to such exacting responses. There are others in the play who will help the audience to have its vengeance straight. The "hellish villain" is excoriated before their very eyes by his own wife. And he is to be tortured: it is a promise. Similarly, in *King Lear*, even as the pitiful burdens of the old man's helplessness begin to mount upon us, the audience is audibly gratified, murmuring contentedly, when Kent lets loose his manly invective against Oswald.

But Bradley does make a remark usable for our purposes when he says of Emilia: "From the moment of her appearance after the murder to the moment of her death she is transfigured; and yet she remains perfectly true to herself, and we would not have her one atom less herself. She is the only person who utters for us the violent emotions which we feel, together with those more tragic emotions which she does not comprehend." To be sure, Bradley is here still talking as though there had been some surprising change in her *character*, whereas we would have him approach such matters more directly, in terms of a transfiguration in her *role*. Because of her relation to Iago within the conditions of the play, because of the things she alone knows, she is in the best position to take over the vindictive role we eagerly require of *someone* at this point. Or, you could state it thus: Some disclosures are due, she is in a position to make them, and if she makes them venomously, she will do best by our pent-up fury, a fury still further heightened by the fact that Desdemona died Christlike.

But when Bradley writes of Emilia, "What could better illustrate those defects of hers which make one wince, than her repeating again and again in Desdemona's presence the word Desdemona could not repeat . . .", here is sheer portraiture, and done in a way that conceals the functioning of the play. The dramatist must continually keep vibrant with the audience, as an essential element in the psychosis, the animal words for sexuality. Iago, of course, carries the main burden of this task. But when he is not about, others must do it for him. It is important that the audience simultaneously associate Desdemona with such motives, and dissociate her from them. Here is the very centre of the tension. Iago does not often speak to Desdemona; and even when he does, within the conditions of the play he could not plausibly speak to her thus, without lowering her in our esteem. But Emilia is perfectly suited to maintain this general tenor of the imagery, so necessary for retaining the exact mixture of pudency and prurience needed for exploiting the tension. And besides thus keeping the motive vigorous, Emilia's use of such terms gives Desdemona's avoidance of them a *positive* or *active* character—and activation, actualization, is sought for always.

At first glance, one might expect us to welcome Thomas Rhymer's notion that Emilia's remarks, after the willow scene, are designed merely as relief ("that we may not be kept too long in the dumps, nor the melancholy Scenes lye too heavy, undigested in the Stomach"). But the theory of "comic relief" has been repeated too often to be trustworthy. And at the very least, we might look at it more closely. In one sense a tragic playwright should have no interest in giving his audience "comic relief". At least, we'd expect him to be as overwhelmingly and protractedly tragic as he could, without risk that the audience might rebel.

In forms such as Cornelian tragedy, "comic relief" was ruled out by the conditions of the game. The conventions required that the ceremonious gesture be sustained throughout. So-called "comic relief", on the other hand, allows for a shift in tonality that permits the dramatist to relax the tension without risking the loss of the audience's interest. He can turn suddenly to a different mode, which allows him later to start building anew from a lower intensity. In this respect, the device at least gives relief to the dramatist. But we would suggest this possibility: Rather than treating such a device merely as "comic relief", might one discern in it a subtler diplomacy? When the audience is carried beyond a certain intensity, it threatens to rebel, for its own comfort. But the playwright might engage it even here too, by shifting just before the audience is ready to rebel. However, he will shift in ways that subtly rebuke the audience for its resistance, and make it willing afterwards to be brought back into line. For in the "comic relief", he makes sure that the rebellion is voiced by "inferior" characters, as when Emilia, very nearly at the end of the fourth act, throws doubt on the entire system of "values" motivating Othello, Desdemona, and Iago, all three.

Desdemona has said, "Wouldst thou do such a deed for all the world?"—and Emilia answers, "The world is a huge thing; 'tis a great price / For a small vice." She continues in this vein, and as the act ends, this motive is strong with us. Yet she here utters the basic heresy against the assumptions on which this play is built. What of that? We would explain the tactics thus:

A tragic plot deals with an *excessive* engrossment. Hence, many average members of the audience might be secretly inclined to resist it when it becomes too over-wrought. Accordingly, one might think it unwise of the dramatist to let their resistance be expressed on the stage.

However, Emilia is present among the big three as an average mortal among the gods. Thus, though in her role she represents a motivation strong with the audience, she is "low" while tragedy is "high". Hence in effect she is suggesting that any resistance to the assumptions of the tragedy are "low", and that "noble" people will choose the difficult way of Desdemona. And since, by the rules of the game, we are there for elevation, her voicing of our resistance protects, rather than endangers, the tragic engrossment. For the members of the audience, coming here to be ennobled, would bear witness to their high spiritual state by fearing the right things, as Aristotle in the *Nichomachaean Ethics* reminds us that there is a nobility in fear when we fear properly.

But let us return to Bradley. When discussing the contrast between Iago's "true self and the self he presented to the world in general", Bradley writes: "It is to be observed . . . that Iago was able to find a certain relief from the discomfort of hypocrisy in those caustic or cynical speeches which, being misinterpreted, only heightened confidence in his honesty. They acted as a safety-valve, very much as Hamlet's pretended insanity did."

Just as I was trying to make clear why I think these remarks malapropos, Bradley helped me by bringing in this reference to Hamlet's "pretended insanity". Passing over the fact that Hamlet's use of insanity as a ruse, while playing for time to avenge the murder, was part of the traditional story from which Shakespeare presumably adapted his own play, we would note other kinds of tactical considerations here.

Thus, when analyzing the plays of Shaw, we have noticed that, by introducing the use of a cantankerous character among the dramatis personae, Shaw could always guaranty himself a certain minimum of flurry on the stage. If nothing else was going on, he could let this character exercise for a while, in spirited Shavian fashion, until the plot was ready to resume. In *The Cocktail Party*, Eliot gets a similar effect by a situational device. It is doubtful whether his personal temperament includes the kind of spirited character that came easy with Shaw. But within his means, he could get an equivalent effect situationally, by vexations, as characters enter at the wrong moment, return suddenly when they are supposed to have left for good, phone or call from the other room inopportunely, the whole adding up to a series of interruptions that is a secular equivalent of mortification, and contrives at the very least to keep things amusingly stirred up. Now, why could we not similarly note that Hamlet's malingering is an excellent device for maintaining a certain minimum of dramatic tension? And the device could serve further to give his utterances an oracular tone. For oracles traditionally speak thus ambiguously; hence the tomfoolery, combined with Hamlet's already established solemnity, could well help place his remarks under the sign of a fate-laden brooding.

The device also aided well in covering up one great embarrassment of the work. For the job of delaying Hamlet's vengeance until the fifth act, whereas he was so clearly in a physical position to kill the king in the first, and had unmistakably established the king's guilt in the third, threatened to arouse the audience's resentment. But the problematical aspect of Hamlet (made picturesque and convincing by the gestures of madness) could be of great assistance to the playwright. And only insofar as the tactics of delay were acceptable would the continuation of the play be possible. On the other hand, if it was necessary to explain Hamlet's pretended insanity as a "safety-valve", why did not so articulate a playwright as Shakespeare stress the point?

Bradley says of Iago: "Next, I would infer from the entire success of his hypocrisy—what may also be inferred on other grounds, and is of great importance—that he was by no means a man of strong feelings and passions, like Richard, but decidedly cold by temperament. Even so, his self-control was wonderful, but there never was in him any violent storm to be controlled."

Here again, looking at the matter from the standpoint of the principle we would advocate, we note rather that Shakespeare has no need for a turbulent figure like Othello here. Iago is properly the principle of steely suspicion that works upon the passions. And if he already has a complete function to perform in accordance with such a character, why should Shakespeare shower irrelevant traits upon him?

Shakespeare is making a play, not people. And as a dramatist he must know that the illusion of a well-rounded character is produced, not by piling on traits of character, until all the scruples of an academic scholar are taken care of, but by so *building a character-recipe in accord with the demands of the action that every trait the character does have is saliently expressed in action or through action*. Here is the way to get "actualization". And such dramatic perfection of expression, whereby the salient traits are expressed in action, may then induce us to fill in (by inference) whatever further traits we may consider necessary for rounding out the character. The stress upon character as an intrinsic property, rather than as an illusion arising functionally from the context, leads towards a non-dramatic explanation. And one can end by attributing to a character certain traits, or trends of thought, for which no line of text can be directly adduced as evidence.

I do not object categorically to such impressions. I would merely suggest that the line of inquiry with relation to them should be altered. *They are the preparatory material for critical analysis, not the conclusions*. If the critic feels that the spectacle of the character in action leads him spontaneously to round out the character, in his own mind, by inferences that Shakespeare has not explicitly sought to establish as motives in the play, then his job should be not just to show that he makes such inferences, nor just to record his exaltation in the contemplation of them; but rather he should aim to explain how, by the few traits which *are* used for the actualizing of a role, the playwright can produce the illusion of a rounded character.

Whereas it has become customary to speak of Shakespeare's figures as of living people, the stupidest and crudest person who ever lived is richer in motivation than all of Shakespeare's characters put together—and it would be either a stupidity or a sacrilege to say otherwise. It is as an artist, not as God, that he invents "characters". And to see him fully as an artist, we must not too fully adopt the Coleridgean view of art as the "dim analogue of creation".

The risk in "portraiture" of the Bradleyan sort (and Samuel Johnson has done it admirably too, also with reference to *Othello*) is that the critic *ends* where he should *begin*. As Jimmy Durante has so relevantly said, "Everybody wants to get into the act." In this sense, impressionistic criticism would write the work over again. Let the critic be as impressionistic as he wants, if he but realize that his impressions are the *beginning* of his task as a critic, not the *end* of it. Indeed, the richer his impressions the better, if he goes on to show how the author produced them. But the great risk in "conclusive" statements about a work is that they give us the feeling of *conclusions* when the real work of analysis still lies before us.

Bradley even asks us to "look more closely into Iago's inner man." The expression almost suggests that Iago is so real, one might profitably hire a psychoanalyst to get at the roots of him. And in the same spirit, after noting that "Shakespeare put a good deal of himself into Iago", Bradley continues: "But the tragedian of real life [sic!] was not the equal of the tragic poet. His psychology, as we shall see, was at fault at a critical point, as Shakespeare's never was. And so his catastrophe came out wrong, and his piece was ruined."

When Bradley says of Iago, "He was unreasonably jealous; for his own statement that he was jealous of Othello is confirmed by Emilia herself, and must therefore be believed (IV, ii, 145)," here we would offer another kind of purely poetic consideration, in contrast with Bradley's novelistic portraiture. In line with Francis Fergusson's discussion of "analogy" in his analysis of *Hamlet* (*Idea of a Theater*), we would note that Iago is here placed in a position analogous to that which is finally forced upon Othello. Such analogy at the very least gives greater consistency to a work, carrying out the principle of repetitive form, by varying a theme. But it does more. For the area of similarity between Iago and Othello here serves also to point up the great difference between them. (Coleridge reminds us dialectically that *rivales* are opposite banks of the same stream.) Hence, Iago's *ignoble* suspicions by contrast make Othello's suspicions seem *more noble*, thereby helping induce us to believe that he killed Desdemona not just in jealousy, but for the sake of "honour". Or, otherwise put: here is the principle of the "reflector", discussed in one of Henry James's prefaces. If you have several characters all looking at the *same* object, you can thereby point up the differences in their perceiving of it. And in attributing to Iago a suspicion analogous to the one he would arouse in Othello, the poet thus is in his way using the "reflector" principle. Also, at the very least, Iago's suspicion helps motivate his vindictiveness, and "rationally". For situations where "honour" is taken as a primary motive, it usually follows that *vengeance* can serve as "rational" motivation of an act (a point to be remembered always, when considering motivations purely on the level of the intrigue).

But let us, in concluding this section, make sure that we do not take on more burdens than we must. To read Stanislavsky's notes on the staging of *Othello* is to realize that, in our novel-minded age at least, the actor is helped in building up his role by such portraiture as Bradley aims at. We will hypothetically grant that the novelistic method may be best for aiding the actor to sink himself in his role. Give him a "physical task", such as Stanislavsky looks for, to make sure that in each scene he can operate on something more substantial and reliable than his mood and temperament. Then, once you have made sure of this operational base, allow for as much novelistic improvising as can give the actor a sense of fullness in his role. Maybe so. But we would still contend that, *so far as the analysis of the playwright's invention is concerned*, our proposed way of seeing the agent in terms of the over-all action would be required by a dramaturgic analysis of the characters.

IV

Peripety

This section, to be complete, should trace the development of the plot, stressing particularly the ways in which the playwright builds up "potentials" (that is, gives the audience a more or less vague or explicit "in our next" feeling at the end of each scene, and subsequently transforms such promises into fulfilments). The potentialities of one scene would thus become the actualizations of the next, while these in turn would be potentials, from the standpoint of unfoldings still to come.

Bradley's remark, "Iago's plot is Iago's character in action," is excellent, unless it tempts us, as it did him, to reverse the order of our inquiry, looking at Iago's conduct as though it were the outgrowth of his character, rather than looking at his character as having been so formed by the playwright that it would be a perfect fit for the kind of conduct the play required of him. But in any case, since Iago's schemings are to be appreciated as such, and since they form the plot itself, the audience is somewhat invited to watch the plot as plot.

However, we shall here confine ourselves mainly to the peripety, Act III, scene iii.

Iago has promised so to manipulate the meaning of events that Othello will be led to misinterpret what goes on before his very eyes (and the eyes of the audience, who know exactly the nature of his errors). Iago now faithfully fulfils his promise; and after proper preparation of the audience under the guise of preparing Othello, he finally becomes like a fiend goading an elephant, making the ungainly beast rear on its hind legs, thrash in bewilderment, and trumpet in anguish. As the scene begins, no suspicion of Desdemona has crossed Othello's mind (unless you except the warning of Brabantio's which at least had brought up the topic, as ambiguous foreshadowing, in Othello's presence).

In the first scene of the third act, after mild horseplay with clown and musicians, a strong potential was established: Iago got his wife to arrange for Cassio's meeting with Desdemona. Never missing an opportunity to keep the innuendoes vibrant, the playwright has Emilia tell Cassio of Othello's desire "To take the saf'st occasion by the front" for reinstating Cassio. Thus with the assurance that Cassio will be where we need him, there follows a brief scene of seven lines, wherein the playwright helps Iago help the playwright get Othello properly placed. Then, along with the usual references to Iago as "honest" (which, since they call for an easy kind of translating, thereby also help induce the audience to collaborate in the making of the play) we hear Desdemona assuring Cassio that she will importune Othello in his behalf. (For potential, as regards

"Cassio's suit", she states her intentions fatally: "Thy solicitor shall rather die / Than give thy cause away.") We are now ready for the grand interweavings, as Othello and Iago enter at a distance, Cassio leaves, and Iago mutters, "Ha! I like not that."

> *Othello.*   What dost thou say?
> *Iago.* Nothing, my lord: or if—I know not what.
> *Othello.* Was not that Cassio parted from my wife?
> *Iago.* Cassio, my lord? No, sure, I cannot think it
> That he would steal away so guilty-like
> Seeing you coming.
> *Othello.*   I do believe 'twas he.
> *Desdemona.* How now, my lord!
> I have been talking with a suitor here,
> ["suitor"—ill-starred word!]
> A man that languishes in your displeasure.
> *Othello.* Who is't you mean?
> *Desdemona.* Why, your lieutenant, Cassio
> [who, we vibrantly learn, "has left part of his grief" with her.]

Thus, by his stutterings, Iago has taken an incident actually neutral, and made it grim for Othello. The audience now has a pattern for creating vigorously: *translating* (the inducement to an audience's self-persuasion that resides in the use of dramatic irony). Desdemona continues to importune (and the playwright helps her help Iago by having her, in the course of remarks, say to Othello: "What! Michael Cassio, / That came a wooing with you, and so many a time, / When I have spoke of you dispraisingly, / Hath ta'en your part"). After Desdemona has left, Othello sums up the motivations perfectly: "Excellent wretch! Perdition catch my soul, / But I do love thee! and when I love thee not, / Chaos is come again." Whereupon, Iago resumes his pattern, making non-committal remarks that invite Othello to do the committing for himself:

> *Iago.* My noble lord,—
> *Othello.*   What dost thou say, Iago?
> *Iago.* Did Michael Cassio, when you woo'd my lady,
> Know of your love?
> [We now see the full dramatic utility of Desdemona's reference to Cassio "a wooing."]
> *Othello.* He did, from first to last: why dost thou ask?
> *Iago.* But for a satisfaction of my thought;
> No further harm.
> *Othello.*   Why of thy thought, Iago?

Iago. I did not think he had been acquainted with her.
Othello. O! yes; and went between us very oft.
Iago. Indeed!
Othello. Indeed! ay, indeed; discern'st thou aught in that?
Is he not honest?
[Fatal word. If the devil Iago is honest, then Cassio and Desdemona, being honest, will be devils.]

Iago.   Honest, my lord?
Othello.   Honest! ay, honest.
Iago. My lord, for aught I know.
Othello. What dost thou think?
Iago.   Think, my lord!
Othello.   Think, my lord!
By heaven, he echoes me.
As if there were some monster in his thought
Too hideous to be shown. Thou dost mean something:
I heard thee say but now, thou lik'st not that,
And when I told thee he was of my counsel
In my whole course of wooing, thou criedst, 'Indeed!'
As if thou then hadst shut up in thy brain
Some horrible conceit. If thou dost love me,
Show me thy thought.

Here the Moor's magnificent upsurge is built around his own description of Iago's tactics. Thus not only is the device used, but in a dramatized way the audience is informed that it is being used, and what its nature is.

Thence to a new device: Iago, to bring up the theme of jealousy, doubts himself, blames himself, begs Othello to make due allowances: "As, I confess, it is my nature's plague / To spy into abuses, and oft my jealousy / Shapes faults that are not." The topic is thus introduced, under the guise of asking that it be avoided. A drastic variant of the *praeteritio*, and one that will soon be developed further, as Iago proves himself a master of the "Say the Word" device whereby the important thing is to see that the summarizing word, the drastically relevant motivating title is spoken. For in its nature as imagery, inviting one to make oneself over in its image, no "no" can cancel it; it could only be abolished by another image—not by a negative, but by a still stronger positive, and the only stronger one, as we shall see later, will not overwhelm it, but will serve as the ultimate reënforcement of it.

Meanwhile, after some near-puns on treasure ("Who steals my purse steals trash," etc. . . . "but he that filches from me my good name," etc.), near-puns, since they half suggest other kinds of repository, likewise to be conceived in association with one's good name—next Iago can exploit directly the topic that he had introduced roundabout: "O! beware, my lord, of jealousy; / It is the green-ey'd monster which doth mock / The meat it feeds on." But now he is gathering momentum, and he rounds out his statement by adding another term, "cuckold", just as a topic, not yet explicitly pointed. And he contrives to Say the Word by another route: "Good heaven, the souls of all my tribe defend / From jealousy!"

Then, as regards the audience, Othello makes the next important contribution: "Think'st thou I'd make a life of jealousy, / To follow still the changes of the moon/ With fresh suspicions?" The involvements of property here take a momentous step forward. By the catamenial theme, time and the very motions of the heavens begin to interweave themselves with Othello's endangered treasure; or, otherwise put, the personal and social nature of such property now begins to move towards ultimate transmogrification, made part of nature, and cosmologized.

But now a new tack is needed. Othello must show strong resistance, too. Otherwise, this bullfight will not be spectacle enough. So after himself introducing the topic of "goat", which Iago will exploit later, he swings into revolt against these ingeniously inculcated obsessions, ending on a demand for proof.

During the discussion of proof, Iago adopts the role of one who is himself looking for proof. Iago is not arguing with Othello ever (quite as a good dramatist would never think of arguing with his audience). Rather, he takes the role of one who is joining with Othello to get the matter clear, and would himself rejoice if his suspicions were proved wrong. But, as if half grudgingly (after having talked of feminine deception generally), he does recall how Desdemona had once deceived her father. He glancingly suggests that Othello is not "Of her own clime, complexion, and degree." He contrives to keep the theme going by a hint of a pun his author was much given to, as he speaks of "her country forms". Then he leaves the stage (whereat Othello can sum up by musing, "This honest creature, doubtless, / Sees and knows more, much more, than he unfolds"); then returns to make a special point of the plot potential, in asking that Othello leave Desdemona free to meet with Cassio.

Left alone this time, Othello muses on the problems of his sweet property: "O curse of marriage! That we can call these delicate creatures ours, / And not their appetites. I had rather be a toad, / And live upon the vapour of a dungeon, / Than keep a corner in the thing I love / For others' uses." And as Iago had previously told Roderigo that "they say base men being in love have then a nobility in their natures more than is native to them," so Othello here likewise considers love in hierarchic terms: "Yet, 'tis the plague of great ones; / Prerogativ'd are they less than the base."

Then, after Desdemona has made her invaluable contribution to the plot by losing her handkerchief, ("Your napkin is too little," Othello had said), and Iago has come into possession of it (informing the audience that he will "in Cassio's lodging lose this napkin, / And let him find it"), Othello sums up the major cluster of his motives, yielding now frankly to his suspicions:

> O! now, for ever
> Farewell the tranquil mind; farewell content!
> Farewell the plumed troop and the big wars
> That make ambition virtue! O, farewell!
> Farewell the neighing steed, and the shrill trump,
> The spirit-stirring drum, the ear-piercing fife,
> The royal banner, and all quality,
> Pride, pomp, and circumstance of glorious war!
> And, O you mortal engines, whose rude throats
> The immortal Jove's dread clamours counterfeit,
> Farewell! Othello's occupation's gone.

In accordance with our method, we cannot lay too much stress upon this speech. For the audience is here told explicitly what the exclusive possession of Desdemona equals for Othello, with what "values" other than herself she is identified. Here they are listed: Ambition, virtue, quality, pride, pomp, circumstance, glory, and zest in his dangerous occupation. Within the magnificently emotional utterance, there is thus an almost essay-like summary. Over and above what she is, Othello tells us in effect, here are the things she *stands for*. All these non-sexual elements are implicit in her sex, which is enigmatically, magically, by the roundabout route of courtly mystery, the emblem of them. For such reasons as this, he could later call himself "an honourable murderer", saying that he did "all in honour" in slaying the charismatic figure who once had announced her intention "to preserve this vessel for my lord." (In the fourth act, a similar identification will be mentioned briefly: "O, the world has not a sweeter creature; she might lie by an emperor's side, and command him tasks.")

When he threatens to turn his fury against Iago, as he spasmodically doubts his own torrents of doubt, Iago now lets loose upon the audience Shakespeare's best rhetoric of *enargeia*, in bringing the particulars of infidelity before Othello's, and thus the audience's very eyes, first obliquely, then finally by his lie that implicates Desdemona in the lascivious movements and treacherous mutterings attributed to Cassio in his sleep.

Now is the time for the *materializing* of these fatal errors, concentrated in the handkerchief as their spirit made manifest. Iago: "But such a handkerchief— / I am sure it was your wife's—did I today / See Cassio wipe his beard with." Within the explicit conditions of the plot, it has been charged with fatal implications— whereat the scene, like the raging Pontick which Othello likens to himself (no ebb tide, all flood), now takes its "compulsive course", with "violent pace", while amidst shouts of "black vengeance", "hollow hell", "aspics' tongues" and "bloody thoughts", Iago and Othello come to kneel together, swearing vengeance and loyalty in vengeance and then, finally, once more, a variant of the Say the Word device, introducing the theme while ostensibly speaking against it:

Iago. My friend is dead; 'tis done at your request:
But let her live.
Othello. Damn her, lewd minx! O, damn her!
Come, go with me apart; I will withdraw
To furnish me with some swift means of death
For the fair devil.

Kneeling together, and well they should, for they are but two parts of a single motive—related not as the halves of a sphere, but each implicit in the other.[2]

V

"The Wonder"

"So much ado, so much stress, so much passion about an Handkerchief! Why was not this call'd the *Tragedy of the Handkerchief*? . . . We have heard of *Fortunatus his Purse*, and of the *Invisible Cloak*, long ago worn threadbare, and stow'd up in the Wardrobe of obsolete Romances: one might think, that there were a fitter place for this Handkerchief, than that it, at this time of day, be worn on the Stage, to raise every where all this clutter and turmoil. Had it been *Desdemona's* Garter, the Sagacious Moor might have smelt a Rat: but the Handkerchief is so remote a trifle, no Booby, on this side Mauritania, cou'd make any consequence from it."

"*Desdemona* dropt her Handkerchief; therefore she must be stifl'd."

"Here we see the meanest woman in the Play takes this *Handkerchief* for a *trifle* below her Husband to trouble his head about it. Yet we find, it entered into our Poet's head, to make a Tragedy of this *Trifle*."

—Thomas Rhymer

"Sure, there's some wonder in this handkerchief," Desdemona had confided to Emilia; "I am most unhappy in the loss of it." And well she might be. For the handkerchief will sum up the entire complexity of motives. It will be public evidence of the conspiracy which Othello now wholly believes to exist (and which, according to our notions on the ironies of property, *does* exist). And by the same token, it will be the privacy of Desdemona made public. If she is enigmatic, emblematic, the gracious fetish not only of Othello, but of all who abide by these principles of spiritual ownership, then her capital as a woman is similarly representative, the emblem of her as emblem. Hence, this handkerchief that bridges realms, being the public surrogate of secrecy, it is an emblem's emblem—and in his belief that she had made a free gift of it to another, Othello feels a torrential sense of universal loss. Since it stands for Desdemona's privacy, and since this privacy in turn had stood magically for his entire sense of worldly and cosmological order, we can readily see why, for Othello, its loss becomes the ultimate obscenity. But there is a further point to be considered, thus:

Aristotle has said that accidents are best accepted in a tragedy when they are placed before the play's beginning, unless they can be made to seem fate-guided. Explicitly, there is no attempt here to show that the handkerchief is lost and found by supernatural guidance. The bluntness of the convenience is tempered by two devices of the plot: (1) Othello, by talking about it, calls the audience's clear attention to it when it falls; (2) since Emilia finds it and gives it to Iago, rather than Iago's finding it himself after having talked of wanting it, the addition of this intermediate step provides a certain tactful modulation between Desdemona's losing it and Iago's getting it. (Also, incidentally, this roundabout approach supplies complications that will later enable the plot to operate somewhat "of itself", when things must turn against the great impresario, Iago, Emilia having been given the information that leads to the exposing of him.)

But our main point is this: There is a kind of magic in the handkerchief, for the audience as well as for Othello—and this property serves as the *equivalent* of a fate-guided accident (the miraculous). It is this miraculous ingredient in the handkerchief that makes the audience willing to accept, so late in the play, the accident whereby Iago came into possession of it after giving notice that he wanted it. Or we'll state our position in modified form: Insofar as the accident is resented, the audience has not felt the equivalent for the fate-guided that we have in mind.

As we began with the subject of pollution (the subject of catharsis), so here, when on the subject of wonder (the other great lure of tragedy) we must return to it. Some psychoanalytic theorists have written of instances where, in dreams, the various secretions of the human body may become interchangeable. "The gist of the matter," Freud says, "is the replacement of an important secretion . . . by an indifferent one." And in accordance with this principle, we believe that some of the "wonder" in this object derives from such ambiguities, which Othello had been made to suggest remotely when he said to Desdemona, "I have a salt and sorry rheum offends me. / Lend me thy handkerchief." Perhaps we are looking too closely; but the adjective "salt" previously appeared in Iago's expression, "As salt as wolves in pride," used when first stirring Othello to jealousy. (*Oxford*—Pride: mettle or spirit in a horse, 1592; sexual desire, "heat", esp. in female animals, 1604.) A related usage appears in Act II, scene i, where Iago, lying to Roderigo about Cassio, speaks of "his salt and most hidden loose affection."

In any case, we can see for a certainty how Shakespeare proceeds to identify the handkerchief at the beginning of the fourth act, where Iago shifts from talk of one "naked with her friend a-bed" to talk of a hypothetical handkerchief. And the playwright bluntly reënforces the identification by having Othello fall "into an epilepsy" precisely from the strain of repeating, in great frenzy, this same drastic association of ideas which Iago had imposed upon him. As with the speech that ended, "Othello's occupation's gone", a simple "essayistic" listing of associated topics underlies the expression here too. Indeed, since the intensity of Othello's agitation calls properly for a disregard of syntax, the speech at the beginning and the end does merely state the topics to be associated in our minds:

> Lie with her! lie on her! We say, lie on her, when they belie her. Lie with her! That's fulsome. Handkerchief,—confessions,—handkerchief! . . . Pish! Noses, ears, and lips. Is it possible?—Confess!—Handkerchief!— O devil! [Falls in a trance.]

Shakespeare thus does all he can to make sure that this object be the perfect materialization of the tension which the play is to exploit, or "imitate". Again, note that it has both intimate and public aspects, being sometimes tucked away, sometimes held in full view. It thus has likewise the pontificating attributes best suited to such an object, and to the kind of mock-revelation it is to supply.

Othello mostly carries on the work of endowing it, for the audience, with a full range of magic properties. Thus, while speaking of it to Desdemona, in warning her belatedly against its loss, he uses such resonant expressions as these, all turned in the direction of the magical: "Egyptian" . . . "to my mother" . . . "charmer" . . . "subdue my father" . . . "but if she lost it" . . . "she dying gave it me" . . . "To lose 't or give 't away, were such perdition / As nothing else could match" . . . "magic" . . . "A sibyl, that had number'd in the world / The sun to course two hundred compasses" (one should also contrive to implicate the story meteorologically) . . . "prophetic fury" . . . "dy'd in mummy. . . . conserv'd of maidens' hearts". (And, he could add, what all these ingredients are but deflections of: Vessel now standing for a hierarchic nest of roles; the public emblem of Desdemona's privacy, which principle in turn is but the concentrate of Desdemona, herself charismatically infused, visibly, tangibly, embodying the tensions, or mysteries of property, as thus personalized with a grace in Desdemona that sets off, and is complemented by, the Othello–Iago grandeur).[3]

Truth, too, is implicated here, terrifyingly. In ownership as thus conceived, our play is saying in effect, there is also forever lurking the sinister invitation to an ultimate lie, an illusion carried to the edge of metaphysical madness, as private ownership, thus projected into realms for which there are no unquestionably attested securities, is seen to imply also, profoundly, ultimately, estrangement; hence, we may in glimpses peer over the abyss into the regions of pure abstract loneliness. All this condition follows from the fact that, if Cassio had wiped his beard with the handkerchief, as Iago lyingly said he had, then by the logic of the emotions, by the mad-magical-metaphysical principle of *falsus in uno, falsus in omnibus* (particularly when the supposed falsity involved a *one* that itself stood for an all), then this beard had by the same token obscenely scratched against Desdemona's cheek or pillow.

And, as projected absolutely, all culminated in a last despairing act of total loneliness. Hence Othello's suicide said, in the narrative terms for the defining of essence, that investment as so conceived is essentially reflexive; for this great male lover, surprisingly, goaded by a man, ends on an imagery of self-abuse, doing himself violence as, having seized "by the throat" a "circumcised dog," he "smote him thus," and thereby "threw a pearl away" that possessed a richness other than the tribal. So Othello is "beside himself," as he must be, for one portion of himself to slay the other, and as he was "in principle," when Iago had kneeled with him in joint vows of vengeance, a posture that was a lie, when considered rationalistically in terms of the intrigue only, but was profoundest truth, as regards its purely ritual design.

Thereafter, the play must be brought to a close swiftly. In a summarizing couplet, Othello will say, as regards the underlying design of the major theme: "the kiss, the kill; the kill, the kiss." Cassio, the second theme, will reaffirm the hierarchic motive in its purity: "For he was great of heart." And to Lodovico is entrusted the job of recapitulating the connotations generally: "O bloody period" . . . "the tragic loading of this bed" . . . "O Spartan dog" (for Iago is called a dog only a few lines after Othello's ingenious reference to another figure, a "circumcised dog," which the audience interpreted as an allusion to himself, had terminated startlingly in a twist of sense whereby the *allusion* could merge into an *act* here and now; and since he called this hypothetical figure a Turk, we might properly recall that Iago earlier, in banter with Desdemona, had referred to himself as a Turk) . . . "the fortunes of the Moor . . . succeed on you" . . . "the censure of this hellish villain" . . . "the time, the place, the torture" . . .

Myself will straight abroad, and to the state
This heavy act with heavy heart relate.

NOTES

1. It will become clear, as we proceed, that we by no means confine our analysis of appeal to such "topical" consideration. But "topics", as discussed in Aristotle's *Rhetoric*, mark one of the points where the work, over and above the appeal of its internal relations, appeals by reference to "non-aesthetic" factors. The "allusive" nature of the work need have no literal bearing at all. That is, it would be "allusive", and correctly allusive, in the sense we have in mind, even though you could prove that in all the history of Western culture no single "Blackamoor" ever arose to such office as Othello's, married a white woman, and as the result of jealous misunderstandings, strangled her.

Longinus' *On the Sublime* offers us the bridge we want, for getting from the recognized use of topics in Rhetoric to their possible unrecognized presence in Poetry. For on many occasions he cites instances of oratory, but treats them as instances of poetry.

Critics systematically recognized that orators employed "topics" to "move" audiences in the practical meaning of the word "move" (inducing them to make practical decisions, etc.). But when they came to the analysis of poetry (with its purely aesthetic way of being "moving"), instead of reference to "topics" they shifted the stress to "imagery". (Longinus himself is a good instance of this change, as his treatise, in contrast with the low rating placed on imagination in classical works generally, assigns to images and imagination the high place they attain in nineteenth-century idealism and romanticism.)

"Images," however, are but one aspect of "topics". And the shift of terms conceals a continuity of function. Or, otherwise put: if the topic is said to figure in the appeal when a given line of oratory is being analyzed, what happens to such appeal when this same line is appreciated purely as poetry? Does the topical appeal drop out of the case entirely? Or are such considerations retained, but in disguise, as critics focus the attention upon "imagery," with its varying capacity for inducing moods or forming attitudes?

2. Note that, as the scene progresses, Iago's part in the development gradually diminishes. And his contribution is in inverse ratio to Othello's increasing engagement. At first he must act vigorously, to set Othello into motion. But once Othello has been fully aroused, and is swinging violently, Iago's role is reduced to a series of slight additional pushes, each just enough to maintain the sweeping rhythm of Othello's passion.

3. As for Rhymer's assertion that the handkerchief is trivial: Shakespeare answered it in advance when Desdemona, talking to Cassio about Othello's agitation, says that some such concern as matters of state must have "puddled his clear spirit." (III, iv, 140.) For in such cases (we would call them hierarchically motivated) "Men's natures wrangle with inferior things, / Though great ones are their objects." In thus pleading for the emblematic, she puts heroically what Rhymer puts meanly. In effect, she says to the audience: "You, who have come here for tragic ennoblement, remember that Othello's tragic excess is noble." (Incidentally, our term "excess" here is used advisedly. The Greek word *hubris*, often used to designate the hero's "tragic flaw", is in many contexts translated "excess". Indeed, a river on the rampage is said to "hubrize", whereat we might relevantly recall Othello likening his mood to the violence of the "Pontick sea".)

1956—Robert B. Heilman. "*Othello*: The Unheroic Tragic Hero," from *Magic in the Web: Action and Language in Othello*

Robert B. Heilman (1906–2004) was for more than 20 years the chairman of the English Department at the University of Washington. He wrote and edited many books on Shakespeare and other literary topics.

The problem of character presented by Othello's collapse before Iago's machinations in 3.3 is handled in three main ways. According to one view, the problem is insoluble: Othello believes Iago only "by virtue of the convention of the calumniator credited." Among the analysts of character, the older tradition is that Othello is the victim of Iago and remains pretty much the "noble Moor" throughout; he is guilty only of being too innocent or foolish or simple or trusting or of losing his usual self-control. According to the other main approach through character, Othello is not the "noble Moor" at all but has serious defects of character which cause his downfall—defects such as habitual flight from reality and as pride. Resultant protests against the deidealizing of Othello may in part be due to the fact that, after the long dominance of the Bradley view of Othello, the discoverers of his flaws tend to take his virtues for granted—courage, desire to do and be right, normal inclination to be open, the impalpable elements summarized as "charm," relative freedom from pettiness and duplicity. But these virtues may coexist with serious defects. I began my study holding the orthodox view of Othello's "nobility" but found the impression gradually modified by repeated readings of the lines. There is something in Othello's own rhetoric, I suspect, which can simultaneously support conflicting impressions of his personality. The sweep, the color, the resonance, the spontaneity, the frequent exoticism of the images—all this magniloquence suggests largeness and freedom of spirit, and it is at first easy to forget that self-deception, limitedness of feeling, and egotism may also inhabit this verbal expansiveness. If there is this ambiguity in the style, then the style is a fitting instrument for a complexity of character that we may subconsciously resist because of the obvious elements that have nourished the long tradition of calling Othello "simple." There is no master term for Othello—"nobility" or "simplicity" or "passionateness under control" or "pride" or "romantic idealism." In following his role one needs a number of different terms, as different facets of his personality come to the fore, or as one is attempting to name a moral quality or a secret impulse. In trying to trace a kind of weakness that leads to the quest for what, though neither satisfied with the term nor able to hit on an equally compact alternative, I call "positional assurance," I also use such terms as "puritanism," "stoicism," "self-love," "self-deception," and so on. Whatever the cost in uniformity, some such plurality of terms cannot be avoided, I believe, without imposing schematic readings.

The arguments that Othello's yielding to Iago in 3.3 is explicable in terms of his character usually turn on such points as these: Iago's irresistible technique and his long reputation for honesty; Othello's fine but simple "extrovert" nature, suited for action but not for perception and reflection; his deeply passionate nature, at best held under precarious control; his submerged sexuality, likely under stress to break out in violence; his unfamiliarity with Venetian ways; a "racial" self-consciousness, inferiority, and perhaps savagery. It is possible that Othello's characteristic quest for assurance of position may reflect in part an ethnic anxiety; once or twice he speaks in terms that may imply an alien's special doubt. Yet such passages are few and incidental; the ideas do not come up again and again as they would do if they were naggingly present in his mind. Though Iago takes some trouble to work on Othello as an outsider and to arouse the suspicions of the foreigner, Othello's passions simply do not mature according to this mold. He thinks of himself as the victim of women generally ("these delicate creatures . . . / . . . their appetites"—3.3.269–270), as the victim of marriage in high life (273ff.), as the "horned man" (4.1.63), rather than, let us say, as the "despised Moor." (Cf. Shylock's awareness of being a Jew.) Shakespeare strives, not for a particularist vulnerability and rancor, but for the human essence, and Othello's scope is lost sight of if we can understand him only by racial psychology. *Othello* is not a treatise on mixed marriages, but a drama about Everyman, with the modifications necessary to individualize him. Othello's Moorishness, if it is anything more than a neutral heritage from Cinthio, is less a psychological or moral factor than a symbol of characteristic human problems currently denoted by such overly familiar terms as "insecurity" and "rejection." Moorishness, in this sense, is one of the ills that flesh is heir to.

The breakdown of Othello from Act 3 on is a collapse of certain props of assurance—the assurance of being loved and the assurance of position—upon which his personality rests and which, as we see long before then, he needs after the manner of a habit. When he murders Desdemona he no longer has the assurance of being loved, but, under the pressure of an alert instinct, he has provided himself with a new "positional assurance." This experience appears to me to be representative rather than idiosyncratic.

* * *

Cause, Sacrifice, Murder

The murder scene requires and fulfills all the careful characterization of Othello that has gone before, for this exactly determines the tone and movement of the scene. It is the high point of the themes of violence and justice. It is another in a series of legal actions; like that in Act 1, it is concerned with a charge of sexual misconduct. In Act 1 there were a defendant, a corroborating witness, a judge, and a plaintiff given to recklessness but not incapable of reason and patience. Here we have only the defendant and the plaintiff—a plaintiff given to self-deception and passion.

* * *

After Desdemona awakes, the dialogue repeatedly draws upon court procedure. She pleads, "guiltiness I know not" (39) and is warned by Othello:

"Take heed of perjury" (51). But the irony is that Othello undermines his own role:

> Therefore confess thee freely of thy sin;
> For to deny each article with oath
> Cannot remove nor choke the strong conception
> That I do groan withal. Thou art to die.
>   (53–56)

The court has made up its mind in advance and sentenced her. The judge loses his composure, cites the circumstantial evidence that Iago gave him, and abuses the prisoner: "By heaven, I saw my handkerchief in's hand! / O perjur'd woman!" (62–63). If Shakespeare had dramatized evil only by such travestying of justice, he would have been very effective. But he has gone further.

Othello is not content with the role of judge. Note these lines:

> Have you pray'd tonight, Desdemon?
>
> If you bethink yourself of any crime
> Unreconcil'd as yet to heaven and grace,
> Solicit for it straight.
>
> *Des.* Then heaven
> Have mercy on me!
> *Oth.* Amen, with all my heart!
> Think on thy sins.
> Therefore confess thee freely of thy sin.
> *Des.* Then Lord have mercy on me!
> *Oth.* I say amen.
>   (25, 26–28, 33–34, 40, 53, 57)

Though some of these lines might be spoken by a Christian judge, they belong rather to the Christian priest, especially the priest in the role of confessor. This, then, is Othello's climactic means of placing himself on a pinnacle of assurance and of blinding himself to the true nature of what he does there. Though he has already inclined to assume the role of priest, only now has he invested it with a brief air of dignity, which Shakespeare uses skillfully to dramatize the horror of Othello's conduct: to the coolness, the prayerfulness, the almost gentle calmness of the priest is added the frankness of the killer: "I would not kill thy unprepared spirit. / No, heaven forfend! I would not kill thy soul" (31–32). Repeatedly Othello talks of "killing" her—his voice quiet and controlled—at the same time that he urges her to save her soul. The shock is that of a murder by rite, of an exotic depravity in which the selfless spiritual concern and the wholly selfish violence are confounded. The priest as killer is a remarkable dramatic conception: an ultimate violence is expressed by doing violence to all our preconceptions. This strategy is used doubly: the priestly role is worked out alongside the judicial role, so that we also have the judge as killer. But then the judge, we recall, is also the plaintiff and the prosecutor: and now he becomes also the executioner—as well as the confessor bent on the spiritual salvation of the criminal. In this merging of incompatible roles is the apex of Othello's self-deception, and here at last we can see that Othello was so easily deceived, so easily taken in by appearances and the false physician and the honesty game, because he had such great talent, and even a need, for self-deception. As we look further, we see that even his actions as confessor are equivocal: for if Desdemona confesses what he is convinced she must confess, she will give him the final assurance of his rectitude as judge and executioner. The revenger assumes the priest to hide the revenge; but even then he is not content but must convert the priestly function into an instrument of self-justification.

*   *   *

The End of the Case

Othello holds court until the end of the play: the judge (the judge-prosecutor-priest-executioner) has to find his own crime (in the tragic pattern created by Sophocles). The court which had heard only one witness must in time, simply by being a court—and this is one virtue of Othello's ritualizing impulse to be judicial—hear other witnesses. The late criminal returns from death to charge, "O, falsely, falsely murder'd!" (117), turning against Othello one of his favorite words of accusation, and to plead again, "A guiltless death I die" (122). Othello's assurance is never dependable; the court is promptly thrown on the defensive, reviles the victim (128ff.) to questioning Emilia, asserts, on the penalty of being "damn'd," that it "did proceed upon just grounds" (138), takes up the "honest Iago" defense of the sole witness and of itself (148, 154), and then, authority fading before the indignation of Emilia, fails into a slump while Emilia calls for help, cross-examines Iago, and blasts his testimony (169ff.). Othello confesses the death of Desdemona and then patiently, concessively (203, 210), almost wearily resumes the defense of the court action (200ff., 210ff.). This part of Act 5 is arranged with especial skill, since the movement comes inevitably from the characters and leads to maximum dramatic effect. There is an alternating rhythm of passion in Othello and Emilia: the first violence of his defense is overborne by her shock and incredulity, and when these have almost exhausted her, he is ready to present an orderly and relatively unimpassioned summary of the evidence. And it is just this complete judicial review of the case which leads at last to the hero's self-recognition in error (discovery of his "mistake" if not complete discovery of himself) that distinguishes tragedy from the brute disaster that impinges only on the beholders. For Othello's defense of the court must name the handkerchief, and this arouses Emilia to a new frenzy in which she tells the true story of the handkerchief (219 ff.). This is the ironic climax of the court metaphor: in the end the handkerchief does have evidential value—but the reverse of what Othello had supposed. The circumstantial evidence which he had admitted and relied on and which once apparently revealed Desdemona to Othello, now partly reveals Othello to himself.

Othello's first impulse, after his new vision of truth, is to execute summary justice on Iago, whom he attacks twice, the first time acting as a self-appointed deputy for an apparently tardy or ineffectual divine justice: "Are there no stones in heaven . . . ?" (234). Here is something again of Othello's inclination to spectacle, to the large mouth-filling stage effect; and the impulse to blame the outer agency of evil and thus avert recognition of inner responsiveness to it. But he does come to the judging of himself, according to his abilities; thus the spirit of justice persists; human order is served by an implicit extension of the very ritual of the court that earlier permitted Othello to gloss over the role of revenge. The instinct for ritualization, though it may be directed toward self-deception, is related to the instinct for justice which includes self-judgment. The principle of the court is brought into play, and the individual is subordinated to it, regaining community. Iago, on the other hand, in the end simply closes up, hardens up in silence and resistance, hugs himself to himself in a shut-off, private world that, though it may break under the cruder instruments of retributive justice, is impermeable to spirit (cf. Othello's "free and open nature"—1.3.405).

It is possible to view the bowing before justice sentimentally, as we know from the turn which drama aspiring to seriousness took in the eighteenth century. It is, indeed, one of the more difficult feats to achieve a submission to justice—an acknowledgement of one's own errors—which is not also a prostration of dignity; in this the dramatist wrestles with the paradox of the attainment of self in the eclipse of self, and he becomes committed to cardinal problems of spirit. The greatness of Othello is not generally of that dimension. Shakespeare approaches the personality rather in terms of a not wholly overt conflict between the sense of justice and a vague appetite for eluding or circumventing its implications: he gives us a series of self-judgments whose rigor is modified by men's partiality to other objectives.

*   *   *

Othello appears before the court of his own conscience, is sentenced to death by himself, and executed by himself. He takes on the same multiplicity of roles that had led to gross injustice in his dealing with Desdemona; his incompetence in the earlier case he purges by his sentencing himself now; justice is served finally by the death of the judge.

Perhaps we should say only that "overt justice" is served. For the foreground action of the court (judicial self-judgment) is modified by a background action of the feelings (personal self-judgment) that admits a charity which is excluded from the sentencing itself. The total self-judgment is colored by elements of personality that we have discerned in other parts of the play. In other words, we have again a provocatively ambiguous court scene, but one which tellingly reverses the terms of the trial of Desdemona: there the private emotion was primary but was qualified by the form of justice; here the act of justice is primary but is qualified by the habits of private feeling. Two elements are tightly interwoven, and we would lose sight of one or the other if we judged Othello to be only the upright executor of justice or, conversely, only the self-regarding loser sunk in self-pity and self-justification.

He speaks accusingly of his failure to kill Iago and keeps his own weapon (5.2.243, 270–271). But here, too, is something of his love for executive despatch: the man who disposed quickly and neatly of the cases of Cassio and Desdemona has been inefficient in dealing with Iago, and on top of that he is hemmed in by Gratiano. He is able to check the comfort of warrior's memories—"O vain boast!" (264) but falls into the sheer defensiveness of "Who can control his fate?" (265), as if he were not actively concerned in the disaster. But, in another attempt to face the moral issue, he turns to Desdemona's body: "at compt," he says, "This look of thine will hurl my soul from heaven, / And fiends will snatch at it" (273–275). Yet even here he in some way slights the present by leaping from past to future: he less defines the quality of his act than anticipates its consequences. In fact, he is a little disposed to revel in the hellish aftermath: "Whip me, . . . / . . . / Blow me about in winds! roast me in sulphur! / Wash me in steep-down gulfs of liquid fire!" (277–280). Here is the tendency to violence, even to spectacle; the summoning of such penalties has a histrionic side. Indeed, Othello, the tough man of war, the stoic in body, equates punishment with physical torment, which, as he portrayed himself in Act 1, is just what he can best endure. "Facing the consequences," when these mean anguish of the flesh, may be a lesser task than facing one's spiritual state. When Lodovico asks Othello, in effect, to explain himself, Othello replies: "An honourable murderer, if you will; / For naught did I in hate, but all in honour" (294–295). Othello does say "murderer," and it is possible that combining "honourable" with "murderer" may be a bitter irony at his own expense. But the second line, as well as Othello's general incapacity for the oblique, makes it very likely that he means, not "nothing but a murderer, trying to look honorable," but "though, alas, a murderer, still an honorable man." "Naught . . . in hate" again displays self-deception: Othello does not know how close hate is to love, and he has forgot the intensity of his passion to destroy. In "all in honour" there is his old quest of assurance of position. Honor is a surrogate for the justice that has gone utterly wrong: in lieu of the lost "cause" it implies a code that ennobles the private lust for punitive action. Yet by "honor" he means less the "active honor" that implies obligation of self to others than the "passive honor" that asserts the obligation of others to oneself and one's accompanying privilege of imposing penalties on those who fail.

Amid spasmodic attacks on Iago, Othello approaches humility at only one moment: when he asks Cassio's pardon for plotting his death (300). His terms of abuse for Iago are more frequent and more severe than the terms of judgment for himself. On hearing the final details of the handkerchief story, Othello cries "O fool! fool! fool!" (323). His epithet reminds him only of the least of his errors. He somehow conveys the impression that his big mistake was not so much murder and revenge as it was depriving himself of Desdemona; he less repudiates the violence than deplores the silly mistakes which wiped out a very nice girl. To understand the incompleteness of the self-judgment we have only to recall the stern self-appraisal of Roderigo: "O, villain that I am!" (5.1.29). The impression of a not wholly disciplined partiality persists even in his death speech, that ingenuous apologia in which Othello bids the onlookers, "Speak of me as I am" (342), and then, with no more self-awareness than before, labors to present an "I am" which will at the last minute give all the assurance possible to a man about to be executed and all the help possible to those willing to "extenuate" his history. Othello's death sentence does represent a self-judgment or at least an invocation of justice as a public act; but while it is a penalty, it is also an act of desperation, a flight from bereavement. The guilt is never specified, but the extenuating circumstances are. The judge and prosecutor becomes, in the end, his own defense attorney, accepting the ultimate legal penalty but throwing himself morally on the mercy of the court of public opinion. He has "done the state some service, and they know't" (339); what the observers of these events must report is "unlucky deeds" (341), as though no will had been involved; he was "wrought, / Perplex'd in the extreme" (345–346)—words which do not report that there was no effort at the delay that might have untangled the maze of difficulties; he "threw a pearl away"—a note of pitiable loss rather than of misconduct; his eyes "Drop tears" (350) rapidly—the marks of a grief and tenderness that appeal for sympathy and that might err but not overtly do evil. "Set you down this" he goes on (351), as if he (who in Act 1 thought in terms of "cue" and "prompter") and they were collaborating on a work of dramatic art. As in Act 1, Othello is conscious of his role and of his audience, particularly now when he sharply focuses all eyes and ears on himself and his last words and theatrically punctuates his death statement with the death blow. His final stroke in the picture of himself is this:

> And say besides that in Aleppo once,
> Where a malignant and a turban'd Turk
> Beat a Venetian and traduc'd the state,
> I took by th' throat the circumcised dog
> And smote him—thus
>
> (352–356)

In a last effort at security (self-esteem and popularity) he invites the Venetians to remember him as a hero of both state and religion. Ironically, his analogy—in which, as earlier (2.3.170), he plays for stock response of turkophobia—also has the effect of making him a malignant dog. They may be a self-betrayal or, as I suggested earlier, a symbolic effort at recovery by self-definition. But the effect of the moral judgment of self is obscured by the showmanship. Othello's last court plays for at least a murmur of applause.

Othello is the least heroic of Shakespeare's tragic heroes. The need for justification, for a constant reconstruction of himself in acceptable terms, falls short of the achieved selfhood which can plunge with pride into great errors and face up with humility to what has been done. All passion spent, Othello obscures his vision by trying to keep his virtues in focus. The Moor, the warrior, the survivor of exotic adventures, the romantic historian of self, is oddly affiliated with the middle-class hero, and in his kind of awareness we detect a prevision of later domestic drama.

It is these aspects of Othello's personality that are lost sight of when his ending is pictured as a rather glorious affair. His very defensiveness and sentiment and sense of loss and of good intention not quite explicably gone awry win an affection which a stern facing of spiritual reality might not. In Othello, the hero is—a rare thing—very close to Everyman in his latent capacity for violence and in all his ordinary self-protective devices. This is the underlying, though unidentified, reason why it is easy to "feel with" him. It is easy to feel with him, also, because he ends things with a beguiling masterfulness; he commands attention, without a disaffectingly conspicuous ostentation: his very use of reckless power matches a secret impulse. With his uninhibitedness, he provides the observer with a release for the unredeemed, though normally controlled, egotism that can aspire secretly both to self-justification and to easy authority over the eyes and hearts of others. Mature men resist the gratifications of these impulses when they come separately; if they are offered together, the double beguilement requires a sharper-eyed resistance. But Othello offers not only these satisfactions that may slide in unperceived; he is, besides, carrying out at least a partial justice. If he is not facing himself in the full truth of his deeds, he is unmistakably sentencing himself to the ultimate penalty—as a pusillanimous person could not do. And finally, to increase his claim upon our feelings, there come into our memories, beyond that seductive union of spectacle and self-punishment before our eyes, impressions of other qualities of his—of the zealous soldier, the loyal servant of the state, the candid and uncalculating man who, unlike Iago, desired the good. This is the complex, and not easily resistible, recipe for the "noble Moor." And a portion of that nobility, of the largeness of the public figure, is there. So are the failures, the self-centeredness, the blindness, the spiritual immaturity that we have described. Though it is easy to call Othello "simple," the characterization is far from simple, and it exacts of us the same double awareness as the trait of his which we may call aspiration—an impulse which may lead to nobility or to flight from actuality, or to something of both at once. In all his major actions there is a comparable ambiguity.

In trying to win approval, from others and himself, Othello includes in his summation a one-line definition of himself which has been remembered better than any other part of his apologia—as "one that lov'd not wisely, but too well" (344). Was his vice really an excess of a virtue? Or should he have said "not wisely, nor enough"? One can guess that the constant quest of assurance might mean less a free giving of self than a taking for self.

—⁓⁓— —⁓⁓— —⁓⁓—

1961—W. H. Auden.
"The Joker in the Pack," from *Encounter*

W. H. Auden (1907-1973) was one of the most famous poets of the century; his criticism was also influential. This essay was first published in the journal *Encounter* and later appeared in Auden's collection of essays *The Dyer's Hand*.

Reason is God's gift; but so are the passions.
Reason is as guilty as passion.

—J. H. NEWMAN

I

Any consideration of the *Tragedy of Othello* must be primarily occupied, not with its official hero but with its villain. I cannot think of any other play in which only one character performs personal actions—all the deeds are Iago's—and all the others without exception only exhibit behavior. In marrying each other, Othello and Desdemona have performed a deed, but this took place before the play begins. Nor can I think of another play in which the villain is so completely triumphant: everything Iago sets out to do, he accomplishes—(among his goals, I include his self-destruction. Even Cassio, who survives, is maimed for life.

If *Othello* is a tragedy—and one certainly cannot call it a comedy—it is tragic in a peculiar way. In most tragedies the fall of the hero from glory to misery and death is the work, either of the gods, or of his own freely chosen acts, or, more commonly, a mixture of both. But the fall of Othello is the work of another human being; nothing he says or does originates with himself. In consequence we feel pity for him but no respect; our aesthetic respect is reserved for Iago.

Iago is a wicked man. The wicked man, the stage villain, as a subject of serious dramatic interest does not, so far as I know, appear in the drama of Western Europe before the Elizabethans. In the mystery plays, the wicked characters, like Satan or Herod, are treated comically, but the theme of the triumphant villain cannot be treated comically because the suffering he inflicts is real.

A distinction must be made between the villainous character—figures like Don John in *Much Ado*, *Richard III*, Edmund in *Lear*, Iachimo in *Cymbeline*— and the merely criminal character—figures like Duke Antonio in *The Tempest*, Angelo in *Measure for Measure*, Macbeth or Claudius in *Hamlet*. The criminal is a person who finds himself in a situation where he is tempted to break the law and succumbs to the temptation: he ought, of course, to have resisted the temptation, but everybody, both on stage and in the audience, must admit that, had they been placed in the same situation, they, too, would have been tempted. The opportunities are exceptional—Prospero, immersed in his books, has left the government of Milan to his brother, Angelo is in a position of absolute authority, Claudius is the Queen's lover, Macbeth is egged on by prophecies and heaven-sent opportunities, but the desire for a dukedom or a crown or a chaste and beautiful girl are desires which all can imagine themselves feeling.

The villain, on the other hand, is shown from the beginning as being a malcontent, a person with a general grudge against life and society. In most cases this is comprehensible because the villain has, in fact, been wronged by Nature or Society: Richard III is a hunchback, Don John and Edmund are bastards. What distinguishes their actions from those of the criminal is that, even when they have something tangible to gain, this is a secondary satisfaction; their primary satisfaction is the infliction of suffering on others, or the exercise of power over others against their will. Richard does not really desire Anne; what he enjoys is successfully wooing a lady whose husband and father-in-law he has killed. Since he has persuaded Gloucester that Edgar is a would-be parricide, Edmund does not need to betray his father to Cornwall and Regan in order to inherit. Don John has nothing personally to gain from ruining the happiness of Claudio and Hero except the pleasure of seeing them unhappy. Iachimo is a doubtful case of villainy. When he and Posthumus make their wager, the latter warns him:

> If she remain unseduced, you not making it appear otherwise, for your
> ill opinion and th'assault you have made on her chastity you shall answer
> me with your sword.

To the degree that his motive in deceiving Posthumus is simply physical fear of losing his life in a duel, he is a coward, not a villain; he is only a villain to the degree that his motive is the pleasure of making and seeing the innocent suffer. Coleridge's description of Iago's actions as "motiveless malignancy" applies in some degree to all the Shakespearian villains. The adjective *motiveless* means, firstly, that the tangible gains, if any, are clearly not the principal motive and, secondly, that the motive is not the desire for personal revenge upon another for a personal injury. Iago himself proffers two reasons for wishing to injure Othello and Cassio. He tells Roderigo that, in appointing Cassio to be his lieutenant, Othello has treated him unjustly, in which conversation he talks like the conventional Elizabethan malcontent. In his soliloquies with himself, he refers to his suspicion that both Othello and Cassio have made him a cuckold, and here he talks like the conventional jealous husband who desires revenge. But there are, I believe, insuperable objections to taking these reasons, as some critics have done, at their face value. If one of Iago's goals is to supplant Cassio in the lieutenancy, one can only say that his plot fails for, when Cassio is cashiered, Othello does not appoint Iago in his place. It is true that, in Act III, Scene 3, when they swear blood-brotherhood in revenge, Othello concludes with the words

. . . now thou are my lieutenant

to which Iago replies:

I am your own for ever

but the use of the word *lieutenant* in this context refers, surely, not to a public military rank, but to a private and illegal delegation of authority—the job delegated to Iago is the secret murder of Cassio, and Iago's reply, which is a mocking echo of an earlier line of Othello's, refers to a relation which can never become public. The ambiguity of the word is confirmed by its use in the first line of the scene which immediately follows. Desdemona says

Do you know, sirrah, where the Lieutenant Cassio lies?

(One should beware of attaching too much significance to Elizabethan typography, but it is worth noting that Othello's lieutenant is in lower case and Desdemona's in upper). As for Iago's jealousy, one cannot believe that a seriously jealous man could behave towards his wife as Iago behaves towards Emilia, for the wife of a jealous husband is the first person to suffer. Not only is the relation of Iago and Emilia, as we see it on stage, without emotional tension, but also Emilia openly refers to a rumor of her infidelity as something already disposed of.

> Some such squire it was
> That turned your wit, the seamy side without
> And made you to suspect me with the Moor.

At one point Iago states that, in order to revenge himself on Othello, he will not rest till he is even with him, wife for wife, but, in the play, no attempt at Desdemona's seduction is made. Iago does not make an assault on her virtue himself, he does not encourage Cassio to make one, and he even prevents Roderigo from getting anywhere near her.

Finally, one who seriously desires personal revenge desires to reveal himself. The revenger's greatest satisfaction is to be able to tell his victim to his face— "You thought you were all-powerful and untouchable and could injure me with impunity. Now you see that you were wrong. Perhaps you have forgotten what you did; let me have the pleasure of reminding you."

When at the end of the play, Othello asks Iago in bewilderment why he has thus ensnared his soul and body, if his real motive were revenge for having been cuckolded or unjustly denied promotion, he could have said so, instead of refusing to explain.

In Act II, Scene 1, occur seven lines which, taken in isolation, seem to make Iago a seriously jealous man.

> Now I do love her too.
> Not out of absolute lust (though peradventure
> I stand accountant for as great a sin)
> But partly led to diet my revenge
> For that I do suspect the lusty Moor
> Hath leaped into my seat; the thought whereof
> Doth like a poisonous mineral gnaw my vitals.

But if spoken by an actor with serious passion, these lines are completely at variance with the rest of the play, including Iago's other lines on the same subject.

> And it is thought abroad, that twixt my sheets
> He's done my office: I know not if't be true
> Yet I, for mere suspicion in that kind.
> Will do, as if for surety.

It is not inconceivable, given the speed at which he wrote, that, at some point in the composition of *Othello*, Shakespeare considered making Iago seriously jealous and, like his prototype in Cinthio, a would-be seducer of Desdemona, and that, when he arrived at his final conception of Iago, he overlooked the incompatibility of the *poisonous mineral* and the *wife-for-wife* passages with the rest.

In trying to understand Iago's character one should begin, I believe, by asking why Shakespeare should have gone to the trouble of inventing Roderigo, a character who has no prototype in Cinthio. From a stage director's point of view, Roderigo is a headache. In the first act we learn that Brabantio had forbidden him the house, from which we must conclude that Desdemona had met him and disliked him as much as her father. In the second act, in order that the audience shall know that he has come to Cyprus, Roderigo has to arrive on the same ship as Desdemona, yet she shows no embarrassment in his presence. Indeed, she and everybody else, except Iago, seem unaware of his existence, for Iago is the only person who ever speaks a word to him. Presumably, he has some official position in the army, but we are never told what it is. His entrances and exits are those of a puppet: whenever Iago has company, he obligingly disappears, and whenever Iago is alone and wishes to speak to him, he comes in again immediately.

Moreover, so far as Iago's plot is concerned, there is nothing Roderigo does which Iago could not do better without him. He could easily have found another means, like an anonymous letter, of informing Brabantio of Desdemona's elopement and, for picking a quarrel with a drunken Cassio, he has, on his own admission, other means handy.

> Three lads of Cyprus, noble swelling spirits
> That hold their honours in a wary distance,
> The very elements of this warlike isle
> Have I to-night flustered with flowing cups.

Since Othello has expressly ordered him to kill Cassio, Iago could have murdered him without fear of legal investigation. Instead, he not only chooses as an accomplice a man whom he is cheating and whose suspicions he has constantly to allay, but also a man who is plainly inefficient as a murderer and also holds incriminating evidence against him.

A man who is seriously bent on revenge does not take unnecessary risks nor confide in anyone whom he cannot trust or do without. Emilia is not, as in Cinthio, Iago's willing accomplice, so that, in asking her to steal the handkerchief, Iago is running a risk, but it is a risk he has to take. By involving Roderigo in his plot, he makes discovery and his own ruin almost certain. It is a law of drama that, by the final curtain, all secrets, guilty or innocent, shall have been revealed so that all, on both sides of the footlights, know who did or did not do what, but usually the guilty are exposed either because, like Edmund, they repent and confess or because of events which they could not reasonably have foreseen. Don John could not have foreseen that Dogberry and Verges would overhear

Borachio's conversation, nor Iachimo that Pisanio would disobey Posthumus' order to kill Imogen, nor King Claudius the intervention of a ghost.

Had he wished, Shakespeare could easily have contrived a similar kind of exposure for Iago. Instead, by giving Roderigo the role he does, he makes Iago as a plotter someone devoid of ordinary worldly common sense.

One of Shakespeare's intentions was, I believe, to indicate that Iago desires self-destruction as much as he desires the destruction of others but, before elaborating on this, let us consider Iago's treatment of Roderigo, against whom he has no grievance—it is he who is injuring Roderigo—as a clue to his treatment of Othello and Cassio.

When we first see Iago and Roderigo together, the situation is like that in a Ben Johnson comedy—a clever rascal is gulling a rich fool who deserves to be gulled because his desire is no more moral than that of the more intelligent avowed rogue who cheats him out of his money. Were the play a comedy, Roderigo would finally realize that he had been cheated but would not dare appeal to the law because, if the whole truth were made public, he would cut a ridiculous or shameful figure. But, as the play proceeds, it becomes clear that Iago is not simply after Roderigo's money, a rational motive, but that his main game is Roderigo's moral corruption, which is irrational because Roderigo has given him no cause to desire his moral ruin. When the play opens, Roderigo is shown as a spoiled weakling, but no worse. It may be foolish of him to hope to win Desdemona's affection by gifts and to employ a go-between, but his conduct is not in itself immoral. Nor is he, like Cloten in *Cymbeline*, a brute who regards women as mere objects of lust. He is genuinely shocked as well as disappointed when he learns of Desdemona's marriage, but continues to admire her as a woman full of most blessed condition. Left to himself, he would have had a good bawl, and given her up. But Iago will not let him alone. By insisting that Desdemona is seducible and that his real rival is not Othello but Cassio, he brings Roderigo to entertain the idea, originally foreign to him, of becoming a seducer and of helping Iago to ruin Cassio. Iago had had the pleasure of making a timid conventional man become aggressive and criminal. Cassio beats up Roderigo. Again, at this point, had he been left to himself, he would have gone no further, but Iago will not let him alone until he consents to murder Cassio, a deed which is contrary to his nature, for he is not only timid but also incapable of passionate hatred.

> I have no great devotion to the deed:
> And yet he has given me satisfying reasons.
> 'Tis but a man gone.

Why should Iago want to do this to Roderigo? To me, the clue to this and to all Iago's conduct is to be found in Emilia's comment when she picks up the handkerchief.

My wayward husband hath a hundred times
Wooed me to steal it . . .
    what he'll do with it
Heaven knows, not I,
I nothing but to please his fantasy.

As his wife, Emilia must know Iago better than anybody else does. She does not know, any more than the others, that he is malevolent, but she does know that her husband is addicted to practical jokes. What Shakespeare gives us in Iago is a portrait of a practical joker of a peculiarly appalling kind, and perhaps the best way of approaching the play is by a general consideration of the Practical Joker.

II

Social relations, as distinct from the brotherhood of a community, are only possible if there is a common social agreement as to which actions or words are to be regarded as serious means to a rational end and which are to be regarded as play, as ends in themselves. In our culture, for example, a policeman must be able to distinguish between a murderous street fight and a boxing match, or a listener between a radio play in which war is declared and a radio news-broadcast announcing a declaration of war.

Social life also presupposes that we may believe what we are told unless we have reason to suppose, either that our informant has a serious motive for deceiving us, or that he is mad and incapable himself of distinguishing between truth and falsehood. If a stranger tries to sell me shares in a gold mine, I shall be a fool if I do not check up on his statements before parting with my money, and if another tells me that he has talked with little men who came out of a flying saucer, I shall assume that he is crazy. But if I ask a stranger the way to the station, I shall assume that his answer is truthful to the best of his knowledge, because I cannot imagine what motive he could have for misdirecting me.

Practical jokes are a demonstration that the distinction between seriousness and play is not a law of nature but a social convention which can be broken, and that a man does not always require a serious motive for deceiving another.

Two men, dressed as city employees, block off a busy street and start digging it up. The traffic cop, motorists and pedestrians assume that this familiar scene has a practical explanation—a water main or an electric cable is being repaired—and make no attempt to use the street. In fact, however, the two diggers are private citizens in disguise who have no business there.

All practical jokes are anti-social acts, but this does not necessarily mean that all practical jokes are immoral. A moral practical joke exposes some flaw in society which is a hindrance to a real community or brotherhood. That it should be possible for two private individuals to dig up a street without being stopped is a just criticism of the impersonal life of a large city where most people are strangers to each other, not brothers; in a village where all the inhabitants know each other personally, the deception would be impossible.

A real community, as distinct from social life, is only possible between persons whose idea of themselves and others is real, not fantastic. There is, therefore, another class of practical jokes which is aimed at particular individuals with the reformatory intent of de-intoxicating them from their illusions. This kind of joke is one of the stock devices of comedy. The deceptions practiced on Falstaff by Mistress Page, Mistress Ford and Dame Quickly, or by Octavian on Baron Ochs are possible because these two gentlemen have a fantastic idea of themselves as lady-charmers; the result of the jokes played upon them is that they are brought to a state of self-knowledge and this brings mutual forgiveness and true brotherhood. Similarly, the mock deaths of Hero and of Hermione are ways of bringing home to Claudio and to Leontes how badly they have behaved and of testing the genuineness of their repentance.

All practical jokes, friendly, harmless or malevolent, involve deception, but not all deceptions are practical jokes. The two men digging up the street, for example, might have been two burglars who wished to recover some swag which they knew to be buried there. But, in that case, having found what they were looking for, they would have departed quietly and never been heard of again, whereas, if they are practical jokers, they must reveal afterwards what they have done or the joke will be lost. The practical joker must not only deceive but also, when he has succeeded, unmask and reveal the truth to his victims. The satisfaction of the practical joker is the look of astonishment on the faces of others when they learn that all the time they were convinced that they were thinking and acting on their own initiative, they were actually the puppets of another's will. Thus, though his jokes may be harmless in themselves and extremely funny, there is something slightly sinister about every practical joker, for they betray him as someone who likes to play God behind the scenes. Unlike the ordinary ambitious man who strives for a dominant position in public and enjoys giving orders and seeing others obey them, the practical joker desires to make others obey him without being aware of his existence until the moment of his theophany when he says: "Behold the God whose puppets you have been and behold, he does not look like a god but is a human being just like yourselves." The success of a practical joker depends upon his accurate estimate of the weaknesses of others, their ignorances, their social reflexes, their unquestioned presuppositions, their obsessive desires, and even the most harmless practical joke is an expression of the joker's contempt for those he deceives.

But, in most cases, behind the joker's contempt for others lies something else, a feeling of self-insufficiency, of a self lacking in authentic feelings and desires of its own. The normal human being may have a fantastic notion of himself, but he believes in it: he thinks he knows who he is and what he wants so that he demands recognition by others of the value he puts upon himself and must inform others of what he desires if they are to satisfy them.

But the self of the practical joker is unrelated to his joke. He manipulates others but, when he finally reveals his identity, his victims learn nothing about his nature, only something about their own; they know how it was possible for them to be deceived but only why he chose to deceive them. The only answer that any practical joker can give to the question: "Why did you do this?" is Iago's: "Demand me nothing. What you know, you know."

In fooling others, it cannot be said that the practical joker satisfies any concrete desire of his nature: he has only demonstrated the weaknesses of others and all he can now do, once he has revealed his existence, is to bow and retire from the stage. He is only related to others, that is, so long as they are unaware of his existence: once they are made aware of it, he cannot fool them again, and the relation is broken off.

The practical joker despises his victims, but at the same time he envies them because their desires, however childish and mistaken, are real to them, whereas he has no desire which he can call his own. His goal, to make game of others, makes his existence absolutely dependent upon theirs; when he is alone, he is a nullity. Iago's self-description, *I am not what I am*, is correct and the negation of the Divine *I am that I am*. If the word *motive* is given its normal meaning of a positive purpose of the self like sex, money, glory, etc., then the practical joker is without motive. Yet the professional practical joker is certainly driven, like a gambler, to his activity, but the drive is negative, a fear of lacking a concrete self, of being nobody. In any practical joker to whom playing such jokes is a passion, there is always an element of malice, a projection of his self-hatred onto others, and in the ultimate case of the absolute practical joker, this is projected onto all created things. Iago's statement, "I am not what I am," is given its proper explanation in the Credo which Boito wrote for him in his libretto for Verdi's opera.

Credo in un Dio crudel che m'ha creato
Simile a se, e che nell'ira io nomo.
Dall viltà d'un germe e d'un atomo
Vile son nato,
Son scellerto
Perchè son uomo:
E sento il fango originario in me
E credo l'uom gioco d'iniqua sorte
Dal germe della culla
Al verme dell'avel.
Vien dopo tanto irrision la Morte
E poi? La Morte e il Nulla.

Equally applicable to Iago is Valéry's "Ebauche d'un serpent." The serpent speaks to God the Creator thus

> O Vanité! Cause Première
> Celui qui règne dans les Cieux
> D'une voix qui fut la lumière
> Ouvrit l'univers spacieux.
> Comme las de son pur spectacle
> Dieu lui-même a rompu l'obstacle
> De sa parfaite éternité;
> Il se fit Celui qui dissipe
> En conséquences son Principe,
> En étoiles son Unité.

And of himself thus

> Je suis Celui qui modifie

the ideal motto, surely, for Iago's coat of arms.

Since the ultimate goal of Iago is nothingness, he must not only destroy others, but himself as well. Once Othello and Desdemona are dead his "occupation's gone."

To convey this to an audience demands of the actor who plays the role the most violent contrast in the way he acts when Iago is with others and the way he acts when he is left alone. With others, he must display every virtuoso trick of dramatic technique for which great actors are praised, perfect control of movement, gesture, expression, diction, melody and timing, and the ability to play every kind of role, for there are as many "honest" Iagos as there are characters with whom he speaks, a Roderigo Iago, a Cassio Iago, an Othello Iago, a Desdemona Iago, etc. When he is alone, on the other hand, the actor must display every technical fault for which bad actors are criticized. He must deprive himself of all stage presence, and he must deliver the lines of his soliloquies in such a way that he makes nonsense of them. His voice must lack expression, his delivery must be atrocious, he must pause where the verse calls for no pauses, accentuate unimportant words, etc.

III

If Iago is so alienated from nature and society that he has no relation to time and place—he could turn up anywhere at any time—his victims are citizens of Shakespeare's Venice. To be of dramatic interest, a character must to some degree be at odds with the society of which he is a member, but his estrangement is normally an estrangement from a specific social situation.

Shakespeare's Venice is a mercantile society, the purpose of which is not military glory but the acquisition of wealth. However, human nature being what it is, like any other society, it has enemies, trade rivals, pirates, etc., against whom it must defend itself, if necessary by force. Since a mercantile society regards warfare as a disagreeable, but unfortunately sometimes unavoidable, activity and not, like a feudal aristocracy, as a form of play, it replaces the old feudal levy by a paid professional army, nonpolitical employees of the State, to whom fighting is their specialized job.

In a professional army, a soldier's military rank is not determined by his social status as a civilian, but by his military efficiency. Unlike the feudal knight who has a civilian home from which he is absent from time to time but to which, between campaigns, he regularly returns, the home of the professional soldier is an army camp and he must go wherever the State sends him. Othello's account of his life as a soldier, passed in exotic landscapes and climates, would have struck Hotspur as unnatural, unchivalrous and no fun.

A professional army has its own experiences and its own code of values which are different from those of civilians. In *Othello*, we are shown two societies, that of the city of Venice proper and that of the Venetian army. The only character who, because he is equally estranged from both, can simulate being equally at home in both, is Iago. With army folk he can play the blunt soldier, but in his first scene with Desdemona upon their arrival in Cyprus, he speaks like a character out of *Love's Labour's Lost*. Cassio's comment

Madam, you may relish him more in the soldier than the scholar

is provoked by envy. Iago has excelled him in the euphuistic flirtatious style of conversation which he considers his forte. Roderigo does not feel at home, either with civilians or with soldiers. He lacks the charm which makes a man a success with the ladies, and the physical courage and heartiness which make a man popular in an army mess. The sympathetic aspect of his character, until Iago destroys it, is a certain humility; he knows that he is a person of no consequence. But for Iago, he would have remained a sort of Bertie Wooster, and one suspects that the notion that Desdemona's heart might be softened by expensive presents was not his own but suggested to him by Iago.

In deceiving Roderigo, Iago has to overcome his consciousness of his inadequacy, to persuade him that he could be what he knows he is not, charming, brave, successful. Consequently, to Roderigo and, I think, to Roderigo only, Iago tells direct lies. The lie may be on a point of fact, as when he tells Roderigo that Othello and Desdemona are not returning to Venice but going to Mauritania, or a lie about the future, for it is obvious that even if Desdemona is seducible, Roderigo will never be the man. I am inclined to think that the story Iago tells Roderigo about his disappointment over the lieutenancy is a deliberate fabrication. One notices, for example, that he contradicts himself. At first he claims that Othello had appointed Cassio in spite of the request of three great ones of the city who had recommended Iago, but then a few lines later, he says

> Preferment goes by letter and affection,
> Not by the old gradation where each second
> Stood heir to the first.

In deceiving Cassio and Othello, on the other hand, Iago has to deal with characters who consciously think well of themselves but are unconsciously insecure. With them, therefore, his tactics are different; what he says to them is always possibly true.

Cassio is a ladies' man, that is to say, a man who feels most at home in feminine company where his looks and good manners make him popular, but is ill at ease in the company of his own sex because he is unsure of his masculinity. In civilian life he would be perfectly happy, but circumstances have made him a soldier and he has been forced by his profession into a society which is predominantly male. Had he been born a generation earlier, he would never have found himself in the army at all, but changes in the technique of warfare demand of soldiers, not only the physical courage and aggressiveness which the warrior has always needed, but also intellectual gifts. The Venetian army now needs mathematicians, experts in the science of gunnery. But in all ages, the typical military mentality is conservative and resents the intellectual expert.

> A fellow
> That never set a squadron in the field
> Nor the division of a battle knows
> More than a spinster . . . mere prattle without practise
> Is all his soldiership

is a criticism which has been heard in every army mess in every war. Like so many people who cannot bear to feel unpopular and therefore repress their knowledge that they are, Cassio becomes quarrelsome when drunk, for alcohol releases his suppressed resentment at not being admired by his comrades in arms and his wish to prove that he is what he is not, as "manly" as they are. It is significant that, when he sobers up, his regret is not that he has behaved badly by his own standards but that he has lost his reputation. The advice which Iago then gives him, to get Desdemona to plead for him with Othello, is good advice in itself, for Desdemona obviously likes him, but it is also exactly the advice a character-type like Cassio will be most willing to listen to, for feminine society is where he feels most at home.

Emilia informs Cassio that, on her own initiative, Desdemona has already spoken on his behalf and that Othello has said he will take the safest occasion by the front to restore him to his post. Hearing this, many men would have been content to leave matters as they were, but Cassio persists: the pleasure of a heart-to-heart talk with a lady about his fascinating self is too tempting.

While he is talking to Desdemona, Othello is seen approaching and she says;

Stay and hear me speak.

Again, many men would have done so, but Cassio's uneasiness with his own sex, particularly when he is in disgrace, is too strong and he sneaks away, thus providing Iago with his first opportunity to make an insinuation.

Cassio is a ladies' man, not a seducer. With women of his own class, what he enjoys is socialized eroticism; he would be frightened of serious personal passion. For physical sex he goes to prostitutes and when, unexpectedly, Bianca falls in love with him, like many of his kind, he behaves like a cad and brags of his conquest to others. Though he does not know who the owner of the handkerchief actually is, he certainly knows that Bianca will think that it belongs to another woman, and to ask her to copy it is gratuitous cruelty. His smiles, gestures and remarks about Bianca to Iago are insufferable in themselves; to Othello, who knows that he is talking about a woman, though he is mistaken as to her identity, they are an insult which only Cassio's death can avenge.

In Cinthio nothing is said about the Moor's color or religion, but Shakespeare has made Othello a black Negro who has been baptized.

No doubt there are differences between color prejudice in the twentieth century and color prejudice in the seventeenth and probably few of Shakespeare's audience had ever seen a Negro, but the slave trade was already flourishing and the Elizabethans were certainly no innocents to whom a Negro was simply a comic exotic. Lines like

> . . . an old black ram
> is tupping your white ewe . . .
> The gross clasps of a lascivious Moor . . .
> What delight shall she have to look on the devil

are evidence that the paranoid fantasies of the white man in which the Negro appears as someone who is at one and the same time less capable of self-control and more sexually potent than himself, fantasies with which, alas, we are only too familiar, already were rampant in Shakespeare's time.

The Venice of both *The Merchant of Venice* and *Othello* is a cosmopolitan society in which there are two kinds of social bond between its members, the bond of economic interest and the bond of personal friendship, which may coincide, run parallel with each other or conflict, and both plays are concerned with an extreme case of conflict.

Venice needs financiers to provide capital and it needs the best general it can hire to defend it; it so happens that the most skillful financier it can find is a Jew and the best general a Negro, neither of whom the majority are willing to accept as a brother.

Though both are regarded as outsiders by the Venetian community, Othello's relation to it differs from Shylock's. In the first play, Shylock rejects the Gentile community as firmly as the Gentile community rejects him; he is just as angry when he hears that Jessica has married Lorenzo as Brabantio is about Desdemona's elopement with Othello. In the second place, while the profession of usurer, however socially useful, is regarded as ignoble, the military profession, even though the goal of a mercantile society is not military glory, is still highly admired and, in addition, for the sedentary civilians who govern the city, it has a romantic exotic glamour which it cannot have in a feudal society in which fighting is a familiar shared experience.

Thus no Venetian would dream of spitting on Othello and, so long as there is no question of his marrying into the family, Brabantio is delighted to entertain the famous general and listen to his stories of military life. In the army, Othello is accustomed to being obeyed and treated with the respect due to his rank and, on his rare visits to the city, he is treated by the white aristocracy as someone important and interesting. Outwardly, nobody treats him as an outsider as they treat Shylock. Consequently, it is easy for him to persuade himself that he is accepted as a brother and when Desdemona accepts him as a husband, he seems to have proof of this.

It is painful to hear him say

> But that I love the gentle Desdemona
> I would not my unhoused free condition
> Put into circumscription or confine
> For the sea's worth

for the condition of the outsider is always unhoused and free. He does not or will not recognize that Brabantio's view of the match

> If such actions may have passage free,
> Bond-slaves and pagans shall our statesmen be

is shared by all his fellow senators, and the arrival of news about the Turkish fleet prevents their saying so because their need of Othello's military skill is too urgent for them to risk offending him.

If one compares *Othello* with the other plays in which Shakespeare treats the subject of male jealousy, *The Winter's Tale* and *Cymbeline*, one notices that Othello's jealousy is of a peculiar kind.

Leontes is a classical case of paranoid sexual jealousy due to repressed homosexual feelings. He has absolutely no evidence that Hermione and Polixenes have committed adultery and his entire court are convinced of their innocence, but he is utterly possessed by his fantasy. As he says to Hermione: "Your actions are my dreams." But, mad as he is, "the twice-nine changes of the Watery Starre" which Polixenes has spent at the Bohemian court, make the act of adultery physically possible so that, once the notion has entered his head, neither Hermione nor Polixenes nor the court can prove that it is false. Hence the appeal to the Oracle.

Posthumus is perfectly sane and is convinced against his will that Imogen has been unfaithful because Iachimo offers him apparently irrefutable evidence that adultery has taken place.

But both the mad Leontes and the sane Posthumus react in the same way; "My wife has been unfaithful; therefore she must be killed and forgotten." That is to say, it is only as husbands that their lives are affected. As king of Bohemia, as a warrior, they function as if nothing has happened.

In *Othello,* thanks to Iago's manipulations, Cassio and Desdemona behave in a way which would make it not altogether unreasonable for Othello to suspect that they were in love with each other, but the time factor rules out the possibility of adultery having been actually committed. Some critics have taken the double time in the play to be merely a dramaturgical device for speeding the action which the audience in the theatre will never notice. I believe, however, that Shakespeare meant the audience to notice it as, in *The Merchant of Venice*, he meant them to notice the discrepancy between Belmont time and Venice time.

If Othello had simply been jealous of the feelings for Cassio he imagined Desdemona to have, he would have been sane enough, guilty at worst of a lack of trust in his wife. But Othello is not merely jealous of feelings which might exist; he demands proof of an act which could not have taken place, and the effect on him of believing in this physical impossibility goes far beyond wishing to kill her: it is not only his wife who has betrayed him but the whole universe; life has become meaningless, his occupation is gone.

This reaction might be expected if Othello and Desdemona were a pair like Romeo and Juliet or Antony and Cleopatra whose love was an all-absorbing Tristan–Isolde kind of passion, but Shakespeare takes care to inform us that it was not.

When Othello asks leave to take Desdemona with him to Cyprus, he stresses the spiritual element in his love.

> I therefore beg it not
> To please the palate of my appetite

Nor to comply with heat, the young affects
In me defunct, and proper satisfaction,
But to be free and bounteous to her mind.

Though the imagery in which he expresses his jealousy is sexual—what other
kind of images could he use?—Othello's marriage is important to him less as a
sexual relationship than as a symbol of being loved and accepted as a person, a
brother in the Venetian community. The monster in his own mind too hideous
to be shown is the fear he has so far repressed that he is only valued for his social
usefulness to the City. But for his occupation, he would be treated as a black
barbarian.

The overcredulous, overgood-natured character which, as Iago tells us, Othello
had always displayed is a telltale symptom. He had *had* to be overcredulous in
order to compensate for his repressed suspicions. Both in his happiness at the
beginning of the play and in his cosmic despair later, Othello reminds one more
of Timon of Athens than of Leontes.

Since what really matters to Othello is that Desdemona should love him as
the person he really is, Iago has only to get him to suspect that she does not, to
release the repressed fears and resentments of a lifetime, and the question of what
she has done or not done is irrelevant.

Iago treats Othello as an analyst treats a patient except that, of course,
his intention is to kill not to cure. Everything he says is designed to bring to
Othello's consciousness what he has already guessed is there. Accordingly, he has
no need to tell lies. Even his speech, "I lay with Cassio lately," can be a truthful
account of something which actually happened: from what we know of Cassio,
he might very well have such a dream as Iago reports. Even when he has worked
Othello up to a degree of passion where he would risk nothing by telling a direct
lie, his answer is equivocal and its interpretation is left to Othello.

Othello: What hath he said?
Iago: Faith that he did—I know not what he did.
Othello: But what?
Iago: Lie—
Othello: With her?
Iago: With her, on her, what you will.

Nobody can offer Leontes absolute proof that his jealousy is baseless: similarly,
as Iago is careful to point out, Othello can have no proof that Desdemona really
is the person she seems to be.

Iago makes his first decisive impression when, speaking as a Venetian with
firsthand knowledge of civilian life, he draws attention to Desdemona's hood-
winking of her father.

Iago: I would not have your free and noble nature
Out of self-bounty be abused, look to't:
I know our country disposition well:
In Venice they do let God see the pranks
They dare not show their husbands: their best conscience
Is not to leave't undone but keep't unknown.
Othello: Dost thou say so?
Iago: She did deceive her father, marrying you:
And when she seemed to shake and fear your looks,
She loved them most.
Othello: And so she did.
Iago: Why, go to then!
She that so young could give out such a seeming
To seal her father's eyes up, close as oak.
He thought 'twas witchcraft.

And a few lines later, he refers directly to the color difference.

Not to affect many proposed matches,
Of her own clime, complexion, and degree,
Whereto we see in all things nature tends,
Foh! one may smell in such a will most rank,
Foul disproportions, thoughts unnatural.
But pardon me: I do not in position
Distinctly speak of her, though I may fear
Her will, recoiling to her better judgment
May fall to match you with her country-forms,
And happily repent.

Once Othello allows himself to suspect that Desdemona may not be the person she seems, she cannot allay the suspicion by speaking the truth but she can appear to confirm it by telling a lie. Hence the catastrophic effect when she denies having lost the handkerchief.

If Othello cannot trust her, then he can trust nobody and nothing, and precisely what she has done is not important. In the scene where he pretends that the Castle is a brothel of which Emilia is the Madam, he accuses Desdemona, not of adultery with Cassio, but of nameless orgies.

Desdemona: Alas, what ignorant sin have I committed?
Othello: Was this fair paper, this most goodly book
Made to write whore upon. What committed?
Committed? O thou public commoner,

> I should make very forges of my cheeks
> That would to cinders burn up modesty
> Did I but speak thy deeds.

And, as Mr. Eliot has pointed out in his farewell speech, his thoughts are not on Desdemona at all but upon his relation to Venice, and he ends by identifying himself with another outsider, the Moslem Turk who beat a Venetian and traduced the state.

Everybody must pity Desdemona, but I cannot bring myself to like her. Her determination to marry Othello—it was she who virtually did the proposing—seems the romantic crush of a wily schoolgirl rather than a mature affection; it is Othello's adventures, so unlike the civilian life she knows, which captivate her rather than Othello as a person. He may not have practiced witchcraft, but, in fact, she is spellbound. And despite all Brabantio's prejudices, her deception of her own father rather makes an unpleasant impression: Shakespeare does not allow us to forget that the shock of the marriage kills him.

Then, she seems more aware than is agreeable of the honor she has done Othello by becoming his wife. Where Iago tells Cassio that "our General's wife is now the General" and, soon afterwards, soliloquizes

> His soul is so enfettered to her love
> That she may make, unmake, do what she list
> Even as her appetite shall play the god
> With his weak function

he is, no doubt, exaggerating, but there is much truth in what he says. Before Cassio speaks to her, she has already discussed him with her husband and learned that he is to be reinstated as soon as is opportune. A sensible wife would have told Cassio this and left matters alone. In continuing to badger Othello, she betrays a desire to prove to herself and to Cassio that she can make her husband do as she pleases. She is frightened because she is suddenly confronted with a man whose sensibility and superstitions are alien to her.

Though her relation with Cassio is perfectly innocent, one cannot but share Iago's doubts as to the durability of the marriage. It is worth noting that, in the willow-song scene with Emilia, she speaks with admiration of Lodovico and then turns to the topic of adultery. Of course, she discusses this in general terms and is shocked by Emilia's attitude, but she does discuss the subject and she does listen to what Emilia has to say about husbands and wives. It is as if she had suddenly realized that she had made a *mésalliance* and that the sort of man she ought to have married was someone of her own class and color like Lodovico. Given a few more years of Othello and of Emilia's influence and she might well, one feels, have taken a lover.

IV

And so one comes back to where one started, to Iago, the sole agent in the play. A play, as Shakespeare said, is a mirror held up to nature. This particular mirror bears the date 1604, but, when we look into it, the face that confronts us is our own in the middle of the twentieth century. We hear Iago say the same words and see him do the same things as an Elizabethan audience heard and saw, but what they mean to us cannot be exactly the same. To his first audience and even, maybe, to his creator, Iago appeared to be just another Machiavellian villain who might exist in real life but with whom one would never dream of identifying oneself. To us, I think, he is a much more alarming figure; we cannot hiss at him when he appears as we can hiss at the villain in a Western movie because none of us can honestly say that he does not understand how such a wicked person can exist. For is not Iago, the practical joker, a parabolic figure for the autonomous pursuit of scientific knowledge through experiment which we all, whether we are scientists or not, take for granted as natural and right?

As Nietzsche said, experimental science is the last flower of asceticism. The investigator must discard all his feelings, hopes and fears as a human person and reduce himself to a disembodied observer of events upon which he passes no value judgment. Iago is an ascetic. "Love" he says, "is merely a lust of the blood, and a permission of the will."

The knowledge sought by science is only one kind of knowledge. Another kind is that implied by the Biblical phrase, "Then Adam knew Eve, his wife," and it is this kind I still mean when I say, "I know John Smith very well." I cannot know in this sense without being known in return. If I know John Smith well, he must also know me well.

But, in the scientific sense of knowledge, I can only know that which does not and cannot know me. Feeling unwell, I go to my doctor who examines me, says "You have Asian flu," and gives me an injection. The Asian virus is as unaware of my doctor's existence as his victims are of a practical joker.

Further, to-know in the scientific sense means, ultimately, to-have-power-over. To the degree that human beings are authentic persons, unique and self-creating, they cannot be scientifically known. But human beings are not pure persons like angels; they are also biological organisms, almost identical in their functioning, and, to a greater or lesser degree, they are neurotic, that is to say, less free than they imagine because of fears and desires of which they have no personal knowledge but could and ought to have. Hence, it is always possible to reduce human beings to the status of things which are completely scientifically knowable and completely controllable.

This can be done by direct action on their bodies with drugs, lobotomies, deprivation of sleep, etc. The difficulty about this method is that your victims will know that you are trying to enslave them and, since nobody wishes to be a slave, they will object, so that it can only be practiced upon minorities like prisoners and lunatics who are physically incapable of resisting.

The other method is to play on the fears and desires of which you are aware and they are not until they enslave themselves. In this case, concealment of your real intention is not only possible but essential for, if people know they are being played upon, they will not believe what you say or do what you suggest. An advertisement based on snob appeal, for example, can only succeed with people who are unaware that they are snobs and that their snobbish feelings are being appealed to and to whom, therefore, your advertisement seems as honest as Iago seems to Othello.

Iago's treatment of Othello conforms to Bacon's definition of scientific enquiry as putting Nature to the Question. If a member of the audience were to interrupt the play and ask him: "What are you doing?" could not Iago answer with a boyish giggle, "Nothing. I'm only trying to find out what Othello is really like"? And we must admit that his experiment is highly successful. By the end of the play he does know the scientific truth about the object to which he has reduced Othello. That is what makes his parting shot, "What you know, you know," so terrifying for, by then, Othello has become a thing, incapable of knowing anything.

And why shouldn't Iago do this? After all, he has certainly acquired knowledge. What makes it impossible for us to condemn him self-righteously is that, in our culture, we have all accepted the notion that the right to know is absolute and unlimited. The gossip column is one side of the medal; the cobalt bomb the other. We are quite prepared to admit that, while food and sex are good in themselves, an uncontrolled pursuit of either is not, but it is difficult for us to believe that intellectual curiosity is a desire like any other, and to realize that correct knowledge and truth are not identical. To apply a categorical imperative to knowing, so that, instead of asking, "What can I know?" we ask, "What, at this moment, am I meant to know?"—to entertain the possibility that the only knowledge which can be true for us is the knowledge we can live up to—that seems to all of us crazy and almost immoral. But, in that case, who are we to say to Iago—"No, you mustn't."

1983—A. D. Nuttall. "*Othello*," from
A New Mimesis: Shakespeare and the Representation of Reality

A. D. Nuttall, who died in 2007, was a professor at Oxford and one of the most admired Shakespearean scholars of recent years. His last book was *Shakespeare the Thinker*.

Shakespeare's play about Venice, *Othello*, has been the occasion of a classic dispute in Transparent criticism. There is disagreement about the hero: is he, in fact, heroic? Othello's speech at the end of the play causes most of the trouble:

> Soft you; a word or two before you go.
> I have done the state some service, and they know't—
> No more of that. I pray you, in your letters,
> When you shall these unlucky deeds relate,
> Speak of me as I am; nothing extenuate,
> Nor set down aught in malice. Then must you speak
> Of one that loved not wisely, but too well;
> Of one not easily jealous, but, being wrought,
> Perplexed in the extreme; of one whose hand,
> Like the base Indian, threw a pearl away
> Richer than all his tribe; of one whose subdu'd eyes,
> Albeit unused to the melting mood,
> Drops tears as fast as the Arabian trees
> Their med'cinable gum. Set you down this;
> And say besides that in Aleppo once,
> Where a malignant and a turban'd Turk
> Beat a Venetian and traduc'd the state,
> I took by th'throat the circumcised dog.
> And smote him—thus.
> (He stabs himself)
> (V. ii. 341–59)

T. S. Eliot in 'Shakespeare and the Stoicism of Seneca' observed that in this speech Othello seems to be 'cheering himself up': 'He is endeavouring to escape reality, he has ceased to think about Desdemona, and is thinking about himself.' F. R. Leavis in his 'Diabolic intellect and the noble hero' picked up a word applied by Eliot to the Stoic hero, 'self-dramatization', and said that this speech by Othello, though it begins in quiet authority, ends precisely in self-dramatization: no tragic hero this, but one who has learned nothing from his misfortune and would rather rant than think. On the other side stands Dame Helen Gardner. In her article, 'The noble Moor', she reaffirmed the essential nobility of Othello, his generosity, the greatness of his heart, his absoluteness and disinterestedness; and many felt that the cynics had been silenced.

My general argument has been that Shakespeare's mimesis is unusually comprehensive. He moves forward on a total front. He imitates individuals but he also imitates contexts. My response to this disagreement of Transparent critics is to stand further back for a while. There are more things in this play than the figure of Othello, and it may be that in understanding some of them we shall understand him. To begin with we may be utterly formalist and ask what kind of play *Othello* is.

Shakespeare's plays have come down to us in the triple division into comedies, histories and tragedies laid down by the editors of the First Folio. There is in this division a large measure of editorial accident, for the three categories are not co-ordinate. *Richard II* is, clearly, a history, but, equally clearly, it is also a tragedy. Indeed it is formally a better tragedy than *Othello* in that it deals with the fall of a prince. *Othello*, on the other hand, is about an almost bourgeois Italian household, a misunderstanding and a murder at a level which involves no repercussions among nations. Its social milieu is that normally inhabited by comedy. This social difference is enough to stamp *Richard II* as central tragedy and *Othello* as peripheral tragedy.

Othello, to be sure, is not the only Shakespearean tragedy to deal with upper-middle-class goings-on. *Romeo and Juliet* refers to a similar section of society, but then it has long been commonplace to observe that *Romeo and Juliet* opens like a comedy. The long dynastic rivalry of Montagues and Capulets brings us nearer to the proper political stature of central tragedy than anything that can happen behind Othello's closed front door.

But there is the phrase 'domestic tragedy'. Is this appropriate to *Othello*? The phrase 'domestic tragedy' is commonly used to connote a distinct genre: all those Elizabethan and Jacobean plays which dealt with real-life murders and scandals, such as Jonson's and Dekker's *The Lamentable Tragedy of the Page of Plymouth*, Yarrington's *Two Lamentable Tragedies*, *A Yorkshire Tragedy* (about a man who murdered his two children) and *Arden of Faversham* (about the murder in 1551 of Thomas Arden by his wife), Wilkin's *The Miseries of Enforced Marriage*, Heywood's *A Woman Killed with Kindness*. It is fairly obvious that these plays catered for appetites which are served today by the more sensational Sunday newspapers. The title pages of these domestic tragedies repeatedly strike a note of prurient censoriousness which is immediately recognizable. *Othello* is not in any straightforward manner a member of this class, although we may note in passing that both *The Miseries of Enforced Marriage* and *A Woman Killed with Kindness* deal, like Othello, with the then uncommon theme of marriage. Moreover, Michel Grivelet has pointed to the popularity among writers of domestic tragedy of the novellas of Bandello, Boccaccio and Cinthio. The principal source of *Othello* is a novella by Cinthio. Again, the stories of domestic tragedies tend to crop up later in ballads. This is true of *Arden of Faversham* and it is also true, as it happens, of *Othello*.

The authors of these plays seem not to have used the term 'domestic tragedy' themselves. The word 'domestic' was used of 'what goes on in a house' (in accordance with its etymological derivation from *domus*, 'house') and also of national as opposed to foreign affairs. Thomas Heywood does occasionally play on this ambiguity, but in the only place where he uses 'domestic' to designate genre ('domestic histories') he is referring to chronicles of England. The earliest example in the *Oxford English Dictionary* of *domestic* as opposed to *regal* (where the *Dictionary* offers the slightly misleading gloss 'devoted to home life') is from Davenant's *Playhouse to be Let*:

> Kings who move
> Within a lowly sphere of private love,
> Are too domestic for a throne.

Nevertheless, it is plain that the idea of a contrast between the tragedy of courts and the tragedy of private, household events was current in Shakespeare's time. The unknown author of *A Warning for Fair Women* (1599) refers to his play as 'a true and home-born tragedy'. Yves Bescou has remarked that in *A Woman Killed with Kindness* the house is itself a principal character. But in the common run of Elizabethan domestic tragedy there is admittedly little sense of tension between the idea of tragedy and the idea of domesticity.

Here Shakespeare is unlike the rest. For if we say that *Othello* is his domestic tragedy we must note that in this case the term connotes a paradox, domestic and yet a tragedy, tragic and yet domestic. If this is acknowledged the phrase has a certain utility as a description of the play. Thomas Rymer's celebrated attack on *Othello*, published in 1693, turns primarily on the fact that the play is bathetically domestic. Speaking of its moral, he says,

> First, This may be a caution to all Maidens of Quality how, without their
> Parents consent, they run away with Blackamoors . . . . Secondly, This
> may be a warning to all good Wives, that they look well to their Linnen.

Othello's tragedy indeed is strangely—and formally—introverted; it consists in the fact that he left the arena proper to tragedy, the battlefield, and entered a subtragic world for which he was not fitted. *Othello* is the story of a hero who went into a house.

Long ago A. C. Bradley observed that, if the heroes of *Hamlet* and *Othello* change places, each play ends very quickly. Hamlet would see through Iago in the first five minutes and be parodying him in the next. Othello, receiving clear instructions like 'Kill that usurper' from a ghost, would simply have gone to work. Thus, as the classic problem of *Hamlet* is the hero's delay, so the classic problem of *Othello* is the hero's gullibility. The stronger our sense of Othello's incongruity in the domestic world, the less puzzling this becomes. Certainly, *Othello* is about a man who, having come from a strange and remote place, found his feet in the world of Venetian professional soldiership—and then exchanged that spacious world for a little, dim world of unimaginable horror. 'War is no strife / To the dark house and the detested wife' comes not from *Othello* but from a comedy, but it will serve here. Its note of peculiarly masculine pain and hatred can still score the nerves. It is therefore not surprising that Shakespeare avails himself of the metaphor of the caged hawk. Desdemona says, 'I'll watch him tame', at III. iii. 23. The real process of taming a hawk by keeping it awake and so breaking its spirit is described at length in T.H. White's *The Goshawk* (1953). Othello turns the image round when he says of Desdemona,

> If I do prove her haggard,
> Though that her jesses were my dear heart-strings,
> I'd whistle her off and let her down the wind
> To prey at fortune.
>
> (III.iii.264–7)

He speaks formally of Desdemona, but it is hard not to feel that in the last words it is his own dream of liberty which speaks.

Othello is also about insiders and outsiders. The exotic Moor finds when he leaves the public, martial sphere that he is not accepted, is not understood and cannot understand. The Venetian colour bar is sexual, not professional. Iago plays on this with his 'old black ram . . . tupping your white ewe' (I. i. 89–90) and the same note is struck by Roderigo with his 'gross clasps of a lascivious Moor' (I. i. 127). Othello's gullibility is not really so very strange. Coal-black among the glittering Venetians, he is visibly the outsider, and in his bewilderment he naturally looks for the man who is visibly the insider, the man who knows the ropes, the sort of man who is always around in the bar, the 'good chap' or (as they said then) the 'honest' man. And he finds him.

There are two schools of thought on the sort of actor who should play Iago. School A chooses a dark, waspish fellow. School B chooses a bluff, straw-haired, pink-faced sort of man, solid-looking with no nonsense about him. In production School B triumphs, for the role, cast in this way, becomes both credible and terrifying. Although Iago is everywhere spoken of as a 'good chap', he has no friends, no loves, no positive desires. He, and not Othello, proves to be the true outsider of the play, for he is foreign to humanity itself. Othello comes from a remote clime, but Iago, in his simpler darkness, comes from the far side of chaos—hence the pathos of Shakespeare's best departure from his source. In Cinthio's *novella* the Ensign (that is, the Iago-figure) with a cunning affection of reluctance, suggests that Desdemona is false and then seeing his chance, adds, 'Your blackness already displeases her.' In Shakespeare's play we have instead a note of bar-room masculine intimacy, in assumed complicity of sentiment. Iago says, in effect 'Well, she went with a black man, so what is one to think?' (III. iii. 232–7). Othello's need to be accepted and guided makes him an easy victim of this style. The hero is set for his sexual humiliation.

From the beginning of the play Othello is associated with outdoor weather, with openness: 'The Moor is of a free and open nature' (I. iii. 393); 'But that I loved the gentle Desdemona, / I would not my unhoused free condition / Put into circumscription and confine / For the sea's worth' (I. ii. 25–8). Note the important word 'unhoused' and the powerful emphasis on the last four monosyllables. In II. i, set on the quayside in Cyprus, the language bursts into profusion of images of wind and weather, before it brings Othello down from the high seas into the encircling arms of his wife. The effect is best represented by sporadic quotation: 'What from the cape can you discern at sea? / Nothing at all, it is a high-wrought flood. / I cannot twixt the heaven and the main/Descry a sail. / Methinks the wind hath spoke aloud at land; / A fuller blast ne'er shook our battlements. / . . . The chidden billow seems to pelt the clouds; / The wind-shaked surge, with high and monstrous mane, / Seems to cast water on the burning Bear, / And quench the guards of th'ever fixed Pole. . . . The town is empty; on the brow o'th'sea / Stand ranks of people, and they cry "A sail!" . . . . Great Jove Othello guard, / And swell his sail with thine own powerful breath, / That he may bless this bay with his tall ship, / Make love's quick pants in Desdemona's arms. . . . O my soul's joy! / If after every tempest came such calms' (II. i. 1–6, 12–15, 53–4, 77–80, 182–3). The diminuendo is marvellously managed: the bay becomes the arms of Desdemona, the tall ship Othello himself. When, in III. iii, Othello thinks his married happiness is irretrievably lost, he makes a formal speech of valediction. This speech turns insensibly from a farewell to married contentment into the real farewell, the real loss, which is the loss of that military action and freedom in which alone Othello's true personality could move:

> I had been happy if the general camp,
> Pioneers and all, had tasted her sweet body,
> So I had nothing known. O, now for ever
> Farewell the tranquil mind! farewell content!
> Farewell the plumed troops, and the big wars
> That makes ambition virtue! O, farewell!
> Farewell the neighing steed and the shrill trump,
> The spirit-stirring drum, th'ear-piercing fife,
> The royal banner, and all quality,
> Pride, pomp and circumstance, of glorious war!
> And O ye mortal engines whose rude throats
> Th'immortal Jove's dread clamours counterfeit,
> Farewell! Othello's occupation's gone.
>   (III. iii. 349–61)

The word 'big' in line 353 is exactly right. He is surrounded by things which are too small to fight with, things like handkerchiefs. When, later in the same scene, he envisages a dark release from the dreadful circumscription of the house, once more a great flood surges in the language of the play:

> Like to the Pontic sea,
> Whose icy current and compulsive force
> Ne'er feels retiring ebb, but keeps due on
> To the Propontic and the Hellespont;
> Even so my bloody thoughts, ...
>
> (III. iii. 457–61)

Othello's gradual disintegration is mirrored in his style of speech, at first swiftly authoritative, then broken and at last full of a barbaric extremism. The thing is done slowly through the play, but there are certain speeches in which the entire triple development is gone through in little. When near the beginning of the play the truculent gang comes crowding in with weapons and torches, Othello easily controls them:

> Keep up your bright swords, for the dew will rust them.
>
> (I. ii. 59)

When he is brought before the Duke and the Senators in I. iii he is at first similar. Asked to account for his conduct he gives the reverend 'signiors' a very gentlemanly account (smooth, unflustered, almost majestic) of the way he won Brabantio's daughter (I. iii. 128–70). There is no sign of any break in this style until we reach line 260. Here Othello's language suddenly becomes problematic, so much so that most editors assume that the text is corrupt. The speech appears in Alexander's edition of the *Works* in the following form (Desdemona has just asked to be allowed to go with him to the wars):

> *Othello*: Let her have your voice.
> Vouch with me, heaven, I therefore beg it not
> To please the palate of my appetite;
> Nor to comply with heat—the young affects
> In me defunct—and proper satisfaction;
> But to be free and bounteous to her mind
> And heaven defend your good souls that you think
> I will your serious and great business scant
> For she is with me.
>
> (I. iii. 260–8)

The crux occurs in the baffling third and fourth lines, which remain puzzling even after they have been amended and repunctuated, as here, by a modern editor. In the case of this play, it is not easy to determine whether the first Quarto of 1622 or the Folio of 1623 has the higher authority. In the crux before us, however, this thorny problem fortunately does not arise, for the two are virtually identical. The first Quarto gives: 'Nor to comply with heat, the young affects in my defunct, and proper satisfaction'. The difficulties are evident. Is 'affects' a noun, in apposition to 'heat', or a verb (the relative pronoun 'which' having been elided) which would turn 'young' into a noun, the object of 'affects'? Should we change 'my' to 'me' (as Alexander did) so that we can read 'the young affects in me defunct' as an absolute construction, equivalent to 'the youthful passions being dead in me'? Does 'proper' mean 'legitimate' or 'my own'? Quite obviously, the sentence is a mess. But a Transparent reading may suggest that nevertheless we can accept it as it stands; that is, if we look through the fractured form to the possible person we may understand the forms as we never could if we looked at form alone.

A certain meaning comes through, and indeed it is strange. Othello seems to be saying, 'Do not think that I am asking for this out of lust, for I am past all that, rather I am interested in Desdemona's mind.' This does not have to be a full profession of impotence (though the powerful word *defunct* might be held to imply that), but only of diminished desires, but this in a newly married hero is sufficiently arresting. Attempts to make *defunct* bear some such meaning as 'discharged' or 'freed' by analogy with the Latin *defunctus periculis* ('freed from perils') will not do. This sense is not found elsewhere in English and, even in Latin, only emerges when there is an accompanying ablative (*periculis*). If Othello had said, 'defunct *from x*', this gloss might have been defensible, but he did not. No audience hearing these words would understand 'discharged'. Othello, beginning to explain that his request does not arise from lust, for the first time loses control of his sentence and so, we may infer, of his thoughts. Why?

Desdemona has just intervened in the men's world of senatorial debate with a sexual candour almost as startling as Othello's sexual retreat:

> My heart's subdu'd
> Even to the very quality of my lord:
> I saw Othello's visage in his mind;
> And to his honours and his valiant parts
> Did I my soul and fortunes consecrate.
> So that, dear lords, if I he left behind,
> A moth of peace, and he go to the war,
> The rites for why I love him are bereft me,
> And I a heavy interim shall support
> By his dear absence. Let me go with him.
>   (I. iii. 250–9)

There is no serious doubt that 'rites' in line 257 is a reference to the consummation of the marriage. This is what throws Othello off balance. She began by speaking of his mind—that part was excellent, carried no danger in terms of the stereotype of the lascivious Moor—but then she asked to be allowed to consummate the marriage. Othello's status in Venetian society is strong as long as it is kept separate from questions of sexuality. His speech is a stumbling, eager attempt to quash the implication of lasciviousness and to recover balance by catching at Desdemona's initial emphasis on mental affinity. The two speeches, Desdemona's and Othello's, are chiastically arranged: ABBA, mind, desire, desire, mind, but Othello's answering version is strangled and broken. To emend is to make it smooth. But the very roughness can be seen as correct, if one intuits a person in the part.

The editorial questions may still need answers (I think 'affects' is probably a noun and that 'proper' means here 'my own') but an actor can deliver the speech as given in the first Quarto, if he is allowed to stammer or hesitate. It remains true that the speech, thus unamended, would count as the most extreme piece of naturalistic confusion in the canon (though Leontes' speech, 'Affection! thy intention stabs the centre' in *The Winter's Tale*, I. ii. 138–46, comes very close). The collapse of Othello's language is microcosmic of the collapse of his personality in the entire tragedy.

Othello was perplexed in the extreme before Iago went to work on him. Marriage itself disoriented him. Naturally, his valediction of marital happiness became a valediction of the military life. It was there that he last knew himself. We are now in a position to return to his final speech before he stabs himself (V. ii. 341–59). Othello quietly stops the captors who would lead him away; he speaks briefly of his service to the state and then asks that, when the story of his actions and his fate is told, it should be fairly told; if it is fair, it will tell not of a pathologically jealous man but rather of a confused man, one who threw away a treasure and weeps for it; moreover the story should also include the slaying of the Turk long ago in Aleppo. As he tells of the slaying of the Turk, he kills himself on the clinching word 'thus'.

In this speech the pathos of the outsider reaches a climax. It is true that Othello has not attained full understanding, but there is a kind of dignity, for that very reason, in 'perplexed in the extreme' (V. ii. 349). In the course of the speech his mind flinches away from the mangled, unintelligible scene around him, back to his heroic past, when he had an honoured part to play. It is no accident that Othello's memory, in its search for a feat proper to be remembered, should light on the slaying of the turbanned Turk. To assert his Venetian status to the full he needs as enemy a spectacularly foreign figure. Yet, as we watch him, we *see*, not a Venetian but—precisely—a spectacularly foreign figure. That this is art of the highest order rather than accident is brought home by the conclusion of the speech. For at the moment when Othello comes, in his remote narrative, to the slaying of the foreigner, before our eyes he stabs himself, in a horrific parallelism. It is as if as his last act of devoted service, his last propitiatory offering to the state, he kills the outsider, Othello.

Let us now turn to the questions we posed at the outset. Is the rhetoric of his speech self-dramatizing, histrionic, or is it noble? I answer, it is noble, but its nobility is tragically deracinated. I said before that Othello's tragedy lay in the fact that he left the arena proper to tragedy. The logical 'shimmer' of this suggestion affects our perceptions of his final speech. Nobility thus isolated and astray is infected with absurdity, but the very absurdity is tragic. Othello's rhetoric is the rhetoric of a shame-culture. . . . Othello's shame-culture is more primitive, more thoroughly pre-Stoic than Coriolanus's, and his difference from the society around him is also greater.

Othello is actually *simpler* than those around him. A shame-culture identifies glory and virtue. The manner in which this survived in Shakespeare's time (and, to some extent in ours) was in the notions of honour and reputation. Thus Cassio harps desperately on his 'reputation' as 'the immortal part' of himself (II. iii. 253–7). But it is in Othello that we find the notion of reputation, not as something extrinsic but as the centre of his moral identity, operating with enough force (as Iago knows) to kill him. At I. iii. 274 Othello says, in the first Quarto, 'Let . . . all indign and base adversities / Make head against my reputation.' There he is insisting still on a confidence which is seriously threatened. But then, in a marvellous scene, Iago gets to work within Othello's mind, thinking his thoughts aloud for him and he knows well on which nerve he should press:

> But he that filches from me my good name
> Robs me of that which not enriches him
> And makes me poor indeed.
> (III. iii. 163–5)

In the world of professional military action Othello was a human being. When he passed through the door of the house he became a kind of nothing. The word 'occupation' is in our day and was in Shakespeare's a relatively colourless word (it had a few extra meanings then, but that is by the way). Shakespeare is therefore doing something very deliberate when he places it at the climax of Othello's speech of valediction at 111. iii. 349–61: 'Othello's occupation's gone.' He is making sure that we notice that the idea of profession or métier has an ethical status in Othello's mind which it does not naturally have in ours.

Venice in *Othello* is the same city we [see] in *The Merchant of Venice*. Othello is thus no feudal baron or chieftain, but a professional mercenary, paid by the state. Thus a certain continuity of economic reference links the two plays. But in *Othello* Shakespeare plays down the references to money. Instead he develops at greater length something which is also present in *The Merchant of Venice*. At III. iii. 31 Antonio said, 'the trade and profit of the city / Consisteth of all nations.' Venice is the landless city where different kinds and races meet in a strangely abstract effort of aggrandizement. The sea is the medium of their wars as money is the medium of their wealth. This, in *The Merchant of Venice*, yielded the endlessly fruitful contrast between a Jewish and a Christian consciousness. In

Othello it permits the study of a primitive consciousness yoked to the service of a complex, civic society. Venice is for Shakespeare an anthropological laboratory. Itself nowhere, suspended between sea and sky, it receives and utilizes all kinds of people.

Othello in his last speech is reverting to the earlier phase. Utterly beaten by his domestic environment, he goes back into his heroic past and delivers his formal vaunt (characteristic of the shame-culture hero from the boasts of the Homeric warrior to the *beot-word* of the Anglo-Saxons, and thence to the 'I killed me a b'ar when I was three' of the American folk hero) though, at the beginning of his speech at least, Othello is restrained by his civilized environment. The speech, properly delivered, should not sound more and more shrilly histrionic as it goes on. On the contrary, it should gather strength and confidence. The actor must draw himself up to his full physical height. Of course there is immense pathos. For—though we dispute their judgement—we are now in a position to account for the reaction of Eliot and Leavis. Othello's behaviour, if judged by the *mores* of the city, *would* be merely theatrical. It may really have a therapeutic function, if not of 'cheering him up,' of galvanizing muscles trained to kill. But ultimately all talk of self-dramatization is a product of the discrepancy between Othello's own nature and the place in which he finds himself. Shame-culture is more concerned than later cultures with outward behaviour; indeed, it locates identity in outward features. Thus for a shame-culture what in us would be artificial posturing may be a means of recovering one's true self. For all the pathos of incomprehension Othello is at last more authentically himself than at any time since the beginning of the play. This recovery of self, however achieved, corresponds to the 'moment of insight' customary in tragedies and successfully prevents *Othello* from turning into a 'sick' paraphrase or serious parody of tragic form. The core of Othello's nobility is real. He has reached a clearing in the forest, a small but sufficient open space in the labyrinth. He has come to a place where, once more, he has a job to do—a job like the jobs he did before—and he knows how to do it well. It is to kill himself. His words recall his feats against the foreign dog and his conclusion is another feat, both like and horribly unlike those.

Thus *Othello* joins the basically economic insight into cultural variation which we find in *The Merchant of Venice* to the contrast of heroic and civic cultures which is so finely treated in the Roman plays. Although Othello postdates Coriolanus and is more primitive than he, there is nevertheless implicit in what I have been saying a shadowy version of the 'evolving human nature' we [see] in the Roman plays. The civic state naturally succeeds the heroic. Othello does not merely belong to another culture but to an earlier one. In the first of the three great dramatists of ancient Greece, Aeschylus, there is virtually no distinction between motive and public situation (this is a continuation of a shame-culture refusal to separate inner and outer). The dilemma of Orestes is essentially public: one god says 'Do this,' another god says, 'Do that.' There is no question of attributing hesitation or procrastination to Orestes as a feature of his character (indeed, he can hardly be said to have character). This holds to some extent for Othello, or for Othello's conception of Othello. Remember here Bradley's remark, cited earlier, about Hamlet and Othello changing places. One thing Othello does not suffer from is hesitation or infirmity of purpose. Between the thing which is to be done and the doing of it no mental shadow falls.

At a later stage of cultural evolution people become aware that their actions are not only provoked by the outside world but are also inwardly motivated. The notion of self, as we saw, begins to contract. The shame-culture hero *is* his strength, his gleaming arms, even, at times, his cloud of assisting goddesses. Later we begin to assume that the self is separate from such external factors; we say 'Oh, yes, she did well in the four-hour examination, but that's just because she happens to have a strong constitution—it's not *merit*.' I suppose this is the present phase for most of us. Can one *imagine* a further phase? By continuing the trend, we would get an even more narrowly contracted ego, perhaps one which might even view its own motives as separate from itself. Certainly a person like that would seem civilized—rather horribly so—and would be a proper product of a world grown very old.

One cannot ascribe to *Othello* as developed a conspectus of evolving human nature as we find in *Julius Caesar* and *Coriolanus* but it may be, nevertheless, that in *Othello*, some four or five years later than *Julius Caesar*, Shakespeare began to push harder at the idea I have just let fall. If Othello is the underevolved man, who is overevolved? The answer is Iago. For if the workings of Othello's mind recall the oldest literature we have, Iago's evoke a literature as yet unwritten, the literature of existentialism, according to which any assumption of motive by the ego is an act of unconditional, artificial choice. Mark Antony is strange but Iago is far stranger. Mark Antony exploits the emotion he really feels; Iago chooses which emotions he will experience. He is not just motivated, like other people. Instead he *decides* to be motivated. He concedes that he has no idea whether Othello has had sexual relations with his wife. He simply opts, in a vacuum, for that as a possible motive.

I think I know how this astonishing idea occurred to Shakespeare. In the seventh story of the third decade of the *Hecatommithi* of Giraldi Cinthio, the following passage occurs (I quote from the careful translation by Raymond Shaw, given in an appendix to M. R. Ridley's New Arden edition of *Othello*):

> The wicked ensign, caring nothing for the loyalty due to his wife or the friendship, loyalty and duty he owed the Moor, fell passionately in love with Disdemona and turned all his thoughts to seeing whether he might enjoy her. . . . Everything that the ensign did to kindle in her a love for him was useless. So he imagined that the reason was that Disdemona had become enamoured of the captain and so decided to put him out of

the way. Furthermore he changed the love that he bore the lady into the bitterest hatred.

The important phrase is 'So he imagined' and the crucial word is 'so'. The Italian, which Shakespeare may have read, reproduces this feature. I assume that in fact it is merely verbal slackness on Cinthio's part. But, taken literally, it implies that the ensign *deliberately* imagined that something was the case, and this impression is reinforced by the active voice of 'changed' a few lines below where we might have expected 'his love changed'. Most readers would hardly notice these two tiny anomalies. But Shakespeare, I suspect, did notice them, and paused in his reading. For here is the germ of the existentialist Iago.

1992—Harold Bloom. "Introduction," from *Iago*

Harold Bloom is a professor at Yale University. He has edited dozens of anthologies of literature and literary criticism and is the author of more than 30 books, including *The Western Canon* and *Shakespeare: The Invention of the Human*.

To see Iago as affiliated with his fellow-Machiavel, Edmund, is traditional; to see his troubling affinities with some aspects of Hamlet, the counter-Machiavel, is not altogether untraditional. Hamlet and Iago alike are theatrical geniuses, though the Prince of Denmark's genius is universal, whereas Iago, who prides himself upon his military talents, displays throughout a dramatic grasp of the power of fantasy that rivals Shakespeare's own. I cannot therefore agree with the late C. L. Barber and Richard P. Wheeler when, in their very useful book, *The Whole Journey*, they say of Iago: "What he seeks is to become the Moor by making the Moor enact his fantasies, fantasies that will destroy them both. When that is accomplished, he can stop." Iago is too aware of the incommensurateness between his godlike general and himself to seek to become Othello, and dreadfully enough the fantasies that Iago makes the Moor enact are authentically Othello's own uneasy imaginings. Shakespeare's grand negations, at their strongest, are figures in a kind of negative poetics, even a kind of dramatic negative theology. Iago, like Hamlet, is a great improviser. He does not set out to become the Moor, or to destroy the Moor; it may be that he does not even begin with the desire to destroy Desdemona. I think we need to start farther back with Iago, in order to see more fully how original a character he was, and is. Iago is not a skeptic, but a believer. His religion is war, and his god is Othello, and so his fury when Cassio is preferred to him is the fury of the priest or worshipper who has been found unworthy, or at least less worthy than another who lacks the intensity of his own devotion. Iago becomes instead a priest of Resentment, fit ancestor for many current pale clerks whose faith has been thwarted.

Iago, as Harold Goddard wisely said, is the incarnation of the spirit of modern war, indeed a prophecy of total war, the religion of war. His truest forerunner in Shakespeare is not Richard III but Ulysses, the theoretician of war, indeed its positive theologian, as opposed to its negative theologians in Iago and Edmund, and its fantastic imagination in Macbeth. Just as the relationship between Lear's Fool and Lear, or between Falstaff and Hal, cannot be understood without our recognizing the extraordinary ambivalence of the Fool towards Lear, and of Hal towards Falstaff, so we need to comprehend Iago primarily in terms of his apocalyptic ambivalence in regard to Othello. Even as the play opens, we confront in Iago's ambivalence something very close to its descendant in Melville's Ahab. Ahab's Othello is Moby Dick, conceived as a great Gnostic Demiurge, a cosmic principle that inspires hatred and revenge. Iago's Moby Dick is the superb Othello, greatest of captains, worshipped by Iago as the God of War, but the worship has become hatred and a spur to revenge. Moby Dick has crippled Ahab, perhaps castrated him, but the permanent mystery of Shakespeare's tragedy is that Othello has done nothing to Iago, except failed to give him preference over Cassio. Yet in a perspective granted by the negative theology of war-as-religion, Iago's malignancy is anything but motiveless. For Iago, God or Othello is everything, because war is everything, and if Othello prefers Cassio, then Iago is nothing, as Cain felt he was nothing when Abel was preferred by Yahweh, or as Satan in *Paradise Lost* believes himself to be nothing when he belatedly hears Christ preferred by Milton's God. Iago is neither Cain nor the Devil, but something far worse: a priest of Moloch or Mars who is also a master psychologist, a great playwright and a theologian of the primal Abyss. Iago's cognitive power is his most astonishing attribute; his intellect is as quick and fecund as Hamlet's, though vastly less comprehensive.

Iago's incessant war is against being itself, which he has identified with Othello. That identification, granted Iago's perspective, is no hyperbole; cultural change and loss accounts for our tendency to undervalue Othello. Iago's Othello is far closer to the *Iliad*'s Achilles than he is to Shakespeare's Achilles in *Troilus and Cressida*, though I mean a closeness in ontological force, rather than in personality. The given in Shakespeare's *The Tragedy of Othello, the Moor of Venice*, is Othello's splendor of being, his unquestioned magnitude, his absolute authority and perfection in the camp and field of war. We do not much exalt the purity of arms, but Shakespeare sometimes does, or at least allows some of his plays to entertain the possibility of such exaltation. Iago believes in nothing but his captain Othello, loves nothing but the captain in Othello, and destroys Othello, but not as captain, not as the pure warrior. Even his destruction of Othello the man remains a negative celebration of Othello the captain, a negative affirmation of the reality of the God of War.

A worship that is hatred is best expressed by Iago's marvelous boast: "I am not what I am," which echoes and undoes St. Paul's "By the grace of God I am what I am." By Othello's refusal of grace or preference, Iago is driven to the negation: "I am not what I am." That statement is not a mere insistence that he is not Othello's "honest Iago," the ensign or standard-bearer pledged to die rather than to yield Othello's colors to the enemy. I hear a kind of religious despair in it as well: "I am not what I am," I am nothing, if the only ontological being that I acknowledge has failed to acknowledge me. Reality has abandoned Iago, and his revenge is a rebellion that in the first place is against himself. He will not, cannot walk away from Othello to another captain: he now hates God, but continues to believe in him. That ambivalent regard for Othello demands expression through a passion for destruction that is also a creative passion. Primal ambivalence fires the whole substance of Iago's being, and fathers his genius: the would-be second-in-command emerges as a Machiavel, as a poet who writes with people rather than with words, and most fascinatingly as the first High Aesthete, a dramatic critic adoring his own achievement as a dramatist. Richard III's gusto, his savage delight in his own villainy, is replaced by Iago's subtly perverse sadistic pleasure in his power of manipulation. Richard manipulates both his equals and his underlings. Iago manipulates as he chooses, but he knows that his negative greatness achieves apotheosis only by manipulating the fall of his mortal god, Othello. Iago's motive is Sublime: he debases, humiliates, and finally destroys the only authority he recognizes; his enterprise finally intends nothing less than the death of God. The God of War, having failed to recognize his true son in Iago, must be horribly punished. Falstaff, the God of Wit, is punished for having recognized his true son in Hal, who may once have accepted the recognition, but now recoils from it in a profound ambivalence. Hal cannot allow himself to know that he both loves and hates Falstaff, but consciously regards the fat knight as a kind of superior fool or jester. The ambivalence, transferred from Henry IV to Falstaff, destroys Falstaff and strengthens Hal. Iago, when we first encounter him, has been rejected for Cassio, and is conscious only of his great hatred for Othello. As he works upon Othello, Iago is delighted and surprised by his ease and aesthetic wonder of accomplishment. The delight could not have its intensity and largeness of dimension if Iago did not retain a reverence and passion for the magnitude of what he was ruining. A great captain, for Iago and for Shakespeare, is a masterpiece of nature, an Adamic splendor falling from godlike to something less than human status.

I think we must dismiss any speculation that Iago has a repressed sexual desire for Othello, which is about as useless as the notion that there was a sexual relationship between Falstaff and Hal. An extreme negative theologian or Gnostic does not lust after God, and what Freud learned from Shakespeare was the terrible ambivalence of our longing for reconcilement with the father while wishing also to murder the father. Freudian readings of Shakespeare, as I have remarked elsewhere, give us neither Shakespeare nor Freud, but a Shakespearean reading of Freud is capable of giving us both. Iago is subtler than Freud, as negative theology is frequently subtler than moral psychology. Reconcilement with Othello is not possible, Iago realizes, because it is Othello who must atone for the rejection of Iago. The degradation of God, a Gnostic concept, is Iago's project: the involuntary atonement of Othello through his debasement. The murder of Othello is not, cannot be Iago's project. A negative theologian does not seek to slay the father, nor to replace the father. It is enough that the father descend into the Abyss, there to suffer uncreation, to return to the void formlessness of night.

For me, the Shakespearean question to ask concerning Iago is: how does he change in the course of the drama? Unlike Macbeth, Iago does not progressively have control of his own imagination. What makes *The Tragedy of Othello, the Moor of Venice* so harrowing a work is the total triumph of Iago, until he is brought down so unexpectedly by his wife's outrage at the victimage of Desdemona. Iago's changes, until Emilia's courage ends him, are marches of triumphalism, in which he perpetually astonishes himself by his own manipulative genius. Yet that is only part of the story, the emergence of Iago as appreciative dramatic critic of his own power in composition. There is another side to this triumphalism, and that is the extent to which Iago, as great improviser, traps himself also in his own web. More successful at manipulating Othello than he could have imagined, he is forced into a situation where he must prove Othello's love a whore, or himself be slain by Othello. His extraordinary status as pure negation gives at once unlimited intellect, an overwhelming sense of nothingness, and a primal ambivalence towards Othello's massive, ontological presence that drives him beyond even his worked-out plottings. In this he differs from Edmund, who keeps to plan until the bodies of Goneril and Regan are brought in. Iago changes with each fresh confrontation, whether with Othello or with Desdemona, until he enters the final changelessness of his silence, prompted by outrage at Emilia's courageous devotion to the murdered and slandered Desdemona.

Iago tells us that he is nothing if not critical, and that he has never found a man that knew how to love himself. We can apply both these self-judgments to one of the most extraordinary moments in the play, when Emilia has given Iago the handkerchief and then been sent away by him (Act III, scene iii, lines 318–29). Alone on stage, Iago exults at his own mastery, and then is moved to a marvelous and horrible aesthetic apprehension of the ruined Othello, the fallen god of honorable war, and now Iago's masterpiece:

I will in Cassio's lodging lose this napkin
And let him find it. Trifles light as air

Are to the jealous confirmations strong
As proofs of Holy Writ. This may do something.
The Moor already changes with my poison:
Dangerous conceits are in their natures poisons,
Which at the first are scarce found to distaste,
But, with a little, act upon the blood,
Burn like the mines of sulfur. I did say so.

                                        Enter Othello.

Look where he comes! Not poppy nor mandragora,
Nor all the drowsy syrups of the world,
Shall ever medicine thee to that sweet sleep
Which thou owedst yesterday.

We shudder and yet, for this great moment, we are Iago, or perhaps Iago is already John Keats and Walter Pater, particularly as he rolls out those sensuous negatives: "Not poppy nor mandragora, / Nor all the drowsy syrups of the world . . ." For he is nothing if not critical, and he chants an appreciation of his own poisonous art, relishing each syllable of "poppy" and "mandragora" and "drowsy syrups" and "sweet sleep." Aesthetic awareness in our modern sense, the poetic self-consciousness of Keats and Pater and the sublime Oscar Wilde, is invented by Iago in this grand negative moment. The excited apprehension of: "This may do something" leads to the conscious pride of "I did say so," as Iago hymns the power of his own "dangerous conceits." It is only a step from this to that still more dangerous prevalence of the murderous imagination that will triumph even more sublimely in the strongest of all Shakespearean negations, Macbeth.

OTHELLO
IN THE TWENTY-FIRST CENTURY
ॐ

At the start of the twenty-first century, it seems that the issues in *Othello* that primarily concern, trouble, and excite critics are those related to race and gender. Some of the foremost current critics, however, examine these issues in the light of an older tradition, one that emphasizes character and aesthetics. An example is Frank Kermode's essay from his book *Shakespeare's Language*, excerpted here.

Othello is often used to reflect contemporary realities and even to comment on social issues. A 2006 production staged in Decatur, Alabama, which included images of the World Trade Center towers, emphasized the military aspect of the play, putting most of the cast in uniforms and making Cyprus suggestive of Bagdad. In 2005, the BBC broadcast a two-hour *Othello*, adapted by Andrew Davis, in which John Othello, a detective in Scotland Yard, is confronted by the problems of racial discord, anxiety about terrorism, and gender inequality currently disturbing English tranquility. In 2001, Tim Blake Nelson's film, *O*, transformed *Othello* into a teen movie about a black high-school basketball star, his envious best friend, and his white girlfriend.

2000—Frank Kermode.
"Othello," from *Shakespeare's Language*

Frank Kermode is one of Britain's most respected literary critics. He has written many highly acclaimed books, including *Shakespeare's Language*, *The Age of Shakespeare*, and *Pieces of My Mind*, a collection of his essays.

If we are to believe the latest Arden editor, *Othello* is closer in date to *Hamlet* than we used to think, for he says it was composed in "late 1601." At any rate, there is a cluster of plays near this date, a year or two after *Hamlet* and probably close to *Twelfth Night* and *Troilus and Cressida*.[1] Others prefer a date nearer 1604; that would twin the play with *Measure for Measure*, the plot for which derives from the collection of stories by Giraldo Cinthio. The issues are very complicated, and there is little certainty in any of the results.

The existence of two texts (the Quarto of 1622 and the Folio of 1623) creates problems different from those encountered in *Hamlet* or *King Lear* but no less difficult. They remain unlikely to be solved in such a way as to command anything approaching editorial consensus, and I do not in any case aspire to assist the editors in their enquiries, but with *Othello* as with *Hamlet* it is necessary on occasion to say where a particular reading originates and why one has chosen it. Textual scholars, loving their trade, will not agree, but critics hoping to comment on the language of the plays must think it unfortunate that the texts of three of the greatest of them should present these virtually intractable textual problems. Fortunately the plays remain for the most part intelligible, and susceptible to comment on their greatly varying styles.

What is extraordinary is the extent of the differences between plays written, one after another, in the first years of the new century. The style of *Othello* we may think of as having been formed while Shakespeare was reading for the task—mostly of Cinthio's novella, which he handles with notable skill and freedom, but also current books about the Mediterranean world.

Since the principal characters of the story were soldiers, the setting couldn't be other than military in character. Shakespeare had plenty of experience doing the military—the life of various kinds of soldier is amply recorded in the History plays and *All's Well*, and is not absent from *Hamlet*—but he had not hitherto attempted that almost invariant type, the foul-mouthed N.C.O. I myself have memories, happily remote, of Iago-like warrant officers, sycophantic self-seekers, the main difference being that Iago has a surprisingly educated vocabulary. At its core, however, is filth.

The first word of the play is Roderigo's "Tush," and Iago's reply begins with an oath: "'Sblood." His first word to Brabantio is "'Zounds" (85), repeated at line 107. None of these expletives is to be found in the Folio text. Honigmann counts fifty cases where the profanities of Q are deleted or modified in F probably because the latter, dependent on a manuscript written by the scribe Ralph Crane, was produced after 1606, when the Act to Restrain the Abuses of the Players forbade the use of oaths or the name of God.[2] "Tush" and "pish" may sound like Rosalind's "pretty oaths that are not dangerous" (*As You Like It*, IV.i.189), but their elimination along with others more shocking makes a considerable difference to the tone of the play, and especially to the characterisation of Iago. The profanities occur not only in soldierly contexts, where they could be taken simply as appropriate to the language of the camp, but more significantly in the context of sexual disgust to which Iago's thoughts repeatedly refer themselves.

The opening scene, as always with Shakespeare carefully excogitated, never simple narrative exposition, is here worth particularly close attention. It does provide some necessary exposition but also describes an evil soldierly prank:

you may think Roderigo must be half drunk to be seduced into the noisy demonstration outside Brabantio's house—as dangerous to him as it is useful to Iago. There have been critics, led by Dr. Johnson, who have wished away the first act of the play, and indeed Boito eliminated it when writing the *Otello* libretto for Verdi. But this move, however correct Johnson might think it and however economical in terms of lyric theatre, would not be sufficient compensation for its cost.

This opening scene outside Brabantio's house, with the subsequent interruption of the wedding night of Othello and Desdemona, seems to me a version of charivari. Charivari was an old custom: if you disapproved of a match as being incongruous in some way, for instance if you deplored a disparity in age (or in colour) between bride and bridegroom, you could call your neighbours and make a disturbance outside their dwelling. The practice was at one time reflected in the clamorous reaction to eclipses, also instances of order disrupted, as Othello remembers in V.ii.99–101, "Methinks it should be now a huge eclipse / Of sun and moon, and that th' affrighted globe / Did yawn at alteration."

Iago will use the noise of the charivari, this "rough music," to his own ends. In the passage before they start making a row, while he and Roderigo are still whispering in the street, we judge the violence of his emotion by his vocabulary: if I don't hate Othello "Abhor me . . . Despise me" (1.i.6, 8), with a hint that, since he knows his own foulness, these are indeed the proper responses to him. Unlike Roderigo, he need not make himself known to Brabantio, and can use what sexual insults he pleases: "Even now, now, very now, an old black ram / Is tupping your white ewe" (88–89) is Iago's way of informing the senator that his daughter has eloped, and this voyeuristic and disgusted attitude to sex is constant in him. They are at it at this very moment! Imagine it! And the man is black, a devil: the senator's daughter is being "cover'd with a Barbary horse" (111), is "making the beast with two backs" (116). Brabantio recognises the speaker as a "profane wretch" (114), "a villain" (117), but Iago has disappeared before the senator has made ready to hurry with Roderigo to the Sagittary, there to continue the process of charivari and disturb the wedding night of Othello and Desdemona.

Iago's onslaught on Brabantio's susceptibilities is kept up by his pupil Roderigo ("the gross clasps of a lascivious Moor" [126]); but he is required to be somewhat civil, as Iago is not. One striking aspect of the scene is that there are echoes of *Hamlet*'s habitual hendiadys. As George T. Wright demonstrated, Othello comes second only to *Hamlet* in the frequency of its use of hendiadys, though it offers less than half as many instances;[3] Shakespeare's enthusiasm for the device was waning, as one can see as *Othello* proceeds. But the habit of expansive doubling continues at the outset of this new one: "as loving his own pride and purposes," "trimm'd in forms and visages of duty," "The native act and figure of my heart," "by night and negligence," "your pleasure and most wise consent," "play and trifle with your reverence," "an extravagant and wheeling stranger / Of here and every where," "flag and sign of love," "the property of youth and maidhood"—all these occur in the first 170 lines. Othello's opening speech in the next scene carries it on: "my life and being," "my unhoused free condition / Put into circumscription and confine" (I.ii.21, 26–27). Brabantio continues the habit in his protest to the Duke:

> my particular grief
> Is of so flood-gate and o'erbearing nature
> That it engluts and swallows other sorrows . . .
>   (I.iii.55–57)

And:

> I therefore apprehend and do attach thee.
> For an abuser of the world, a practicer
> Of arts inhibited and out of warrant.
>   (I.ii.77–79)

There is another trace of the device in the senators' war council ("Neglecting an attempt of ease and gain / To wake and wage a danger profitless" [I.iii.29–30]). Later instances are Brabantio's "a judgment main'd and most imperfect" (99), "thin habits and poor likelihoods" (108), "indirect and forced courses" (111). The Duke calls the proposed expedition "stubborn and boist'rous" (228) and Othello refers, in Hamletian vein, to "the flinty and steel couch of war" (230), asking for Desdemona "such accommodation and besort / As levels with her breeding" (238–39); and, in a very strained expression, referring to his sight as "My speculative and offic'd instruments" (270). Desdemona, addressing the Senate, catches the habit in her speech proclaiming her part in the wooing: "That I did love the Moor to live with him, / My downright violence, and storm of fortunes, / May trumpet to the world" (I.iii.248–50). Here her own sense that the unconventionality of her choice amounts to a kind of social violence is emphasised by hendiadys ("My downright violence, and storm"). Later we have "quality and respect," "honesty and trust" (I.iii.282, 284), "worldy matter and direction" (299), and so on. The habit has spread to almost every character, but examples become harder to find as the play discovers and develops its own dialect, becomes less fond of semantic collision and contraction.

Hamlet can be coarsely bawdy, and seems to mean to offend Ophelia by being so, but although in future plays Shakespeare was to be capable of rendering deep sexual disgust (for example in *Troilus and Cressida*, *Timon of Athens*, and *The Winter's Tale*, and in one or two sonnets) Iago is probably his most disgusted and disgusting character, claiming precedence over Thersites and Apemantus by virtue of his centrality to an action of which he is indeed the sole agent. Mention of Desdemona having sex is all that is needed to make him talk dirty: Othello "hath boarded a land carract" (I.ii.50) means that he has gone aboard her, almost as an act of piracy or rape, as if any other explanation of the relationship were out of the question. The scene ends with a prose discussion between Iago and Roderigo, and here Iago offers the young man he means to push deeper into corruption an account of his beliefs and habits. Although it may suggest a similar self-hatred, this confession in no way resembles the Credo written by Boito for Verdi, which makes of Iago a gloomy nineteenth-century atheist. Yet it does offer a kind of philosophy.

Roderigo is in love with Desdemona, and Iago cannot think of love as anything but lust: the beloved object is a guinea hen, a loose or worthless woman; the lover is behaving like a baboon. Roderigo claims that it is not in his "virtue" or nature to stop being "fond," whereupon Iago delivers an extraordinary speech comparing the body to a garden, considered as a piece of coarse nature that the gardener, or human will, can amend. The fluency and power of this speech are remarkable—the persuasiveness of the analogy and the conceptual clarity of the conclusion drawn:

> If the beam of our lives had not one scale of reason to poise another of sensuality, the blood and baseness of our natures would conduct us to most prepost'rous conclusions. But we have reason to cool our raging motions, our carnal stings, our unbitted lusts . . .
> (I.iii.326ff.)

Iago's opening exclamation ("Virtue? a fig! 'tis in ourselves that we are thus or thus" [319]) ensures that the speech begins with the equivalent of an obscene gesture, but the argument that the will should have "power and corrigible authority" is perfectly conventional. This is good doctrine, the reason controlling the senses, the lower powers of the soul. Roderigo's admission that he cannot wield such control, his will being presumably unequal to the task, is met with another piece of advice: love "is merely a lust of the blood and a permission of the will" (334–35), which means that love is possible only because the will has abdicated its power over the senses. Iago's deception of Roderigo depends on the young man's willingness to believe that Desdemona is sexually corruptible, that he can buy her with presents, taking comfort meanwhile from the thought that the violent beginning of Desdemona's love for Othello will surely be followed by a movement of revulsion, as Iago's philosophy of lust would lead him to expect. And for good measure Othello will surely, in his turn, grow sick of Desdemona. "The food that to him now is as luscious as locusts, shall be to him shortly as acerb as the coloquintida" (347–49). The locust was a very sweet fruit, the food of John the Baptist in the wilderness; coloquintida was bitter and used as a purge. Iago can look about quite widely for his similes. The union of the lovers is a match between "an erring barbarian and a super-subtle Venetian" (355–56), a black man and a well-born Venetian lady; they had, at least among the vulgar, reputations, the black man for superior sexual powers, the Venetian lady for love affairs.

The aptness of this talk, and its lexical resourcefulness, display a mind, almost the mind of a poet, made formidable and alien by the context of corruption, a mind capable of seeming honest when honesty is called for but soured with its own baseness. Iago's baseness is more fundamental than a mere desire for revenge against Cassio and Othello; it is darker than Edmund's in *King Lear*. The whole point of the dialogue between Desdemona and Iago on the wharf at Cyprus (II.i) is to demonstrate that Iago, though apparently willing to pass the time of day with women, cannot quite manage to keep suppressed his loathing of them; he hates them for being sexed. That Cassio delights in touching them, smiling, taking their hands, and so forth makes him a man whom Iago hates less for his lieutenancy than for his sexual freedom, his ease with women:[4] "a most profane and liberal counsellor," he calls him (163–64); and although there is here a tinge of puritanical contempt for the libertine, Iago's next exchange with Roderigo, which follows hard upon the rapture greeting Othello's safe arrival, again dwells on the image of Desdemona engaged in "the act of sport" (227). He knows that she is to be credited with a "delicate tenderness" (232), but he uses that knowledge only to persuade Roderigo that she will come to "disrelish and abhor" the Moor—"very nature will instruct her" to do so (233–34). Her flirting with Cassio is lechery, and after it copulation must inevitably follow: "hard at hand comes the master and main exercise, th' incorporate conclusion. Pish!" (261–63 [F]). (Othello, infected by Iago's corruption, echoes this "Pish!" in IV.i.42.)

In the course of the play this kind of talk is contrasted with the innocently excessive courtesies of Cassio, the secret rebelliousness of Emilia, and of course the honesty of Othello himself, before his fall. Cassio's language is so near the extreme of doting admiration that Iago can profess to believe that his "civil and humane seeming" is only a cover for his "salt and most hidden loose affection" (II.i.239–41). Of course his immediate intention is to gull Roderigo; the art of the play is to make his claim seem not quite implausible. Cassio's extravagances, however disinterested, may sometimes go over the top, as when he expresses his hopes that Othello will arrive safely in Cyprus, and "Make love's quick pants in Desdemona's arms" (II.i.80); here he uses a trope from erotic poetry, to be found also in Thomas Carew's poem "A Rapture": "Yet my tall pine shall in the Cyprian strait / Ride safe at anchor, and unlade her freight." Cassio has a touch of the libertine, and his relationship with Bianca is important to the plot, but he is incapable of the language of Iago; he combines a politely seductive way of talking[5] with a matter-of-fact attitude to sexual satisfaction, a not unusual combination.

A dialogue in Act II is carefully inserted to make plain this capital difference between Iago and Cassio. Iago says Othello has left early to be with Desdemona: "He hath not yet made wanton the night with her; and she is sport for Jove."

> *Cas.* She's a most exquisite lady.
> *Iago.* And I'll warrant her, full of game.
> *Cas.* Indeed she's a most fresh and delicate creature.
> *Iago.* What an eye she has! Methinks it sounds a parley to provocation.
> *Cas.* An inviting eye; and yet methinks right modest.
> *Iago.* And when she speaks, is it not an alarum to love?
> *Cas.* She is indeed perfection.
> *Iago.* Well—happiness to their sheets!
>   (iii.18ff.)

This keenly written passage (some of which F tries to render as verse) contrives a social encounter that can only make Cassio uneasy; his position is such that despite his being the superior officer he cannot reprove Iago, only withhold assent to his slyly voyeuristic propositions and provide more courtly alternatives. When Iago invites him to drink to the health of "black Othello" (32), he tries to decline the invitation, such toasts being a courtesy he disapproves of because, as he explains, he has a weak head for drink. This is candid, but Iago seems to have known about this weakness already. Cassio makes a mistake when, having himself been addressed as "lieutenant" (13), he replies with "good Iago" (33), a patronising form of address like "honest," a word which from now on becomes central to the play. Iago resents it, for it is a word normally used of inferiors, but he makes use of it, since a reputation for good-humoured servile reliability suits his ends.[6] Cassio indeed loses this match, since it is as if he were explaining or defending his more delicate sexual attitudes by deriving them from his higher rank and class, a certain coarseness in these matters being exactly what one would expect of a social inferior.

Iago naturally has no use for the language of courtship; all love-making for him is merely the submission of the will to the base passions of the body. He assumes that Othello is a "lusty Moor" (II.i.295), perhaps because he is black, and the ideas of blackness and sexual potency were already twinned, or perhaps because he just assumes that all men are lusty. Othello himself has explained to the Duke that he wants Desdemona to come to Cyprus with him, "Nor to comply with heat (the young affects / In me defunct) and proper satisfaction; / But to be free and bounteous to her mind" (I.iii.264–66). (Here "affects" means "passions," "defunct" means not "dead" but "spent, a matter of the past," and "proper" means "personal" or even, in this context, "selfish."[7]) Othello is to him a gross and grossly privileged body, so deficient in the cunning of intellect that he

is easily duped. Iago doesn't seem to be particularly lustful himself; he may take
that to be a source of strength, while still envying others who are.

All this we infer only from the language of the individual characters. As it
happens, Iago's is least interesting when he is thinking in verse; his soliloquy
at the end of II.i is unconvincing, almost an admission of confusion in the
author as well as the character, a muddle of implausible motives where none
was needed other than the established foulness of the man's imagination.[8]
Even when Othello asks him to explain the reason for the brawl (II.iii.176ff.)
he speaks of the peaceful merriment that preceded it as being "in terms like
bride and groom / Devesting them for bed." His obsession gets uninhibited
play when he later tells Othello what he experienced when sharing a bed with
Cassio (III.iii.413–26)[9] and again expresses his obsessive interest in what
people do in bed ("kiss me hard . . . laid his leg / Over my thigh"). When
Boito rewrote this for Verdi ("*Era la notte, Cassio dormia*"), he had to leave this
kind of thing out, as too strong for a polite late-nineteenth-century audience;
Verdi supplied the feeling with eery music, giving the speech the air of an
erotic dream.[10]

The pivotal scene of the play is III.iii, which from the outset, with Iago's
"I like not that" as Cassio withdraws, to the end, when Othello has accepted
the charge against Desdemona and planned her death and Cassio's, is fewer
than five hundred lines long, probably less than half an hour of stage time.
It is extraordinarily bold. Desdemona aids the process, twice commending
Iago's honesty, a conviction of which in the other characters is now essential
to his design; at her exit Othello speaks of his love for her and the chaos that
will follow if his love should ever cease. It is at exactly this point (93) that
Iago goes to work, sowing doubts about Cassio. The dialogue is spare, at first
sounding almost like casual chat between a superior, who calls his interlocutor
"thou," and a subordinate, who must use "you" but who, without ceasing to be
deferential, can count on his boss's trust and on a long acquaintance:

Iago. My noble lord—
Oth. What dost thou say, Iago?
Iago. Did Michael Cassio, when you woo'd my lady,
Know of your love?
Oth. He did, from first to last. Why dost thou ask?
Iago. But for a satisfaction of my thought,
No further harm.
Oth. Why of thy thought, Iago?
Iago. I did not think he had been acquainted with her.
Oth. O yes, and went between us very oft.
Iago. Indeed!
Oth. Indeed? ay, indeed. Discern'st thou aught in that?

Is he not honest?
Iago. Honest, my lord?
Oth. Honest? ay, honest.
Iago. My lord, for aught I know.
Oth. What dost thou think?
Iago. Think, my lord?
Oth. Think, my lord? By heaven, thou echo'st me,
As if there were some monster in thy thought
Too hideous to be shown . . .
. . .
        If thou dost love me,
Show me thy thought.

                    (93–116)

In the first exchange the pentameters are broken up, giving the passage a peculiar uneasiness, which is reinforced by the triple "honest" and the triple "think," especially where two usages collide. "What didst not like?" asks Othello, seventy-five lines after Iago planted the expression. The question whether Cassio is or merely "seems" honest (unlike Iago, whom Othello accepts as honest all through) is now adroitly raised. "I dare be sworn I *think* that he is *honest*." "I *think* so too . . . Why then I *think* Cassio's an honest man":

Nay, yet there's more in this.
I prithee speak to me as to thy thinkings,
As thou dost ruminate, and give thy worst of thoughts
The worst of words.

                    (130–33)

At which point Iago expresses moral indignation, again with sound doctrine, explaining that even a slave can keep his thoughts to himself, and that one may have "uncleanly apprehensions" (139) without revealing them. But Othello insists that if Iago *thinks* him wronged he should make known his "thoughts" (143–44); "By heaven, I'll know thy thoughts" (162).

Here we are only at the beginning of a storm; no high colours, no blasts of rhetoric; the words "honest" and "think," "thinking," "thoughts" have to do all the work. After a while Iago, who has spoken of his own "jealousy" (147), meaning something like "envy" or "undue curiosity," but without sexual implication, uses the word again, now with full sexual reference and direct application to Othello's case: "O, beware, my lord, of jealousy! / It is the green-ey'd monster which doth mock / The meat it feeds on" (165–67). The seventy or so lines of verse that have elapsed before there is any direct accusation of Cassio and Desdemona have brought Othello to "misery" (171). He soon asserts that he could never suffer cuckoldry, adding that Desdemona's infidelity, if it existed, could not be attributed to any weakness in himself: "For she had *eyes*, and chose me" (189). And now the insistence is on eyes: "I'll *see* before I doubt" (190) . . . "*Look* to your wife, *observe* her well with Cassio, / Wear your *eyes* thus, not jealous nor secure" (197–98) (not suspicious but not overconfident); "In Venice they do let God *see* the pranks / They dare not show their husbands" (202–3) . . . "She that so young could give out such a seeming / To seel her father's *eyes* up" (209–10) . . . "If more thou dost *perceive*, let me know more; / Set on thy wife to *observe*" (239–40). This string of words will culminate in Othello's demand for "the ocular proof . . . Make me to *see* 't" (360–64). A passage of high tension, generated by all the words that have been in play: "honest," "think," "see":

> *Oth.* I do not *think* but Desdemona's honest.
> *Iago.* Long live she so! and long live you to *think* so!
>   (225–26)

Iago then touches on the disparity or disproportion between Othello and his Venetian wife, already become, through his assiduity, a credible cause of concern:

> *Iago.* To be direct and honest is not safe.
> *Oth.* Nay, stay. Thou shouldst be honest.
> *Iago.* I should be wise—for honesty's a fool . . .
>   (378–82)

> I *think* my wife be honest, and *think* she is not;
> I *think* that thou art just, and *think* thou art not.
> I'll have some proof.
>   (384–86)

"I see, sir, you are eaten up with passion . . . You would be satisfied? . . . but how? How satisfied, my lord? / Would you, the supervisor, grossly gape on? / Behold her topp'd?" (391–96) (here he uses to Othello himself the word Roderigo had used to Brabantio in the opening scene: "the gross clasps of a lascivious Moor" [126] and "Your daughter . . . hath made a gross revolt" [133–34], as well as "top," a variant of the word "tupping" in line 89).

> It were a tedious difficulty, I *think*,
>   To bring them to that *prospect*, damn them then,
>   If ever mortal eyes do *see* them bolster
> More than their own. What then? How then?
> What shall I say? Where's satisfaction?

It is impossible you should *see* this,
Were they as prime as goats, as hot as monkeys . . .
                          (397–403)

The only "satisfaction" available is Iago's account of his night with Cassio.

It becomes clear, in this masterly dialogue, that Iago's interest in sex is to watch others doing it, or at least to think about them doing it. It was important therefore to develop these ideas of seeing, these increasingly coarse descriptions and conjectures. The tone has grown calculatedly immodest—"damn them then"—and this is achieved before the story about Cassio in bed, and before the handkerchief provides what looks like satisfactory ocular evidence. For the tactician Iago has correctly guessed Othello's reaction even to the possibility of his wife's unfaithfulness, and at first with all the hesitations proper to an honest man (and an inferior) communicating such a suspicion, he infects Othello with his own disgust. Following the uses of "honest," "think," and "see," with their derivatives, one begins to understand how compact and fierce this writing is. Even after the account of Cassio's dream, when Othello is ready to tear his wife to pieces, the honest man can admit "yet we see nothing done; / She may he honest yet" (432–33)—which is the moment to introduce the handkerchief, something which can be seen, something with which Iago can claim to have seen Cassio wiping his beard. And the scene ends with the pair swearing a joint oath of loyalty and vengeance.

Considering the scantiness, or absence, of incriminating evidence, and the completeness of Othello's collapse, it would be easy to read this scene as an allegory of demonic possession, a reading Othello himself for a moment considers but dismisses in the last scene of the play: "I look down towards his feet; but that's a fable. / If that thou be'st a devil, I cannot kill thee" (V.ii.286–87). The success of Iago is "diabolic" only in the sense that his temptation has discovered in Othello a horror of his tempter's apparent knowingness about sex. Once more the effect is got by reiteration: "honest," "think," etc. The magical force of this rhetoric is what makes the scene possible.

Soon the handkerchief, the false substitute for "ocular proof," becomes itself the means of equally terrible reiteration. Othello credits it with an occult power that has now become appropriate to the occasion. The Egyptian or gipsy who gave it to his mother "could almost read / The thoughts of people" (III.iv.57–58). It had the power of controlling his father's love for his mother; if she lost it he would loathe her. He is talking about his own love for Desdemona: "there's magic in the web of it" (69).

The ensuing dialogue with Desdemona—she lying about the handkerchief and crazily resuming her plea for Cassio, while he says almost nothing but "handkerchief"—is as brilliantly conceived as the Othello–Iago dialogue, and it is hard to imagine a dramatic poetry more minimally perfect:

Oth. Is't lost? Is't gone? Speak, is't out o' th' way?

Des. Heaven bless us!

Oth. Say you?

Des. It is not lost; but what and if it were?

Oth. How?

Des. I say, it is not lost.

Oth. Fetch't, let me see't.

Des. Why, so I can, sir, but I will not now.

This is a trick to put me from my suit.

Pray you let Cassio be receiv'd again.

Oth. Fetch me the handkerchief, my mind misgives.

Des. Come, come;

You'll never meet a more sufficient man.

Oth. The handkerchief!

Des. I pray talk me of Cassio.

Oth. The handkerchief!

Des. A man that all his time

Has founded his good fortunes on your love,

Shar'd dangers with you—

Oth. The handkerchief!

Des. I' faith, you are to blame.

Oth. 'Zounds![11]

                                    (III.iv.79–98)

It has often been remarked, by G. B. Shaw with derogatory intent, that Othello is the most operatic of Shakespeare's tragedies; think, for example, of the duet at the end of III.iii (where Verdi has the advantage of Shakespeare that he can make Iago and Otello swear their oath together instead of having to do it one at a time). This intense Shakespearian scene, too, is in its way equally musical. This kind of writing, by quasi-musical, quasi-magical means, achieves a rawness of passion, a conflict between innocently suicidal enquiry and a rage almost beyond words. Rage beyond words was not something the early Shakespeare would have even thought of aiming at. Here, as in Hamlet, a long experience of theatre has taught him a new way of writing poetry.

The strangest line in Desdemona's part comes in IV.iii. Othello has just grossly insulted and struck her in the presence of Lodovico, the Venetian envoy. Now he orders her to bed. Talking with Emilia, she remembers the maid Barbary and her song, but before she sings it she says, with apparent inconsequence, "This Lodovico is a proper man" (35). None of this passage (30–52) is included in Q. There must have been some good reason to exclude the Willow Song (perhaps the temporary unavailability of a boy actor who could sing), and the line about Lodovico was lost along with the song. Some modern editors, including

Honigmann, give the line to Emilia, but only because it seems "out of character" for Desdemona.[12] Despite his treatment of her, she has continued submissive and loving to Othello, even when he acted out his horrible pretence that she was a whore and Emilia her bawd. After Othello's aria "Had it pleas'd heaven / To try me with affliction . . ." (IV.ii.47ff.) she hardly complains: "I hope my noble lord esteems me honest," and "Alas, what ignorant sin have I committed?" (65, 70). Even at her boldest, as when she insists on going to Cyprus, she has deserved Lodovico's compliment, "Truly, an obedient lady" (IV.i.248). Yet now, at a moment of intense marital distress, her thoughts wander momentarily to another man. Very shortly she listens with amazement to Emilia's avowal that she would be unfaithful to her husband if the reward was great enough. Desdemona says she would not behave so "For the whole world" (IV.iii.79). The fine speech (not in Q) in which Emilia stands up for women's right to sensual life against the restrictions imposed by tyrannical men is not the sort of thing Desdemona would ever have spoken (IV.iii.84–103). Yet she is rather taken by Lodovico, and at a very odd moment.

It is true that she can say unexpected things; she is represented as suffering a kind of loss of attention: after the horrible brothel scene when cast as "that cunning whore of Venice / That married with Othello" (IV.ii.89–90), she declares herself "half asleep" (97) and hardly understands what Emilia says next. These moments may contribute to any secret disposition in an audience to agree that it was less than seemly of this young woman, ignoring the "curled darlings of her nation," to marry a man so alien and so much older, an "extravagant and wheeling stranger" (I.i.136), a general whose social standing, though high, depends entirely upon his military rank in an embattled state. (As Auden remarks, Brabantio was happy enough to have Othello to supper and hear his tales, but that was another matter from having him as a son-in-law.[13]) And she is made to lie[14]—about the handkerchief, and about the identity of her murderer. Many of these traits may be attributed to a strain of feminism in the play, a hint of the ways in which women might sometimes escape the regime imposed by their husbands—a little quiet talk with another woman, a venial fib or two. Yet the fact remains that there is a faint ambiguity in her character as we try to see it as a whole, and this is notoriously true also of Othello's.

There have been some celebrated criticisms of Othello's generally orotund way of speaking, which may be regarded as a sort of innocent pompousness or, if you dislike it, a self-regard that is not so innocent. It is easy enough to explain the choice for Othello of this particular mode of speech. He is meant to be a man whose sole reason for existence is command—after all, he is responsible for the security of an empire, Cyprus being a province that must be defended. The self-esteem of such a man can be rendered in the naturally hyperbolical terms of military glory. It has been observed that Londoners of the time were familiar with the idea of magnificent North African potentates. "The black, or tawny,

soldier-hero was a figure in festivals long before he reached the Elizabethan stage
. . . These Moorish shows were resplendent, soldierly and sensual . . . the role of
the Moor in public spectacle was to enrich the public conception of power and
sexual potency in the early stages of Tudor empire."[15]

The example of Marlowe's *Tamburlaine* was fairly recent, but Othello does
not have his out-and-out bombast, and there is a touch of modesty and courtesy
in his speech. His first line, "'Tis better as it is" (I.ii.6), is intended to promote
calm in the face of Iago's pretended anger on his behalf; he has nothing to fear
from Brabantio, he says, because of his services to the state. Here he claims
royal birth, like a sultan in a Lord Mayor's Show; he will not boast of it except
by mentioning it, but the final effect is not quite modest. When he speaks of
his "demerits," the word (as in *Coriolanus*, I.i.275) means "merits." It is an odd
word since it can also mean its opposite; but I think the point of it is to have
Othello use a strange word rather than a familiar one—something he does on a
good many other occasions. Its oddness makes it stand out against the bustling
language of the messages concerning the military crisis, and his character
is already pretty firmly established as calm, grandiloquent, unaware of his
vulnerability, by the famous line "Keep up your bright swords, for the dew will
rust them" (I.ii.59). This invulnerability is founded in a soldier's courage, and it
does not, as he supposes, extend to the dangers of civilian life.

Arriving in the Senate House, where all the talk is practical, he utters
an oration on the topic of his marriage ("Most potent, grave, and reverend
signiors" [I.iii.76ff.]) and on his wooing of Desdemona, "Wherein I spoke of
most disastrous chances: / Of moving accidents by flood and field, / Of hair-
breadth scapes i' th' imminent deadly breach, / Of being taken by the insolent
foe / And sold to slavery" (134–38)—a speech of forty-one lines celebrated for
their grandeur, which is enhanced by the tinkling couplets and plain prose of
the following speeches by the Duke and Brabantio. The speech is completely
successful; the Duke is proud that his warrior deputy talks exactly as he would
be expected to fight, superbly. And the grandeur depends partly on Othello's use
of unusual words like "demerit" and "agnize" and "indign." The one word he finds
no synonyms for is "honest," twice applied to Iago in this scene (284, 294) and
repeatedly in later scenes. And it is the honest Iago who will, in the course of the
play, reduce Othello's language as well as his honour.

Before the temptation scene it is impossible to imagine Othello using the
vocabulary of Iago; indeed, he rarely uses language appropriate to prose. It is
essential to the character that until he collapses he speaks grandly. Later come
the anguished repetitions of "handkerchief," the questioning of the sense in
which Iago uses the word "lie," the pathetic stress on "honesty," the unaccustomed
langue verte picked up from Iago, and the vile berating of Desdemona, whom he
calls a whore, which suits his action in striking her.

Othello's final speech has been much commented upon. In a famous essay T. S. Eliot noted that in his self-pitying grandeur, his boasting about his weapon and his past achievements, he stresses his claim to be serving the state but makes no mention whatever of Desdemona. "Humility is the most difficult of all virtues to achieve; nothing dies harder than the desire to think well of oneself... I do not believe that any writer has exposed this *bovarysme*, the human will to see things as they are not, more clearly than Shakespeare."[16] This view has been much attacked, but it has not lost all its force. Eliot does not support his observation by comment on the language of the speech, which has some resemblance to that of Othello's speech to the Senate at the outset. It repeats the point made in I.ii.18 about the respect he has won by "My services which I have done the signiory," but important differences arise from the fact that he cannot now allow himself to speak of "My parts, my title, and my perfect soul" (I.ii.31). Instead, he compares himself to Judas ("the base Indian") who "threw a pearl away / Richer than all his tribe" (V.ii.347–48).[17] He claims not to be jealous except when "wrought." He cannot confess to weeping without explaining that it isn't his usual practice. And he ends with a recollection of one more notable service to the state.

We need not suppose that Shakespeare was contemptuous; only that, as his language suggests, Othello was human, the victim of long habit, and wanting, as he ended his life, to enter a plea for merciful interpretation. That he did not get it in the play, and has not always had it subsequently, merely shows how variable interpretation must be when it has to work on language as complex as that of *Othello*.

NOTES

1. *Othello*, ed. E. A. J. Honigmann (Arden edition, 1997). The date is discussed in Appendix I, pp. 344–50, the text in Appendix 2, pp. 351–67, which summarises the arguments in Honigmann's book on the subject, *The Texts of "Othello"* (1996).

2. On the cleaning up of F. see Honigmann. p. 352.

3. "Hendiadys and *Hamlet*," *PMLA* 96, pp. 168ff.

4. W. H. Auden thought otherwise, arguing that Cassio is easy only with "women of his own class." "The Joker in the Pack," in *The Dyer's Hand* (1963), p. 262.

5. Auden speaks of Cassio's "socialized eroticism," p. 262.

6. See Empson's essay "Honest in *Othello*," in *The Structure of Complex Words*, pp. 218–49. The preceding chapters, "Honest Man" and "Honest Numbers" (pp. 185–217), are also relevant.

7. See the discussion of "defunct" in Hulme, *Explorations in Shakespeare's Language*, pp. 153–54. I think the best of her suggestions is that it means "past danger." The sense of "proper" seems to be misunderstood by Honigmann ("in conformity with rule").

8. Auden, who describes Iago as a practical joker, goes so far as to say that he ought to act brilliantly when being all the varieties of himself as presented to Othello, Cassio, Desdemona, etc., but badly in the soliloquies: "He must deliver

the lines of his soliloquies in such a way that he makes nonsense of them" ("The Joker in the Pack," p. 258).

9. On the importance in the play of the word "bed," which occurs more than twenty times, see R. R. Heilman, *Magic in the Web* (1956).

10. *Otello* is not only the finest of Shakespearian operas but in certain respects offers an intelligent commentary on its source. It has been remarked that Boito underlined certain passages in the play, for example Iago's description of love as "merely a lust of the blood and a permission of the will," but Verdi did not set them; I take these to indicate that Boito saw the importance of the lines but, feeling he could not use them, indicated that the music must somehow convey their sense. See James A. Hepokoski, *Otello* (1987), for a study of Boito's dealings with Shakespeare.

11. F weakens this exit by substituting "Away" for "'Zounds."

12. This is the reason why some editors transfer Miranda's excoriation of Caliban (*The Tempest*, I.ii.351–62) to Prospero. But the motive is not a good one, for it assumes that editors already know all they need to about the limits of the character.

13. "The Joker in the Pack," p. 263. Auden remarks that in a mercantile and warlike society like Venice there was need of foreign soldiers and also of usurers, the latter being Jews and socially unacceptable despite their utility. "No Venetian would dream of spitting on Othello as on Shylock, but a line was drawn nevertheless, and it excluded marriage to a high-born Venetian woman."

14. "Lie" is another reiterated word; "lie/lies" occurs twenty-five times in the play. It provides the theme of Desdemona's talk with the Clown (III.iv), a scene which prepares us for Iago's casual and obscene punning in the horrible IV.i: "Lie—With her? / With her? On her; what you will . . . / Lie with her? lie on her? We say lie on her, when they belie her" (34–37)—at which point Othello has his fit. This device of hammering away at certain words is, as we have seen, a habit of the mature Shakespeare.

15. Philip Brockbank, "The Theatre of *Othello*," in *On Shakespeare* (1989), p. 200. Brockbank's information comes from *The Calendar of Dramatic Records in the Books of the Livery Companies of London*, 1485–1640, eds. D. J. Gordon and Jean Robertson (1954).

16. "Shakespeare and the Stoicism of Seneca," in *Selected Essays* (1932), pp. 131–32.

17. "Judean" is the reading of F; Q (and F2) read "Indian." The arguments for and against are summarised by Honigmann in the Arden edition, p. 342.

BIBLIOGRAPHY

᪥

Adamson, Jane. *"Othello" as Tragedy: Some Problems of Judgment and Feeling* (Cambridge: Cambridge University Press, 1980).

Booth, Stephen. *"King Lear," "Othello": Indefinition and Tragedy* (New Haven: Yale University Press, 1983).

Campell, Lily B. *Shakespeare's Tragic Heroes: Slaves of Passion* (Gloucester, Mass.: Peter Smith, 1973).

Davies, Anthony. *Filming Shakespeare's Plays: The Adaptations of Laurence Olivier, Orson Welles, Peter Brook and Akira Kurosawa* (Cambridge: Cambridge University Press, 1990).

Draper, John William. *The Othello of Shakespeare's Audience* (New York: Octagon Books, 1966).

Elliott, George Roy. *Flaming Minister: A Study of "Othello" as a Tragedy of Love and Hate* (Durham, N.C.: Duke University Press, 1953).

Fiedler, Leslie A. *The Stranger in Shakespeare* (London: Croom Helm, 1973).

Greenblatt, Stephen. *Renaissance Self-Fashionings: From More to Shakespeare* (Chicago: University of Chicago Press, 1980).

Kolin, Philip, ed. *Othello: New Critical Essays* (New York: Routledge, 2001).

Leavis, F. R. "Diabolic Intellect and the Noble Hero: or The Sentimentalist's *Othello*," from *The Common Pursuit* (London: Chatto & Windus, 1952).

MacDonald, Ann-Marie. *Goodnight Desdemona (Good Morning Juliet)* (Toronto: Coach House Press, 1990).

Neely, Carol Thomas. "Women and Men in *Othello*," from *The Woman's Part: Feminist Criticism of Shakespeare*, edited by Carolyn Ruth Swift Lenz, et al. (Urbana, Ill.: University of Illinois Press, 1980).

Rosenberg, Marvin. *The Masks of Othello* (Berkeley: University of California Press, 1961).

Snyder, Susan. *Othello: Critical Essays* (New York: Garland, 1988).

Vaughan, Virginia Mason. *Othello: A Contextual History* (Cambridge: Cambridge University Press, 1994).

313

Vaughan, Virginia Mason, and Kent Cartwright, eds. *Othello: New Perspectives* (Rutherford, N.J.: Fairleigh Dickinson University Press, 1990).

Vogel, Paula. *Desdemona: A Play about a Handkerchief* (New York: Dramatists Play Service, 1994).

ACKNOWLEDGMENTS

❧

Twentieth Century

A. C. Bradley, "Othello," from *Shakespearean Tragedy* (London: Macmillan, 1904).

T. S. Eliot, "The Hero Cheering Himself Up" (1927), from "Shakespeare and the Stoicism of Seneca," reprinted in *Selected Essays 1917–1932* (London: Faber and Faber, 1932).

G. Wilson Knight, "The *Othello* Music," from *The Wheel of Fire* (London: Methuen, 1930), pp. 97–119.

William Empson, "The Best Policy," from *Life and Letters To-Day* 14, no. 4 (summer 1936), pp. 39–45.

Harold C. Goddard, "*Othello*," from *The Meaning of Shakespeare,* vol. 2 (Chicago: University of Chicago Press, 1951), pp. 69–106. © 1951 by the University of Chicago.

Kenneth Burke, "'Othello': An Essay to Illustrate a Method," from *The Hudson Review* 4, no. 2 (summer 1951), pp. 165–200. Reprinted by permission of *The Hudson Review.*

Robert B. Heilman, "*Othello*: The Unheroic Tragic Hero," from *Magic in the Web: Action and Language in Othello* (Lexington: University of Kentucky Press, 1956), pp. 137–168. © University of Kentucky Press.

W. H. Auden, "The Joker in the Pack," from *Encounter* (August 1961). Reprinted in *The Dyer's Hand and Other Essays* (New York: Random House, 1962), pp. 246–272.

A. D. Nuttall, "*Othello*," from *A New Mimesis: Shakespeare and the Representation of Reality* (London: Methuen, 1983), pp. 120–143. © 1983 A. D. Nutall.

Harold Bloom, "Introduction," from *Iago* (New York, 1992), pp. 1–5.

Twenty-first Century

Frank Kermode, "Othello," from *Shakespeare's Language* (New York: Farrar, Straus and Giroux, 2000), pp. 165–182. © 2000 by Frank Kermode. Reprinted by permission of Farrar, Straus and Giroux.

INDEX